AN APPETITE FOR
CRIME

The Memoirs of former Detective
Superintendent Ron Chapman

by

Ron Chapman

Grosvenor House
Publishing Limited

The right of Ron Chapman to be identified as the author of this
work has been asserted in accordance with Section 78
of the Copyright, Designs and Patents Act 1988

The book cover picture is copyright to Ron Chapman

This book is published by
Grosvenor House Publishing Ltd
28-30 High Street, Guildford, Surrey, GU1 3EL.
www.grosvenorhousepublishing.co.uk

A CIP record for this book
is available from the British Library

ISBN 978-1-78148-948-2

Disclaimer

We have tried to recreate events, locales and conversations from the memoirs
of our father. In order to maintain anonymity in some incidences we have
changed the names of individuals and places. We may have also changed
some identifying characteristics and details such as physical, properties,
occupations and places of residence. We do hereby disclaim any
liability to any party for any loss, damage or disruption caused by
errors or omissions whether any such errors or omissions result from
negligence, accident or any other cause.

Contents

Foreword

We have published Ron's memoirs of his outstanding police career to share with friends and family and also with those who have an interest in the policing and detective work from an earlier era. Ron worked so hard on these memoirs, including great levels of detail and often referring to notes made over forty years previous; it is almost as if he planned to write this book the day he joined the Met.

He had an absolute passion for, love of, and dedication to 'the job'. That is not only evident from what is enclosed within these chapters but from all the memories we share of Ron and the times we spent together. As a family we have many of our own tales from Ron's time in the police; nights out spent trailing suspicious-looking characters, driving lessons touring the houses of known villains and the early morning phone calls that indicated another serious murder had occurred.

We have deliberately left the works unedited and unfinished as we wanted to keep the book true to his voice. We hope you will hear this as you read through the chapters. The title is the one he had already chosen and reflects well his stories, both in terms of his complete devotion to the pursuit of criminals and his enjoyment of a wide range of London eateries in the process.

We hope that as you read this book you get the same warm glow as we do – it feels like Ron is there telling his story, with all the details you may or may not possibly need. Whilst we are so very sad that he is not still with us and able to finish his memoirs, we hope you can enjoy these memories that he had planned to share with you all.

Chapter One

Explosion at Camden Hill Square

Glancing at my watch I saw that it was 9.20am as I brought my vehicle to a halt, its bonnet nudging the white tape, strung across the busy Holland Park Avenue, forming an outer cordon to the venue of the latest bombing incident in Central London. The usual heavy flow of rush hour traffic, initially halted, was now in the process of being diverted by uniformed Officers. Commuters dispersing from the nearby Notting Hill Gate and Holland Park Underground Stations, turned onlookers, as they gathered at the cordons, some drawn to the scene having heard the explosion, others curious to learn what had interrupted their journeys. I knew without doubt this was yet just one more incident in a protracted and intensifying campaign by the Provisional IRA unit, who had been terrorising the population of Central London for many months. The attempted assassination of the Right Honourable Sir Hugh Fraser, MP, who only eight months previous, in conjunction with Margaret Thatcher had challenged Edward Heath for leadership of the Conservative Party. What I did not know at that time was that Caroline Kennedy the 17-year-old student daughter of the late Senator John F. Kennedy was a house guest staying at the Fraser's house in Kensington, whilst attending a course at Sotheby's.

As one of the police constables manning the cordon, approached my vehicle, I wound down my driver's door window, to address him. It was not a marked police vehicle but my own private car an Austin Maxi Saloon, used when off duty as a family car, for my wife and three young daughters. I was however authorised to drive it on duty, and it had been fitted with a covert police radio, Call Sign 'Central 707', the medium through which

I had first been notified of the incident, just before 9am that Thursday morning, 23rd October 1975.

I'd received the call whilst driving to Scotland Yard from my home in Essex. The venue of the incident was given as Camden Hill Square, but never having served in the Kensington Area, I'd brought my vehicle to a halt to consult a street map and revise my route.

Ironically I'd stopped in Neville Road Stoke Newington, almost opposite the 'Neville Arms' public house. The spot where some fifteen years previous, as a young off duty, probationer P.C., having pursued two men through various side streets, I'd finally managed to arrest one of them, for Shop breaking, despite a violent struggle. This off duty arrest, coupled with other 'Crime Arrests', I'd effected during my brief spell in uniform, had not only given me a taste for crime, but marked me out as a likely candidate for the CID. Subsequently I'd been attached as an Aide to CID, some two months before completing my Uniform Probationer period. My prisoner, George Ince, after serving a sentence of two years imprisonment, continued his career, in a life of crime. This was later to see him arrested for the Silver Bullion Robbery at Mountnessing, and then twice stand trial for the murder of Bob Patience, in what became known as 'The Barn Restaurant Murder'. His acquittal, being finally secured by the disclosure of his affair with Dolly Kray, wife of the imprisoned Charlie, elder brother of the infamous twins Ronnie and Reggie.

"Detective Inspector Chapman, Bomb Squad Duty Officer," I said, reaching behind me to access the wallet in my hip pocket which contained my police warrant card. Then as the constable and a colleague raised the tape to facilitate my entry, I surveyed the scene on the far side. An assortment of emergency service vehicles were parked in no particular fashion, their occupants having departed hastily, each to deal with their own particular professionalism.

Standing amongst a group of senior uniformed police officers in the centre of the road within the inner cordon, I spotted the familiar figures of Detective Chief Superintendent Jim Nevill and Detective Superintendent Peter Imbert. Wearing the distinctive protective jackets and hard hats issued to officers of all ranks, on appointment to C.1. (4) Department at New Scotland Yard, otherwise known as 'The Bomb Squad' they stood out from their uniform colleagues. The presence of two of my senior officers was of some comfort to me. Although I was a seasoned detective with considerable experience in dealing with murder, as well as a variety of offences across the criminal spectrum, I had only transferred to this branch some five weeks previous and this was my first visit to a bomb scene.

Parking my car in one of the few remaining spaces between the cordons I donned my own protective clothing, before making my way over to join them.

"What kept you Ron?" enquired Jim Nevill, the vaguest suggestion of a knowing smile appearing beneath his twinkling blue eyes.

"It's all right for you West London Officers," I retorted respectfully, "I was at Stoke Newington when the explosion occurred, it's taken me half an hour to get here."

I refrained from mentioning that as Duty Officer for 24 hours I had been on Standby at Scotland Yard until midnight the previous evening.

Having joined my colleagues, I was then able to view the scene in the West Side of Camden Hill Square. Within the inner cordon, the remains of a 4.2 Jaguar Saloon lay broadside on its roof in the middle of the road, a mixture of smoke and steam still emanating from its carcass. The vehicle owned by Sir Hugh Fraser had been parked overnight outside his address at number 52. I was to learn that the explosion had killed a neighbour and his body lay in the front garden of that house. Tragically, the victim was suspected to be Gordon Hamilton-Fairley a Professor of Medical Oncology at St. Bartholomew's Hospital, who resided next door at number 53 and who had been out walking his dogs at the time of the explosion.

Jean Leyland, a Children's Nanny employed by Sir Hugh and Lady Antonia Fraser, had witnessed the explosion. She having taken their eight-year-old son Orlando to school, from Lady Fraser's address in Launceston Place, was driving the latter's car down Camden Hill Square, intending to pick up any mail for her, the couple having recently separated. I was to learn later from local officers that she was now living with the famous playwright Harold Pinter. As the Nanny approached the Fraser's house she noticed a man bending down beside Sir Hugh's parked Jaguar and looking under it. She then saw the man approach the rear wheel and noticed an object under the car which the man bends down to examine. The object was fawn about the size of book, which Ms Leyland thought might have been a wooden wedge on account of the steep slope. She was some two-car length from the Jaguar when it suddenly blew up. Leaping from her car she ran back up the hill, whilst her vehicle, with no handbrake in operation, careered into a tree on the near side pavement.

There were trees situated every twenty feet on the footway, as well as numerous trees and shrubs situated within the railed garden area in the middle of the Square, where Major Jim Greenwood the Duty Explosives Officer, was particularly concerned that a secondary device could have been secreted.

The explosion had unfortunately caused a premature autumnal fall of leaves, which now carpeted the whole scene, thus hampering the search within the inner cordon, where police sniffer dogs were being deployed to search for any secondary devices or residue explosives.

I learnt later that two uniformed police officers, John Harwood and Martin Harland, had been sat in a Police Panda Car alongside the gardens, on the west side of Camden Hill Square, watching the nearby traffic lights, when the explosion had occurred. Being only some twenty yards from the seat of the explosion, their vehicle had rocked violently from the blast and the officers had felt the ground shake beneath them, as debris from the car landed around them. Numerous houses in the area received shattered windows brought about by the explosion. Sir Hugh Fraser who had been working at his desk, in a first floor front room used as a study, had been spattered with shards of broken glass, one of which grazed his temple.

Two other officers had been in a police wireless car in Holland Park Avenue, held up in heavy traffic when the explosion occurred. They had been near enough to see pieces of metal debris land in front of them. Two others had been travelling in a police van to Ladbroke Grove when they heard the explosion, which rocked the van from side to side. These officers between them had first summoned the fire and ambulance services, before evacuating nearby residents and tending to various pedestrians who were suffering from shock, or had received minor injuries from the blast.

Once the area had been declared safe, further detailed photographs were taken of the scene. Once officers acting under the supervision of the Exhibits Officer – Detective Constable Pat O'Connor had collected debris in the immediate area of the Sir Hugh's House, we were able to view the body of the victim of this terrible atrocity. It was lying inside the front garden of number 52 a distance of about twelve to fifteen feet from the pavement edge where the jaguar had been parked. There was an iron-railing fence bordering the front garden, some three foot six in height, which the force of the explosion had propelled the victim over. Suffice to say the body was badly mutilated. On the pavement nearby lay the remains of a small white dog.

Meanwhile various officers from my team assisted by local uniform and CID officers were engaged in interviewing and taking statements from members of the public. Many people, who had been in the vicinity at the time of the explosion, had received minor injuries or found pieces of debris in and around their properties. For this purpose, C.13 Department had the use of a dedicated and specially equipped, 'Incident Control Van', which we parked between the inner and outer cordons and which acted as a focal point for the initial investigation. Although equipped with a work surface and two seats for statement taking, it was only of value in the initial stages of an incident. An Incident Room was therefore opened at Kensington Police Station, within a few hours and the local Detective Inspector Brian Riley and a number of his officers were deputed to assist our investigation.

The majority of officers on my team were however still dealing with enquiries into a bombing incident at the Hilton Hotel in Park Lane on 5th September. An incident, which had occurred a few days before I joined the Branch and in which two people had been killed and some 63 injured. The assistance of CID officers from Kensington Police Station was therefore greatly appreciated. I had however barely time to make the acquaintance of Brian Riley and his colleagues before attending Westminster Mortuary with Peter Imbert, where Dr James Hamilton-Fairley, identified the body of the deceased as that of his 45-year-old brother, Professor Gordon Hamilton-Fairley M.D. F.R.C.P.

The unfortunate victim had been currently working at St. Bartholomew's Hospital as a Professor of Medical Oncology. He was the father of four children; his wife Daphne I recall was on a visit to China on the day of the explosion.

St. Bartholomew's Hospital subsequently honoured his memory by naming a Hospital Ward after him. I was to be reminded of this fact some six years later when I became an in-patient in an adjacent ward after ten days in Intensive Care, fighting for my life after a mystery illness that had caused me renal failure.

In the first few hours of any murder or major enquiry, where numerous officers are busily engaged in interviewing potential witnesses in the street, or injured parties at hospitals and taking statements and gathering evidence, the information gleaned needs to be assimilated by those leading the enquiry. It also needs to be shared with all persons on the investigating team. Being the Duty Officer when this incident occurred, the day to day running of this investigation was now down to me and I arranged a Team Meeting to be held at the first available opportunity, which in this instance was on my return from Westminster Mortuary.

One interesting piece of information came from Tessie Candasan the resident Philippine cook employed by the Fraser's. In the absence of Sir Hugh the evening prior to the bombing she answered a telephone call from an unknown man who enquired as to whether Mr Fraser was in and whether he would be home before midnight. When advised that she did not know the time of his return, the caller asked what time Mr Fraser would be going out the next morning. He was informed that it was usually between 8.30am and 9am, but declined to leave his name. Sir Hugh had in fact returned home and parked his Jaguar at 12.45am.

At about 7.30am on the morning of the explosion Miss Candasan went out onto the porch at No 52 to collect the newspapers. She then noticed an object, which she thought, looked like a large stone, it being grey in colour, which was behind the front wheel of Mr Fraser's car. At the time she thought Mr Fraser might have put a stone behind the wheel to stop it rolling down the hill. She therefore made no mention of this to Mr Fraser when serving his breakfast soon afterwards. A little later she noticed Mr Hamilton-Fairley walking up the hill with his two white dogs. It was shortly after this that the windows of the house were blown in by the force of the explosion.

There were numerous statements from persons who been in the vicinity at the time of the explosion, several of whom had received minor injuries or suffered from shock or damage to their property. There were mentions of various vehicles seen being driven in Camden Hill Square, late the previous evening or earlier that morning, but no indication that their occupants could in anyway be connected with placing the device. Steps would however be instigated to trace and eliminate these vehicles.

Sir Hugh Fraser the intended victim of the car bomb, having been spattered with broken glass whilst seated at his desk, had also witnessed his wife's car, driven by Miss Leyland the Nanny, collide with a tree causing him to rush into the street in his dressing gown and pyjamas. Having satisfied himself as to the safety and condition of his nanny his cook and his houseguest Miss Kennedy, Sir Hugh dressed and proceeded to the House of Commons.

Miss Caroline Kennedy who had been staying as a guest of the Fraser's, whilst attending a course in London, had been in a front first floor bedroom when the explosion occurred outside, she felt the whole house shake as glass from the windows was blown in. Fortunately she was not injured.

The explosives officer James Greenwood had expressed the view, that the explosion was caused by the use of a mechanically timed, or a booby trap of a pressure or release type, device. Doubtless the perpetrators of this attempted political assassination, were the same unknown members of the Provisional Irish Republican Army, Active Service Unit that had been responsible for many similar incidents in past months, we were however no nearer apprehending them and bringing them to justice.

The following morning together with Detective Superintendent Peter Imbert, I attended Westminster Mortuary, where I formally identified the deceased to Professor Keith Simpson, MA. MD. FRCP. FRC.Path, who then carried out a post mortem examination in our presence. His findings, as expected, were that the victim, had died as a result of multiple explosive injuries concentrated on his right side and lower limbs.

Attending Post Mortems was one of the more unpleasant duties of a senior-investigating officer. Normally not having been acquainted with the victim, it was possible to remain detached, focusing on the findings of the pathologist and how they might affect or progress your investigation. Having learnt that our victim was not only an innocent neighbour, but an eminent professor whose life's work, had been devoted to fighting cancer, in order to save other's lives, I could not but let my thoughts dwell on the futility of his death.

Had I known then those responsible for this dastardly deed, had but two months of liberty left, to cause further death and destruction throughout London, before surrendering after a week long siege, I would have slept more easily. Particularly if I'd known that I would have the pleasure of raiding one of their two residences and recovering guns, explosives and other evidence, as well as the satisfaction of interviewing their ringleader and hearing him claim responsibility for this and many other violent deaths.

But that was in the future. A future in which I would also find myself investigating further terrorist incidents; various murders; including the political assassination of the Bulgarian dissident, Georgi Markov, by use of a ricin laden pellet, discharged by a man carrying an umbrella on Waterloo Bridge. But before venturing there, let me go back in time and recall some of the events that led me to this point in my career. A career that was to prove as interesting, exciting and challenging as any young man could wish. A career that would see me rise through the ranks from being a humble police cadet, to serve for seven years as a Detective Superintendent, investigating armed robberies and murders.

Chapter Two

Career Choice

"What made you join the police force?" This is a question I and I'm sure many of my former colleagues, must have been asked on many occasions throughout our careers. In my particular circumstances it was a decision I made just prior to leaving school, but in retrospect I had no concept of what being a police officer really entailed, nor did I have the vaguest idea of what a challenging, interesting but fulfilling career I had chosen.

Born in Balham South London during the early part of the Second World War, I grew up in nearby Tooting Bec, living the majority of my childhood with my parents; two sisters and a brother in a large double fronted Victorian House where my parents rented the upper two floors.

At sixteen years of age and a pupil at Tooting Bec Grammar school, I realized that many of my school friends had decided on their future careers, which included banking, insurance, teaching and such occupations, none of which particularly appealed to me. Art and mathematics being my strong subjects, my father, a self-employed painter and decorator, suggested I consider Architecture, but I had no wish to work in an office environment, I wanted to get out and about and meet different people. My knowledge of what life had to offer was however, very limited despite perusal of careers literature. Passes in Art, Mathematics, and Biology, at 'O' level, had not particularly enhanced my career prospects. I had enjoyed the Sciences and expected a pass in physics, I therefore returned to school for an additional term with the intention of re sitting this subject. It was during this final school term that a Police Career first came to mind and I can remember quite clearly how it came about.

Walking home from school one afternoon I noticed a uniformed figure talking to another pupil from my school. As

I drew near I recognized the figure as that of John Davidson, the elder brother of a school friend and himself a former pupil. He was wearing the uniform of a Police Cadet. I had however no knowledge up until that meeting, of the existence of a Police Cadet Corps. John looked extremely smart and when he told me about his job and the training he had just undergone and how he was now attached to a local police station, my interest grew. I was aware that John's father was a local police sergeant, who was a familiar and well-known figure in the neighbourhood. It was doubtless through him, that he had gained first-hand knowledge of police work and of the Police Cadet Corps.

Although National Service was destined to terminate prior to my eighteenth birthday, I had had, a brief taste of the discipline involved in the wearing of a uniform. Third year pupils and upwards at my school, were obliged to participate in the school's Combined Cadet Force. I'd therefore spent many a Thursday evening, with a hot iron, blanco, brass and boot polish, preparing my uniform for inspection, during the following afternoon's parade and drill. In addition, I had long been an active member of the Scout movement, which had developed a competitive spirit in me. I had been one of a pair of Senior Scouts, who had won our district 'Hike/Camp' competition, for two consecutive years. The Police Service promised therefore, both a new challenge and a future career.

Not discouraged by the thoughts of shift work, following discussion with my father, concerning the pros and cons of a police career, I wrote off for the necessary literature and application form. Prior to then, I had considered the Police Service, but the recruitment age of nineteen did not satisfy my immediate needs for employment. I was therefore pleased that at last I felt I had found not only a suitable career, but also one that I could embark on within a matter of months. I saw the Police Service as a career where I could help people in need, which appealed to me as something I could aspire to do, with training. Although I probably didn't appreciate it at the time, the example my father had always set probably pointed me in that direction.

Dad was always helping other people, often when we were on a family day out, on his motorcycle combination. If he saw another motorcyclist or a motorist broken down, he would always stop to see if he could be of assistance. Sometimes we never reached our intended destination, which was usually a South Coast resort. I can well remember unpacking our Primus stove to brew a cup of tea on some grass verge, whilst dad was helping a stranded motorist. I'm sure my mother found this frustrating, but I was quite proud of his actions. Although he drove a hard bargain when making any major purchase, he would always point out to a shop assistant if he had been given too much change. The thanks he received at such gestures made me realise at an early age, that it was more pleasurable to be honest, than profit from such situations.

It was not long before I found myself with an appointment to attend the Metropolitan Police Recruiting Centre, which was then situated at Beak Street, London, W.1. I was aware that in addition to undertaking a written test, I would be required to undergo a thorough medical examination, before being interviewed by a selection board. I had long been a keen swimmer and played rugby for my school under 15's Rugby Team, so had no qualms about my fitness. My biggest concern however was the eyesight test, as I knew my left eye to have a weakness. This had resulted in the prescription of N.H.S. spectacles for me, for several years earlier in my school days. Their design had done little to encourage me to wear them, so I had no way of knowing whether my current vision would prove adequate for the Police Service.

In recent times it is now possible for police recruits to wear spectacles on duty as long as their vision is of an acceptable standard. I will never know whether my left eye had acceptable vision, because, when asked to hold a card over my right eye, in order to test my left one, I left a slight gap between the card and my nose. This enabled me to read the test card with the aid of my right eye as well, to ensure I did not fail the test. Needless to say I passed and it was many years later, when being considered for driving duties, before I was obliged to have another eyesight test.

Once formally accepted for enrolment as a Police Cadet, I had to await notification of the date when there would be a vacancy for me to attend the Metropolitan Police Cadet Training School at Hendon. I left school at the end of that term and in order to obtain some income, took a job as trainee sales assistant, at Meakers men's wear shop in Balham. Had I made it known that I was awaiting a date to start my cadet training, I would never have got the position. There were however no temporary jobs available so I was obliged to commence training as a shop assistant. Although this was only to be for about two months, it reinforced my view that my future did not lie in, either retail or an office environment.

On 25th February 1957 I presented myself at Beak Street Recruiting Office and following issue of a uniform was dispatched with a number of eager aspirants, by coach to the Hendon Police Cadet Training Centre. A mature stern faced Station Sergeant accompanied us whose name was Stubbs and who was to be our Class Instructor for the next four weeks. Sgt Stubbs instructed us to address him as 'Sir' at all times and 'move lively' when obeying commands. Clearly it was necessary to lick us into some kind of shape in the short time available, before letting us loose on the unsuspecting public and the police stations where we were to be deployed.

The Police Cadet System was introduced by many Forces to aid recruitment, by attracting the interest of persons under the age of nineteen, the age at which, if suitable, one could be attested as a police constable. It has been varied many times since its inception, particularly with regard to the recruitment qualifications, the length and type of training and the duties that are performed. At the time when I joined there were 'Junior Cadets', with enrolment at a minimum age of sixteen years and two months and 'Senior Cadets' from the age of eighteen years and four months. Senior Cadets received the same basic 10 week training afforded to recruits aged nineteen or over. Consequently, on the first Monday following their nineteenth birthday, they were attested as Police Constables and posted to Divisions to commence service.

I was somewhat surprised to find I was one of the few Londoners in my intake, with my fellow cadets coming from all parts of Great Britain, some never having even visited London prior to applying to join. They were a good crowd however and there was plenty of mickey taking about the broad accents some had. The initial Cadet training we received included an insight into the rank and organisational structure of the Metropolitan Police, including the communications systems; basic foot drill; a brief understanding of the legal system and the differences between Criminal and Civil Law. In addition we acquired some basic typewriting skills and were instructed and rehearsed in the manner of performing school crossing patrol duties.

Having been trained, it was the norm for Junior Cadets to be posted for periods of six months to various police stations, Traffic Patrol garages or to some central departments at New Scotland Yard. Those cadets, who normally resided in the Metropolis, were allowed to live at home, whilst Section House Accommodation was provided, for those whose families were domiciled elsewhere in the Country.

My initial posting was to Brixton Police Station, which was situated only a few miles from my home address. There were a number of other cadets already serving there attached to the Chief Superintendent's Clerk's Office and Divisional Office. I was attached to the Communications Room, although each of the cadets was on a rota to undertake school crossing patrol duties at relevant times.

The Communications Room was staffed by a civilian switchboard operator and one police constable, who in addition to taking telephone messages and operating a tele printer machine, gave advice to the public as required. Brixton as well as being a busy station in its own right, also housed the Senior Officers for 'L' Division, and I was soon instructed in the method of operating the switchboard and filing and cross referencing the various copies of tele printer messages. This was for me a very interesting introduction to the police service. To be at the hub of activity and able to monitor the various communications that emanated from or were received at the station, as well as the manner in which they were dealt with by officers, was a useful introduction to policing.

The School Crossing Patrol duties also gave me the opportunity to get to meet some of the public and provided me with what I suppose was my first embarrassing moment in uniform. One day whilst on school crossing duties in Coldharbour Lane outside a school, I was asked by the driver of a lorry if I could direct him to Barnwell Road. Taking out my brand new A-Z purchased especially for this purpose I thumbed through the index, finally located the relevant page and the location, only to realise it was the turning alongside the very school where I was standing. I did feel a fool.

Two other road names I'll always recall were Somerleyton Road, and Geneva Drive. It was in these two roads that the majority of the first West Indian immigrants had taken up residence during recent years, mainly attracted by employment opportunities that had arisen. Many of the houses stood out from others in the neighbourhood as they were gaily decorated with brickwork painted in bright colours reflecting the personality and origins of their occupants. Crime was certainly not rife in this area then, the only troubles deriving from the occasional late night noisy party. I'm sure nobody serving at Brixton in those early days, could have anticipated the riots, involving the second generation that were to envelop these very streets in 1981.

Gradually, as I became more familiar with the Police Service and those around me, I learnt that not all police officers were in favour of the cadet system, for whilst the majority were friendly enough, some were outwardly intolerant. This in part emanated from the fact that National Service, which had been undertaken by most young men between the ages of 18 and 20, years, had only recently ended. There had however, been an option for Police Cadets to opt out of National Service, if serving as a cadet prior to attaining the age of 18. This sometimes aroused suspicions as to whether an individual's motivation was a police career or the avoidance of National Service. There was also the position that young men like myself, were becoming police officers at the age of 19 years. At this age some officers were considered naive or immature and lacking in life experiences or self-confidence and the reference by certain officers that an individual was an 'Ex Cadet', took on a sinister overtone.

I also became aware that some Junior Cadets were under employed, in that there was insufficient work suitable for them in the department where they were posted. Sometimes two cadets were deployed in the same office, where one would suffice. Often they were considered only useful as tea boys and this led to individuals skiving off to the canteen or the snooker room and then not being to hand if required. Since the meal breaks were only for three-quarters of an hour, the presence of cadets using the snooker table, albeit in their lunch break, was like a red rag to a bull with certain officers. I was grateful to be kept busy in the Communications Room and could soon be left alone to operate the switchboard, which I enjoyed.

My next posting was an attachment to the Plan Drawer responsible for Balham Sub Division, which encompassed the Sections of Earlsfield and Wandsworth Common Police Stations, with an office at the latter. Plan drawing was one of the many inside jobs or special functions that contribute to the efficient workings of police duty, but of which I had no prior knowledge. Gerry Chamberlain the plan drawer, to whom I was seconded, was a long serving officer with a 'drawing office' background and he was very experienced in this particular field. His prime function was to supply certified maps for prosecutions and the majority of his work involved detailed plans of road junctions, where Road Traffic Accidents had occurred resulting in a prosecution. Gerry was a dry old stick, but quite likeable once you got to know him. His prime concern with any new attachment was to describe the fate that would befall anyone careless enough to spill ink over his drawings. Having a cadet to assist him was obviously a great help to him particularly when he was out on locations, using a tape measure to check road widths and distances from signs.

His mode of travel was by bicycle and fortunately having one of my own and living only 15 minutes from the station, this posed no problem to me. Whenever Gerry received a request for a plan of a particular road junction he would check to see if he had a copy of a previously drawn one to work from. If he had, it would only be a matter of a quick visit to check that the junction had not been altered or any additional road signs or markings installed, before he could prepare a fresh original plan. I was frequently dispatched to check up on such matters enabling Gerry to get on with his drawings. When no previous plan was to hand the procedure was for Gerry to measure off the copies of Ordnance Survey maps he held, to get the basic layout and then add in local features and signs following a visit to the location.

It was whilst working with Gerry that I had my first insight into a major crime and this came about one day when we attended a house facing onto Clapham Common. There had been a murder at the house a few days previous, a man having killed his two young children. The C.I.D needed a plan of the inside layout to assist with the eventual prosecution and court proceedings. I was quite unprepared for what we found inside the house, having no prior knowledge of the details of the incident. Once inside the children's bedroom the extensive patterns of fresh blood staining on the wallpaper, clearly silhouetted the position where the headboards of two small beds had been, before being removed as exhibits. It transpired that the father had gone berserk and lashed out with a hammer at the heads of his two sleeping children, after his wife had left him. The extent of the blood splashes bore witness to a number of blows having been struck, during this horrendous crime.

We were both grateful to be spared the shocking sight that the first officers at the scene must have encountered, prior to the removal of the children's mutilated forms, during routine forensic examination. This scene, watched over by prematurely redundant dolls and soft toys on shelves, brought a chill to my spine, both at the time of our visit and during subsequent recollection.

Little did I know at that time that I was soon to be indoctrinated with the sordid detail of many other serious and often tragic crimes, for following my posting to the Plan drawer, I was transferred to the Forensic Science Laboratory at New Scotland Yard. Both at that time and on many occasions in my later service I contemplated how fortunate I had been to experience such an interesting informative and prestigious posting so early in my career.

The name Scotland Yard has been associated with the Metropolitan Police since 1829, when Sir Robert Peel, the Then Home Secretary, first established the Force. The task of organising and designing the new police was deputed to Colonel Charles Rowan and Richard Mayne (later Sir Richard Mayne). They set up headquarters at 4, Whitehall Place adjacent to a courtyard and premises formerly used as the London home of the Kings and Queens of Scotland prior to the Union. Other adjacent premises were subsequently taken over for use as police headquarters.

In 1890 the Metropolitan Police Headquarters were moved into a purpose built building designed by the architect Norman Shaw, located between the Victoria Embankment and Derby Gate, just off Parliament Street. This building, which became known as 'New Scotland Yard', was built in somewhat gothic style as a square with an inner court and with four great chimney stacks. The materials used were a mixture of red brick, Portland stone and Granite, the latter being quarried by convict labour at Dartmoor and other prisons to offset costs. Although it was both impressive and dominant alongside the River Thames, almost immediately it was found to be too small for the forces growing needs. An additional building was designed by the same architect and constructed to the South side, linked to the original by a bridge over a public road.

Another extension called the Curtis Green Building after its architect, was opened to the north of the first building in 1940 and linked to it by two enclosed bridges. The headquarters of the Metropolitan Police remained in these three buildings until 1967 when the need for larger and more modern accommodation, resulted in the move to the current site. The two Norman Shaw buildings North and South are now integral parts of the Parliamentary Estate, housing Members' of Parliament's offices and services.

The Metropolitan Police Forensic Science Laboratory was originally located on the 5th and 6th floors of the more modern Curtis Green extension of New Scotland Yard. It was here at the age of 17 that I found myself posted on my third placement of Service as a Police Cadet. Prior to this posting my visits to Scotland Yard had consisted of a brief tour as part of my training and thereafter the odd visit to collect urgently required plans that were copied and printed there. In addition to the laboratory, at that time Scotland Yard housed many other departments, those in later years were to be devolved or relocated to more suitable sites. In fact the Metropolitan Police Laboratory was subsequently renamed the Home Office Forensic Laboratory and re located into a purpose built building in Lambeth.

I found the Laboratory to be under the Directorship of a Dr Nicholls, but the police staff was few by comparison to current levels and consisted of Detective Chief Superintendent George Salter, Detective Inspector John McCafferty and Detective Constable Norman Brown. Norman in fact began his attachment to the laboratory on the same day as me, as a result of an increase in the police establishment. Although initially somewhat nervous and overawed, I can still recall how honoured I felt to be a member of the police staff, albeit very junior, in such illustrious company.

My prime role was to assist in the creation of relevant files and assist in packing or unpacking or transporting exhibits sent in for forensic examination, not only by the various Metropolitan police divisions, but also the Home Counties Forces. I was therefore privy to reading the explanatory reports of the investigating officers when items were received, as well as the reports of the findings of the various scientists, when packaging items for return. This was a real eye opener for me, to learn what practices went on in the world around me, particularly with offences of a sexual nature.

The laboratory work at that time was divided between the Biology Department and the Chemistry Department, whilst Ballistic work was generally undertaken by the DI John Mc Cafferty, in liaison with one of the scientists. I learnt that the Biology department was concerned very much in the examination and grouping of blood, saliva, or semen stains, found on articles submitted for examination. The identification and comparison of hairs and fibres and the maintenance of an index of various woods, such as those used in the sawdust composition of safe ballast, formed an equally important part of its work.

The staff of the Biology department numbered only about five at that time and one of these was a young Scientific Officer, Margaret Pereira whose work on blood analysis was to result in her becoming one of the Countries leading authorities on the subject in later years. Another topic being pioneered within the department at that time, was the collation of the sole patterns of footwear and methods of lifting footprints in dust or blood, for comparison with the footwear of suspects if arrested.

It was practice at that time to use samples of fresh blood of a known group, to help ascertain the group identity of samples sent for examination. Most of the scientific and civilian staff's blood groups were listed and it was not long before I was being called upon on occasions, to have a finger jabbed with a flat needle to provide a specimen. As each donor received a fee of two shillings and sixpence to cover 'pain and suffering' and my weekly wage was just over £3, I was always ready with a finger, whenever a fresh blood grouping case was being commenced. Unfortunately, my then hobby of motor cycle mechanics, sometimes conflicted with my ambitions as a blood donor and my finger was occasionally passed over in preference for one, uncontaminated with a week ends involvement with grease and carbon.

The Chemistry Department dealt with the examination and comparison of glass and paint samples, the examination of tool or jemmy marks at scenes of crime and comparison with items recovered from suspects, as well as cases involving drugs and poisons. It also had a handwriting expert on the staff. One of the most fascinating pieces of equipment for me was the spectrograph machine, which produced a graph showing the various chemical components of samples. This was particularly useful where paint chippings, consisting of several layers of different coloured paints, needed to be compared with control samples taken from a suspect's vehicle in fatal accident cases, or a jemmy in burglary cases. It was also fascinating to witness the reappearance of die stamped serial numbers, previously erased by criminals from stolen motor vehicle engines and the like, when treated with chemicals by the scientists.

In addition to the two scientific departments, there was a Gun room where handguns used or suspected of being used in crime were test fired and the Detective Inspector John Mc Cafferty undertook such cases. I believe John had been a chemist prior to joining the police service and this experience, doubtless resulted in his appointment to the laboratory. I learnt that a few years previous, he had been very much involved in the examination carried out at 10, Rillington Place, following the discovery of human remains buried and concealed there after murders perpetrated by the now infamous John Christie.

It was however in the field of ballistics that I was often called upon to help and found particularly interesting. I was to learn how most weapons other than shot guns were tooled during manufacture on the inside of the barrel with a spiral groove, to cause fired ammunition to spin and thus enhance accuracy. Contact with the barrel resulted in striation marks being scored into the side of bullets. Unless these marks were damaged or distorted by the bullet flattening on impact with a hard substance, it was possible to prove conclusively that a bullet had been fired from a particular gun, should it be traced. In the absence of the weapon it was possible to connect seemingly unrelated shooting incidents by comparison of bullets recovered at the scenes of crimes. Likewise the examination and comparison of the marks made by the striking pin or ejector mechanism on cartridge case could also link weapons to crime scenes.

In order to test fire a weapon and recover the spent bullet in an undamaged condition, it was fired through a hole in one end of a long wooden coffin like box, tightly packed with cotton wool. The box, which had a removable lid was divided into 12-inch sections by thin cardboard inserts, these were removed after a firing, in order to determine in which section the bullet had come to rest. I recall how amazed I was at the retarding effect of mere cotton wool. The spinning action of the heated bullet soon became tangled with an ever-increasing mass of cotton wool, which quickly slowed down its passage through the box. Doubtless, the principal evolved to the present day use of Keflon material in bulletproof clothing. I was often entrusted with the task of ferreting through the box to recover the sample bullet, which would then be examined by scientists with the aid of a comparison microscope.

During the period of my attachment, DI Mc Cafferty decided to carry out an experiment involving striation marks. He, therefore, arranged for the acquisition of two revolvers from a leading manufacturer, specifying that they be consecutively manufactured particularly with regard to the rifling of their barrels. It was his intention to examine any similarities in the striation patterns on ammunition fired from each weapon, both initially and after firing a specified number of rounds. This was with a view to being able to negate if required, any Defence Counsels inference that the striation marks on a particular bullet, could have been made from another gun manufactured at the same time as the one in question.

For the purpose of this experiment I accompanied him to Chelsea Barracks where arrangements had been made to use their range. Within a short time of commencing firing one of the weapons appeared to suffer a misfire. Whilst DI Mc Cafferty was examining the rear of the chamber with a puzzled expression on his face, standing to his side I suddenly noticed a slight bulge on the exterior of the barrel which I quickly pointed out. Further examination proved that the last fired round had somehow lodged in the barrel. This unfortunate incident put paid to the experiment, but only after the DI had congratulated me on my powers of observation, which had prevented a nasty accident. Unfortunately my period of attachment to the laboratory came to an end before new weapons could be obtained to continue with the tests.

Various tasks I was deputed would necessitate my crossing from my somewhat modern surroundings, into the old Norman Shaw Building. The contrast was striking, if not a little eerie and I felt a real sense of being somewhere special. Beige-coated messengers shuffled along the corridors, pushing trolleys heavily laden with files and correspondence, as part of the internal despatch system. The silence as I walked along the broad carpeted corridors, only broken by the occasional squeak from one of their trolleys. The nature and content of any conversations from within the various offices, was kept secret by the stone walls and heavy timbered doors. As I passed through these hallowed corridors, I would gaze in awe at the various door signs, reading the names of the diverse departments and their occupants. I often recognised familiar names of high ranking detectives, who'd featured in murder investigations in the national newspapers, which only two years earlier I had been delivering, before attending school.

My aspirations at that age were to progress through my Cadet Service to become a fully-fledged Constable for a career in the Police Service. Little did I realise that one day I would have an office at Scotland Yard, albeit in the more modern characterless present building. Having once visited the infamous Black Museum in the basement and seen its macabre exhibits, it never entered my head that, this museum would ultimately feature, an exhibit from a case I had investigated and the tiniest exhibit ever. A platinum iridium pellet smaller than a pin head, but drilled at right angles to provide channels to contain ricin, an almost unknown and undetectable poison, used in a political assassination.

Following my three, six months postings as a Junior Police Cadet I returned to the Hendon Police Training College, where I was enrolled as a Senior Cadet. There I was issued with my Instruction Book, known as the 'I.B.' or police officers bible, which set out procedures for dealing with almost any eventuality, as well as the relevant legislation and punishments. I then underwent the ten weeks intensive training, identical to that undertaken by Police Recruits. This included learning word perfect, various definitions within the Criminal Law such as the Larceny Act of 1916 (Later Repealed) the Offences Against the Person Act 1861, the Vagrancy Act of 1824 and many others. It was also essential to learn the intricacies of the different powers of arrest existing under Common Law and various Statutes.

Our training also involved a good deal of role playing, by instructors acting out different scenarios of incidents we might have to deal with, once finally attested as Constables. We had also to practice filling in the various report booklets, for Road Traffic

Accidents and practice giving evidence, in a mock courtroom within the training centre. Early morning parades; Uniform Inspections; Foot Drill; Self-Defence Training; Life Saving; First Aid Training and general sporting activities, punctuated our academic day. Thus it was ensured that we were neither bored, nor capable of anything other than a good night's sleep at the end of each day.

We were allowed to return to our respective homes at weekends. Those cadets from the provinces, who had occupied Section House accommodation as Junior Cadets, were obliged to stay at Hendon, when distance from their families precluded travel. In any event, much of our weekends, involved studying and learning, but those of us able to return to our families had the benefit of a change of diet and a mum to do our laundry. In addition to various Senior Cadet Courses at Hendon, older applicants for a police career were undergoing identical training courses there as Police Recruits. There was also another training establishment for Recruits only and this was at the Peel Centre in Regency Street, London. SW1.

Within a few days of our training commencing we were informed that the Annual Boxing Competition between Peel House and Hendon Police Recruits, was due to take place during our term there. As it was intended to have a few bouts of inter cadet boxing on the same bill, volunteers who either had boxing experience or an interest in competing, were required to undergo boxing training in the lunch period.

As a boy, my father, who was interested in boxing, had encouraged me to take up the sport. He wanted me to be able to stand up for myself and so, I had for a number of years received boxing training. Initially aged about 9 years on Sunday mornings he took me to Merton, where a former boxer was training young lads, in a large shed kitted out as a gym in his rear garden. I believe this also gave my dad an excuse to meet up with his brother Bill, whose son Alf my cousin also attended. Soon afterwards I joined the Earlsfield Boxing Club (later renamed the Wandsworth Boxing Club) which met twice weekly at Waldron Road School, in Garrett Lane Tooting.

Thinking back this was probably my first contact with the criminal element in society, as us juniors shared changing facilities with the seniors and whilst we were changing after training, the older lads would arrive. I overheard many a tale in the changing room, concerning brushes with 'The Law' some of them had had. In addition some of them would occasionally be absent for periods of time and it was apparent from conversation on their return, that they had either been on remand, or serving short terms of imprisonment. Indeed the standard of ability of one senior club member, when he first joined, raised questions as to how he was not known on the local boxing circuit. It transpired that he had in fact won a Borstal Championship. Needless to say this contact in no way impinged on my wellbeing, it providing merely a broader insight into society. The training and experiences I gained from amateur boxing, apart from keeping me fit, developed my self-confidence and proved useful on one occasion, when three school bullies picked me on. Indeed one of them impressed at my stance and ability approached me about joining my club.

Subsequently I had boxed as a junior at a number of local Amateur Boxing Shows. I had also, at the age of 14, managed to win the South West London, Schoolboy Championships, at 8st. 2oz. The next round of the championships in 1955, saw me due to compete against a lad named Sid Chapman (no relation), the South East London Champion. Whilst queuing up for the weigh in at Lewisham Baths, I casually picked up a local newspaper opened at the sports page, only to read that my opponent that night, had the previous year won the London Schoolboy Championships and was strongly fancied to proceed further this time.

Needless to say this did little to boost my confidence and my progress in the Championships ended in the first round. My corner threw the towel in, or so I was told afterwards, for I only remember seeing stars, following a barrage of blows from which I was unable to recover. That fight effectively ended my boxing activities as a schoolboy, as for several days I suffered a severe migraine and vomiting. Thereafter I also suffered the onset of occasional long lasting headaches, for which no apparent cause could be found, despite referral to a Specialist at Guys Hospital. The only consolation on my part was to see my opponent progress to win the Great Britain Schoolboy Championships, later that year.

Despite the three-year gap, I volunteered to undertake boxing training at the Cadet School. As the competition drew near, we were required to do early morning training, thus being excused Parade and rewarded with 'Special Diet' breakfasts. These were at least a slight improvement, on the usual trays of plastic looking fried eggs that resulted from mass catering. Ultimately I boxed a fellow cadet at the Inter School Competition. I was matched against a lad named Andy Beaton, who was a strong lad, being a keen swimmer, but who displayed more guts than boxing skill. Although I won my bout, it was a hollow victory, for there was a dearth of boxing experience amongst my fellow cadets. Little did I realise at that time; my boxing experience was to play a significant part in my future posting as a Police Constable and my life thereafter.

On successful completion of my training I found myself posted to Balham Police Station, in Cavendish Road. Here I was deployed on a Relief with fully-fledged constables and learnt beat duty. This involved patrolling the streets with various officers, on weekly alternating late and early shifts. I also had brief periods of attachment to the area Traffic Patrol Garage and the local South West London Magistrates Court, the latter proving a real eye opener to me, as to what went on in my local neighbourhood.

Working with a variety of experienced officers, seeing how each dealt with day to day problems and incidents and how they interpreted the various Acts of Parliament, I had just spent ten weeks studying, proved a useful education. One salutary lesson I did learn came about one Saturday afternoon in a busy part of Balham High Road when we witnessed an obvious altercation within a group of men, one of whom punched another. I immediately began to run towards them until reigned back by my P.C. tutor telling me to take my time. We then continued to approach the men at a steady walking pace. This however gave time for the group to see us coming and warn the two protagonists.

As a result, when we reached the group, the disturbance had ceased and our presence was merely needed to offer 'words of advice'. My colleague then pointed out that had we both run into the situation, we could have become embroiled in a general free for all, with us possibly losing control or exacerbating the situation. The steady approach had not only allowed the situation to cool, but gave us thinking time to analyse the situation. It also allowed a few seconds to consider, how or where we might obtain assistance, should it be required, for there were no such thing as personal radios let alone phones at that time.

Chapter Three

On the Beat

On 27th April 1959 the first Monday following my nineteenth Birthday, I presented myself at New Scotland Yard and together with a number of other cadets, as well as some new recruits, was duly attested as a Constable. I learnt that I was to be posted to 'N' Division, which I only knew to be north of the Thames. I was a bit surprised as although one undertook to serve anywhere in the Metropolis, I had anticipated that I would be posted somewhere in South London, where I had grown up and had some local knowledge of. This was also going to drastically affect my social life in particular my involvement with helping to run a Scout Troop in Balham, where the alternate late shifts as a Senior Cadet had already restricted my availability.

I discovered that the area covered by 'N' Division was roughly Stoke Newington, South Tottenham, Holloway, Highbury, Islington and Kentish Town. I had only knowingly travelled north of the river Thames on three occasions each as a schoolboy, on the pillion seat of my father's motorcycle combination. Once to Holloway Bus Garage, when I had left my school satchel, containing my French homework on a bus. Another time was when Fulham, whom we supported, were drawn against Tottenham Hotspur in a cup round and finally on a day out to Epping Forest.

The headquarters of my new Division was Stoke Newington, so it was here that I reported to Divisional Chief Superintendent Beresford Paul, a ruddy faced jovial man, who greeted me with a warm handshake which helped to put me at ease. Almost his opening words as he came from behind his desk were, "I understand your interests include boxing and rugby"

He then proceeded to show me his Trophy Cabinet and point out the various cups and awards his Division had won.

"We always enter a team in the Lafone Cup," he informed me and knowing this to be an Inter Divisional Novice, Boxing Event, it began to dawn on me that my posting might have been no mere coincidence.

"You'll be attached to St. Ann's Road, but when the boxing training starts your duties will be arranged so you can train in our gym downstairs."

I was also advised to contact inspector Spears at Caledonian Road Police Station, who ran the Divisional Rugby Team. There were a few words of warning about the dangers of associating with married women, which I later discovered arose over another recruit's recent indiscretions. He wished me luck and the interview was over.

On meeting my Sub Divisional Superintendent, I was informed that I was allocated the Divisional Number 268 'N' and was in fact being posted to St. Ann's Road Police Station, a Sectional Station under the command of Stoke Newington which covered the area of South Tottenham and Haringey. Being single, I was allocated Section House Accommodation but as the Section House adjacent to Stoke Newington Police Station had no current vacancies, I was to live in Section House accommodation, over Tottenham Police Station on "Y" Division, until a vacancy occurred. There followed a visit to the Divisional Clothing Store to be fitted out with a Constables uniform and other relevant items of kit, before being deposited by police van at my new abode.

This I found to consist of a small sparsely furnished partitioned cubicle, on the second floor. There were however a number of communal facilities such as washroom, television lounge and Residents Canteen. My cubicle, which overlooked Tottenham High Road, was one of about twenty, in two rows divided by a central access passage. The partitioning stopped about 18 inches short of the ceiling, so I soon learnt it was possible to have a conversation with one's neighbours without leaving your cubicle. It also became a regular almost daily occurrence to hear someone else's alarm clock going off at about 5am for the Early Turn shift. Although most of my fellow inmates were based on 'Y' Division, so none worked as my station, living in such close proximity, it didn't take long to get to know them. I made some lasting friendships in the time I was there.

Since a great deal of a Police Officer's time was to be spent giving evidence in various traffic or crime cases, part of our training had been to practice giving evidence in a mock court, with instructors taking the part of the Magistrates. This was quite unreal however, so, the first few weeks of a new recruit's posting to a Sub Division, were spent attending the local Magistrates Court. This was to familiarise themselves with the building, staff, local procedures and any idiosyncrasies of individual Magistrates. St. Ann's Road's Station area was situated mainly in the County of Middlesex, and served by Tottenham Magistrates Court, where Justices of the Peace held a Crime Related Court on Thursdays. A small area however was part of the northern most part of the County of London, served by North London Magistrates Court, where a Stipendiary Magistrate sat daily. I was therefore tasked to attend this court on a daily basis, but Tottenham Court on the Thursday. Having booked on duty by telephone from North London Court for two days, and still not having set foot inside my new place of work, I and another recruit also 'Learning Courts', decided to call in on the Thursday to book on personally on our way to Tottenham Magistrates Court.

Unbeknown to us, that day Local Elections were being held and all available Police Manpower was needed to man Polling Stations. Consequently we had both been rostered for this duty, He 6am-2pm and I, 2pm-10pm. Since neither of us had been informed, my colleague was three and half-hours late for duty, whereas I was four and half-hours early. I reported back at 2pm and was directed how to find the relevant school and told I would be relieved for refreshments in due course. I was due to spend my first few weeks after 'Learning Courts' in the company of seasoned officers teaching me the various beats and imparting local knowledge to me. Instead of this, here was I in a completely strange environment hoping I didn't get lost on my way to the Polling Station where I was due to relieve an Early Turn Officer. What was more worrying was that throughout my training,

Polling Station Duty had never been mentioned. I was therefore very unsure what I was supposed to do at a Polling Station but hoped the officer I was to relieve would be able to brief me.

I needn't have worried, his 'brief' amounted to, "Just make sure no one nicks the Ballot Box" and he was off. Some four hours and numerous cups of tea later, a Sergeant arrived, Bill Cutler who was destined to be one of my Relief Sergeants. He looked somewhat crestfallen to learn I had walked to the Polling Station, then handed me his cycle clips insisting I borrowed his bike, saying "I don't want to be here all night." He was a lot taller than me and I found I could only just reach the pedals, so with a bit of a wobble and feeling very vulnerable, I cycled back to the Station, praying no one would need my services on the journey.

Once finally attached to my relief I found it to consist of about ten Constables and three Sergeants, though we were never all on duty at the same time, when Leave Days, Holidays etc. took their toll. All probationers are allocated a reporting Sergeant and mine was Jack Bannister. He was a very likeable personality, well built with close cut, greying hair, a broken nose and a twinkle in his eye. He possessed a wealth of experience and self-confidence and was an ideal role model. I was pleased to ascertain that with the exception of one Officer, who was still a Probationer, (having less than two years' experience), the remainder were all seasoned officers. Some were in the twilight of their careers, with war service and therefore an abundance of experience for me to draw on if necessary. As we were a Sectional Station, only Police Constables and Sergeants were based at St. Ann's Road, supervised by an Inspector from Stoke Newington, where all other management and admin offices were located. There was however a CID office staffed by detectives of similar ranks.

It was a requirement that officers paraded for duty a quarter hour before commencement of their shift. This was to be briefed regarding any 'All Station' messages that might be relevant to our tour of duty, including details of lost or stolen motor vehicles in the Metropolitan Police District (M.P.D.). In addition messages from other stations with requests to interview or pass on information to individual members of the public would also be given out, for in those days only a minority of households had telephones.

Officers were also required to produce their 'Appointments' which consisted of a duty armband a whistle, a Police Box key, a truncheon, a wallet containing Report Books a Pocket Book and, if on Night Duty, a set of 'Marking Instruments', more of which will be mentioned later. During the briefing officers were allocated various Beats or Patrols and Refreshment times to ensure that some officers were always out on the streets. With myself rostered to 'Learning Beats' for the first few weeks: each day a different officer would be deputed to take me with him on his Beat. Their purpose being to familiarise me not only with the various streets I was to patrol for the foreseeable future, but also some of the diverse characters both good and bad, that frequented or resided in the locality.

The area covered by our Section comprised six beats in the Haringey (later re-named (Haringey) area. St. Ann's Road Police Station was conveniently situated in the centre of its area of responsibility.

My first day's beat duty was on Early Turn with Bill Lineham, one of the veterans on our relief and probably old enough to be my father. He was an imposing figure of a man who I found to be quiet, but amiable, as we headed off west towards Green Lanes passing the adjacent St. Ann's Road Hospital and the Ever Ready battery factory. After a brief introduction to the female news vendor outside the Salisbury public house, we headed south along Green Lanes, a busy bus route lined either side by shops, and many run by the local Cypriot population. Passing Haringey Railway Station, we reached Haringey Stadium, which I knew to have been the venue of some great professional boxing bouts in bygone years. Adjacent to this was Haringey Greyhound Track, which I learnt currently featured greyhound racing on Mondays and Fridays and made demands on police manpower.

Walking up the hill, Finsbury Park was pointed out just across the road, which I learnt to be part of the Hornsey Sub Division. Reaching the top of Green Lanes at its junction with Seven Sisters Road, we arrived at a major road junction where the Manor

House pub and Underground Station were situated, here we crossed over to a Police Box situated by one of the Gated entrances to Finsbury Park. Surveying the busy junction, I little realised that within a few months I would be out in the middle of this junction, directing traffic, whilst a new traffic light system was being installed.

The now obsolete Police Boxes were then strategically placed, usually bordering neighbouring Beats and often, adjacent Divisions. A small wicket door was available for the public to access a telephone, which directly communicated with the switchboard of the local police station. Alongside was the narrow entrance door fitted with a universal lock, for which all officers were issued with a key. Their appearance from without, painted in regulation blue with police insignia and a central revolving roof light, may have been imposing, but within there was barely room for two officers to stand, a fitted shelf for report writing taking up the space behind the telephone compartment with a stool underneath.

Hand held personal radios had yet to be developed and introduced throughout the force. Officers were therefore tasked to 'Ring In' to their Station at fairly specific times, once before their meal break and once afterwards, so the Police Boxes were from where these 'Rings' were made. Should a station have an urgent need to contact an officer, the Police Box Pulsating Light could be activated, in the hope of attracting an officer's attention.

Continuing along the busy bus route of Seven Sisters Road, we passed a number of large blocks of council flats which I learnt was the Woodberry Down Estate. I was by now completely disorientated, but was soon pleasantly surprised when I realised we had arrived back at an intersection with St. Ann's Road This enabled us to return to the Station in time for our meal break. Nothing untoward had occurred during the first part of our patrol, but it had given me my first taste of beat duty as a constable and a brief introduction to the neighbourhood.

During the ensuing days I was deputed to work with other officers on their Beats each day, gradually getting to know the area and personalities of the team with whom I was to work for the foreseeable future. Also getting experience in the completion of Accident Reports and reporting of motoring offences known as 'Process'. On my third week of 'Learning Beats' due to a shortage of manpower, an officer from Stoke Newington, whose name I can only recall as Bill, was posted to work Late Turn at St. Ann's Road and I was rostered to work with him. We had almost completed our uneventful tour of duty when we arrived at the Police Box situated at the top of Stamford Hill, our joint boundary. Bill lived in Stoke Newington and so he told me he intended to smoke a roll up in the box and would then book off duty by phone from there. Instructing me not to get into any trouble we parted company and I headed back, but by 9.40pm I was in St. Ann's Road almost within sight of the Police Station. I still had 20 minutes to kill before finishing my shift at 10pm, so I decided to patrol down Cissbury Road one of the residential side turnings, turn left and take the next left South Grove which I knew would bring me back on route and on time.

As I turned left at the first junction my attention was drawn to two youths on the opposite side and at the junction with South Grove, some 100 yards away where I could see a shop premises. They were stationary, but looking all around in a suspicious manner. It was dark and I did not think they had seen me as I had instinctively ducked down behind a parked car. A few moments later the pair of them came running round the corner down the middle of the road in my direction with one of them pushing something inside his coat. I could feel the adrenaline flowing as I crouched, waiting and timing my move. Then leaping out from behind the car I grabbed the lad with something down his coat. The other one ran on then stopped some twenty yards further on to look back. Shouting in voice which I didn't recognise as my own I said, "Come here you" and to my surprise he did.

Inside the first boy's coat I discovered a small box containing nine rolls of sweets, which they admitted having stolen by pushing in some hardboard covering a previously broken window. It was used as a serving hatch at the shop; a confectioner's adjacent to South Grove School. Both youths were aged 15, but fortunately seemed resigned to their fate, as I walked them holding the upper arm of each, towards the Station. I then began to think about whether Bill would be in trouble for letting me return on my own and wondered if I could get him on the phone before he left the police box. I reached the Station just as the shift hand over had taken place. I was obliged to explain to the night Duty Sergeant Bill Hicks who I had barely met. "Don't worry about being on your own son," he said, "you'll probably be a sergeant by next week" this flippant remark having put me at ease, details of my two culprits were obtained and their parents were sent for. Both lived quite close and two fathers shortly attended to be present during proceedings. No sooner had the Custody Sergeant related the facts to them and their offspring acquiesced in their guilt, than one father a burly lorry driver with hands like bunches of bananas, stepped forward and slapped his son round the face almost knocking him off his feet. We were completely taken by surprise at this dispensation of summary justice and stepped between father and son to intervene. Seeing a red hand shaped wheal appearing on the cheek of this lad, I did feel that perhaps justice had been done and proceeding could have ended there.

The following week I found myself at Tottenham Juvenile Court about to give evidence for the first time. Although both youths had admitted the theft they had been charged with burglary and as this was a technical matter, i.e. the reaching into premises to steal from within, they had been advised to plead 'Not guilty'. My mind raced back to the mock court practice I had had some months previous. The Court Usher hands you a copy of the New Testament then a card on which the Oath is typewritten. You raise the New Testament in your right hand to head height, the Usher reads out the Oath, one line at a time and you repeat that line after him reading from the card. I had almost finished the Oath before I realised the hand I had raised was my left one with the Oath card in it, my right arm holding the Testament was down by my side. If anyone noticed they said nothing and I gave my evidence with a very red face vowing not to make that mistake again. Both youths were subsequently convicted and fined.

After six weeks of day duty 'Learning Beats' adhering to the normal relief pattern of alternating Early Turn 6am – 2pm and

Late Turn 2pm – 10pm shift. There was a three week Night Duty tour 10pm – 6am, this I found completely different. For the early part of the shift whilst the public houses were still open there was quite a lot of activity on the ground and apart from dealing with any disturbances, most officers would patrol, checking the security of the various shops and factories on their beat. As one of our boundaries was the river Lea we had a number of large timber merchants with businesses adjacent to the river. There were also a number of furniture manufacturers doubtless emanating from the local timber supplies. There were also some very extensive factories such as Gestetners, who made printing machines; Maynards the sweet manufacturers and Courtney Popes the shop fitters. Together with Greyhound Meetings twice a week, this made for an interesting area to police. After midnight the ground would quieten down and it was possible to focus on the activities of any vehicles or persons still moving. It was a bit of a revelation to learn the varied different reasons people had for being abroad in the early hours and how many other services and business operations worked twenty four hours such as us. I recall spending some time watching two men with torches in the distance along Seven Sister Road, seemingly loitering near parked cars, only to find on approaching they were Water Board employees testing water pressure in roadway hydrants.

On night duty I found that it was the practice to check the security of any shop premises as soon as possible on commencement of the shift, and this meant trying door handles or pulling on padlocks, as the case may be, to check them. One would also repeat this practice at the end of your shift. In between times it was up to the individual officer where and when he patrolled the remainder of his given Beat, as long has he kept to his schedule for 'Ringing In' and taking refreshments. If premises were found to be insecure or there were signs of unlawful entry or attempts thereat, such as an alarm bell ringing, it would be necessary, having checked for intruders, to mind the premises until arrival of a Key holder. This could be up to an hour, of more if you were unlucky and keep you away from the remainder of your beat. I was to learn that some alarms were prone to activate whenever it was very windy, whilst others only went off when there was a genuine attempt to break in. With increasing demands on police over the years the practice of minding premises, just because an alarm had been activated has been discontinued and legislation has been introduced so that alarms must cease ringing after twenty minutes. Anyone residing in a flat over high street shops must be truly grateful for this piece of legislation.

Many of the shop premises had rear access yards or alleyways and as this was the most likely point of entry for any would be burglar, it was necessary to visit these at night. It was here that officers' 'Marking Instruments' could come into their own. This would consist of a small pouch or tobacco tin in which to carry any item such as a reel of dark cotton and some pins. The idea being that if a rear alleyway or unlocked gateway led to a number of different vulnerable premises, once checked you could stretch a length of cotton across between two posts or fences at the entrance and if intact on your return, this could save time in further checks. With communal gateways a small piece of paper held in place by a door against the doorjamb, was a useful indicator of any access having been made.

By the time I had completed my 'Learning Beats' I was more than ready to face the great British public on my own. I was by no means an expert at anything, but possessed of a lot more confidence in dealing with people and situations. As a probationer I still had to attend weekly, an Instruction Class held by an Inspector at Stoke Newington, for their were further examinations to be taken at nine and fifteen months from date of appointment. Jack Banister my supervising sergeant would also be submitting 'returns of work' on a regular basis. This listed the numbers of Arrests, Traffic Process and Verbal Warnings I had undertaken. My first Crime Arrest had pleased Jack, but he did have to chase me to up my figures for traffic process on occasions.

Our busiest shopping area was Green Lanes Haringey so much so that in addition to being part of a Beat, it was a 'Patrol' and one officer was posted just to that Road. Drivers would regularly stop on the yellow 'No Waiting' lines, whilst their spouses popped into shops thus reducing two possible lanes of traffic into one. Some would move on seeing me approach, others would brazen it out saying, "I'll only be a few minutes officer". What they failed to consider was the disruption to fellow motorists in those few minutes and the fact that others would follow their example and effectively restrict traffic flow all day. I generally took the view that if drivers who remained with their vehicles accepted a 'Verbal Warning' and moved when approached or spoken to, I saw no need to report them. Sympathetic to the lack of convenient parking I would turn a blind eye to those who parked in the restricted section of side roads if they were not blocking turning vehicles.

To spend all day reporting offending motorists would be both tedious and counter-productive, it was certainly not what I had joined the police force to do. There were however some motoring offences that I considered either dangerous or irresponsible, such as 'parking in the approach to' or 'failing to accord precedence to pedestrians' at pedestrian crossings and using a vehicle without insurance and I had no hesitation in reporting offenders for such offences. Quality rather than quantity was my watchword, but already my appetite had been whetted by my first arrest for Crime.

I had not been serving many months before I became a victim of crime myself. I was still resident in Tottenham Section House at the time and several of us who had motor cycles were in the habit of going swimming at Tottenham Lido in the morning before Late Turn. I had a six-year-old 350cc Ariel motor cycle, which was stolen from the Lido car park one morning. I got a lift back with one of the others and reported the theft at Tottenham Police Station. Needless to say there were quite a few officers keeping a look out for my bike. I scrutinised every approaching motor cycle whether on or off duty for the next few days, and was surprised how many ariels were to be seen, but not mine. About a week later I received a phone call at the Section House from one of the PC's at St. Ann's Road, to inform me my bike had been found abandoned beside a school wall in Seaford Road. To add insult to injury Seaford Road was on 15 Beat to which I was currently posted. Fortunately no damage had been caused.

About a week or so later having finished a shift of Night Duty on a Sunday morning, I drove straight to my parent's home at Tooting Bec and went to bed. I was awakened some hours later by my mother telling me a police officer was at the front door asking to see me. Still bleary eyed I went down and found myself being questioned about the ownership of my motorcycle which was parked outside. The P.C. then informed me he had received a message from Woodford Police requesting that I be interviewed and reported for 'Failing to Notify the Licensing Authority of Change of Ownership' of my vehicle. It transpired that on the morning my bike was stolen a youth had been stopped whilst driving it, but before I had reported it stolen. He claimed to have recently purchased it and having given a false name and an address in Tottenham, had been allowed to continue on his journey which he stated was to visit Southend. He had been issued with a form H.O.R.T./1, to produce his licence and insurance, but before it was learnt that his details were false, an enquiry had been instigated to interview and report the 'previous owner'. I subsequently spoke with the officer who had made the 'stop', he was very apologetic, but was able to supply me with brief description of the suspect. The false address was a road about half a mile from where my motorcycle was found on Tottenham Sub Division and although I made a few further enquiries with the local Collator the culprit's identity remained unknown. I was however grateful he had not damaged my bike in any way.

One evening whilst walking through the car park of the greyhound stadium just before racing finished, my attention was drawn by a flickering light to a group of men huddled together with their heads bent down observing something in their midst. I strolled over curious as to what was engaging their attention and peered over the shoulders of the back row to see that a game of Crown and Anchor was in progress on a board, supported on a makeshift table of cardboard boxes illuminated by several candles. My first indication that this was illegal, was when the chap operating the game looked up and obviously saw the top of my helmet. He then grabbed his board and made off in the opposite direction, letting the candles fall to the ground and the small crowd disperse, with disapproving glances in my direction. I found myself somewhat bemused by this as I had no wish to spoil anybody's entertainment, the crowd were all race goers and therefore gamblers and if they wished to risk their bus fare on a last chance to break even, I had no wish to stop them. Technically there was an offence of Gaming in a Public Place, but the car park was isolated and only used by the racing crowd and I personally saw no harm in their game. I had been aware that certain officers were deployed in plain clothes to deal with teams operating the 'Three Card Trick' who set up games near the approaches to Manor House Station, but naively I was unaware that Crown and Anchor featured in these illegal activities.

The Manor House was always a busy spot during the early evening, particularly when there was greyhound racing at Haringey Stadium. Many punters would exit the Piccadilly line underground there and frantically look for a taxi to take them the half mile to the track. It was common knowledge that taxi drivers would fill up their cabs with as many individuals as they could, often exceeding their quota of four persons and then charge a flat fee per head. By sharing with others, race goers reduced their taxi fare and the cabbies charging a flat rate per head, for a full cab on a short run were well rewarded. What it did mean however, was that cab drivers were pulling up all over the place often double parking and doing 'U' turns to the detriment of other traffic. It was also difficult for anyone seeking a cab to go anywhere other than the dogs, to get one. By law once a cab displaying a 'For Hire' sign had been hailed and the driver had stopped to speak to a customer, he was obliged to accept the hiring. Seeing a lady standing on a central reservation in the middle of Seven Sister Road hail a taxi on a race night, I was surprised to see her walk away after the driver had stopped and spoken with her. I quickly approached her and enquired where she wished to go. She replied "St. Ann's Road Hospital, but the driver's only going to the Dog Track". Opening the door of the cab, which had not moved off, I said to a startled looking cab driver," This lady wants to go to St. Ann's Hospital, right?"

"Yes governor," he replied sheepishly as he opened the door for his solitary passenger.

Helping a deserving member of the public was very satisfying but that was not to be the case for my next 'Good Deed', which was on behalf of a fellow motorcyclist and also occurred on a race night. One of the police duties associated with greyhound racing at Haringey was to man a traffic point in Green Lanes at the 'T' junction with Hermitage Road, which provided access to the rear entrance to the track. Whilst performing this duty standing in the middle of this junction one evening, looking to my left I saw a solo motorcyclist approaching I then noticed that the side, 'kick stand' was down in the open position. This I knew from personal experience could be a potential safety hazard, as when one lay the bike over to perform a left turn, the end of the stand, protruding forward against the return spring, could stab into the road surface and cause the bike to jump suddenly. Fearing for this motorcyclist's safety, as he passed in front of me I called out "Your stands down". I immediately regretted my action, for he looked back over his right shoulder in my direction and I saw his bike gradually swerved to the left across the road, to where a motor cycle combination was parked, some twenty feet further on. Its rider had just left his house and mounted the bike when the handlebars of the solo struck him in the back. I was horrified to say the least. I ran to their assistance and explained what had occurred, fortunately no serious damage or injury had been caused, although the rider of the combination had hurt his back and decided to visit the Prince of Wales Hospital for a check-up. Being fellow motor cyclists both understood and accepted my explanation and this was a great relief. My biggest problem thereafter was when completing the Personal Injury Accident Report Book under the Section 'How Accident happened'. I did have visions of being sued, but fortunately never heard any more about it.

It did not take me long to realise the work ethic of officers varied with their age and personality. Naturally young officers like myself were keen to do the job they had recently been trained to undertake, but among the longer serving officers there were those who never seemed to get involved in anything, whilst others were always to the fore where arrests or process were necessary. This commitment to the job was probably more apparent on night duty, where certain officers seemed to think that nothing much happened after about 1am and they would drag out their refreshment break or find excuses to be in the station in the early hours. True when parading for duty at night you would learn of any crimes committed the previous night and often there were none. I however took the view that various criminals, even if not breaking into premises on our Section, could be driving through it in stolen vehicles, or in possession of property previously stolen elsewhere. Given that there were far fewer people out and about during the night, I tended to treat everyone with suspicion until I knew otherwise. That is not to say I would stop and search everyone, sometime I would engage passers-by in general conversation asking them if they had far to travel and such like and in this way learn their reason for being out and about. I would follow up with a more direct approach if they seemed nervous or unwilling to converse with me. On other occasions I would conceal myself in a darkened shop doorway just watching who was driving up and down.

We did suffer smash and grabs from jewellers and electrical retailers from time to time and I considered I would be more likely to catch someone doing this, if I kept a low profile. When we were short staffed you could find yourself allocated two or more beats to cover and it was then permissible to use a pedal cycle to cover the area. My cycle had dynamo-powered lights and on night duty I often reached back and flicked the dynamo off the tyre. This was usually when going down side streets or factory estates in the early hours, so as to give me an element of surprise should there be any criminal activity going on. Occasionally a car would pass before I had time to put the lights back on and a motorist would flash his headlights, I often wondered what thoughts crossed this motorist's minds at such times.

One of the most important things to get to know was the location of all the telephone kiosks on any given beat, particularly on night duty when shops and businesses were closed. Although there were four Police Boxes they were all situated on the extremities of our Section and if one needed assistance or to communicate urgently with the Station, other than a couple of all night petrol stations, there was only public telephone kiosks to fall back on. We were of course issued with a whistle, but I personally have no recollection of ever blowing it, other than to remove the odd bit of fluff. This now redundant item was only ever of use when manpower levels were such that another patrolling officer was likely to hear it. On a more personal level, I liked to familiarise myself with the location of various vending machines for drinks or confectionery and would usually make sure I had a supply of relevant coins when going on night duty. One of my favourites was a machine at Stamford Hill adjacent to the Police Box, which dispensed hot drinks. This was something I looked forward to on a cold night. I was very frustrated one night having inserted my sixpence and selected the Chicken Soup, to realise that it had run out of paper cups, and I could only watch as the soup was dispensed onto the pavement.

It was a bar of chocolate that nearly impeded by first big arrest on Night Duty some few months into my service. It was about 12.30am on 5th August and I had just acquired myself a bar of chocolate from a vending machine in Green Lanes. I was patrolling towards the railway bridge alongside Haringey Railway Station and discreetly breaking a square of chocolate from the bar in my right pocket and nibbling it as I walked along. The station was served by two entrance paths at right angles to the roadway, one north and one south of the railway bridge. A short tunnel through the railway embankment beneath the lines connected these paths. Walking into the north pathway I turned right into the darkened tunnel and was now facing the booking office which was located on the south pathway at the far end of the tunnel a distance of about twenty yards. I had barely taken a couple of steps when I heard whispering and then a shaft of light appeared from centre of the double doors to the office. In the light I saw the silhouette of a man he appeared to be conversing with someone inside the office through the gap between the doors. I stepped to my left as close to the tunnel wall as I could so as not to be seen. Then as the man turned so his back was to the doors they closed and the light disappeared I could now no longer see the man but knew he was still standing in the doorway. He was obviously a 'look out' for whoever was inside the office, and he was facing directly towards me, but unable to see me, as only the two pathways were illuminated casting a dark shadow within the tunnel hiding my presence.

I was only about 15 feet from a telephone kiosk which I had just passed on the north pathway before entering the tunnel, but to get to it I would have to step out into the lighted area in direct line of sight to the 'look out'. Like a child in a game of statues, I stood still whilst I assessed the situation, my right hand still holding a square of chocolate. I was trying to gauge whether I could drop it without it being heard, hoping there was no silver paper adhering to it. I needed my right thumb free, to feel for the loop in leather strap of my truncheon. This was to give me some protection when I moved in, other than the rubber torch I held in my left hand. I knew I had the element of surprise on my side whilst I remained still, so I decided my only option was to rush forward and endeavour to grab the lookout before he realised what was occurring. Fortunately the chocolate square landed quietly and drawing my truncheon I darted forward. I would love to have seen the look on the guy's face as I appeared out of the darkness but the distance was too far and I never even saw his face as he fled down the pathway without any warning to his accomplices. Realising he had too much of a start on me I settled for apprehending whoever was in the office. Being unfamiliar with the two heavy wooden doors I first pushed then pulled at them before they opened, the noise reverberating loudly in the still of the night. I found myself suddenly in the brightly lit booking hall, facing two startled looking men, one with socks over his hands was holding a cold chisel whilst the other was holding a wood chisel. There was a table knife on a shelf by the glass service window of the ticket office, from which the beading had been removed and propped against the wall.

In retrospect they may have thought I was not alone for they would not have known their look out had fled and avoided arrest. The men probably didn't realise that I was nearly as startled as they were, as I instinctively grabbed their chisels and the knife without resistance put them in my coat pocket. Then still holding my truncheon and rubber torch managed to link my forearms round their upper arms and manoeuvred them down the tunnel like the front row of a rugby scrum, to the telephone kiosk on at the other end. I was not aware that either of them made any attempt to struggle free. I felt I had to be quick, as I was unsure whether the lookout would return to aid his accomplices. Looking back it was probably a combination of my decisive action and the element of surprise that gave them no time to think of evading arrest. Having thrust the two of them into the phone box, there was just enough room for me to reach in and dial 999 then stretching the flex through the doorway I took the handset outside, requested assistance and stood guard on the door, my unused truncheon in hand.

Assistance came in the form of the local Q Car an unmarked car driven by a Class 1 Police Driver in plain clothes with a Detective Constable and an Aide to CID as crew. They seemed quite surprised that I had managed to capture two burglars on my own, whilst my concern was about the look out and how far he could have travelled in the time available. With the assistance of other units that arrived, a search was made for the third man but to no avail. My prisoners subsequently identified as Colin Nutt aged 20 and Paul Goodsell aged 21, who when searched was found to be in possession of a screwdriver, were duly charged with Office breaking and Possessing Housebreaking Implements by Night. Both later pleaded 'Guilty' to these charges before the Hon. Ewan Montagu Q.C. at Middlesex Sessions.

In respect of these arrests, on 17th November 1959 I was awarded my First Commendation by Commander 2 Area for 'vigilance and ability' in effecting the arrest of the two men. Although it is nice to have one's efforts noted in this way, nothing can compare with the personal feeling of satisfaction I felt at the time of this incident, despite the initial trauma when dealing with the situation. My colleagues on the relief were clearly impressed on the night of this event, but for me it was a just reward for the hours spent conscientiously patrolling when nothing untoward had occurred.

I found nothing brings you down to earth more than being on day duty. In particular directing traffic and I was to spend several weeks on this duty at the Manor House whilst new Traffic Signals were being installed, and later at Seven Sisters Road, when the excavations for the Victoria Line were first commenced. Despite relief by colleagues directing traffic is physically and mentally tiring and what little satisfaction there is from achieving a free flowing junction, can so readily be thwarted by inconsiderate or incompetent motorists.

One of my most embarrassing, yet humorous incidents however, occurred whilst I was directing traffic. On this occasion I was controlling a Pedestrian Crossing on Stamford Hill for the convenience of schoolchildren and their parents attending Olinda Road School. Normally specially employed School Crossing Patrols were employed to carry out these duties. As Olinda Road abutted the busy North South thoroughfare of Stamford Hill and was located half way down the hill, it was considered too dangerous for a civilian School Crossing Patrol. The P.C. on that beat before and after school therefore controlled this Crossing. A lot of heavy lorries used this road and particularly when travelling down the hill it was necessary to give them ample opportunity to brake. I had done this duty many times and where possible looked for a convenient gap in the approaching downhill traffic, before stepping out into the road to signal vehicles to halt. On this particular day most of the parents and children had accessed the school and I was nearly due to complete crossing duties, when I saw a young mother hurrying along Olinda Road approaching the crossing from the far side. She was holding the hand a small preschool aged boy and I could tell from the way she was almost dragging the child that she was in a hurry. Glancing at the approaching traffic, I realised it was an opportune time to step out giving adequate notice to oncoming vehicles, so I stepped into the road and duly halted the traffic. Realising that no one had crossed in front of me I glanced to my left and there at the kerbside was the young woman holding up the leg of her son's short trousers, as he urinated into the gutter at the edge of the crossing. There were no other pedestrians wishing to use the crossing so I had halted the traffic to watch this spectacle. I felt myself blush with embarrassment, but the drivers of halted vehicles were laughing their heads off.

One of the less pleasant duties that Police Officers are called upon to perform relates to sudden deaths, either in notifying relatives or friends or dealing with bodies found. The first time I ever saw a dead body was as a P.C. with a colleague Tom Collins. We were requested to break into a house in Woodberry Grove, where a man had not been seen for several days and was thought may be ill or injured. He had in fact committed suicide by electrocuting himself. He was lying in his hallway with bare wires wound several times round each of his thumbs; the other ends of the wire flex were connected to a three-pin plug located in a wall socket. One of the most unpleasant things was the odour of early decomposition, but once a doctor had attended and certified death, I found an air spray used by the undertakers to have an even more repulsive aroma. I was grateful when Tom offered me a roll up, as although not a regular smoker, I found it helped to mask the smell.

On another occasion a night club hostess was found murdered in Clifton Gardens and I was sent to the scene to assist. The Detective Superintendent then asked me to find the nearest house with a telephone to use as a point of contact. Examining the telephone wires from a nearby telegraph pole, I found one set led to a house only three doors away and the occupants duly obliged. I was then tasked to man this phone and had only been doing so for a few minutes when a member of the Press telephoned to ask the occupant about their neighbour whose body had been found. He was a little taken aback to find himself talking to a police officer but nevertheless persisted with his enquiry. I declined to assist him, but within a short apace of time, he knocked on the door, following up his enquiry. This was my first dealing with the Press and I was amazed how quickly they had learnt of the incident and how resourceful they could be.

During my time in uniform at St. Ann's Road, I became aware that a local girl originally from Stoke Newington, an up and coming actress named Barbara Windsor was living in a flat over one of the shops on Grand Parade, Green Lanes. More significantly she was the girlfriend of Ronnie Knight, a suspected-armed robber who was of interest to the Criminal Intelligence Department at Scotland Yard. At that time he regularly drove a two tone Ford Zodiac the Registration number of which I can still recall – YOT 606 and I was familiar with where it would be parked, as I frequently saw it arrive back at her flat late at night. If I saw him using a different vehicle I would report details to the yard.

Another young woman living in a nearby flat off Green Lanes was also to feature in my life during these early days of my career, but cause me considerable embarrassment and angst. This resulted from the period when Divisional Boxing Training was being organised in a basement gymnasium at Stoke Newington Police Station. Another young P.C. Bob East, who was on a different Relief at St. Ann's Road, was also involved in boxing training and so the two of us were paired together and posted to 'Accident Prevention' duties. 8am – 4pm. We were free to patrol anywhere on our Section and report motorists for serious traffic offences, in particular with two of us and one either side of a junction we could catch offenders jumping red traffic lights. This duty also enabled us to travel to Stoke Newington during training hours. Bob like myself was single, originally from south of the river and had a motor cycle for transport. We got to know each other and I learnt he was practically engaged to a girl from back home in Richmond. After a few weeks, Bob told me his girlfriend and another girl who worked for the same firm, were taking a flat in Paignton Road just off St. Ann's Road. Ultimately I was introduced to this girl, Peggy who was from Co. Down, Northern Ireland and we began seeing each other. I learnt that she had only recently come to England following the breakdown of a relationship back home. After a couple of months, she decided to get a room on her own just off Green Lanes. I by now was living in Stoke Newington Section House some 15minutes away and at first everything was fine, although she found she was financially stretched with the amount of money consumed by the gas and electric meters. Like me she was paid weekly in those days, but by the Thursday she was skint whereas I was paid on Wednesdays, so I frequently gave her some money to get her through until Friday, when she was paid. I did however become increasingly aware that other than work colleagues, she had no real friends over here and was becoming increasingly dependent on me for company. On one occasion as I went on night duty I found her waiting outside the station and she insisted on walking along with me as I began my patrol, causing a few raised eyebrows from my colleagues.

With Peggy increasingly expecting me to see her in the evenings or weekends, when not working, I realised I was getting too deeply involved. I tried to ease the situation by arranging to see her less frequently each week. She however, resented this and so one evening I told her I needed a bit of space and whilst not wishing to terminate the relationship did not want to spend all my available time with her. When I left to return to the section house that night, she was still quite distressed which did concern me, but I felt I had to stand my ground. Back at the Section House I was still concerned about her and a little uneasy that some money I had left with her earlier in the evening had included a quantity of silver and several shilling pieces. Peggy had certainly not intimated she might do anything to harm herself, but I knew she was feeling very sorry for herself. Around midnight I decided to ring the communal telephone of the house which was occupied by a number of females renting rooms. There was no reply to my call so I returned to bed and eventually went to sleep. It must have been around 2.30am when I was awakened by a knock on my room door. I opened it to find two uniform PCs from 'Y' Division who I did not know, one of who was holding an envelope with my name of it. My heart sank I knew instinctively their presence was something to do with Peggy. They told me that she was in the Prince of Wales Hospital having attempted to commit suicide by using her gas oven. Fortunately she had been thwarted by the intervention of two of the other girls who had heard her crying and become concerned on hearing her putting a number of coins in the gas meter in the hallway. The officers then took me to the

Hospital where I learnt that Peggy was expected to recover satisfactorily.

Attempting to commit suicide was a Criminal Offence at that time, although proceedings were seldom taken other than when the offence involved two or more persons involved in a pact. The incident had therefore been recorded as a 'Crime' at St. Ann's Road and in view of my involvement, a report was awaiting the arrival of my Superintendent later that morning. I was duly summoned to his office where I explained the situation to him. He was sympathetic and as myself, grateful that the attempt had been unsuccessful. He suggested that in the circumstance it might be best if she returned to her family in Ireland, offering to arrange a Travel Warrant if she wished to return. When I spoke with Peggy she was full of remorse for her actions. We talked things over and I made it clear that my position was unchanged, ultimately she agreed that it was in her own best interest to return home for a while and I was greatly relieved when she finally departed. I received a couple of letters shortly afterwards and then about six months later she telephoned me at the Section House to say she was back over here working as a barmaid in Covent Garden, I wished her well but made no arrangements to see her.

Chapter Four

Section House Life

After the first few months of my service I had transferred to Stoke Newington Section House, a building which accommodated about 40 residents and was situated behind Stoke Newington Police Station at the rear of the police station yard. The accommodation there was much better than Tottenham, in that it was purpose built and each resident had his own room. Whilst most of the men were aged in their twenties, there were a few older confirmed bachelor types, but all residents were stationed on 'N' Division and they were a good crowd. There was a Resident's Canteen with limited facilities to cook your own food if preferred a Snooker Room and a Television Lounge. I had learnt by now that card playing was a regular past time in the force, usually during refreshment breaks in canteens, but even more so in Section Houses when off duty. Although not a gambler, I personally enjoyed card games and had regularly played snooker before joining the police, so fitted in with the routine. Most evenings a group of lads would go to a nearby pub for a few drinks and a game of darts and on pay-days a Chinese or Indian meal was often consumed to round the evening off. There was a good rapport amongst the lads and I soon felt quite at home. There was also an all-night coffee stall a few hundred yards down Stoke Newington High Street at the junction with Amhurst Road, where hot steak and kidney pies were a favourite of many of us, particularly late at night when the canteen was shut.

One of my Section House friends was Clive Bean, a Geordie with a dry sense of humour, who was in the rugby team with me and who had a bit of a reputation as a big eater. Clive also enjoyed the pies at the coffee stall and around midnight one day at the end of December, the two of us went over there and found it was quite busy. Clive was queuing up for our pies and I was stood back a bit, there were a number of people standing around eating and drinking as usual and behind me was a wire fence enclosing the grounds of a church. The church grounds consisted of trees and shrubs extending northward back to the next junction which was Evering Road. Suddenly I heard the sound of a burglar alarm, which seemed to ring for a few seconds and then stop, the sound had come from the direction of Evering Road and I knew that an electrical shop was situated on the corner. As the sound had stopped, I thought at first it could be someone locking up after working late or end of year stocktaking. Moving towards the junction with Stoke Newington High Street and looking through the shrubbery to get a better view, my attention was drawn to two men running southward, but diagonally across the high street from the direction of the electrical shop. I instinctively ran up Amhurst Road and across the high street after them and as I did I saw a uniform constable run out of the end of Evering Road, increasing my suspicions that a burglary may have been committed or attempted. As the men ran down a side turning on the far side, the nearest one had a lead of about 25 yards on me and the P.C. was about 75 yards further back. Being very fit I gradually closed the gap between the nearest fugitive and myself and after turning left and right the two men gradually came to a halt still some distance apart. We were all breathless, but I managed to grab hold of the nearest one, he started to struggle and his mate approached as if to help and I managed to shout out I was a police officer, whereupon he decided not to intervene. There was no sign of the uniform P.C. so with an arm lock on my prisoner I began walking along one of the side turnings in the general direction we had come. I knew we were about half a mile from Stoke Newington Police Station. I was hoping to find a telephone kiosk but my prisoner having recovered his breath was now trying to get free, so on seeing a door bell outside a public house I rang the bell, whereupon a woman poked her head out of an upstairs window to complain. I told her I was a police officer and asked her to phone for assistance, but she was not best pleased at having her slumbers disturbed and referred me to a telephone kiosk just round a bend in the road I was in. I managed to get my prisoner there and call for assistance. A police car arrived almost instantaneously having been called to assist the pursuing officer I had seen earlier and my prisoner and I, were conveyed to Stoke Newington Police Station.

My prisoner was a man in his early twenties named George Ince who gave an address in Bow. It transpired that he had already served a term of 9 months imprisonment for assaulting an off duty police officer and six months imprisonment for smashing a man on the head with a bottle. The key holder of the electrical shop was called to his premises and found they has been forcibly entered and a small amount of cash stolen. The CID took over the case and Ince was subsequently charged with shop breaking. His accomplice was never identified. I learnt that the officer, who I had seen earlier, was a P.C. Dave Omer. He was a new recruit on his first tour of night duty and just on his way back to the station, when he had heard the alarm and seen the two men appear from the direction of the shop. On seeing the officer, the two men had run off and when he saw me running behind them he'd thought I was their lookout. When I heard this I was pleased he had not been able to catch up with me as I might have received a truncheon blow to my head. As for my steak pie, when I met up with Clive the next evening he informed me that as he had no idea where I had suddenly disappeared to, he had eaten it on my behalf. Little did I realise at the time that this arrest was to have a more significant effect on my future health than the loss of a steak pie.

George Ince having appeared at North London Magistrates Court on two occasions was granted bail until a future date when Committal proceedings were due to take place. Thereafter he failed to answer to his bail and an Arrest Warrant was issued. Some initial enquiries would have been made by the CID Officer in the case at his home address without success, but as I was to learn during my service, there are many such offenders who having jumped bail, lie low and eventually carry on living as before. Such people remain 'Wanted' by police, but often it is only when arrested for some other offence that they dealt with for their original offence. Whilst such fugitives may feel every police officer is on the lookout for them, such is the state of crime that this is not possible. It is often only local officers who know a particular criminal and are aware of his being 'Wanted', that are actively keeping an eye out for him. When I had last seen Ince he was leaving the court and I saw him get into a fairly new two tone Vauxhall Estate car. The address he had given on arrest was in Ida Road Bow. So during the following weeks I decided to drive over to Bow on my motorcycle in my off duty time and see if Ince's car was parked up near his address. The address was not far from Bow Road Police Station and if I had seen his, car my intention was to call in there and seek assistance.

It was whilst returning from my third such unsuccessful visit, that tragedy befell me. Three attractive young females walking along on my right as I was driving north up Cambridge Heath Road distracted my attention. Re-directing my gaze in front of me I was to see I was about to hit the far kerb of a side turning on my left, which protruded out restricting the width of the road I was on. I had no choice but to hit the kerb at right angles with my front tyre and try to steer the bike back onto the roadway. Unfortunately a pole which was supporting the power supply line of the still in vogue trolley buses, was situated in front of me and I clipped this with the handlebars of my bike. I was propelled into the far carriageway as my bike smashed into the pole. I lay in the road unable to get up, but an oncoming bus driver thoughtfully pulled his bus right up close to shield me from any overtaking traffic. I was conveyed by ambulance to the nearby London Hospital where I was found to be suffering from a severe laceration to my left shin and bruising to various parts of my anatomy, but no broken bones. After a few days I was transferred to the Metropolitan Police Nursing Home at Denmark Hill, where I was treated for several weeks. One of the other patients in my room was a lovely man a real gentleman, a Chief Inspector Tom Shepherd, who I learnt was employed in plainclothes as a Protection Officer with the Royal Family. He was not permanent with any particular family member, but a relief officer so had worked with all of the Royal Family at various times. It was fascinating to hear about his work and what was involved in providing security for the Royal Family both here and abroad. For a young officer like myself in my first year of service, I felt privileged to be in such illustrious company. I got to meet Tom's wife Margaret several times when she visited him. Later, once Tom had resumed duty, they sent me a postcard bearing the Balmoral Castle postmark, which I still have, and although we met up once for afternoon tea, we didn't keep in touch.

I was finally recommended for a two-week visit to the Police Convalescent Home near Brighton and was allowed home for a weekend to prepare and pack some clothes. My biggest concern however was my motorcycle, which initially had been taken to Bethnal Green Police Station. My dad had arranged for his brother to collect it in his works van and it had been taken to my dad's lock up garage in Tooting. Dad had told me the front forks needed replacing and the sump was cracked, which meant the engine being stripped right down to fit a new crankcase. As this was my main means of transport, I needed to get the bike repaired as soon as possible. I therefore spent the whole weekend round dad's garage stripping the bike down so new parts could be ordered as required. When I returned to Denmark Hill on the Sunday Evening for transfer to the Convalescent Home, I was careful not to let anyone see my hands as they no longer resembled those of someone who'd spent five weeks in bed.

The Convalescent Home served many Police Forces and it was interesting to meet colleagues from other parts of the country and discuss Policing in rural areas. I was intrigued to learn that Sheep Dipping required a police officer's presence, but I'm still not sure why. After convalescence I spent another weekend putting my motorcycle back together again before returning to the Section House and normal duty. As for George Ince he remained unlawfully at large and our paths were not to cross for nearly two years.

On occasions, St. Ann's Road was asked to supply manpower to our Sub Divisional Station at Stoke Newington. It was not the practice however for Probationer PCs to be posted on loan until they had successfully completed their Probationer Examinations, which occurred at 9 and 15 months service. Having reached this point in my service and being resident at Stoke Newington, I was a natural candidate to go on loan to Stoke Newington on a night duty shift on 4th November 1960, when they were short staffed. Living there, this was convenient although my knowledge of the Section related mainly to the major thoroughfares, the High Street Shops and some of the public house and restaurants I'd frequented. At about 3.45am in the morning I was patrolling along Stoke Newington Church Street some 50 yards or so from the T-junction with Stoke Newington High Street. The silence of the night was suddenly broken by the sound of an approaching vehicle. I then saw car containing three men drive past the end of the road, travelling north towards Stamford Hill. Although there was no traffic in Stoke Newington Church Street, the traffic lights were at green, which meant the passing car must have gone through a red traffic signal. I ran to the end of the road and just caught sight of the vehicle as it continued on up the hill through another set of red traffic lights. Seeing a car approaching in the same direction I stepped into the road and signalled it stop. I was pleased to see it was a black cab, so I instructed the bemused driver to 'follow that car'.

As we drew near the junction with Manor Road some half mile further on, opposite Stoke Newington Railway Station, I saw the vehicle stationery in the middle of the carriageway with the driver just raising the bonnet. The cabby duly stopped just behind the car and had I been a more seasoned traveller I would no doubt have been out of the cab in a jiffy. But unfamiliar with its interior, I had great difficulty in the dark, locating the handle on the cab's large door, however with the driver's assistance; I finally located it and alighted with a hurried 'thank you', but no time for a tip.

The car driver seeing me approach, said, "It's all right governor. I have got some trouble with the engine and couldn't stop." Both he and his two passengers were in their twenties. I began inspecting the vehicle; the front passenger remained both silent and seated looking straight ahead. I opened the rear door to be confronted by a man who gave the appearance of being asleep, slumped back with a hat half over his face, I was not convinced by this charade. I noticed a radio and some bottles of spirits on the seat and the floor. Fortunately at that moment I heard a car slowing down on the far carriageway, looking over I recognised the driver as Ron Ace a Detective Sergeant at St. Ann's Road. He was the night duty CID Officer and with him was John Simmonds, who was an Aid to CID, stationed at Highbury Vale. Their timing could not have been better and with their assistance the boot was opened and found to be full of boxes of toys and dolls, the rear passenger rudely awakened from his slumbers was found to have his coat pockets stuffed with cigars. Conflicting stories concerning the ownership of the property and their movements that night, resulted in them being arrested for unlawful possession of the goods and taken to Stoke Newington Police Station.

Also on loan to Stoke Newington that night was Sergeant Bob Hope, who was on my relief at St. Ann's Road. Bob was a nice enough man, but had a nervous habit of fiddling with his tie or his shirt cuffs and blushing when stressed or needing to exert his authority, an unfortunate habit, which had earned him the nickname of 'Collar and Cuffs'. On entering the Charge Room the prisoners were seated on a bench whilst the CID Officers explained the arrest to Sgt Bob Hope in the front Station Office. I was left alone with the prisoners briefly but could see Bob with the CID officers, through the glass door. Suddenly one of the men said to me "Here you better have this you're going to find it anyway" and handed me a small starting pistol. Taking it, I asked if it was loaded and he said he didn't know, I thought this odd, but examined the pistol and could see no sign of any cartridges. There was a space where I thought they might fit, but I had never handled this type of pistol before. Just to make sure, I foolishly pointed the pistol at the floor and pulled the trigger. There was an almighty bang and a cloud of smoke enveloped the prisoners and me. A brief silence followed during which, glancing through the Station Office door, I saw the colour drain from Sgt Bob Hope's face, before people came rushing from every direction. Alan and James Burton aged 23 and 27 respectively, together with George Wicker aged 20 were subsequently charged with breaking and entering a house in Downs Park Road, Hackney. The starting pistol was in fact part-proceeds of the burglary, hence the prisoners lack of knowledge about it.

Although I only had some 18 months service and was still serving my Probation period, I had by now realised that arresting people for crime was by far the most appealing and satisfying aspect of police work as far as I was concerned. The pathway into the C.I.D at that time was to serve, firstly as an Aide patrolling in plain clothes, as one of a pair, until recommended for a Selection Board for Appointment to the CID. Any Aides I had met usually had at least 4 years' service in uniform before becoming an Aide. During a week's attachment to the CID Office however, I had spoken with Ralph Fewell the Detective Sergeant who had dealt with the Haringey Railway Station arrests. He showed me the 'Application Book' for anyone who wanted to be considered as a future Aide, I pointed out that I had not yet finished my Probationary 2 years, and he said, "There's nothing to stop you putting your name in the book now." There were a couple of names already on the waiting list and so with little expectation I entered my name and warrant number.

At around the same time I had responded to an invitation for officers to volunteer to work 'Aid to Marylebone Lane Police Station' in uniform, to assist with Christmas Shopping Crowd Control. On the first day having been given a sketch map of the Sub Division on which all major Stores, Roads and Public Buildings were marked, I was allocated a short patrol in Orchard Street. My map indicated this to be a stretch of Road about 500 yards in length between Oxford Street and Portman Square, alongside Selfridges Store. I was a bit disappointed to have such a short stretch of road to patrol. As a Londoner whose main visits to the centre had been to the Museums in School Holidays and more latterly the Curry Houses in the evenings, with Section House friends, I had no idea how busy the West End would be in the run up to Christmas. I must have directed half a dozen people to the American Embassy whilst walking along Oxford Street, before I even got to my Patrol and my first request from a member of the public for the nearest telephone kiosk, had me flummoxed, these not being marked on my map. I assured the enquirer there were bound to be phones in the nearby Underground Station at Bond Street, only to find later there were none. In short I was becoming a Tourist Guide, but found time passed quite quickly. If so minded, by way of entertainment one could play 'Cat and Mouse' with the Unlicensed Street Traders selling cheap jewellery and perfume out of suitcases outside Selfridges as we had been briefed about these individuals and their fake wares. The advice from local officers was to remove your helmet and approach behind a group of shoppers to avoid being spotted by their lookouts. But no sooner had they been arrested and bailed than they were back on the street operating as before, so when they finally appeared at court in January they were pleading 'Guilty' to twenty or thirty summonses.

As for Crowd Control this entailed officers linking arms to prevent pedestrians from jay walking and committing suicide in the rush hour at traffic light junctions, whilst an officer bellowed instructions with a megaphone. I no longer recollect what made me volunteer for this duty, it may have been the thought of a change of scenery or more likely there may have been a financial inducement. Whatever it was this attachment proved to be no more than an interesting experience and I was glad to be back on own patch over the Christmas holiday and on Night Duty again which would enable me to have Christmas dinner with my family in Tooting.

Once I had experienced Section House life I was glad to be living away from home, but duties permitting I drove to Tooting most weekends not only for my mum's Sunday roast, but to collect clean underwear and socks. The washing facilities in the Section House were limited to hand washing in a normal sink basin and then hanging shirts on wire hangers on a make shift string line in one of the shower cubicles, or alternatively a radiator in your room. I usually hand washed and ironed my uniform shirt and detached collars and fortunately 'Drip Dry' shirts were gaining popularity at that time, so civilian shirts for off duty wear were mainly 'Drip Dry'. There was however one drawback with these, which one would not have expected in a Police Section House.

This was that every so often someone would go to the wash room see if his shirt was dry only to find it missing or showing signs of having been borrowed and worn. This caused both inconvenience and suspicion at times and whoever the culprit, he was careful not to get caught. I was ultimately to suffer at the hands of the phantom 'borrower' in another way just prior to a particularly important event.

One of the senior residents P.C. 'Nobby' Hall based at Stoke Newington, had been a former Prisoner of War held by the Japanese. He never spoke about his past sufferings, but rumour had it that the top half of the built in wardrobe in his room was packed with tinned food, because he'd vowed never to go hungry again. As no one to my knowledge, was ever invited to enter his room, the rumour was unsubstantiated. He certainly didn't sleep well and one would often come across him in the wash room in the early hours, his gaunt figure bent over the sink hand washing his clothes. Nobby was a bit of a loner but with a wry knowing smile on his face would greet you and exchange a few pleasantries on meeting.

Another character was 'Sailor' Wright a former Merchant Seaman and therefore much older than most of the residents. I had first come across him when he was giving evidence at North London Court, as I was 'Learning Courts'. As a result of finding fresh jemmy marks at the rear of a Stoke Newington Shop, he'd staked out the premises on his own for about six hours. This was purely on a hunch that a further attempt would be made to break in. Finally his efforts had been rewarded by the offender(s) returning and being arrested by him. Listening in court when 'Sailor' had given his evidence of the times of his observation I thought I'd misheard him or he'd made a mistake. It was only later, after moving to the same Section House, did I learn that he was such an obsessive and determined character that he operated on a different wavelength to most officers. Handcuffs were not issued to individual officers at that time, but only kept at Stations for use in escorting or transferring potentially violent prisoners. Sailor, however, had purchased his own handcuffs and there was an occasion when having disturbed two offenders, he handcuffed

AN APPETITE FOR CRIME

one to some railings then ran off in pursuit of the other. After a considerable chase he managed to apprehend him, but was then unable to recall where he had 'lodged' the handcuffed associate and had to trawl the area with the Wireless Car to locate him. Sailor owned a black M.G. Convertible sports car and in the summer would wear a Naval Cap when driving with the hood down, a real 'poser', but a great character.

With all the diverse personalities residing in the Section House and new faces appearing to replace those that either married or were transferred elsewhere, it was an interesting place to be living. There was quite a lot of good-natured Mickey taking often by colleagues regarding incidents that had occurred during working hours. One of my friends, Dave Walton who worked at Holloway Station having arrested a man for Drunkenness, took pity on him at the Magistrates Court and paid his fine to prevent him from having to remain in Custody for a day. Dave was a real nice guy and I could understand him doing this if he thought the man was a deserving case. But much to Dave's embarrassment, another officer on his shift broadcast the tale round the Section House. Dave was also a bit accident-prone and on one occasion he twisted his ankle running to retrieve a loose ball, whilst he was a spectator at a football match against Southend Police. He returned to the section House on crutches. Being the only casualty of the game whilst merely a spectator, he came in for a lot of leg pulling on his return. Dave was also prone to bouts of raucous laughter and one afternoon a group of us were in the lounge seated in armchairs that had broad flat wooden armrests, which were handy to support a cup and saucer. Something was said that tickled Dave's fancy and he roared out laughing rocking his armchair right back and I saw his cup of tea slide down the arm of the chair and fall on to the floor much to everyone's amusement.

Residents of the Section House worked at various Stations on 'N' Division and their work often brought them in contact with nurses at a number of local Hospitals. This could be either when dealing with victims of traffic accident or assault cases or where hospital staff required assistance to deal with abusive or drunken patients. Like police officers, nurses worked unsociable shifts with irregular off duty times and single girls lived together, usually in Nurses Quarters or a shared flat, so a good deal of fraternisation occurred. Whenever there was a party involving nurses, whether at a hospital or private flat, a word to just one officer or a phone call to a Section House would ensure the attendance of a good number of eager males.

Of all the residents in the Section House only a few owned motor cars, there were more like myself, who's mode of transport was by motorcycle, some had scooters which were very much in vogue and the remainder relied on public transport or bicycle to get around. In addition to my accident with the trolley bus pole, I had experienced a number of other narrow escapes whilst motorcycling. This together with the inadequacies of the protective clothing I had for inclement weather, led me to believe that my future wellbeing, lay in acquiring a car as soon as I could afford one. I learnt that some of the residents were being given driving lessons by a bus driver who lived nearby. He was well recommended and more importantly his charge of seven shillings and sixpence an hour significantly undercut local driving schools, so I enrolled with him. On my first Driving Test however, when the Driving Examiner moved over suddenly, almost onto my lap, as I passed too close to a stationery lorry, I realised another Test was inevitable and that time I passed.

Looking back I could not expect to have the same luck I had experienced when taking my first Motorcycle Driving Test. I had undertaken this Test at the age of 16, riding a 1938 350cc Ariel with rigid frame and girder front forks, a real old banger, which I had acquired from my uncle for £5. The low price on account of the fact that it was contained in numerous cardboard boxes having been completely dismantled for spares and various parts were missing or needing replacement. Fortunately my father was a motor cycle enthusiast having ridden them since before the 2nd World War, during which he rode as a despatch rider with the Royal Corps of Signals. The mechanical knowledge I gained spending several weekends and various evenings with my dad, whilst he showed me how it all fitted together, was however to prove invaluable in later life. I had subsequently taken my Motor

Cycle Driving Test at Wimbledon and the Test Examiner first set me a short route consisting of right hand turns whilst he watched from a static position. There was a very sharp bend involved driving from the Broadway into Merton Road and as I was mid-way round it with the bike leaning over, the engine suddenly cut out and the loss of power caused the bike to topple so I fell off. I hastily picked myself up moved to the kerbside and tried to kick start the bike into action, whilst looking around to see if I could spot the Examiner. Fortunately although I was shaken up, I had no serious injury, but noticed a tear in my trousers through which I could see a fresh abrasion on my knee. The engine would not start and did not seem to be firing, so checking things over I noticed the ignition lead to the spark plug was hanging loose and a small threaded ferrule was missing from the top of the plug, which I realised must have vibrated undone. I bent down and began to look around for it on the roadway when I heard the Examiner's voice enquire "What's the problem". Making sure my riding coat concealed the tear in my trousers, I explained the engine had cut out and I was missing a spark plug ferrule. He clearly hadn't seen me fall as he went to his car parked nearby and from his toolbox produced a spare ferrule, which one fitted, enabled me to continue and pass my Test.

Chapter Five

Aide to CID

The opportunity to commence working in plain clothes as an Aide to CID came both suddenly and unexpectedly for me in February 1961, when I was approached by the two officers who were currently engaged on this duty at St. Ann's Road, PCs Bob Chambers and 'Digger' Chapman (no relation). It was a pleasant surprise when they told me that a vacancy was about to occur for the post of Aide to CID. It transpired that 'Digger' was leaving the force to return to his native Australia. Having looked at the list of applicants for Aiding duties, Bob Chambers who I only knew in passing intimated he would like me to be his new partner. I pointed out I still had two months to go before completing my Probation Period, but would be happy to oblige. They told me it would have to be authorised by the Superintendent but foresaw no problem, and within a couple of weeks my uniform career came to a somewhat abrupt end as I began my training as an Aide to CID.

I knew the role consisted of working from the CID office mainly patrolling in pairs directing your attention at relevant time to the areas where crimes, particularly housebreaking were being committed. The duties also entailed periods of static observation at times from suitable buildings, if crime trends or intelligence indicated the likelihood of a particular crime being committed nearby. Aides also worked on a rota with an experienced CID Officer to provide cover for the whole Division on night duty. Additionally, there was the occasional opportunity to be posted to 'Q' Car Duties as a radio operator. My first week's duty was in fact spent with another Aide, Terry Richardson from Stoke Newington, as Bob was taking some holiday leave. I learnt from Terry the day to day routine of studying the Crime

Books and Station Messages to familiarise oneself with what had taken place during the past 24 hours. You also needed to get into the habit of recording in a Duty Book, your intended whereabouts when you left the station and expected time of return. Then later recording a Diary of your various duties and any expenses incurred. Aides had to record details on any arrest in the back of their Official Diary and it was both the quality and quantity of these arrests, which ensured an Aide's retention on plain-clothes duty and ultimately any recommendation for permanent deployment as a CID Officer. Diaries of all Aides and CID Officers were submitted to the Detective Inspector for inspection of a weekly basis.

Bob had been a uniform P.C. at Stoke Newington for several years before coming out as an Aide, several months beforehand. He was a couple of years older than myself and was married. Like me he was conscientious and keen to establish himself as a good Aide to CID, with a view to being recommended to attend a Selection Board, for a permanent position as a Detective Constable in due course. We gradually formed a good working relationship and whilst Bob was more experienced, I had a more intimate knowledge of St. Ann's Road Section. With Greyhound Racing on Monday and Friday evenings, parked vehicles in the Haringey Stadium vicinity were often a target for would be thieves, either intent on stealing from parked cars or taking and driving away cars or scooters, so we nearly always worked those evenings. Being in plain clothes gave us the advantage to look out for anyone whose attention was directed at stationary vehicles. Our efforts were to be rewarded from time to time with arrests relating to vehicle crime. In the daytime, we mainly patrolled the residential areas, looking out for anyone showing an unhealthy interest in dwelling houses. There were a few mundane jobs like early morning observations we did in Seven Sisters Road after reports of someone regularly having their milk stolen, which resulted in our arresting a vagrant we caught in the act. At other times we might be called upon to assist one of the CID staff to arrest someone or help process prisoners, but our primary role was patrolling the streets.

Within a few weeks of working together we came across some young lads in possession of good quality pedal cycles one of which was a 'Hetchins' pedal cycle. I was aware that these cycles were handmade and very expensive; furthermore I recalled one had been stolen only a few days previous from outside a local cycle shop. As a result of the evasive answers the lads gave to our enquiries concerning the bikes in their possession, they were arrested. The Hetchins cycle turned out to be the one stolen locally and as our enquiry progressed, we gradually recovered a number of stolen bikes from their homes and gardens. The enquiries continued over a period of several weeks, during which it transpired that about three or four lads were in the habit of cycling all the way to the Imperial War Museum in Kennington, on old bikes then stealing the best bikes they could, from cycle racks there. They would then abandon the bikes they'd travelled on, some of which had been stolen on previous occasions. Furthermore they had been swapping parts and selling them to school friends, which resulted in yet more arrests. The bikes and parts we recovered soon filled our small Station Property Store and eventually one of the interview rooms as well. Bob and I found ourselves quite adept at dismantling various parts as owners came from all over London to try and identify their stolen property. Ultimately when the proceedings were completed, the Commissioner commended us both for 'Persistence and ability resulting in the arrest of a number of troublesome juveniles for larceny'. Whilst it was not the most serious crime in the book, this was an encouraging start to our partnership.

A few weeks later I was fortunate to receive another Commendation, this time from Commander 2 Area for an off-duty arrest I had made. This occurred one night around midnight as I was returning alone to the Section House having visited the coffee stall, yet again. Crossing Stoke Newington High Street to turn into Victorian Grove, I saw a man in front of a cigarette machine, which was affixed to the wall beside a lock up shop, some twenty yards from the High Street. At first I thought he was having trouble getting his money in or cigarettes out, but the noise he made aroused my suspicions and I went to a shop doorway to keep him under observation. He continued to grapple with the machine looking around from time to time, but his bulky frame masked exactly what he was doing. Suddenly I saw a police Area Car cruising slowly South down the High Street, it was in fact just passing the Police Station some 200 yards or so away. I ran back, away from the junction with Victorian Grove in order to flag the car down without it stopping in view of my Suspect. I was pleased to see the plain-clothes observer was Ted Greenacre, one of the more crime-minded officers on my old Relief who had taught me Beats. Ted left the car and joined me in my observations and ultimately it became clear the suspect was intent on forcing the machine open. We decided it was time to intervene and approached the man, as we reached him and identified ourselves he shouted something in German and tried to push us out of his way. We started to question him, but he just shouted again and started to run off. We both caught up with him and attempted to restrain him by grabbing hold of him by the upper arms. As I took hold of his right arm he swung it violently upwards and I saw he was holding a butchers meat cleaver in his right hand. I shouted a warning to Ted and after a violent struggle, we managed to pull the man to the ground and disarm him. We were by now opposite the junction with Shipway Terrace, the Cu-de-Sac giving access to the Police Station Yard, but the man continued to struggle and there was no sign of any other officers coming or going. After what seemed an eternity we finally managed to get him to the Station, where after obtaining the assistance of an interpreter, he was identified and charged with attempted theft. He gave his occupation as a chef and that may well have explained his possession of the meat cleaver. Had I attempted to arrest the man without the assistance of Ted Greenacre, the outcome may have been completely different. The aforementioned Commendation was for 'Devotion to duty whilst off duty and ability in effecting the arrest of a troublesome and violent thief'.

It was by now difficult for me to think in terms of being on or off duty. Working in plain clothes I was spending most of the day walking around observing others, looking for some sign that their intentions were dishonest. It has long been the case that most crimes are committed by young males aged from about 13 to 21. Experience also shows that whilst petty crime such as shop lifting may be committed by a lone individual perhaps on impulse, more serious offences such as housebreaking are usually committed by groups of youths may be two or three in number. When patrolling therefore, apart from perhaps having descriptions of offenders seen at or suspected of recent crimes, one tended to focus on individuals of this age or group. Whilst my German cigarette thief was not in this category his behaviour had been enough to arouse my suspicions and I could not have disregarded my instincts just because I was off duty.

Likewise when off duty, if I saw a fellow police officer dealing with any incident where suspects were being detained or questioned, I instinctively found myself pausing if only briefly to assess whether they had sufficient manpower to handle the situation or needed some assistance. On one occasion a uniform constable at Dalston junction was endeavouring to apprehend an offender for some misdemeanour, but the prisoner would not let go of the pedestrian guard-rails at the edge of the pavement. Each time the office prised one hand off, the prisoner grabbed the rail with his other hand. I was just passing on foot so introduced myself and assisted the officer to get his prisoner away from the rail and he was then able to control him unaided. On another occasion whilst driving to my parents' home in Tooting around midnight, as I reached the Elephant and Castle, I noticed a police Hillman car and one officer speaking to the occupants of a car on the far side of the roundabout. I drove round to see if all was OK and found that the police officer was in fact an Inspector Mc Sherry from Clapham, who had been following the car as he was suspicious of the three occupants. I helped him search the vehicle, which had what appeared to be the proceeds of crime on board. He was then able to radio for more assistance and the suspects were conveyed to Clapham Police Station where I assisted Inspector Mc Sherry with interviews. The prisoners were later transferred to Mitcham where an offence of Burglary had taken place and it was daylight when I finally arrived at my parent's home. Some months later I had to attend Kingston Crown Court to give evidence, all through stopping to help, but I had no regrets as I considered it all part of the 'Job', but hoped that others would do the same for me in similar circumstances.

Shortly after my 21st Birthday, which I had celebrated with a group of Section-House mates on a pub-crawl around the West End, I acquired my first car. It was a 1957 Standard 8. My father had bought the vehicle when new and was part exchanging it for another vehicle. Having completed my Probationary 2 years I had received a pay increment and knowing the history of the car, which was reasonably economical to run, I arranged with the dealer to buy back the car on hire purchase. As only one other of my particular group of Section House friends owned a car, this acquisition was to prove very useful particularly when there was a nurse's party in the offing. I can still recall driving up Muswell Hill in the snow one Saturday night, with five burly coppers in my little Standard 8 unsure whether we would reach the top as the wheels spun and the engine laboured.

One other Saturday night whilst resident at the Section House, was also particularly memorable but for an entirely different reason. On this occasion I had taken to my bed during the day having felt unwell with pains in my lower abdomen. I awoke during the early evening as the pain was getting unbearable, I felt nauseous and I suspected it might be Appendicitis. My room was on the first floor and the only telephone in the building was on the ground floor in a locker room adjacent to the canteen. After a while I knew I need medical help and struggling to the door of my room I called out along the corridor but at 8.30pm on a Saturday not a soul was about. I then made my way to the stone stairwell and shouted down for help and I believe it was an officer on his way to the canteen that must have heard me and I asked him to call my doctor. Most of the Section House residents were registered with the same local GP, who was also the Police Divisional Surgeon with a practice near the Station, so he was not long in attending. Before I knew it I was in the back of an ambulance the siren going as I lapsed into unconsciousness. I was conveyed to the Hackney Hospital, although I knew nothing more until coming round to find myself on a ward, drowsy and unsure of what had transpired. I learnt from a nurse that I had suffered a perforated appendix, which had been removed. I was to remain on the ward for a week or so, during which time some other young male patients and I enjoyed some friendly banter with the nurses. I received a number of visits from Section-House mates who appeared just as keen to suss out the talent as top up my locker with goodies. I did, however, get friendly with one particular Irish nurse and we continued to see each other for a few months after my return to duty.

There was no official police transport for CID officers at St. Ann's Road. In fact the only transport provided for use by certain authorised officers whilst I was on the beat, was one of the Velocette motor cycles which became known as the 'Noddy Bikes'. CID Officers were usually authorised to use their own motor vehicles and paid a mileage allowance, but there was no provision for Aides to have transport other than when posted to the 'Q' Car. It was, however, fairly common practice for Aides to unofficially use their own cars on duty if they had one. My Aiding partner Bob commuted to and from work by scooter so once I had the car, we agreed to put five shillings a week each towards petrol and patrol in my car.

We could now cover so much more ground in a short space of time and if one side of our section seemed quiet, we could quickly travel to the other side and patrol there. Bob was a good six foot and I being five feet ten and half, the pair of us did stand out, particularly if anyone we were watching was being cautious, so the car gave us an element of cover. Whilst my Standard 8 was not equipped with sirens or blue lights for high-speed chases, we could follow any suspect vehicles for limited distances. One of the first instances where I did this was one evening as we were in my car, parked near a long row of lock up garages off Spring Hill. A small van pulled up outside a garage some 50 yards in front of where we were, two men got out, unlocked the garage, entered and returned with some metal objects which we could hear being thrown into the back of the van and the garage was then re-locked. It was about 9pm and very dark where we were, but the sounds we heard were like the sound of metal bars clanging together and the possibility that they were jemmies or crowbars entered both our minds. The headlights of the van then came on and it was driven towards us. Realising our presence would be silhouetted I moved over towards Bob to give the impression we were a courting couple and the van passed us did a 'U' turn and drove back out of the lane where the garages were situated. We were able to see it was an Austin A 35 van and started to follow it. As the van drove alongside Clapton common it indicted a left turn which would take it away from our Section so rather than lose it in traffic or end up miles away, we decided to stop it and speak to the occupants. I flashed my headlight as I managed to overtake it in Upper Clapton Road Bob was waving his warrant card out of the window and I pulled across in front of it before it was able to pick up any speed. We got out of my car and approached the van. I was on the driver's side so I showed my Warrant Card to the driver. I was about to explain why we wished to speak to them when he reversed the car a few yards, turned it to the right in order to get past my car and began to drive towards me. I tried to cling on to the front of the car to prevent his manoeuvre but quickly let go when he showed no sign of stopping and I was thrown into the roadway.

Apart from a few grazes, I suffered only from hurt pride, and we quickly found a phone to circulate the index number of the van VGN 914 I still remember it, but it was never traced. Enquiry of the Vehicle Licensing Authority indicated the vehicle had been sold but the purchaser had supplied false particulars. The rented lock up garage was completely empty when we gained access with the assistance of the owner and the name and address of the tenant also proved fictitious. I have no doubt these men were setting off on some criminal enterprise, probably a shop-breaking, but who they were and what their exact intentions were, remains a mystery. There was however, one subsequent development, which we came across by chance in casual conversation some 6 months later.

In 1960, an American Corporation A.M.F. had converted a building that had been a cinema at Clapton Common, when I first went to St. Ann's Road, into the first Bowling Lanes in this country. My partner Bob Chambers had taken up bowling with a group of PC's from Stoke Newington, and got to know some of the other teams including a group of meat porters from Smithfield Market. We often called in there when in the locality, as a number of the criminal fraternity used it and thefts from bowler's cars became a localised problem. One of the meat porters, who knew Bob, casually mentioned to us one day that he'd recently rented a lock up garage nearby and whilst giving it a good clean out, he'd found a stick of gelignite on top of one of the rafters. Bob and I looked at each other before Bob said," It wasn't a garage off Spring Hill by any chance was it?" It was, but the chap had already disposed of the gelignite by throwing it in the River Lea, so there was little to do other than put it down to experience.

Whilst using my car on duty, to avert suspicion both by householders and suspects, I often displayed 'L' plates on it to give the appearance of receiving driving tuition. There was one occasion when Bob and I were keeping observation near the address of a youth, who we suspected of being responsible for a spate of handbag snatches, as it was our intention to follow him when he left home. Unbeknown to us a resident outside whose house we were parked telephoned the Station to report our vehicle acting suspiciously. By now everyone at the Station knew my vehicle and so the caller's fears were allayed. Our suspect did not come out that morning and when we returned to the Station; we learnt that there had been an armed robbery of the Wages Car for Maynards Sweet Factory in Vale Road. A number of men armed with pickaxe handles had laid in wait in a van nearby the factory and then rammed the car returning with the firm's wages. Unfortunately there had been no suspicious residents to report the presence of that vehicle. That particular type of crime was becoming prevalent throughout London at that time, when most employees were paid weekly in cash usually on a Friday. Even without any inside knowledge, villains could work out that the manager or secretary of a large company would need to visit their local bank in time for wages to be made up and they could target the manager's car, which was inevitably the vehicle used.

Such offences ultimately resulted in the growth of security companies and the deployment of armoured vehicles, operated by guards for bulk cash handling, but the need to stem such robberies at that time, resulted in a Metropolitan Police Operation known as 'Bank Patrols'. This operation involved the deployment of any available transport to pay special attention to Bank premises during their hours of business on Fridays and Aids to CID were deployed on Traffic Patrol Cars diverted from their normal duties to assist this operation. The operation ran for about a few months and Bob and I were each posted to separate Traffic Patrol Cars with their two-uniformed crew. The presence of uniformed vehicles in the vicinity of banks may have had some deterrent effect, but I don't recall any bank robbers being caught during this operation, it did however result in my effecting two arrests.

On one of the 'Bank Patrol' days as we were driving along Upper Clapton Road, and glancing to my right across Clapton Common I noticed a man leaving a tower block of flats carrying a heavy looking holdall. Something about him aroused my suspicions and I knew we had experienced burglaries in these flats on a regular basis. I shouted to the car driver to pull over so I could get out before the suspect spotted their car. I told them of my suspicions and asked them to let me approach the man across the Common, whilst they took the next right so they could observe me and approach once I had stopped him. Everything worked well and as soon as I stopped the chap and told him I was a police officer, I knew by his reaction I was in luck and he readily admitted he had just burgled one of the flats.

The other arrest and the most satisfying came about after I received a telephone call from Dave Norris, who was an Aide at Hackney Police Station. Dave and I often met at North London Court and chatted about various cases. Dave rang me one day to enquire whether George Ince was still 'Wanted'. He explained that whilst on his local Bank Patrol duties he had stopped Ince and recorded his details, but on his return to the Station a Criminal Record Check revealed he was 'Wanted' for a case in which I had been the arresting officer, some 18 months previous. I told Dave that Ince was still wanted for non-appearance at court on the Shop breaking charge. Having checked my availability over the next few days Dave said, if it's alright with you I'll go round and nick him and give you a ring so we both end up with one for the back of the book". He was referring to the fact that by Dave arresting Ince and handing him over to me to continue proceedings, we were both able to record the arrest in the rear of our diaries. I was more than happy with this arrangement, as the address was nearer to Hackney and so within a few days Ince was arrested. He was then committed in custody to the Inner London Sessions (now the Crown Court) for trial. He appeared there in October 1961 and pleaded 'Not guilty' and was represented by an up and coming, but very attractive young barrister Nemone Lethbridge. His defence to the charge became apparent when she cross examined me along the lines that I was mistaken about her client being the man I had seen running from the shop. She first questioned me about the clothing Ince had been wearing and then about my own attire on the night, which by now was some 18 months or so previous. I described the colour of my own clothes, which were a sports jacket and trousers. Then in an effort to cast doubt on my recollection, she persisted with the question, "How can you be so sure officer?" to which I was obliged to reply, "Because that was the only civilian jacket and trousers I owned at that time." There were no more questions, Ince was ultimately convicted by the Jury and after details of his Antecedents and Criminal Record made known to the Court, he was sentenced to two years Corrective Training.

Several interesting matters arising out of this prosecution were that during the course of the trial, one could be forgiven for thinking that Miss Lethbridge was in the habit of using her charm and good looks to influence the Judge and Jury on her client's behalf. This fact was not lost upon one of the elderly Court Ushers, who sidled up to me after I had given my evidence saying, "She won't be getting all the attention in this trial, Patricia Roc is on the Jury." Whilst I would not have recognised Patricia Roc, I certainly knew of her fame as a 1940's Film Star and glancing at the Jury it was easy to spot the lady in question.

George Ince progressed up the criminal ladder to become one of a gang, who hijacked a lorry containing nearly £400,000 in Silver Bullion in May 1972 near Mountnessing in Essex. Prior to his arrest for this offence he became a suspect for the now infamous 'Barn Restaurant Murder' at Braintree in Essex. Bob Patience the owner of the Barn Restaurant, his wife Muriel and daughter Beverley had been shot by one of two men during a robbery at their house, resulting in the death of Mrs Patience. Ince was to twice stand trial for this offence purely on the identification evidence of Bob Patience, his daughter and other witnesses, before finally being acquitted. His alibi for the time of the murder, being provided by a married woman with whom he had been having an affair for a number of years, Dolly Kray wife of Charlie Kray elder brother, of the infamous Kray twins. Subsequently two other men were arrested and convicted of the Murder and Manslaughter during the robbery at the Barn Restaurant. George Ince however, remained in custody to face trial for the Silver Bullion robbery, and after a lengthy trial at the Old Bailey, was convicted on 29th November 1973 and sentenced to 15 years imprisonment. As for Nemone Lethbridge our paths crossed once more at the Old Bailey and she was later to marry a man serving a life sentence for murder, and is currently the Solicitor for the Krays.

The term 'Body Language' is much used today, but it was not a term I was familiar with as a young Aide to CID, yet it was certainly a factor in our daily assessment of any potential suspects. We often observed or followed young men we encountered walking around the residential area, where house-breakings occurred, but what we would be looking for was some sign that they were either going about their innocent everyday activities or whether they were showing more than passing interest in residential premises. The majority of house-breakings are not directed to a particular house, rather the area is selected by would be thieves, who then go looking for a house suitable to their particular method of entry. One tell-tale sign was the behaviour of individuals when they came to road intersections, for if they were a strange neighbourhood or unsure which way to go next they invariably hesitated, glancing in each possible direction, before proceeding further. Whilst passing houses they would glance at each one maybe looking for a tell-tale sign, such as milk on the doorstep or an open ground floor window. Corner or end of terrace houses, were often targeted, as some burglars liked to ensure they had a ready means of escape out a back or side entrance. A lot of premises are forcibly entered by brute force on the front door sometimes by use of a screwdriver or jemmy, but more often than not, by a hefty kick adjacent to the lock. Once inside the burglars would bolt the front door from the inside to prevent them being disturbed by any returning householder. If brute force on the door were to be used, doorways, which were not overlooked by neighbours or were masked by trees or shrubs, would be preferred.

On one occasion as Bob and I were driving along two young boys approached a gateway to a house on our near side. I noticed that the boy, who went to open the gate, reached to his right before locating the latch which was on the left, they then went up to the front door as we drove past. We then saw another young lad standing by a hedge at the next junction, but peering rounds in the direction of the other two. Seeing the hand movements at the latch was enough for me to realise this was not the boy's own house. He may well have been visiting a friend, so I would have pulled up and watched to see what happened next, but the actions of the third boy alone were enough to arouse our suspicions. The boys remained by the house for a while without gaining access and we decided to speak to them. They were clearly very apprehensive and could not give satisfactory explanations for being there. We searched their pockets and a folded piece of paper on one of them turned out to be a plan of the house they had called at and the location of various valuable items within. This was most unusual particularly as the lads were only aged 13 or 14. We arrested them and when questioned later at the police station, it transpired that the elder sister of one of them worked as a cleaner at the house. She, knowing her brother was not averse to a bit of burglary, had tasked him to burgle the premises having given him a 'shopping list'. She was duly arrested and charges of Conspiracy to burgle ensued.

On Clapton Common by the top of Spring Hill, there was a refreshment hut, which was popular with van and lorry drivers, as parking was available and Bob and I occasionally took our refreshments there, rather than return to the Station. There was a good all round view and whilst standing eating one of their fried mince rolls, swigging a mug of tea, we could cast our eyes around. The Common provided a good view to see any potential suspects heading towards the residential properties between Stamford Hill and the River Lea, which suffered the majority of our burglary offences.

On 12th December 1961 we saw two men leaving the refreshment hut and head down Spring Hill and we decided to follow them in my car. They were in their early twenties and appeared to be strangers to the area and once they had walked a short distance we realised they were paying a lot of attention to houses as they passed. We followed them around a few roads all the time their attention was directed at dwelling houses and eventually one of them called at the front door of a house in Leadale Road. It was occupied and after a brief moment's conversation with the female resident, the man re-joined his mate at the gate and the two continued on down the road. We were by now convinced that these two were intent on doing a burglary. Once they were far enough away I stopped by the house and Bob spoke to the occupant, who confirmed that the man had asked for someone who did not live there and she had suggested he may want Leland Road nearby. Shortly afterwards the men called at yet another house and left when the door was answered and again we went there with a similar result to the first house.

By now we were well keyed up. It is hard to describe the feeling you get when you knew you were about to effect an arrest in these circumstances not knowing where or when it will occur, what opposition you might face, or how able you will be to deal with the situation. Had we had any form of communication we could have called for back up to be nearby if needed, but we could not afford to let these two out of our sight for more than a few seconds, knowing in all probability, they would be entering a house somewhere soon.

I was keeping well back particularly when they turned corners out of sight, sometimes doubling back in the car to get a view of the suspects from the far end of any road they turned into.

Finally they turned from Barry Avenue into Rostrevor Avenue. Allowing them time to move away from the junction, I slowly approached just edging the bonnet of my car out until I could see where they were. They had in fact crossed over and I spotted one of them on the doorstep of a house. It was at the far end on a short terrace of about five houses. He was looking in our direction when I first spotted him and must have seen the bonnet of my car slowly emerge, for he suddenly moved forward into the house through the front doorway as though alerted by our presence. I drove down to the house and the front door was closed, bolted on the inside, looking through the letter box I heard a crashing sound coming from the rear and realised they were trying to escape out the back.

There was a garage to my right alongside the house with a flat corrugated asphalt roof. Aided by a low sidewall, I managed to climb up onto the garage roof and run across it. As I did so, I felt and heard the panels cracking beneath my feet, which was a bit disconcerting, but I just kept going. As I jumped down into the rear garden I could see our two suspects clambering over the side garden fence into the neighbouring garden on my left. I went after them and remained once fence behind, as we traversed three or four fences in this fashion like a steeplechase without the horses. I hadn't stopped to wonder where Bob was, but as the two suspects reached the end garden of this short terrace one of them started to clamber up the side fence adjacent to the pavement in Cadoxton Avenue. I saw the top of a police truncheon raining down on the top edge of the fence, as a deterrent to whoever was endeavouring to scale it, and I heard Bob's agitated voice shouting, "Get down!" The fences we had gone over had been about four or five feet in height but this end fence to the side road was a good eight feet. Deterred, no doubt by the height of the fence and the chance of having bruised knuckles, our two suspects ran towards the house.

They then realised there was a side gate, which they managed to unbolt as I reached the final garden. Once out of the garden one went right, chased by Bob and the other went left and up Rostrevor Avenue towards the High Road pursued by me. On reaching the

High road he ran straight across, through the traffic and I finally caught up with him on the far side, outside St. Ignatius Church. We were both completely breathless, but I managed to hold on to him, penning him in against the church railings by holding a rail in each hand with my prisoner sandwiched between the railings and myself while I got my breath back. Looking over my shoulder I could see no sign of Bob or the other suspect, a few pedestrians glanced in our direction, but probably thought it was just men fighting. I thought of asking a passer-by to help me or phone for assistance, but the first fit looking chap that approached, I recognised as one of the Mobbs brothers who had themselves been done for a series of burglaries about a year beforehand.

Next to the church was a school playground so there were no convenient premises I could access a phone. On the far side of the High Road was Stewart and Arden's, a motor repair shop so I decided to get my prisoner there, but having recovered his own breath, he struggled more violently and was trying to bite my hand. I managed to get an arm lock of sorts on him and got him half way across to the central reservation, but as I waited for a suitable gap in the traffic he tried to push me out into the path of oncoming traffic.

Finally I got him into the entrance of the garage workshop and here the pair of us were struggling down on the floor. I was trying to hang on to him and at the same time draw my truncheon, which I kept in a truncheon pocket cut from an old pair of uniform trousers and sewn into my civvies. A bemused group of motor mechanics had by now gathered around us, but at a respectable distance. I shouted out to them, "I'm a Police Officer phone 999 for help."

My prisoner then shouted out, "No he's not." To reach in my pocket for a Warrant Card at this juncture would have meant letting go what little hold I was able to maintain on my prisoner. Seeing a doorway to some toilets, I shouted out, "Lock us both in there and call the police".

The garage foreman then came over and told me he had rung for assistance and he helped me to restrain my prisoner until help arrived in the shape of the local Area Car.

I then learnt from the Area Car crew that Bob had caught his suspect further down the High Road outside a shop, the staff of which had called police. Although I had not used my truncheon I had drawn it as a measure of self-protection and a visible threat to the man I was endeavouring to detain. This had proved beneficial, as the garage foreman told me he had once served as a War Reserve and having recognised my truncheon as police issue, he had finally been convinced of my identity and called for assistance.

The two prisoners Fehily and Chapman (no relation) both had a number of previous convictions and had travelled away from their own locality in Kentish Town, intent on breaking into houses in an area where they were not known and the residences were more attractive to them. When searched at St. Ann's Road Police Station Chapman, who Bob had arrested, was found to be in possession of a small quantity of ladies jewellery including a number of rings.

The house they had been disturbed at, 55 Rostrevor Avenue had had the front door kicked in and the two men had gone out the back via the French windows, which was the sound I had heard on my arrival. We knew there was very little time for them to have stolen anything so it was no surprise when the occupants returned and we learnt that the jewellery did not belong to them. This was put to the two prisoners and Chapman admitted that they had broken into a house earlier that day and stolen the jewellery and £7 in cash, which Fehily had pocketed. He could only recall, it was an end house near a garage and they had on that occasion, broken in round the back. I put this to my prisoner Fehily and he replied.

"Yes that's right there wasn't much there, my mate had those rings and I took the money you found on me. If there had been a bit more cash you wouldn't have caught us doing the other one."

He may well have been right in this observation, but being strangers to the area, the pair had unwittingly returned to the very same road where they had committed their first burglary, before Bob and I had first seen them.

That evening two ladies residing at number 2 Rostrevor Avenue returned to their house to discover it had been burgled. £7 cash and some jewellery was missing, had they returned earlier and called police, the two culprits could well have been back in the vicinity, still in possession of the proceeds.

Fehily and Chapman both pleaded guilty to two charges of housebreaking and with the passage of time I no longer recollect their sentences. Bob had lost his raincoat during the pursuit of Chapman and in accordance with Regulations was able to put in a claim for compensation, it was an old coat and the compensation amounted to more than he was expecting, so he treated me to Chinese meal. On conclusion of the trial, the Commissioner commended both Bob and me for 'Vigilance and Determination in a case of housebreaking'. Nothing however, can be as rewarding as the personal feeling of satisfaction in apprehending two active burglars caught in the act, purely as the result of a gut feeling and with such limited resources as we had. It certainly made up for the many days of fruitless patrolling that were necessary before striking lucky.

Other than the few specific occasions when information or intelligence was to hand, one never knew when an arrest for crime might occur. It was partly the uncertainty of what you might come up against whilst patrolling that kept you on your mettle. In present day times many of the specialist squads target individuals if there is good evidence or intelligence to indicate they are actively engaged in specific serious crimes, but such operations are extremely expensive both with regard to manpower and resources. As the only two Aids on our Section we had to manage our time and the demands made on it to the best of our ability. Although we usually concentrated on the areas where specific crimes were most prolific, our Section was not inundated with crime and you could go several weeks without affecting an arrest. At other times there may have been suspicions that certain individuals were engaged in particular crimes, but there was still the need to obtain concrete evidence, to verify those suspicions.

One such individual was employed as a maintenance man at the Stamford Hill Bowling Alley. He was suspected of stealing from cars parked in the car park there or nearby. He knew the pair of us and knew we suspected him, so if he was out and about in that vicinity and saw us he would scurry back to his work, but we had our day eventually when we saw him tampering with parked vehicles. It transpired he had just stolen a record player and was using the boot of an associate's parked car to store his booty.

Where vehicles were the subject of crime, particularly scooters taken for joy riding it was invariably juvenile males who were responsible often in small groups sometimes hiding a motor bike or scooter then passing in on to school friends the next day for more joyriding. Dealing with juveniles for any offence was always time consuming, as a parent or responsible adult had to be called to the Station to be present during any interviews and extra forms had to be completed. Where prosecutions ensued there was usually several court appearances, with cases remanded for Probation Reports to be compiled on offenders.

There was a period when the Justices at Tottenham Juvenile Court started taking a harder line with Juveniles; particularly those convicted of burglary offences. Instead of remanding them on bail they remanded them in custody for two weeks for Reports, this proved to be a short sharp shock to many, inducing tears from parents and offspring alike. Even if they eventually were placed on Probation or Conditionally Discharged, the two weeks away was an effective deterrent. Greater use of this type of action by Juvenile Courts would in my opinion have acted as a 'wake up' call to both juvenile offenders and their parents and had, far more of a deterrent effect, than many of the penalties handed out. Fortunately many young lads, who are before the courts as Juveniles, do grow out of offending particularly when they start working or seriously courting. Others, however, are destined to live a life of crime.

Although burglary offences were the focus of much of our attention as Aids, I was always conscious that at any given time a number of stolen vehicles must be being used in any given area, either to assist in criminal acts or as everyday transport for those who were willing to take a chance on being caught. The majority of vehicles taken without the owner's consent would be by joyriders and abandoned soon after being taken, in all probability before they had been missed. If it were intended to keep a stolen vehicle for any length of time, possibly to use for crime, it would often be fitted with false index plates and perhaps a stolen and altered Vehicle Excise Licence. More sophisticated car thieves, who altered engine and chassis numbers were more often than not intending to, sell on a stolen vehicle to some unsuspecting member of the public. If therefore, I saw a vehicle with brand new index plates i.e. cleaner than the general condition of the vehicle itself, I always considered it worth a second look. This was normally only possible with parked vehicles, but on the afternoon of 22nd January 1962, Bob and I found ourselves behind such a vehicle whilst driving along High Road Tottenham.

The vehicle a Ford Consul contained two men and I noticed there were scratch marks around the fixing screws on the rear number plate which appeared new. I pointed this out to Bob and we decided to follow the vehicle in the first instance as it was driving north towards Tottenham. Ultimately we left our Section at West Green Road and continued onto Tottenham Section passing the Police Station, but nowhere did the vehicle stop in a convenient place for us to alight and speak to the occupants, which we had now decided to do. As we reached Bruce Grove, the passenger turned in his seat to look at us as, a sign that the driver must have become aware of our continued presence. Driving on, the vehicle then indicated a right turn and turned into a minor side road as did I. It then took a series of left and right turns around back streets, with the passenger now repeatedly looking back at us. I followed every manoeuvre confidant that we were on to something.

Fortunately a left turn, which I thought might give the car access to Lansdowne Road and an opportunity to speed off, proved to be a dead end merely leading into some lock up garages, where the car came to a halt. Neither man made any attempt to get out of the vehicle and with my car right behind, the vehicle's exit was blocked, was nowhere to go nor the driver sat still, surveying us in his rear view mirror. I remained in the driving seat for a brief moment prolonging the cat and mouse game, which had ended so abruptly. Then we approached the still seated occupants and introduced ourselves.

I asked the Driver, a man by the name of Geoffrey Bell, whether the vehicle belonged to him, to which he replied, "It's my mate's here," nodding in the direction of his passenger Kenny Squires. Squires said, "Yes, I'm thinking of buying it from a fellow in Green Lanes." I then instructed Bell to get out of the car so I could speak to him out of the earshot of Squires, and said, "Have you any proof you are in lawful possession of this car?"

Bell then produced a logbook from his jacket and said, "The bloke we were thinking of buying the car from, gave me the log book in case we were stopped."

A quick perusal of this revealed the registration number to tally with the plates on the car. I said, "Have you any licence or insurance?" Bell replied, "I haven't got my licence with me, but my mate's got his."

He then produced a licence in the name Kenny Squires. Returning to the car I said to Squires, "What is your name?" He replied "Paul Hindle." Bell interjected and said to him, "Tell the truth Kenny, he's seen your licence."

Both men then gave us their full particulars, which Bob wrote down whilst I examined the number plates and then the engine. I found a number on the engine, which did not appear to tally with the vehicle logbook, but as this was the first time I had carried out such a check I was unsure whether I was looking at the right number. With the exception of a club hammer I'd found under the drivers' seat, which Bell denied having seen before, the inside of the car was completely clean. It contained none of the usual paraphernalia and litter that gathers in vehicles in everyday use, possibly corroborating the assertion that the vehicle had come from a car salesman. I told the two men that we would need to speak to the owner and check the car properly. In the absence of a telephone or radio we decided it would be best if we went to Tottenham Police Station, which was the nearest and Bell and Squires readily agreed to this course of action.

I suggested to Bob that he should accompany Bell, the driver of the Consul, in that vehicle and Squires should accompany me in my car. In this way we still had an element of control over our two suspects pending our enquiries which would clarify whether the vehicle itself and the facts we had been given were straight. To my surprise Bob declined to accompany Bell in the suspect vehicle on his own. I was completely taken aback, but this was neither the time nor place to discuss the risk factor of this option. So with Squires in the front passenger seat of my car and Bob in the back, I told Bell to drive the consul in front of us to Tottenham Police Station, a distance of about half a mile.

As my vehicle was blocking the Consul in the entrance to the lock ups, I needed to reverse back out into the Cul-de-sac end, of the road and allow Bell the room to do the same with the Consul. Having completed these manoeuvres, Bell drove in front of me for a few yards then suddenly accelerated until reaching the first side turning. Then the driver's door opened and Bell jumped out, leaving the car to career on driverless as he ran off down the side road in the direction of Tottenham High Road. I drove up to where the Consul had come to a halt behind a stationary vehicle and Bob instinctively reached forward grabbing Squires in a bear hug from behind and I left my car and ran off in pursuit of Bell, who by now had a substantial lead on me.

Reaching the busy Tottenham High Road, Bell turned to his right and by the time I reached there, he was still some distance ahead. As I ran across the High Road, I waved down the first available vehicle, which was a large 3-ton van. It mattered not, as the traffic was heavy, and from the high cab position, I was able to see Bell over the cars in front, as he headed past Lansdowne Road. I barely had time to explain my identity to the driver and thank him, before seeing Bell turn off the High Street and go left down a narrow walkway some 500 yards from where I had hailed the lorry. The brief ride had enabled me to regain my breath and Bell who was barely running now, had only a lead of some 20 yards on me as I departed from the lorry. I quickly made up the distance and he was in no fit state to offer much resistance when I finally apprehended him.

Asked why he had run off, Bell said, "I needed time to think." He was to do the rest of his thinking in a cell at Tottenham Police Station for having dialled 999 from a nearby telephone kiosk, I deposited Bell into a Police car which returned me to where I had left my car with Bob Chambers and Kenny Squires. Bob had managed to shout to a passer-by to phone for assistance, which was in attendance by the time I returned and fortunately Squires had not resisted arrest.

The Ford Consul had caused slight damage to a parked car when abandoned by Bell, so the incident had to be fully reported. I knew this would cause questions to be asked by the Duty Officer at Tottenham, in particular how come we were in my private car on duty. Owing to this and the fact that we needed to let our office know where we were, I rang the CID Office at St. Ann's Road and spoke to Arthur Butler who was the First Class Sergeant. Arthur was a really nice guy and a shrewd detective, who had only been at St. Ann's for a few months after a long period of service on the Flying Squad at Scotland Yard. He was a very practical officer and was fully aware that I used my own car on duty (at my own expense), but as this was producing good results he acquiesced in this practise. He was pleased to hear of our two 'Arrests' and suggested that to avoid any difficulties regarding the use of my vehicle he would book us off duty an hour previous. Bell and Squires having declined to identify the person from whom they had obtained the vehicle, were initially charged with unlawful possession of the vehicle which subsequent enquiries revealed was in fact stolen and fitted with false index plates to match the Vehicle Registration Book produced by Bell.

Although I had been taken aback when Bob had declined to accompany Bell in the Ford Consul, I never raised the matter later. Certainly Bell had the appearance of a being a bit of a hard case and had Bob been able to drive my car, I would have happily have accompanied Bell. I was, however, at the peak of personal fitness at that time, for a few weeks later, I was the winning finalist at light heavyweight, when 'N' Division won the Lafone Cup Boxing Competition for the second year running. By deciding to make a run for it, Bell had not only confirmed any suspicions about his guilty knowledge regarding the vehicle, he had picked the wrong copper to try and escape from. A month later, Bob and I, on the recommendation of Arthur Butler were commended by the Area Commander for 'Devotion to duty whilst off duty, vigilance and ability in effecting the arrest of two men for stealing a motor car.' Whether this case would have earned a Commendation had it not been reported as an 'Off Duty' arrest I don't know, but we were both grateful for the support of Arthur Butler in relation to this case.

Once again the personal satisfaction I felt at the time of the detection and arrest of mature criminals, far outweighed any commendation, particularly when the arrests were purely as a result of one's own instincts, sometimes after many days of fruitless patrolling and observations. Life as an Aid was not all hard work, however, for in addition to boxing, I was also playing rugby for "N" Division, whenever duties allowed. In March 1962 our team spent a very pleasant few days in Jersey, where we had the honour of playing the Jersey Rugby Club in the inaugural game on a newly acquired ground, which was formally opened by the Lord Lieutenant of Jersey.

During the all too brief time that Arthur Butler was our First Class Sergeant, we experienced a spate of night-time house burglaries at St. Ann's Road. It soon became apparent that the offences were occurring on Friday nights, at premises bordering railway tracks, with access being gained to the rear mainly where windows had been left open. Many people were still in receipt of weekly pay packets at that time and had retired to bed leaving their money in one of the ground floor rooms only to find it missing in the morning with other small items of jewellery. With the assistance of some of the Aides from Stoke Newington and a number of uniform officers employed in plain clothes, Arthur Butler instigated all night observations on the relevant sections of the railway embankment for a number of Friday nights. I was quite surprised when he turned out himself for several hours of the operation for he was still engaged on normal daytime duties. We did, however, have two different rail lines crossing our Section at right angles. Having focused on the area where the offences had been occurring, the 'night man' changed his activities to a different area and then the offences became more sporadic, so with other demands on manpower, the observations had to be terminated.

About a month later during the early hours of the morning police were called to a house in Stanhope Gardens, where a suspect had been heard tampering with a window at the rear, which was adjacent to railway tracks. After a search of the area P.C. John Corner one of the lads from my old relief who was posted to the Area Car, arrested a man who had in fact broken into a neighbouring house, whilst police were being called. The man was found to have a number of pawn tickets on his person and at his address, for articles subsequently identified as proceeds from our previous night burglaries near railway tracks. It had been thought that our 'Night man' was possibly a railway employee and familiar with the layout to the railway embankments and adjacent premises, but this proved not to be the case. He had found that by using the railway embankment to gain access to rear gardens, a number of people having a false sense of security, left ground floor windows open or unlocked and he could enter at first light and steal small items without disturbing the sleeping occupants. It was a bit frustrating to think that had we been able to continue our night observations a bit longer, we may well have caught the 'night man' ourselves. I was however pleased that John Corner had effected the arrest, as he was one of our boxing team and an applicant for Aide to the CID, so this particular arrest came at a good time for him.

This arrest had come about as the result of an emergency call, responded to by the Area Car. Two uniformed officers manned such Cars and if manning levels permitted a plain-clothes observer. Officers from the Sub Division i.e. Stoke Newington and St. Ann's Road posted to this duty for six weeks would provide the crew. In addition to Area Cars, each Division would have the use of a 'Q' Car, which would be an unmarked high-powered car often a Jaguar or Rover, driven by a Class 1 police driver in plain clothes with an Aide to CID employed as the radio operator. On one shift either a Detective Constable or Sergeant would act as an Observer and on the other shift a Uniform Sergeant in plain clothes, would be selected for this role. The cars covered the whole Division for six weeks, alternating late and early shifts. This was a much sought after duty.

As I became an Aide before completing my Probation period I was never eligible for a posting to the Area Car, I did however enjoy several postings to the 'Q' Car. One of the benefits for me was not having to drive and being able to concentrate fully on whatever was going on around, as well as having a police radio, relaying information concerning any crimes in progress. If any information was received regarding suspects loitering with a view to committing crime, then the operator at Information Room at Scotland Yard would normally allocate the call to a 'Q' Car in the first instance, so discreet observation could be made by plain clothes officers. Where crimes were actually in progress such as house burglaries, then a local Area Car would be dispatched, but a 'Q' Car could assist if in the vicinity. There always existed a healthy competition between the two crews posted to 'Q' Car duties regarding who could achieve the best 'Return of Work', in particular the number of arrests for crime. So when first posted to 'Q Car duties I learnt it was prudent to get around the various CID Offices and let the personnel know that you were on the 'Q' Car. Then, should they have any intelligence relating to crimes or suspects active on their Sub Divisions they might be happy to pass it on, knowing you were interested in acting upon it.

One interesting case arose when I was working with Detective Constable Roy Walpole and P.C. Reg Arthur two excellent Stoke Newington Officers. We received information that a beat duty P.C. at Highbury Vale had seen a Jaguar Car with personalised index plates JRB 123, which were not allocated to a Jaguar Car. The vehicle had been seen parked in several locations in Highbury Hill during the early evening but never being driven. We agreed to look out for the vehicle when posted to the 6pm – 2am shift and within a few days we located the car parked in Highbury Hill. Reg Arthur parked our car further back up the road, from where we were able to keep the Jaguar under observation and within the hour, a smartly dressed young man, got who had been walking up Highbury Hill, got into the vehicle and prepared to drive away.

Reg drove the 'Q' car down to impede his progress and Roy and I detained the chap.

The smart blazer that he was wearing bore the badge of the Arsenal Football Club, where he told us he had just been training as one of their youth team players. He gave the name of John Robert Brown hence the personalised index plate. He initially claimed the car was his, but once confronted with evidence to the contrary, admitted stealing the vehicle. His address was searched and various items stolen from motor vehicles were recovered, including a driving licence belonging to a peer in the House of Lords.

Another interesting case arose from a woman residing in a rented flat in a large house in Upper Clapton Road. A young woman who moved into the flat below hers and who had invited her in for coffee of a few occasions had befriended her. From conversations with her new neighbour and her own observations, she had become suspicious of the activities of this neighbour's boyfriend and on one occasion whilst in the flat, noticed a newspaper cutting about an armed robbery of a Security Vehicle. She decided to report her suspicions to Stoke Newington Police and details were passed on to Roy Walpole whilst we were on 'Q' car duties. After speaking with the informant and making various enquiries, Roy obtained a search warrant for the address and we duly arrested the boyfriend, a man named Foster, who was found to be in possession of some items of stolen property for which he was charged with Receiving. More importantly we recovered the press cutting covering a story relating to 'The first robbery of a security vehicle'; such vehicles for conveying cash in transit, only recently being taken into use. As a result of liaising with the officers dealing with the robbery, Foster's fingerprints were compared with some found on a vehicle used as a getaway car and lo and behold there was a match.

Foster was then interviewed and subsequently charged with the armed robbery, which he denied. In due course he appeared at the Old Bailey and was represented by Nemone Lethbridge, who I had last seen when she defended George Ince. Foster produced a seemingly respectable woman, who gave him a possible alibi for the day of the robbery. It transpired however; that the car had been cleaned the day before it was stolen. Having been used in the robbery, almost immediately thereafter, the jury were invited by the Judge to draw the conclusion that the presence of Foster's fingerprints inside the car was indicative of his involvement in the robbery. He was, however, facing a separate indictment of 'Taking and driving away' the car. Whilst the jury were considering their verdict, in conversation with Ms. Lethbridge, she remarked that if the Jury were to convict on the "Taking and driving away', they must surely also convict her client of the robbery. Such is the perverseness of juries, however, for they found Foster 'Not Guilty' on the Robbery Charge, but 'Guilty' to Taking and Driving Away the car.

The most exciting aspect of working on the 'Q' Car was when answering calls to 'suspects on premises' where someone had reported actually seeing suspects breaking into premises and we often assisted uniform crews in such matters. One amusing incident arose when we were called to a large house in Camden Road, where the residents returned and disturbed a burglar who fled out into their back garden and then climbed into adjacent gardens in an endeavour to escape. On our arrival uniform officers were already searching the rear gardens and so after checking the rest of the house with the tenant, I looked out of a third floor rear window in time to witness the suspect clambering over garden walls followed by uniform colleagues a few gardens away. The suspect then decided to attempt an escape through the rear door of one of the houses. Having entered the house within a few seconds he ran back out, pursued by an elderly male occupant and as he tried to scramble over a side wall the man picked up a yard broom and swung it violently at the back of the suspect striking him several blows. This enabled a uniform P.C. to catch up with the suspect, who was arrested and led through the man's house to access the police car. When we spoke to the arresting officer he was very amused by the fact that the elderly occupant had been sat reading a copy of the Church Times, before laying into the intruder who had disturbed his afternoon read.

In addition to the 'Q' Car there were Nondescript vehicles used mainly for static observation purposes, mostly by Aides to CID but occasionally for uniform cases. There were not many such vehicles and they were shared between Divisions on rota and you considered yourself very fortunate if one was available when a need arose. The vehicles were usually vans, specially fitted out in the rear, with seats and spy holes, sometimes one way glass in the rear doors and equipped with a police radio. Once the officers engaged on the observation were in the back, a plain clothes police driver would drive the vehicle to wherever was considered a suitable location for the observation in hand and then leave the vehicle, locking the drivers cab and walking away to detract any suspicion.

On one of the rare occasions when Bob Chambers and I had secured the use of a Nondescript van, things did not exactly go according to plan. We needed to keep observation on a vehicle, which we suspected of being fitted with false index plates, which was parked near Clapton Common. We arranged for the driver of the Nondescript to meet us nearby and not knowing how long the observation might last, we decided to get some rolls and a drink from the nearby refreshment hut to take into the van with us. Whilst we were doing this the driver went to look for a suitable location to park the van once we were ensconced inside. When he did not return we walked round to the location of the suspect vehicle, only to find our driver had already detained a man, who was in the act of getting into the suspect car as he drove by. It was a rule that wherever possible you tried not to disclose the identity of whatever vehicle was being used as a Nondescript as word soon got around the criminal fraternity. On this occasion, however, our driver had no option and had in fact secured the prisoner in the back of the van awaiting our arrival, much to our embarrassment.

One skill that being a police officer, particularly an Aide to CID, sharpens up, is one's powers of observation, but I never expected that I would spend over a week carefully observing the footwear of my fellow Section House Residents. This came about in the summer of 1962, when a close friend in the Section House,

P.C. Andy Petter, was due to get married. Andy had extended me the honour of asking me to be his Best Man, which I had readily accepted. About a week to ten days before the wedding however, I discovered that my best pair of black shoes, with spit and polished toecaps, had gone missing from the wardrobe in my room. I was aware that items of clothing usually shirts got "borrowed" from time to time, but this was something new and the first time I had been the victim. I was particularly concerned, as they were the only shoes suitable to wear with the suit purchased with the wedding in mind. When they did not reappear, I put a note on the Section House notice board requesting the culprit to return them, pointing out that they were required for Andy's Wedding, which about ten of the other Section House Residents were due to attend.

Being only a size eight and a half, I could eliminate the majority of other residents, whose feet clearly needed sizes nine, ten or eleven. So I found myself studying the footwear of anyone who might be the same size as me, during my off duty time in the Section House. I had long had my suspicions about a nearby resident, who I suspected of shirt borrowing, particularly as outwardly, he always presented a smart image especially when dating girlfriends, but having worn items let them pile up on his armchair instead of putting them away or laundering them. By the eve of the wedding they had still not been returned and although I had a mental short list of possible suspects, I was no nearer discovering the culprit. I had decided that if they had not been returned by the day of the wedding I would have time to purchase a new pair and with this in mind had visited a local shoe shop to study their range. On the morning of the wedding, however, as I left my room to visit the washroom, outside my door I found my missing shoes. I never did find out who had borrowed them, but I'm pleased to say that my main suspect did not remain in the police force very much longer.

The shoe episode, however, proved to be only a minor incident by comparison to later events concerning Andy's wedding, brought about by an unfortunate meeting a few days beforehand. Andy and I and a few of the lads from the Section House were having a drink in a local public house when I spotted a chap I knew as Patsy Kearns, who happened to live nearby. I had first met Patsy in the Charge Room at St. Ann's Road Police Station, whilst a uniform P.C. He was one of five persons arrested in possession of a stolen motor vehicle late one Saturday evening. The men had all come from the Manor House public house just prior to their arrest and Patsy claimed that, having been employed as a drummer in the band at the pub, he had been offered a lift home and knew nothing about the vehicle being stolen. I believe the vehicle had come to police notice a few days before, when someone was seen dumping a small safe in the River Lea. I had had no personal involvement in the case, but had merely been asked to stand guard on the charge room door in view of the number of prisoners therein.

Patsy, who was in his thirties, was a bit of a character, a native of Ireland, short in stature, but long on wit and clearly at his best in the company of others with a pint in his hand. What the outcome of that case was, I don't recall, but it certainly didn't result in any loss of liberty on Patsy's behalf, as I saw him from time to time in and around the local public houses. If he spotted me patrolling, he would greet me and always had a yarn to tell or would try out his latest jokes on me. Ultimately, when I became an Aid to CID, I occasionally saw him in the public gallery at the rear of North London Court. He had told me that as he lived across the road from the court, he often popped in, finding it interesting listening to the various cases and the excuses given by people for their misdemeanours. I'm sure this gave him good fodder for his bar room chats. I had myself had a drink with him on one occasion after I had been to Court, as apart from being good company, being a person with his ear to the ground and doing the rounds as a pub entertainer I considered his local knowledge could prove useful.

It was no surprise therefore that when Patsy saw me, he came over to where Andy and I and our group were having a drink and he was soon in his element telling yarns and jokes. Events thereafter are a little unclear. I do recollect that on learning that the reception was to be held in a local public house, Patsy offered his services as a vocalist or M.C. but no firm arrangement was made.

The wedding went well and lo and behold Patsy turned up at the Reception. He appeared to know the musicians and he was soon entertaining everyone with his competent rendition of a number of Irish Ballads, taking a turn on the drums and acting as an MC by inviting or cajoling a number of people to get up and sing. He was kept well supplied with beer, which he certainly deserved. Ultimately Andy and Christine departed for their Honeymoon and the Reception carried on until the end of the evening. It was at the stage when everyone was departing, that Patsy came out of the cloakroom holding a small black attaché case, just as I was passing. Seeing me he remarked something to the effect, "I brought a few of my tricks along but didn't get to use them".

I said, "Oh you should have said," and bade him good night thanking him for his contribution to the evening's success.

Some 15 minutes or so later I became aware that Peggy one of the Bridesmaids, was looking concerned and she told me she couldn't find her case with her change of clothes in, which she had left in the cloakroom. I asked her what sort of case it was and she described the case I had just seen in the possession of Patsy Kearns. My heart sunk, I realised Patsy must have pinched the case and I felt totally responsible. The case contained only a blouse and skirt and a few cosmetics, but its loss was going to spoil Peggy's day apart from the inconvenience of not being able to change.

Patsy had mentioned that he was working as a potman at the nearby Farleigh Arms and would be going on there after the Reception. After assuring Peggy that someone must have taken her case by mistake and it would surely turn up, I left for the Farleigh Arms, without mentioning my suspicions or intentions to any of my colleagues who were present. On my way my mind was racing, going through all the possible permutations of how to deal with this situation without causing any embarrassment to Andy & Christine, who by now would have been in Jersey on Honeymoon. I would have no compunction, but to arrest and charge Patsy but this would put blight on the Wedding Day, even if the local newspaper didn't pick up on the story.

By the time I reached the Farleigh Arms, to say I was fuming would be an understatement and as I walked in I spotted Patsy immediately on the far side of the lounge in a white jacket carrying a tray of empty glasses. He took one look at me and stopped in his tracks, going over to him I said, "Right, you outside."

He put his tray of glasses down on a nearby table and after I declined his request to go and change out of his bar jacket, he accompanied me out of the pub. It was the first time I had been in this particular pub and only as we crossed to the door, did I become aware it was packed with Saturday night drinkers. I'd paid no heed however to anyone who was in there, other than my quarry it was certainly not a place where I wished to pursue my business.

Once outside, I said, "Where is it?" giving no room for any denial by Patsy, although his body language had already told me he would put up no resistance or pretence.

"At home" he replied meekly,

"Where is that?" I said,

"Bromley Road" replied Patsy.

"Have you still got everything?" I asked,

"Yes, I gave a few bits to my wife".

As we walked the short distance to Bromley Road, I at last felt a sense of relief knowing that I was going to be able to return Peggy's property to her, but still angry at the stupidity of Patsy. He was full of apologies saying, "I'm sorry I don't know what came over me," but I far too annoyed to indulge in petty conversation.

Patsy took me to a first floor bedsit, where his wife was lying on the bed watching T.V. Prior to that day I neither knew whether Patsy was married or single and the poor girl must have wondered what was happening when I first entered the flat late that Saturday night. Patsy handed me the black attaché case and I told his wife what Patsy had done. I told them to replace everything in it exactly as it was when he first opened it, as by now my prime concern was to return it to Peggy intact without her day being spoilt by the knowledge that she had been the victim of a petty theft. I had no knowledge of all the original contents, so was dependent on Patsy and his wife to replace everything intact. She retrieved a blouse and skirt from a small chest of drawers and placed them folded into the case together with a few cosmetics. I didn't bother questioning her as to any guilty knowledge regarding the origin of the property as I was anxious to try and return to the Wedding Reception and reunite Peggy with her property if she had not already left. I had decided that I would wait until after the honeymoon before telling Andy what had occurred, so left a sheepish looking Patsy with a few choice words of advice and the threat of a possible prosecution hanging over him.

It was in fact the next day before I was able to reunite Peggy with her case. I told her that it had been 'taken in error' and as she did not ask any questions, I did not elaborate on the facts. By the time I next saw Andy, after his return from Honeymoon, he had already heard all about the missing case through conversations between Christine and Peggy and had sussed out what had happened. I outlined my actions on the day and neither he nor Peggy wished to pursue the matter further.

Ultimately my Aiding partnership with Bob Chambers came to an end. Bob, who had become a bit despondent about his chances of securing a permanent position with the CID, informed me that he had heard there was a vacancy on the newly formed Juvenile Bureau, which he successfully applied for. I then began a new partnership with Graham Pollock, whose nickname was Sam, and who had been a uniform P.C. at Holloway. We were deputed to work from Stoke Newington Station where a number of other Aides were also employed. Sam was happy to continue with the arrangement I had had with Bob, of using my car and sharing the costs of the petrol. Sam had a great sense of humour and an infectious laugh and like myself was keen to attain a career in the CID so we got on well together. One of our earliest arrests came about when we made a routine stop on a local criminal name Jackson. He was found to have a loaded .22 revolver concealed in the waistband of his trousers, an offence, which was to result in a 6-month sentence of imprisonment, when he appeared at North London Magistrates Court.

One unusual case arose at a time when we were experiencing an increase in housebreaking offences at Stoke Newington, where in addition to the usual valuables, a number of domestic utensils were also being stolen. Whilst driving down Kyverdale Road one afternoon, I noticed a young chap in his early twenties walk from the entranceway of some houses on my near side and continue down the footway as we drove by. There was nothing untoward in this, but about an hour or so later, whilst in the same vicinity, we saw the chap carrying two bulky holdalls which I knew he had not had with him when seen earlier. We decided to do a stop on him and as he was on our offside, I drove across the road and pulled up just in front of him, but no sooner had we began to get out of my car, then he dropped the bags and ran off. I jumped back into the car and drove further down the road stopping some twenty yards in front of him, to enable me time to alight and I managed to catch up with him as he ran across the road. A violent struggle then ensued in the middle of the roadway, with me trying to maintain an arm lock on him, whilst he wriggled and kicked in an endeavour to escape.

The contents of the holdalls were found to be the usual valuables that were stolen in housebreaking offences including some cheap decorative ornaments of no particular value. Our suspect, whilst admitting having just committed an offence of burglary, declined to supply us with an address where he was currently living. Although I could not pinpoint the exact house I had seen him leave earlier, by retracing our steps I narrowed it down to one of a pair and at one address we located the girlfriend of our prisoner. A search of the premises then revealed that it had been furnished almost entirely with the proceeds of a number of recent burglaries, right down to rugs on the floor. He was subsequently charged with four offences of Housebreaking and a number of charges of receiving stolen property. We were ultimately Commended by the Area Commander for 'diligence and initiative' in effecting his arrest.

With the passage of time it is not possible to recall the names of all the various individuals one has dealt with let alone the punishment metered out by the Judiciary. In some cases, only the salient facts are remembered whilst in others it is the events at trial or the verdict of the jury that enables an accurate recall. One such case which arose whilst working as an Aide at Stoke Newington concerned a man known to police as 'Old man Hawkey' or 'Scarface Hawkey'. Although he did have a small facial scar the nicknames were primarily used to differentiate him from one of his sons, who I believe shared the same Christian name and was, like his brothers, fast following in the father's footsteps as a career criminal. 'Old man Hawkey', was certainly in his mid-forties, he lived in Hackney and whilst he had an assortment of previous convictions, was an active housebreaker and petty thief, particularly in the Stoke Newington area. His Modus Operandi (MO) was to walk the streets looking for suitable premises to break into, either where a window had been left open or a front door might succumb to a hefty kick. He would then call at the premises to check whether they were occupied. If they were, he would ask the occupant whether any decorating jobs needed doing so as to allay suspicion. To this end he usually carried a paint sample brochure, a tape measure and a small notebook. These items being his 'insurance' if any suspicious residents alerted police to his activities.

During investigations into house burglaries, when making enquiries at neighbouring premises regarding any suspicious callers, it was not uncommon for detectives to learn than a man of Hawkey's description had called during the relevant period enquiring about decorating work. From an Aides point of view, should Hawkey be seen on the manor, he was a 'must' for keeping under observation, but this wily individual was extremely surveillance conscious.

Such an opportunity came one day whilst patrolling the mainly Jewish residential area, in the vicinity of Cazenove Road off Stamford Hill, where many large Victorian dwelling houses are situated. A colleague and I spotted Hawkey walking along with more than a passing glance at the various houses he passed. Being in my trusty Standard 8, once we had identified our prey, we were able to keep well back to avoid detection ourselves. After a while we saw Hawkey turn into Kyverdale Road and a few seconds later

I drove past the end of that road to see how far he had walked and on which footway he was on. Despite having a clear view of both footways Hawkey was nowhere to be seen; an indication that he must have entered the large front garden of one of the first few houses in Kyverdale Road. Not knowing which garden he had entered, it was too risky to drive into Kyverdale Road. Turning the car round, I drove back past the end of the road and was just in time to see Hawkey hurriedly exit from the front garden of premises some 50 yards away and cross the road, before turning the corner into Cazenove Road.

Thereafter we followed him along several roads without incident until finally in Downs Road, he crossed over and walked onto a footpath on Hackney Downs. It seemed that he was heading back home so we decided to stop and question him regarding his prior movements. Having parked my car, we trotted along the footpath and finally caught up with Hawkey, who was wearing a full-length coat. We had just introduced ourselves and told him we had been watching him, when I glanced down and saw a ladies handbag lying on his shoes, which I realised he must have had concealed under his coat. Despite the bag being on his shoes he denied ever having seen it before. Needless to say he was duly arrested and taken to Stoke Newington Police Station where I learnt that the Area Car had just been called to a small school in Cazenove Road, where the cook had reported her handbag stolen.

The school had an entrance door in Kyverdale Road, which was left ajar and this provided access to the kitchen area from where the theft had occurred. The bag was duly identified by its owner and was intact. Hawkey was charged with an offence of burglary and theft. It occurred to us that Hawkey in crossing Hackney Downs was not only headed in the general direction of the flats where he lived, but his route would have taken him past the public conveniences. This would have been an ideal place to examine the bag and extract any cash or valuables that it contained, before abandoning the bag and any unwanted items. Even when challenged with the evidence that we had seen him coming from the garden of the premises from whence the bag was stolen, Hawkey denied the offence and persisted that he had never seen it before we stopped him. In due course he appeared at North London Magistrates Court and although the case could have been tried there, as no forcible entry was used to effect the burglary, Hawkey elected trial by Jury at the Inner London Crown Court. Granting this request the Magistrate Frank Milton remarked, "This is probably the best course of action as I know this family all too well."

At his subsequent trial having pleaded 'Not guilty' to the offence, Hawkey proffered a defence that he had found the bag that morning in the garden of the premises concerned and was taking it to Hackney Police Station when stopped by us. To add insult to injury his Defence Counsel in addressing the Jury persisted in referring to 'Hackney Downs Police Station', thus giving the impression to the Jury sitting in South London, that the police station was situated on the Downs, whereas the only significant building there was the toilets.

In answer to questions by Prosecuting Counsel, Hawkey merely stated that he always hurried when crossing the road and had not informed the officers who stopped him of his 'find', as he didn't trust them. Ignorant of the true nature of the individual they were trying and the numerous previous convictions recorded against him, the Jury were not persuaded and he was found 'Not guilty'.

Hawkey was experienced enough to know that by electing to go for trial, this enable him time to study the prosecution evidence furnished at Committal proceedings. This would not only enable him time to think up a defence, but by putting his fate in the hands of a jury, there was always chance of an acquittal. In later years legislation was to be passed to prevent defendants hijacking prosecutions in this way, by introducing a defence, which the prosecution had no forewarning of and thereby no chance of rebutting with contrary evidence. This is now embodied in the very words of the Caution an officer must give to every person on arrest viz:

'You do not have to say anything. But it may harm your defence if you do not mention when questioned, something which you later rely on in court. Anything you do say may be given in evidence.'

Losing a case like this is very frustrating, but it does serve to make you realise how defendants can pull the wool over jury's eyes and the need therefore to adduce every possible bit of evidence which might help to prove a case. In this particular case we were at least able to reunite the cook with her handbag and it was not long before Hawkey was apprehended again. Before the aforementioned change of legislation, I was however; to experience a similar fate of being ambushed by the defence much later in my career, this time in relation to the rape and murder of a young female.

In the Spring of 1963 after a period of just over two years as an Aide to CID I was successful in passing a Selection Board for permanent appointment to the CID I then had to wait several weeks to find out where I would be posted. Being single I knew I could be posted anywhere in the Metropolis, but thought I might be posted to an adjacent Division. I was totally surprised however, if not a little disappointed, to find that on 17th June I was to join 'L' Division, which was south of the river encompassing the area of Camberwell, Peckham, Clapham, Streatham, Walworth with Headquarters at Brixton where I had begun my Cadet Training.

My biggest regret was that I would be leaving Stoke Newington Section House. In the four years I had resided there, I had made a number of good friends with whom I spent most of my off duty time and Annual Holidays. There was a great sense of camaraderie between us, which I knew I would miss. Little did I realise that fate was to ensure that I continued to spend a great deal of my off duty time in North London.

About ten days before my transfer, at the end of a tour of duty, I went to a local sports ground where some of my friends were involved in a cricket match. After the match we discussed what we were going to do that evening. The choice narrowed down to staying at the sports club for a few drinks; going back to the Section House for a game of darts in our local pub or the third option was going to a party at a flat in Dalston. A flat shared by a couple of nurses we knew from the Metropolitan Hospital.

We decided to give the party a try, as we had not been to a party at this particular flat before. At the party there were a few familiar faces but one particularly attractive young lady, who I had not seen at any of the previous parties, caught my eye. After a few drinks I plucked up the courage to ask her to dance, only for the record player to break down mid dance. Being more confident at mending things than chatting up young ladies, I went over and helped fix a problem with the stylus, meanwhile the young lady re-joined her group of friends, so having fixed the problem I had to make a fresh approach to continue our dance. Like many of the nurses and several former girlfriends, she hailed from Ireland and I learnt her name was Noeleen, on account of her having been born at Christmas. At the end of the evening she accepted my offer of a lift back to the Nurses Home, after which we arranged to meet again. Within a couple of weeks of this meeting, I was transferred to my new posting as a Detective Constable in South London, but distance was to prove no obstacle to pursuing this relationship.

Chapter Six

Detective Constable

Reporting to Commander 'L' Division on 17th June 1963, I leant that I was to be posted to the CID Office at Carter Street Police Station, in Walworth Road S.E.17 near the Elephant and Castle. My living accommodation was to be a room at Nightingale Lane, a modern purpose built Section House in Clapham, facing the common and only a few miles from where my family resided.

On my first visit to the Station I found the CID office to be almost devoid of staff except a typist, as a number of search warrants were being executed that morning and I was to learn this was a regular almost weekly occurrence. After a successful morning the various officers returned with prisoners and a quantity of stolen property and I was gradually introduced to the staff. The Detective Inspector was about to be transferred and was on leave. The First Class Sergeant Ron Andrews, was a very experienced and amiable character, who was to take me under his wing, until I found my feet in my new role as a Crime Investigator, mindful that I had yet to undertake my ten week course at the Detective Training School. As expected there was nobody there that I had met or served with before, but I was to find that they were very much the usual mixes of personalities that one found in any CID Office.

Although I did not know the area well, I was familiar with the busy East Street Market; just across the road from the Police Station, where East Street extended for some half-mile north to the Old Kent Road. As a young boy I had occasionally visited this market on a Sunday morning, with my father when he was seeking to buy leather to repair shoes. A little further along was Manor Place with its well-known Baths, where Henry Cooper and many an aspiring champion, had boxed in past years.

I was to find that my new Sub Division was densely populated with a mix of Victorian mansion blocks, terraced houses and a few post war council flats. It was almost entirely residential, save for shops and public houses and one small green area – Kennington Park on the southernmost boundary, opposite the Oval underground Station, where the home of Surrey County Cricket Club was located on a neighbouring Sub Division. As with most CID offices it was the practice for the Staff to be split into two shifts Early and Late (9am-5pm and 2pm-10pm) alternating day by day, with a separate rota to provide cover at weekends and Leave Days. Officers on late turn invariably working overtime in the mornings, in order deal with their cases under investigation or prepare papers for, or attend court. I soon settled in to the routine of being allocated crimes to investigate rather than the pro-active patrolling duties as an Aid that I had been used to. I was now officially authorised to use my trusty Standard 8 Saloon on duty and paid a small mileage allowance, as the Hillman Estate car provided for the exclusive use of the CID, was shared between about eight detectives and six Aids as well as the DI.

Every CID office was equipped with a Fingerprint kit, which consisted of a wooden box in the style of a large briefcase. These were fitted out with compartments to hold an assortment of fingerprint dusting powders a magnifying glass, measuring tape, tweezers and sample bottles for any small recovered items found when examining the scenes of burglaries. Once instruction in the use of the equipment, had been received from a Fingerprint Officer, it was practice when allocated burglary offences to investigate, to take the fingerprint box, in order to make an examination for any finger impressions left at crime scenes. By today's standards this examination was very rudimentary. Fingermarks, which are made by a sweat deposit from person's hands, were only detectable on hard smooth surfaces. Examinations were therefore confined to glass; glossy painted surfaces such as doors, window frames and any metal or plastic boxes, such as the coin containers of prepayment gas and electricity meters which were very much the norm at that time. Should suitable marks be found they had to be examined by an expert from Scotland Yard's

Fingerprint Branch. Portable items were conveyed to the local police station, whilst marks on fixed items such as doors and windows required not only the attendance of a fingerprint expert, but a photographer from the Yard's Photographic Branch.

During later years I was to see the development of fingerprint recovery, progress, to include the lifting of finger-marks using an adhesive tape, and the use of chemicals to identify marks on porous surfaces, such as paper, a process that was to assist me in a particularly sadistic murder enquiry. Ultimately for crimes of a violent or sexual nature one could call upon the services of a Detective Sergeant attached to the Police Laboratory. He would carry out any examination of a scene or exhibits, but eventually these various functions were to be combined and carried out by civilians, trained to carry out both fingerprint and forensic examinations and employed as Scenes of Crimes Officers (SOCO's) attached to every Sub Division.

The role of an investigating officer has not changed much over the years only the sophistication of the various services that support the investigation. The basics of investigating any crime, amount firstly to establishing that a crime has been committed; then endeavouring to ascertain who was responsible. This can be achieved by taking written statements from any witnesses; preserving any item(s) that might assist in establishing a suspect's identity or proving the facts; thereafter, circulating a description of any identifiable property or suspect, with a view to tracing them; before finally, interviewing such persons and searching their premises, in order to recover any proceeds or evidence to establish guilt or otherwise.

The most prevalent crimes I encountered at Carter Street, were house burglaries, shop breakings and theft of vehicles laden with property. In addition to speaking to the owner of the property and any known witnesses to the offence, it was practice to make enquires at neighbouring premises particularly in the case of burglaries. People, who were unaware that a crime had been committed, could well be possessed of information that might assist. As with any district there were always people who did not want to get involved in helping police whether they had useful information or not. Such persons were often from families where criminality was part of their everyday culture and Carter Street certainly had a preponderance of these.

I recall whilst making enquiries at a particularly infamous mansion block just off East Street, the front door was opened by a young boy aged about 5 and having asked him if mum or dad were in, he yelled over his shoulder "Mum it's the Old Bill at the door". I was a bit taken aback for I had not been to this flat before and I could only presume he drew his conclusion from my appearance, as I had not deemed it necessary to announce my identity to the child. It was in this same street on another occasion whilst driving the CID car with a colleague, we noticed a group of very young boys carrying parts of a bicycle and as we slowed down to speak to them. They swarmed around the car and we became aware that some were endeavouring to remove the hubcaps of our vehicle as we spoke, prompting us to vacate the area as quickly as possible. Another of my colleagues had the misfortune to return to the CID car late one evening after making some enquiries in a nearby public house, only to find a brick had been thrown through the car's windscreen.

Situated a short distance from our Sub Division was the Headquarters of Great Universal Stores a large Mail Order company the forerunner of Argos Stores. They employed a fleet of Green Austin A.35 vans in which their drivers known as tallymen would deliver goods to customers and collect weekly payments for items previously supplied on credit. These little green vans were to be seen everywhere about the manor and it seemed most of the local population were living on tick and those that weren't stealing the vans and selling the goods to their friends and neighbours. Fridays were a particularly busy day as this was pay-day for most people and the tallymen could ensure they were paid something off their customer's accounts, even if no further purchases were made. Consequently it was a busy day for the thieves or 'Van draggers', as they were known in the trade. On one particular Friday, some five tallymen queued at the front counter in the Station Office, waiting to report the theft of their vehicles. Thieves soon leant the various routes and would not be content with just having one van away and seemed to have no difficulty in overcoming the van door locks. Indeed it was not uncommon for a tallyman to see his vehicle being driven off, just as he knocked at a customer's front door, particularly if it was upstairs at flats and mansion blocks.

One afternoon the manager of a petrol station in Kennington Park Road, reported that a small green tally van had been driven onto his forecourt at speed and abandoned, by two men. They had then jumped out and ran off, just as a police car was driving by with its warning bell activated. Simultaneously the owner was reporting its theft from nearby. It transpired that the police Area Car was responding to an emergency call elsewhere, oblivious of the tally van's presence, but this had obviously alarmed the thieves. From time to time arrests were made for such offences, more often than not by the execution of search warrants at the premises of known offenders. Such was the extent of this particular type of crime that there was always a good deal of intelligence to be had arising either from the description of the offenders, or their vehicle, or from their attempts to dispose of the proceeds within the local community.

The other three Detective Constables, Peter Elliott, Dave Hall and Eric Goddard, came back from executing such a search warrant one morning, soon after I arrived at Carter Street and Dave and Eric could not stop laughing. It transpired that Peter Elliott, who already had the nickname 'Pete the feet', presumably on account of his size eleven shoes, had endeavoured to kick in the front door of the premises to be searched. His foot had struck one of the thin panels which split, with the result that his foot went right through, whilst the door held firm. On extricating his foot he realised his shoe was lying in the hallway of the house, where an irate female occupant, was shouting abuse and refusing to open the door, or return the shoe. Pete was left hopping on one foot outside, remonstrating with the occupant through the split panel whilst Dave and Eric fell about laughing at their colleagues predicament. I don't recall whether any stolen property was found on that particular search although Pete did get his shoe back.

In addition to the normal criminal element that resided on, or frequented our manor and that I was to become familiar with, I was warned in the early days of the presence of one major criminal – Charlie Richardson. Charlie with his brother Eddie operated a Scrap Metal Business on the boundary of our Sub Division, but on the neighbouring Camberwell Section. Although our paths were never to cross, he had his finger in many pies and his name came to the fore from time to time. One such occasion was on 8th August 1963, when I answered a phone call from Detective Sergeant Henry Stevens on the Flying Squad. Henry who had served at Carter Street just prior to my arrival was seeking information from our records regarding the criminal associates of the Richardsons. He was a little surprised that we were unaware that a mail train robbery had occurred in the early hours of that morning, at Sears Crossing in Buckinghamshire. The news of what was to be coined 'The Great Train Robbery' with some £2.6 million being stolen from a mail train, had not yet filtered through to those of us investigating more mundane matters.

Whilst details of serious offences or suspects are usually circulated from one police force to another, other than in cases of instant pursuit, it may take some time before clear evidence emerges, regarding the extent of the offence or details of any suspects have been collated. Invariably it is by the medium of National News Media that matters of anything other than local issues become known. A few months later on 22nd November a member of the public hurried into the front office at Carter Street Police Station where I happened to be, to pass on news regarding the assassination of President John F. Kennedy which he had just heard on his car radio. I was both stunned by the news and moved by the considerate act of this unknown man, who felt the need to pass on such news to others and chose to stop at our station in order to do so.

With regard to the Richardsons, they did not feature in the train robbery and the enquiry about them and their associates was purely speculative, at a time when the Flying Squad would have been compiling lists, of organised criminals with a capacity to finance and carry out such a feat. Whilst serving at Stoke Newington I was aware that the Kray brothers and their criminal associates had interests in and frequented, various local clubs and a snooker hall, but only rumour and innuendo prevailed about the alleged controlling influences they had on such establishments. On my arrival at Carter Street, learning about the Richardsons, I did wonder why no one seemed to be doing anything constructive to investigate the activities of such gangs. I was not alone in my thoughts, for the following year in July 1964; there was speculation about the Kray's infamy in various national newspapers, including publication of a photograph of Lord Boothby a former Conservative MP and television celebrity, in the company of the Kray brothers. This resulted in questions to the Home Secretary in the House of Commons, culminating in Detective Inspector Leonard (Nipper) Read, at Commercial Street Police Station, being tasked to set up a covert operation to 'Have a look at the Krays'. Although a subsequent prosecution for matters relating to a protection racket, was to fail after two trials, despite the best efforts of police, it was reassuring for all to know that such people were not beyond investigation.

Then in March 1966 a fatal shooting incident at Mr Smith's Club in Rushey Green, South East London, resulted in the arrest of the Richardson brothers and associates including Mad Frankie Fraser, on charges of affray and murder. A subsequent police enquiry into the various activities of Charlie Richardson was to culminate in what the press dubbed the 'Torture Trial' with a sentence of 25 years being handed out to him. Ironically, the fatal shooting of Dickie Hart at Mr Smith's Club is rumoured to have precipitated, the shooting of George Cornell by Ronnie Kray, (Hart's cousin) in the Blind Beggar public house, a month later. This and other murders ultimately resulted in the eventual downfall of the Krays following a second enquiry into their activities by Nipper Read on his promotion to Detective Superintendent, in 1967. But these events were yet to unfold as I worked as a young Detective Constable learning my trade at Carter Street.

Some local villains also had a lot to learn at that time, as I was to find one morning when called to an overnight breaking which had occurred at an office in the Walworth Road. Explosives had been use to force open a safe, but enough nitro-glycerine had been used, not only to propel the safe door off its hinges but across the office to become embedded into a beautiful antique roll top desk. The entire contents of the safe were consequently blown to smithereens and fragments of banknotes littered the office like confetti. Whoever carried out this crime was clearly inexperienced in the use of explosives, a fact confirmed by Major Don Henderson GM, the Explosives Expert who attended to make the crime scene safe, by identifying and retrieving any explosive residue.

On another occasion I attended the premises of a sausage distribution business in Camberwell Road, where oxyacetylene cutting equipment had been used to cut off the back of a large safe. On this occasion the owner explained that he did not keep anything in it other than a few old ledgers and papers, as the hinges were stiff making it difficult to open and it had not in fact even been locked. Although this proved to be a useless exercise by the would-be thieves, I received a free sample of Purity Brand pork sausages, for my trouble, which proved very tasty. This unfortunately did not occur on the same day as when I visited an elderly gentleman to investigate the theft of some property from his vehicle and as I was leaving he reached into a drawer before holding out his closed hand saying, "Here is a little present for you". Expecting to receive a couple of toffees or suchlike, I held out my hand under his, then found myself holding two new laid eggs which in order not to offend him I felt obliged to take.

Fortunately like anywhere else a good proportion of the community were on the side of law and order and appreciative of our efforts, going out of their way to make you feel welcome. Not least amongst these were some of the landlords of local public houses who welcomed the visits by the local C.I.D or uniform colleagues at the end of their shifts, as a means of exercising a controlling influence on some of their patrons. Public houses were also a useful place to get to know the faces of some of the criminal fraternity, and the Thomas a Becket and the Bricklayers Arms, both in the Old Kent Road were two pubs that were useful in this respect. Both were premises that provided musical entertainment and they were popular haunts of those responsible for van dragging. This would of course work both ways for whilst certain individuals were being surreptitiously identified by my colleagues, I myself was being clocked by the individuals concerned and their associates as the new 'Old Bill' a popular euphemism in that neck of the woods. Indeed it was not unknown for a round of drinks to suddenly appear, courtesy of some cheeky villains in an adjacent bar, seeking to let us know we had been seen and they were feeling flush.

I had not been at Carter Street long before I experienced the pleasure of receiving a telephone call from Fingerprint Department, at New Scotland Yard informing me that they had made identification on some finger impressions I had found at a house burglary. I recalled that the house in question was being redecorated and the painter had left the bottom sash slightly ajar overnight, to allow the paint to dry. The marks in question were on the bottom of the window in fresh paint where the sash had been raised to effect entry and the painter's radio had been the only item stolen. The person identified was a 15 year old youth, who I ascertained lived in a house the rear garden of which, backed on to the rear garden of the premises concerned. The youth had therefore been able to commit this crime without setting foot on the street. I was fortunate that his fingerprints were on record, as juveniles were not routinely fingerprinted on arrest. This was to become a bone of contention in this case because when I arrested the youth, not only did he deny the offence but also his father refused to give the necessary consent, for me to take his son's fingerprints. I needed them to prove the offence, as evidence of them having been taken on a previous case, would be inadmissible at court. This would be tantamount to informing the court he had previously been in trouble, before a verdict was arrived at on the current case. I pointed out to the father that we already had his son's fingerprints on record and parental consent must have been given on a previous occasion, apparently by the boy's mother. The father still refused to cooperate and I was obliged to attend Juvenile Court and request the Court Inspector to make a formal request to the Justices, for an Order for the fingerprints to be taken. Fortunately the Order was granted, to my great relief, for not having encountered the need for exercising this procedure before, it caused me some anxiety as to whether I would be able to prove my case. At the subsequent hearing the youth endeavoured to ambush the prosecution by mentioning for the first time, that he had in the past been requested by a resident to climb in this window and open the front door. This had allegedly been when they had been locked out, thus explaining the presence of his fingerprints. As the window had only been painted the day before the burglary, any marks left on such legitimate entries (had they occurred) would have been destroyed; a point not lost on the Chairmen of the Juvenile Bench who found him guilty of the burglary.

One day whilst in the company of one of my colleagues, Detective Constable Dave Hall who was driving the C.I.D car in Albany Road, I noticed a BMW car containing two men parked outside a house in a side turning as we drove by. Something about it aroused my suspicions and I asked Dave who had not seen it, if we could turn back and have another look at it. As we were returning Dave told me that there was a known Receiver who lived in one of the houses where I had seen the car parked. After a brief period of observation, during which the men remained in the car, it was driven off and we decided to stop it and check out the occupants. The two men were in their mid-twenties, and on the rear seat covered by a blanket we found a stereo system and other items, typical proceeds of a domestic burglary. Not being satisfied, with the conflicting accounts they gave for their movements and possession of the equipment, we arrested them for unlawful possession.

Ultimately the property was identified as the proceeds of a burglary from a house occupied by several schoolteachers, somewhere near Bexley Heath. This resulted in the discovery that the fingerprints of one of our prisoners matched finger impressions left at that scene. This was particularly significant, as he had not previously been arrested and fingerprinted. But for our actions, the offence may have remained undetected. The men were subsequently charged with the burglary offence and in due course convicted at the Inner London Sessions.

In my off duty time I continued to see Noeleen who I had met just before my transfer. She was then a Staff Nurse in the Operating Theatre and was often 'On Call', even when off duty, so could not leave the hospital. If I was off duty early I would drive over and visit her in the Nurses Sitting Room, the only part of the nurses Home where male visitors were allowed, in times when 'Matron' was a figure to be feared. On other occasions she would be off duty, when I was working late, so she would get a bus to Liverpool Street and another to the Walworth Road, so we could meet for a drink as soon as I finished. As a result of an attempted burglary I had met a nice young couple who ran the Canterbury Arms, a modern public house, built to serve a post war housing estate at the quieter end of our manor, near Kennington Park. This was to prove a useful place to take Noeleen away from the more undesirable elements. On other occasions we would visit the Fox public house, opposite the Metropolitan Hospital known as 'A.4. Ward' by the medical staff that frequented there. The licensees at that time, Bert and Tess were an extremely nice couple. As we sat there drinking halves of Red Bull, I would never have anticipated, that I was sitting over the very cellar, where some £6million proceeds of a Security Express Depot Robbery, would be stashed many years later. Or that Flying Squad colleagues and I would be hunting for it and those responsible.

I still kept in touch with my friends from Stoke Newington from time to time and Noeleen and I would occasionally meet up with them at social functions. Soon after leaving the Section House, I heard that my friend Clive Bean, who had devoured my pie, the night I first arrested George Ince, had managed to improve his reputation as a big eater, by consuming 40lb of bananas. This apparently emanated from casual conversation, during which an idle remark by Clive that he liked bananas and could eat lots of them, progressed into a challenge by another resident, which Clive took up. The task having been completed Clive adjourned to a local hostelry for a few pints, meanwhile someone decided to notify the Guinness Book of Records much to Clive's embarrassment.

Nightingale Lane Section House, where I was then living in Clapham, was a modern purpose built building but more impersonal than Stoke Newington, housing a much greater number of officers. As result of the long hours I was working and seeing Noeleen in my off duty time, I never had much more than a passing acquaintance with most residents. I was also now much nearer to my family home in Upper Tooting. A few of the residents were constables at Carter Street so I had more of an affinity with them, as with a few who were C.I.D officers or Aids based at other stations.

In the spring of 1964 some 9 months after my appointment I was finally sent on a course at the Detective Training School, which was then located at Walton Street, Chelsea. I was pleased to learn that a fellow resident Nick Carter, who was based at Brixton, was also attending the same course, so we travelled together alternating between his car and mine. This proved to be ten weeks of intense learning, of various Acts of Parliament covering every aspect of the criminal code. Subjects covered, including larceny; fraud; offences against persons and property; sexual offences; firearms offences; as well as a whole raft of procedures and Judge's past interpretations of these Acts, by way of 'Stated Cases.' All of which was to stand us in good stead in our future careers as detectives.

The careers of both Nick and I were to change a few months after completing our training, as in November that year we were both transferred to the West End of London, to serve on 'C' Division, at West End Central Police Station in Saville Row. There were in fact two separate CID offices known as 'C.D.1.' and 'C.D.2', each responsible for separate areas of the West End. Whilst 1 was posted to 'C.D.1', Nick was to work upstairs in the office of 'C.D.2". It soon became apparent that our moves and those of several other new faces to these offices, had been precipitated by a number of transfers off 'C' Division, following investigations into alleged malpractice's, by a Detective Sergeant Harold Challenor. This officer, who had been responsible for running a Crime Squad, consisting primarily of Aids to CID, had been the subject of a number of complaints that Challenor and his subordinates had planted evidence on them. One particular case had concerned the alleged planting of pieces of brick, involving a number of people accused of possessing offensive weapons. This had, not only resulted in an acquittal of one defendant and charges being dropped against others, but had culminated in Challenor appearing at the Old Bailey, on 4th June 1964, on a charge of corruption. He was however committed to a mental hospital, having been found unfit to plead. Three other officers were found guilty and received sentences of imprisonment. At the end of this trial, Mr Justice Lawton requested that the Commissioner be informed, of his grave disturbance, that Detective Sergeant Challenor was on duty at all, at the time when these offences were committed in July 1963. This was as a result of evidence from doctors when Challenor was arraigned, to the effect that it seems likely that he had been mentally unbalanced for some time. This resulted in what was to become known as 'The Challenor Enquiry', being set up and was ongoing when I arrived at West End Central.

I don't recall being particularly impressed at this transfer, not least because it meant having to re- locate to Trenchard Section House, in Broadwick Street, Soho, adjacent to Berwick Street, where a busy market was held and street parking was not only restricted, but very limited. I leant from other residents that the only suitable unrestricted places to park ones private car were in Regents Park, or Admiralty Arch by Trafalgar Square and I chose the latter. Whilst it was only a five minute walk to Saville Row each morning, I had to traverse the seamy streets of Soho to access the Section House, after parking my car on evenings out.

The staff consisted of about eighteen CID Officers housed in a large open plan office, and split into two shifts each under the supervision of a First Class Sergeant, mine being Jack Candlish, who I found to be an amiable enough character. The only person I had met before was Dave Dixon, one of the other Detective Constables, who had served on the neighbouring 'G' Division Crime Squad, whilst I was Aiding.

I was to find that there was a vast amount of petty crime to deal with, particularly thefts of property from unattended vehicles. With a number of clubs and bars in the Old Compton Street and Wardour Street area, purse and handbag thefts were a common occurrence, as were assaults. Although shoplifters were dealt with by a special unit, many of the shops in places such as Oxford Street, Piccadilly and Regent Street, had a variety of offices located overhead, where unattended valuables, were a target for 'walk in' thieves. Stolen or fraudulent cheques tended in payment for goods were however dealt with by a Divisional 'Cheque Squad'.

At that time my experience of drug related offences, had been confined mainly to small amounts of cannabis. It was an eye opener therefore, for me to find that drug offences were rife. Amphetamine sulphate tablets, blue in colour and known as 'purple hearts', were the most prevalent and readily available in and around the bars and clubs. Whilst many of the drugs arrests, were effected by uniform officers, including Special Constables, as with any arrest for crime, it fell to the lot of the CID to investigate and prosecute the offenders. Persons arrested solely in possession of suspected drugs, were initially interviewed, and then bailed, pending laboratory examination, to confirm the identity of the substance seized. Thereafter the CID officer would consider any offences disclosed, prefer relevant charges and prosecute the case at court. It was just my luck that one of the first such cases dealt with by me, resulted in a telephone call from the police laboratory informing me that the blue tablets submitted, were in fact Aspirin tablets which had been dyed blue, possibly with diluted ink. The person arrested, had admitted buying them outside a local club, in the belief that they were amphetamines, but he had obviously been conned. Since none of my colleagues had experienced anything similar, I sought the advice of Jack Candlish, as to what I should do next. I was relieved when he suggested a charge of 'attempting' to contravene the Drugs (Prevention of Misuse) Act 1964. Having explained the circumstances of this unusual charge to a bemused Mr Babbington the Magistrate at Bow Street Magistrates Court, he was happy to accept the defendant's 'guilty' plea. He did however express the view that with the increasing number of persons coming before him for possessing amphetamines; it was perhaps no surprise that unscrupulous dealers might resort to such underhand tricks.

Getting used to different Magistrates and Court staff and procedures, that a transfer brought about, could be a harrowing experience and this was particularly so with my transfer to West End Central. There being no direct bus route you needed to allow twenty to thirty minutes to walk there through the busy West End Streets. It was also common practice that if an officer on late turn had a case at court and was not giving evidence himself, he would hand the papers over for an early turn officer to deal with. It was not uncommon to be dealing with four or five separate cases and with two courts sitting at the same time, on more than one occasion I found myself still dealing with a case in one court when my presence was required in the other.

One particular type of crime new to me, but peculiar to the West End, arose from the preponderance of 'Clip Joints' around Soho. These premises also known as 'Near Beer Bars' usually comprised of seedy basement areas, posing as clubs. Scantily dressed females stood in the doorway at pavement level, accosting unsuspecting males, in an attempt to entice them into the premises, on the promise of a strip tease act or similar sex show. Having entered the 'club' the men would find themselves seated at a small table with the girl and encouraged to order drinks for both of them. The girls would always order a particular house drink, which was little more than coloured water, but would prove to be particularly expensive. Other girls who visited numerous such premises during an evening invariably performed the floorshow. Whilst waiting for the show to start, within a short space of time an unsuspecting customer could incur a large drinks bill, with no more than a bit of female company to show for it. These clubs employed doormen or 'bouncers' to deal with customers who protested at the amount of their bill, or were unwilling to pay, sometimes giving rise to allegations of assault.

Customers were often led to believe they would experience more than just a 'Strip Tease' resulting in disappointed and often inebriated customers, attending West End Central Police Station to make complaint. There was little that could be done where they had merely been foolish enough to find themselves in a situation where they had to pay exorbitant prices for drink. On some occasions however allegations amounted to, money handed over on a promise of sexual intercourse, which had not materialised. Monies for such services were sometimes handed over on first entering a particular 'Clip Joint', but delaying tactics such as repeatedly ordering more expensive drinks, meant that the customer eventually left whilst he still had his fare home, but his sexual desires unfulfilled. On other occasions girls would take money from customers and arrange to meet them nearby a short while later but fail to keep the appointment. Such allegations if true amounted to offences of 'Obtaining money by false pretences'. Detailed statement would be taken from complainants in order to identify the premises concerned and the name or description of the female involved. Arrangements would then be made for them to attend Bow Street Magistrates Court in order to apply for an arrest warrant.

Many such complainants however, failed to follow up their initial complaint once they had sobered up and thought the matter through, which doubtless encouraged the offences in the first place. The first such allegation I dealt with involved a married man with seven children who had an artificial leg and resided outside of London. He was adamant that he would return to attend court and pursue the matter, but like many before him, changed his mind after his statement had been typed and a warrant prepared.

When I eventually did deal with a complainant who agreed to pursue his allegation, the suspect female turned out to be Maltese, claiming not to speak English, – although she clearly spoke enough to induce my complainant to part with his money. I was then obliged to obtain the services of an interpreter, before proceeding further with the investigation. The girl pleaded 'not guilty' when the case was finally heard at Bow Street Magistrates Court, but was convicted and sentenced to 3 months imprisonment. She decided to appeal, which involved me in yet more paper work, but her appeal was ultimately dismissed. Fortunately for me my time at West End Central dealing with such sordid cases and the many seedy individuals who frequented the Soho area, was to be short lived.

The formation of the Greater London Council, (GLC) which became effective on 1st April 1965, was to see a massive realignment of Divisional Police Boundaries, to become coterminous with local Borough Boundaries. This involved a re-assessment of the various manpower allocations, resulting in numerous inter-divisional transfers. I found that after barely five months service at West End Central, I was to be transferred back to 'N' Division; in particular to Highbury Vale Station in Blackstock Road, a Sectional Station of Holloway Sub Division. This transfer also involved a change of Section House accommodation to Olive House, a modern purpose built building in the Cannonbury area of Islington, with residents parking facilities; such luxury after the restrictions of living in Soho.

This unexpected move could not have been more welcome, as far as I was concerned. Noeleen and I were now engaged and due to marry in July 1965. Olive House was only ten minutes' drive from the nurses home and I was to work in an area I knew reasonably well as it bordered with Stoke Newington Sub Division.

At Highbury Vale I found myself to be one of four Detective Constables whom together with two Aids and two Detective Sergeants were supervised by a 1st Class Sergeant, Bill Thomas, and a dour Welshman, unflappable and in the twilight of his career. I knew one of the Aides, Tony Mills and two of the other D.C.'s Mick O'Neill and Bob Lonkhurst from my previous service on 'N' Division, so I soon settled in and got to know the others – Stan Morten and Vic Allen two long serving and experienced Detective Sergeants.

In February that year I had been successful in passing the Sergeants Examination, aided by a week of my holiday leave, spent on intense study in Trenchard Section House. But with less than two years' service as a Detective Constable, I knew it would be some time before I would be considered as suitable for recommendation for a promotion Selection Board.

With the exception of the Arsenal Football Club which was situated close by, our policing responsibility was mainly over a residential area, with small local shops and some light industry. In addition a few small hotels were situated in the Finsbury Park area of Seven Sisters Road, in close proximity to the infamous Queens Drive, a well-known haunt of prostitutes. All prosecutions were dealt with at North London Magistrate's court, with which I was already familiar and so assisted my settling in with little difficulty.

My workload consisted of a variety of routine investigations making arrests where possible, as well as dealing with the prosecutions of persons arrested by uniform colleagues. During the football season, Arsenal's home games could bring additional work such as thefts from unattended vehicles and assaults between rival fans. A Detective Sergeant normally dealt with the more serious offences, particularly any sexual offences.

This routine was to be broken on Christmas Day 1965, but not in the way that I had anticipated. Noeleen and I having married in July were renting a small-furnished flat on the top floor of a large house in Ashley Road, Holloway. When the Christmas Leave rota was drawn up, I considered myself fortunate to be off on both Christmas Day and Boxing Day and we'd therefore arranged to spend Christmas with my family in Tooting. We'd planned to drive over on Christmas morning in time for lunch, but early that morning I was awakened by the communal telephone, ringing in the hallway downstairs. On answering, I learnt that a man had been murdered the previous night, in Chapel Market, Islington and that my presence was required on a Murder Squad being formed at Kings Cross Police Station. At any other time I would have been excited at the prospects of working on a murder squad, but not Christmas morning. Somewhat stunned by this unwelcome news I went back upstairs to tell Noeleen, she was still in bed but like myself had been disturbed by this early telephone call.

The news that our festive holiday plans were to be ruined by my having to work brought tears to her eyes. We then realised that we only had enough food in the flat for breakfast. I could not dream of leaving her on her own at this time, but realised that if I could get her over to Tooting at least she would have a Christmas Dinner and some company until I got off duty. I returned to the phone and rang the Detective Chief Inspector at Kings Cross, to explain my dilemma. Fortunately he agreed that I could drive her to my parents' home, before reporting for duty at Kings Cross. As Noeleen hastily prepared breakfast, I rang my parents to inform them of the change of circumstances. On our arrival in Tooting my father proffered me a small whisky, saying "Have this son, it might be the only one you'll get today." How right he was. I wished everyone a 'Merry Christmas' and after appeasing my mother, by assuring her that if she plated up my Christmas Dinner, I'd be more than ready for it, at whatever time I was able to return that evening, I set off for Kings Cross.

As with most murders that occur late at night, a small nucleus of local officers, had been summoned from their beds, to deal with the initial investigation at the scene. Thereafter additional officers from local Sub Divisions, like me, were deputed to build up a squad; in order to handle such enquiries as the investigation demanded. Within a short time of my arrival a briefing took place in which I learnt that following an altercation in the Alma public house, Chapel Market, a man had been stabbed outside the premises a short while later and had died of his injuries. A number of statements had already been taken from family and friends who were in the company of the deceased and witnessed events leading up to and culminating in his demise.

It appeared that the initial altercation ensued after a male customer spilt beer near or over a group of men and women, who like many, were celebrating Christmas Eve in this family public house. Subsequently a confrontation had taken place in the street outside. From initial enquiries it appeared that one of the men in the group had tried to attack the man who had spilt beer, but whilst endeavouring to restrain him, one of his own friends had received a fatal knife blow. The suspected offender was however, currently in custody at the station.

This murder had therefore all the signs of being a drink induced tragedy and not unnaturally with the fatal blow having been inflicted by one of the deceased's own friends, the statements taken initially indicated attempts by some, to hide the truth. Despite the confined nature that this enquiry appeared to have, it was still necessary to trace as many witnesses as possible both to the incident in the Alma as well as the actual stabbing.

One of the procedures then, which still pertains today, was that each individual enquiry needed, was recorded as an 'Action' and allocated to an officer to deal. When a witness was traced and a statement obtained, once typed and checked it would not be unusual for four or five further Actions to be raised by the Office manager, (usually an experienced Detective Sergeant), particularly when the names or descriptions of others present at the scene were disclosed. It was also practice to make enquiries at all neighbouring premises and residences in an endeavour to trace potential witnesses. Within a short time of an Incident room being set up, each officer could be handling anything up to ten different Actions.

In this particular enquiry the most urgent Actions were to re interview the small group of people who had been in the company of the deceased for some clearly had made misleading statements already. One of the Actions allocated to myself was to trace the individual who'd spilt beer and with whom the altercation had taken place. This man's name was thought to be 'Barney' or something similar and initial enquiry of the Alma's licensee revealed that he was a casual porter at Covent Garden Market, so he was not going to be traceable over the Christmas Holiday. Vic Allen one of the Detective Sergeants with whom I worked at Highbury, had also been seconded to the murder squad and so working together and having made what enquiries we were able, by 5.30pm we realised we were both starving. Having missed out on a Christmas Dinner and with no canteen open at Kings Cross Police Station, we looked around to see if there was a restaurant open in the area, but to no avail. Our only option was to use the canteen in Mc Naughton Section House, in Euston, which on arrival we found was due to close at 6pm. Egg chips and baked beans was no substitute for a turkey roast, but I wolfed it down in record time and Vic and I then continued with our various enquiries until about 9pm, when we were stood down and told to report back at 8.30am the following morning.

With virtually no traffic on the roads, I arrived at my parent's home a short while later, but in no real mood to enjoy what remained of Christmas Day or the dinner my mother had dutifully kept warm for me on a saucepan of boiling water. The congealed gravy at the edge of the plate indicated that my arrival had been hoped for sooner. Naturally Noeleen and my family wanted to know all about the Murder. There was however little satisfaction in outlining details of how a man had died through the drink induced actions of one of his friends, particularly when this act of stupidity had already spoilt Christmas for so many.

With the person responsible for this murder having been in custody prior to my arrival on the squad, all enquiries that followed were centred on preserving evidence and tracing witnesses, both to the stabbing and the beer spilling incident in the Alma, which precipitated it. In order to trace the man 'Barney' Vic and I were obliged to visit Covent Garden market at around 6am for several mornings before we were finally successful. Once the Christmas Holiday had passed, being on the murder enquiry team made a pleasant change from normal duties and the experience gained particularly regarding the management of such an enquiry was to prove useful for my future.

After a few weeks, when most of the enquiries had been completed and all potential witnesses had been traced and statements obtained, the enquiry team was reduced to a few local officers. These would be involved in preparing a report for the Director of Public Prosecutions (D.P.P.), who would ultimately brief Counsel to prosecute the case at Trial.

I returned to normal duty at Highbury Vale, but having recently been successful on a Promotion Selection Board, I was awaiting a promotion to Detective Sergeant. In February 1966 I received a telephone call from Detective Sergeant Ron Ace, who I'd worked with at St. Ann's Road. He was now the First Class Sergeant in charge there, (although St. Ann's Road had been moved from 'N' to 'Y' Division during the formation of the

G.L.C.). Ron told me that I was in a Draft Police Order, to transfer to 'Y' Division at the end of the month on promotion to Detective Sergeant. He then asked me if I would be interested in returning to St. Ann's Road, as a vacancy existed for a D.S. I was both pleased at the news that I was moving to 'Y' and that someone of the calibre of Ron Ace wanted me to work with him. I had no hesitation in accepting his offer.

Chapter Seven

Detective Sergeant

On 28th February 1966 after a brief meeting with the Commander of 'Y' Division and my new Detective Superintendent, Sid Bradbury, at Wood Green Divisional headquarters, I reported to Detective Inspector Southeard at Hornsey Police Station. He confirmed that I was to be attached to St. Ann's Road, which as a result of the boundary changes of 1965, had become a Sectional Station of Hornsey Sub Division. As he had one of his Detective Sergeants suspended from duty, however, I was to be based at Hornsey for a few weeks, until the position was ratified. This meant I would have the chance to get to know other colleagues on the Sub Division and have an even shorter journey to work, so I had no qualms with this arrangement. The only staff I knew at Hornsey were Ron Dickinson the First Class Sergeant who I'd met at Holloway, and Bob Green, one of the DC's who had been a fellow player in the 'N' Division rugby team.

I had been at Hornsey only a few weeks when I was rostered to work a weekend. On the Sunday afternoon, I was alone in the CID Office, writing up details of investigations in the Crime Book, when two uniform officers came up and asked if they might borrow the CID car, for a job. One of them, John Denney, explained that there had been a series of indecent assaults on women, in and around Haringey Passage, a pedestrian footpath between houses, in the roads leading from Wightman Road to Green Lanes. He'd just seen a man answering the description of the suspect in that vicinity. A Photo-Fit impression of the suspect was on display in the CID Office, so I was aware of these offences, which involved the suspect grabbing women's breasts, or placing his had under their skirts, whilst they were walking in the street. John and his colleague had obtained the duty officer's permission, to don civilian jackets over their uniform shirts and trousers, to keep observation on the suspect, but whilst admiring their keenness, I knew they would have a limited chance of not being recognized as police, even in the CID car. As the suspect was in the vicinity where offences had been committed the objective was to try and catch him in the act, or at least gain supporting evidence as to his activities before attempting to effect an arrest.

I told them I would accompany them, as being in plain clothes, I would be able to watch the suspect on foot, if necessary, whilst they remained in the car at a discreet distance. John drove us to the area where the suspect had been spotted and within a matter of minutes John pointed out the suspect, as he crossed the road ahead of us. The suspect was a well-built man in his late twenties, fairly smartly dressed with a collar and tie, but one distinctive feature was his pock marked face. Having observed the suspect, I could see he bore a strong resemblance to the Photo Fit impression, I had taken with me. There were no women pedestrians in the area and our suspect after looking around him entered Haringey Passage, a footpath leading to adjacent roads. I directed the two PCs to drive to the next road so they could observe the suspect when he emerged from the passage and told them I would walk along the passage at a discreet distance to try and observe him lest any offences occurred on the footpath. I found the passage to be a narrow walkway meandering between the houses but with no clear view through to the next road. Halfway along I discovered that another narrower pathway crossed the passage, at right angles and this provided rear access to the gardens of the houses.

Our suspect reached the next road without incident and having paused to look around, him crossed over and continued along Haringey Passage. We repeated the operation with the two PCs driving to the next road, but our suspect again crossed over and re- entered the Passage. I then spoke with the two PCs who drove up to liaise with me and found that the distance they had to drive to get from one road to the next, meant the suspect was half way across the road when they arrived. I suggested they drive two turnings along and watch the exit from the Passageway whilst I continued on foot behind the suspect.

I re-entered the Passage, at a discreet distance behind the suspect, who was by then not in view. On reaching the intersection with the rear access pathway, I slowed to peer round lest our suspect had deviated from the main passage. Suddenly I received a violent punch, to the side of my face. I realized the suspect must have been standing in the intersecting pathway, conscious that someone was approaching or following him. Stunned by the weight behind the punch, I managed to grab hold of the suspect's coat, as he attempted to run past me. He immediately reined further heavy blows at my head and I had no hesitation in fighting back, but having let go his jacket, to fend off his attack and throw a few punches of my own, he started to run off again. I ran a few paces and grabbed his arm, which in an ideal situation I would have put in an arm lock. I found however, that he was heavier and stronger than I was, and as I attempted to restrain him he had no hesitation in punching and kicking at me, in a violent manner.

At some stage in the proceedings I shouted out that I was a Police Office but this had no effect and may have made him more determined to escape. During the struggle he wriggled from the jacket I was holding and I instinctively grabbed hold of his necktie. I received further punches to the face, as I held his tie, trying to grab his arm. Unfortunately, he had the advantage of being able to punch me with both fists, whilst I had to maintain my grip on his tie to prevent his escape. With my free right hand I managed to throw a few punches at him and one punch struck him in the face with such force, that the necktie broke at the side of the collar, leaving me holding it in one hand with the knot still intact. Whether from the force of my blow or his endeavours to pull away from my grip, losing his necktie threw him off balance and he fell back against a wooden gate, which gave way, under his weight. We grappled further, on the ground whilst I tried to get him into an arm lock, during which time I could smell that he had defecated in his trousers, but he was too powerful for me and by now, I was both breathless and exhausted. The suspect finally ran back down the passage, in the direction he had come from, but I was too exhausted to follow. My clothes were torn and soiled from our struggle on the floor my face was bruised and bleeding and my watch was missing, but I still had the suspect's jacket.

He was barely out of my sight before the local Area Car crew arrived, in response to an emergency call of 'Men fighting'; the call having been made by the occupants of the house, whose gate we'd demolished. They were followed by John Denney and his colleague, who had been unfortunately been too far away to hear the disturbance and with no means of communicating with me, had rightly held back, not wishing to compromise my observation.

Between us we trawled the locality, but without trace of the suspect and ultimately P.C. Terry Southwell, the Area Car driver insisted on taking me to the local hospital for a check-up. There were no broken bones, but I was in no fit state to resume duty that day. Fortunately the jacket contained a pocket diary, bearing the name of James Douglas, with a nearby address and whilst I was being treated at the hospital, officers sought the assistance of one of my colleagues Det. Sgt Cyril Rodwell who was off duty, but resided locally. He visited the suspect's address with other officers and was advised by a heavily pregnant Mrs. Douglas, that her husband had not returned home after going out for a walk.

Later that evening Terry Southwell and the Area Car crew visited me at my flat in Hornsey to inform me that Douglas a 28 year old meat porter, had attended St. Ann's Road Police Station, with his father and given himself up. He like myself bore all the hallmarks of having been involved in a 'prize fight' and had sustained a fractured cheekbone and sprained wrist. More importantly, he had confessed to three case of indecent assault, when interviewed by Cyril Rodwell.

He subsequently appeared at Highgate Magistrates court and pleaded 'guilty'' to assault on police and three case of indecent assault. His solicitor made great play of his being a man of previous good character, who was experiencing matrimonial difficulties and whose wife was expecting a child. This coupled with the fact that he had himself received injuries, had given himself up and admitted the offences, resulted in him being fined £25 and placed on probation for 3 years. Mr. Derek Johnson Deputy Chairman at Highgate Court, also commended me and I later received a Commendation from Commander 2 Area, for 'determination and courage' resulting in the arrest of Douglas.

Some three months were to elapse before I finally began to work at St. Ann's Road, by which time I had become familiar with all the staff at Hornsey and now had to get to know my new colleagues. Apart from Ron Ace the First Class Sergeant and Margaret Smith the typist, who had first commenced work there whilst I was an Aide, I knew no one. I was however to form a good working relationship and lasting friendship, with my new colleagues and enjoy the next few years of my service, working with Mick Strapp the other Second Class Sergeant and Detective Constables, Brian Goddard, Roger Moulds and Harry Davies.

After a few months I was fortunate to get a posting to the Divisional Q-Car. One afternoon, whilst at Stoke Newington dealing with some prisoners, Arthur King one of the Area Car Drivers, informed me that he had just heard on the police radio that there had just been a shooting incident involving a Q-Car crew on 'F' Division. The date was 12th August 1966 and as news of the event unfolded, it became apparent that all three police officers attached to the 'F' Division 'Q' Car call sign, 'Foxtrot 11', had been shot dead. It was a Crime so horrendous and unprecedented that it defied belief.

I hurried home after my tour of duty in order to catch the news on television, still shocked with disbelief that this could have happened. When the news bulletin displayed service photographs, of the fallen officers, I received a further shock, one of them, Detective Sergeant Chris Head, was not only known to me, he had been a fellow resident in Trenchard Section House, where we had occasionally dined together. He had been a D.C. at Tottenham Court Road, on 'C' Division, whilst I served at West End Central. The other two officers were, P.C Dave Wombwell an Aide to C.I.D. and the driver P.C. Geoffrey Fox. Whilst shocked and saddened at the incident, I had not anticipated, knowing any 'F" Division officers personally, but like myself, Chris had been promoted and transferred from 'C' Division and ultimately, found himself posted to Q-Car duties on 'Foxtrot 11'.

The incident had occurred at 3.30pm in Braybrook Street, Shepherds Bush, and a road bordering the grounds of Wormwood Scrubs Prison. The crew of the Q-Car had stopped a blue Standard Vanguard saloon, containing three men, whose movements had apparently aroused their suspicions. The occupants of the vehicle were, James Witney, the driver; seated alongside him, was Henry Roberts; whilst in the rear passenger seat, was Jeff Duddy. Unbeknown to the officers, Roberts was armed with a handgun; two other weapons were in a bag next to Duddy. The three men had in fact been planning an armed robbery and were looking to steal a further vehicle, until the unfortunate intervention of the Q-Car crew.

It transpired, that having stopped the vehicle; Geoff Fox remained at the wheel of the Q-Car, whilst Chris Head and Dave Wombwell spoke to Witney and Roberts. Then, whilst Dave Wombwell recorded their details in his notebook, Chris Head turned his attention to Duddy, asking him about the contents of the bag. Suddenly, without warning, Roberts shot Dave Wombwell in the head with a luger pistol. As he fell, a second shot was fired and as Chris Head ran for cover behind the police car, he was mortally wounded by a third shot. Then, as P.C. Geoff Fox attempted to reverse the police car at them, he too, fell victim to shots fired by both Roberts and Duddy, before the three suspects made good their escape, in the Standard Vanguard.

Duddy and Witney were arrested in a matter of days, but Roberts went on the run. Such was the publicity and public abhorrence at this dreadful crime that the whole nation was looking for him. Possible sightings of Roberts, were reported everywhere. Whilst posted to Q-Car duties, my crew and I responded to numerous emergency calls, regarding possible sightings of Roberts, but all proved abortive. He was eventually arrested and together with his two associates, was subsequently convicted of these dreadful murders and sentenced to life imprisonment.

Public outrage and sympathy, for the families and dependants of the three officers, resulted in many spontaneous financial gestures; so much so, that the traditional 'Police Widows and Orphans' collection boxes, affixed to the front counter at every police station, proved inadequate. This was particularly so at Shepherds Bush Station, where it became necessary to empty the box, several times daily. The generosity of the British public emanating from this tragedy and their desire to support the officers' families gave rise to the formation, of the 'Police Dependants Trust'.

This horrendous crime also acted as a 'wake up' call to the Metropolitan Police and possibly a number of other forces; with regard to how ill equipped they were, to deal with the increased use of firearms by offenders. Police issue firearms and ammunition, were kept locked in the Station Office Safe at every Police Station and if a situation arose, where it was necessary to deal with an armed criminal, an Inspector could authorize issue of weapons, to authorized personnel. Whilst there should have been a number of officers at each Station, who had undergone firearms training and become, 'Authorized Firearms Officers', absence of officers due to, leave rotas; transfers to other Divisions; and retirements, had created an imbalance or dearth of authorized firearms officers.

Initially a programme was introduced to ensure that at least one CID Officer, at every Sub-Division, was an authorised firearms officer, in addition to existing authorisations, of uniform officers. As a consequence of this, I found myself nominated to attend firearms training at Enfield Small Arms Factory. This training was conducted by a uniform Inspector and involved familiarisation with the .38 Smith and Wesson revolver used by the force, including method of loading; instruction on the law and force regulations regarding drawing and using the weapon and finally discharging about ten single rounds at a target. This very basic training did little to inspire me with any great confidence regarding my future use of the weapon.

The Metropolitan Police was however, in the process of establishing a specialist Firearms Department. I was therefore, subsequently, to witness, firearms training undergoing a complete reorganisation, with vast improvements to facilities, on the

AN APPETITE FOR CRIME

frequent refresher courses that I undertook throughout my service.

During my six week posting to the 'N' Division Q-Car, there was one case that I became involved in that was particularly satisfying, this also involved three active criminals, but of a lower league than Roberts Duddy and Witney. For some weeks, 'Y' Division had experienced a number of night-time smash and grab raids at electrical retailers. On several instances a dark E-type Jaguar car, had been seen involved or seen speeding away from the area, but without the registration number being noted by anyone. There had been cases at Enfield, Wood Green, Muswell Hill and Haringey, with televisions and other electrical goods being stolen in the early hours of the morning. One evening I received a call to contact Det. Sgt Alec Eist, who was based at Wood Green and was the Divisional 'Night Duty CID Officer', that week. I knew Alec, as he and I had attended the same evening classes at Vallance Road School, some years previous, whilst studying to pass the Higher Civil Service Examination, a pre-requisite at that time, to sitting the 1st Class Sergeants Examination.

Prior to his posting to Wood Green, Alec Eist had served on the Flying Squad, where he acquired a considerable reputation as a thief taker. He was known as an officer who cultivated good informants, resulting in the arrest of some very active and professional villains, often as a result of information received from one of his 'Snouts'. It was no surprise therefore when Alec told me he had received information, that the men responsible for the smash and grabs, occupied two flats in a house in Park Avenue, Wood Green. He had obtained a search warrant for these premises, but in view of the frequency with which offences were being committed, he wanted the assistance of the Q-Car. This was in order to stake out the premises, during the times when the raids were being effected – usually between midnight and 1 am, – with a view to catching the raiders red handed. We carried out this operation for several nights without any offences being reported, but on the third night our luck was in. A message came over the police radio of a smash and grab at an electrical shop in the Highgate area. A short while later from our vantage point parked further down the road, we saw a car drive up to the suspect house and through the darkness it was apparent that property was being carried into the house. Alec who was parked up with his crew the other side of the location, radioed that the time for right to execute the Search Warrant and we duly raided the premises. The two flats occupied by the suspects and their girlfriends, were stacked with televisions and assorted electrical appliances. We arrested and after lengthy questioning, later charged, three men, who acting in pairs had been responsible for the series of burglaries using the E-type Jaguar, which had also been stolen.

When Alec had first told me he'd received information about the men responsible for the smash and grabs, I presumed this was from one of his established Informants. The identity of 'Informants' is always closely guarded, usually only known to one or two officers, so I had not questioned Alec about the origin of his information. It was only whilst having a drink with Alec, following the conviction of the three men at Middlesex Guild Hall that he mentioned that his information had come from an elderly female tenant at the same address. She had phoned Wood Green Police Station, to complain about the nocturnal habits of her fellow tenants. She was later to receive a 'Letter of Thanks' and a small reward from the local Commander, who also commended Alec and the other officers and I involved, for 'Determination and team work resulting in the arrest of three persistent breakers'.

Criminal Records Department at Scotland Yard, maintained not only details of all previous convictions of offenders, but albums of their photographs. One section of this department, known as 'Method Index', compiled and maintained records of individuals, who regularly committed crimes using a similar method. As many burglars just use brute force to gain entry to premises, an index of this method would be so vast as to be of little use to an investigating officer. Certain criminals however, use cunning and guile to gain entry to premises, by tricking the occupants into letting them in and then stealing property. Typical of this is persons posing as water board officials, or gas or electricity suppliers, who mainly prey on the elderly. Such offences were known as 'Burglary by Artifice' and Method Index would collate details of offences and suspects, in order to link them with known offenders, or persons arrested in the future, using similar methods.

It was however a young schoolgirl who answered the door of a house in Eastbourne Road, N.15 to be confronted by two coloured men, that was to be my first witness in a case of burglary by artifice. This young girl, a child of mixed race had been persuaded by the men that they were friends of her mother and talked her into letting them in, whilst her mother was out. Whilst one kept her talking the other busied himself looking around for anything of value he could steal. Although deceived by the men, she was a particularly bright and able to give a good description of the two suspects. As there had not been reports of similar crimes locally, I decided to consult 'Method Index', by phone rather than just submitting the descriptive forms of the suspect to them, and I was given details of a possible suspect. His Criminal Record File was duly forwarded to me containing his photograph. I then needed the witness to view the photograph to see if any identification was possible.

Strict rules apply to the manner in which photographs of suspects, are viewed by potential witnesses. A single photograph is never shown on its own, but has to be shown with others of similar age and appearance, much like an identification parade. In order to comply with this practice, I needed a number of other photographs of young coloured men. 'Book 15' was a loose-leaf binder containing a brief record and photographs, of all local, active criminals. The CID staff maintained it at that time, prior to the introduction of Collators. Once photographs were updated in the binder, the old ones were kept together and could be useful to make up a selection, to be shown, along with a suspect's photograph, to witnesses.

Finding myself short of suitable photographs to make up the requisite number, I perused the Book 15 and found two photographs of coloured men that were of similar age to my suspect. I borrowed these from the Book, and to my surprise, when my young witness viewed the group of photographs – which included the suspect's one, supplied by Method Index – she identified an individual whose photograph I had borrowed from Book 15. The girl was very positive and not knowing the individual, I returned to the Station to find out more. I then learnt his last known address had been in Daleview Road, just a short distance from the venue of the offence. My new suspect had various convictions, but none for 'Burglary by artifice'. I rang Criminal Records Office to draw his file and was informed that he had recently been arrested and was due to appear in custody at Stratford Magistrates Court the following Saturday.

Despite the fact that a photographic 'Identification' may have been made by a witness, unless a suspect admits the offence when arrested, he must be placed on an Identification Parade – if he consents. This is to test the witness, particularly as the appearance of some individuals may have changed considerably since their photograph was taken, when last convicted. Having liaised with the officer dealing with my suspect and the Court Inspector, I arranged for an Identification Parade to take place at Stratford Magistrates Court. When the young girl was introduced to the parade she walked up and down looking at the participants, as instructed by the Court Inspector, she then pointed out the suspect, whose photo she had previously identified. Later, when taking a further statement from her, regarding this identification, the girl remarked, "I recognised the man as soon as I entered the room, but I thought I'd better walk up and down and look at the others, like the Inspector told me."

Doubtless she would have made an impressive witness at trial, but she was spared any further court attendance, as the suspect admitted his part in the offence, when I interviewed him after the parade and eventually pleaded 'guilty' to this offence of burglary.

Adjacent to Eastbourne Road was Paignton Road, where I was called one day by an anxious mother, who had become concerned that her young son, who was aged about eight, might have been the victim of an indecent assault. This woman an unmarried mother, lived with her son in the first floor flat.

A middle-aged man, living on his own, who she knew as John, occupied the ground floor flat. There was a communal front door to the premises and over a period of time the young boy had been befriended by John and allowed to visit his flat and watch television with him. Her suspicions were aroused when she went to collect her son one evening and found him sitting on John's lap. As the child got up, she noticed John's trousers were undone at the front. She was aware that her son sometime sat on John's lap, but had had no reason to suspect anything untoward up until this time. She subsequently questioned her son as to whether John had ever touched him in any inappropriate way, and finding that he had fondled his private parts, she reported the matter to police.

I interviewed the boy in his mother's presence and he reiterated the fact that John had sometimes placed his hand up the leg of his short trousers and touched his private parts. Fortunately this act of indecency did not appear to have gone any further than that, but after taking detailed statements, from the boy and his mother, I arranged for the boy to be medically examined, by our Divisional Police Surgeon, who found no evidence of other physical abuse. Typical of young boys who fall prey to this type of abuse, the child welcomed the freedom to visit his neighbours flat, to be given sweets and attention, that might have not have been so readily forthcoming in his own home. He had therefore, not mentioned anything to his mother, concerning John's behaviour, knowing this would curtail any future visits.

I obtained a detailed description of John, from the mother, who confirmed that his surname was Carter, there was however, no trace of him in our local records. I therefore consulted Criminal Records Office, at New Scotland Yard, to find that he appeared identical with a John Michael Charter, who had a string of previous convictions for indecent assault and buggery, for which he had served numerous terms of imprisonment. Having obtained his Criminal Record File, I was horrified to think that someone of this pedigree had been living on our manor, without police knowing. I recall that most of his previous offences had been committed in the provinces.

I arrested Charter, who whilst admitting to having the string of previous convictions for various indecency offences, strongly denied having been up to his old tricks with regard to his neighbour's young son. A search of his premises did not reveal anything that could be considered of any evidential value regarding this allegation. He did not deny that he was fond of the child, who he claimed on some occasions had climbed on his lap uninvited, whilst watching television. He knew as well as I did, that it was his word against that of the boy, unless there were any witnesses. The only evidence tending to support the boy's allegation, was the occasion when his mother saw John's trousers undone whilst the boy had been on his lap. Questioned about this he denied knowledge of such an occasion, claiming, had she seen such a thing it could only have been because he had accidentally forgotten to button his fly.

My dilemma was that because of the boy's age, I knew it would be a matter for a Judge's discretion as to whether he would allow the child to give evidence on oath. He was old enough, but of an age where it would be up to the Judge to question the boy and satisfy himself that the child knew what 'promising to tell the truth' meant, before allowing him to take some form of oath. Even then the law as defined in previous 'Stated Cases', required some corroboration, for it had been held, that, if the only evidence against an accused person was the uncorroborated evidence of an 'unsworn' child, the jury must be directed to acquit. I could not let Charter get away with what he had been doing. I decided to charge him with Indecent Assault on the boy, relying on his mother's evidence and his interview with myself to provide corroboration, if the Judge agreed that the boy could give sworn evidence at trial.

Charter was charged and subsequently remanded in custody at Tottenham Magistrates Court, whilst I submitted a report to the Metropolitan Police Solicitors Branch, for legal representation. Having read my report and considered the evidence, one of the solicitors rang me to discuss the case, expressing the view that they were unsure whether the prosecution should be continued in view of the boy's age and the uncertainty of whether he could give sworn evidence. I explained that I had considered this, but felt that we should not 'second guess' what decision a Judge might take regarding the boy's competence to give sworn evidence and should therefore proceed with, a Committal for trial. He reluctantly agreed to seek Counsel's advice and in due course, the case was committed for trial to Middlesex Crown Court.

On the day of the trial, after details of the case had been outlined to the Judge, the boy was called into Court. The Judge removed his wig and spoke with the child asking him questions as to whether he believed in God and understood what promising to tell the truth meant and so forth, finally deciding that he would allow the boy to give sworn evidence. Following a brief discussion between Defence Counsel and his client, I was both surprised and relieved, to learn that Charter now intended to plead 'Guilty'. I believe his genuine fondness for the boy must have played a part in his coming to this decision. Charter would have known, however, that had the child been required to give evidence and the case been proved, in view of his past record, the sentence of imprisonment, passed by the Judge, could have been substantially increased, for putting the child through such trauma. I was particularly pleased at the outcome of this case, as I felt it fully justified my insistence on pursuing this prosecution. Had I not charged Charter but referred the matter to Solicitors Department for directions, the case might not have been brought.

Whilst appreciating the need for caution before accepting the word of a child in criminal proceedings, I learnt that children were often a lot more attentive to detail, than some of their elders. A particular instance came to light whilst investigating an armed robbery at St. Ann's Road.

The offence took place one weekday lunchtime, when the sub postmistress of a small post office in St. Ann's Road, locked her premises to go home for lunch. Crossing the busy Seven Sisters Road, she only had a short distance to walk to Plevna Crescent, where she lived, a journey taking no more than five minutes. Whilst preparing her lunch she answered a knock at the front door, to be confronted by three men dressed in white painter's overalls. Forcing their way into her home the men threatened her with a knife and demanded the keys to the post office. She was then tied to a chair and guarded by one of their number, whilst the other two left with the keys, which they used to burgle the post office. Once the burglary was completed, a phone call was made to the house and the postmistress was released and left in a state of shock, by the third man who made good his escape.

This offence was investigated by Mick Strapp and me, and during the course of our enquiry we made house to house enquiries, at other premises in Plevna Crescent, looking for potential witnesses. Taking one side of the road each, we called at each house. I did trace one witness a builder who had noticed some men in painter's overalls passing by. He'd thought something was a bit odd, as their overalls seemed too clean, but thought no more of it until spoken to by me. It was however, a thirteen-year-old schoolgirl who proved the most useful witness. She lived about ten doors further along from the sub postmistress and although she was unaware of what had occurred, until spoken to by me, she was a witness. She told me that having come home from school for her lunch, she was sitting by a first floor window, doing her school homework, when she saw some men in white overalls. One of the men was in a saloon car and the other two were talking to the driver through the car window, in the roadway outside her house. She thought the men looked a bit suspicious, as they were looking around them and were strangers to the road.

She was able to give a good description of two of the men and described the car as having a bonnet that sloped down. Having made notes of her description I thanked her and as I was leaving I said, "You didn't happen to notice any of the letters or numbers on the index plate, did you?" and to my surprise she replied, "Oh yes, I wrote the number down on my maths book cover."

Had I not asked that question, the identity of the car may have not have been traced, for she appeared to have forgotten this important detail until prompted by me. The vehicle, a Jaguar saloon, had been reported stolen, but was located the following day, having been abandoned in front of some lock-up garages in Lordship Park, Stoke Newington. Unfortunately the perpetrators of this robbery were never identified, but the details this young schoolgirl was able to give, was a salutary lesson, in the value of making extensive house to house enquiries, in respect of any crime. It was an example I was to quote, on many future occasions, when training young, 'would be' detectives, in the art of crime investigation.

Plevna Crescent was also home to a man who had numerous criminal convictions for a variety of offences mainly relating to burglary. Although not known to me personally, I was familiar with his photograph and past record as he featured on one of the pages of our 'Book 15', the Record of Local Criminals. This individual was at that time in his fifties, but as some years had elapsed since his last arrest, I recall discussing him and similar individuals with my CID colleagues and musing as to what age criminals finally give up their criminal habits.

Ironically a few months later one of the more active PC's Frank Humm, came up to the CID Office and sought my advice about this very individual. Frank like me was familiar with his record and seeing him in Seven Sisters Road during the early hours of one morning, decided to keep an eye on him. Being in uniform this was difficult to do without being noticed and whilst walking at a discreet distance behind him, the officer saw him appear to throw something over a wall as he passed. He subsequently stopped the man who denied having thrown anything and said he was just out walking as he was unable to sleep. He was allowed to continue on his way, but Frank with the assistance of some colleagues later returned to the area where he thought he had seen something thrown and in a yard behind the wall located a cloth bundle, which contained a jemmy and other tools.

Together with a colleague I went and interviewed the suspect who did not seem surprised at our visit. As a result of questioning he admitted having thrown the tools away when realising he was being watched by a Police Officer, and he was duly charged with 'possessing house breaking implements by night'.

On another occasion a young Probationer P.C. came into the CID Office seeking my assistance. This officer. who shall remain nameless, told me that whilst patrolling in Woodlands Park Road, he had entered an area known as Rowley's coach yard, which housed various lockup workshops and provided parking for a number of coaches and other vehicles. In the yard he had seen a man who was in the process of burning off, the outer covering of some lengths of heavy duty copper cable. The usual reason for this practice was to enable the cable to be sold, as scrap copper, which fetched a high price at local scrap yards, so reports of thefts of such cable from road works and building sites were not uncommon.

"Where did he say it had come from?" I enquired.

"Oh, I didn't speak to him, I know you are good at interviewing people and as I knew you were in the Station I thought I'd come and tell you." The officer replied.

Had I not been so flabbergasted, I might have been flattered by this reply.

"The only reason I might be good at interviewing people, is that when I was walking around these streets in uniform like you, if I was suspicious of anything I poked my nose in and started asking questions." I retorted, still not believing what I had just heard. Dropping what I was doing, I drove the half mile to Rowley's Yard with the officer, whilst advising him on how to approach such a situation in the future. It was no surprise however, that all that was to be found at the yard was the burnt remains of the cable covering.

This young officer a somewhat frail looking individual, by comparison with his colleagues, clearly lacked a bit of self-confidence, despite having over nine month's service. He was however conscientious which in my book was perhaps more important, as I knew he would gradually acquire more confidence as he gained experience. I could still recall how vulnerable I had felt when I first stepped out of the station on my own in uniform, but it had not lasted more than a few days probably because I was more self-confident. In time I learnt that the mere wearing of an uniform, gives a police officer an edge over the wrong doer and whilst some individuals can be devious or offensive when spoken too, many offenders particularly first time offenders, readily admit their guilt. Even career criminals can be pleasant to converse with, possessing a sense of humour and treating their being arrested from time to time, as an inevitable consequence of their chosen way of life.

An example of this came to my notice one morning, at Tottenham Magistrates Court, when I was dealing with two men who had been arrested overnight for breaking and entering the factory premises of Courtney Popes, a shop-fitting company, with extensive premises in Vale Road. One of the prisoners told me, that having forced their way into a workshop, they were looking for something to steal, when they became aware that police officers were searching the yard outside. They decided to hide under a work bench, but realising it was only a matter of time before they were discovered, they had tossed a coin to see which one of them should walk out and give himself up, in the hope that the other, would remain undetected. Unfortunately for them P.C. Humm had earlier seen 'two' men, climbing over the perimeter fence, whilst patrolling on his Noddy bike, so when one surrendered, the search continued until his accomplice was located.

One of the more serious cases that I investigated at St. Ann's Road involved a pair of professional criminals, Maurice West and MartinCornwall. These two men armed themselves with a sawn off shotgun, in order to carry out a robbery at the Midland Bank, situated at 33, Grand Parade, Green Lanes, Haringey. Having threatened the staff with the shotgun, the two men, their faces concealed with black balaclavas stole some £1,500 in cash and then attempted to make good their escape in an Austin mini saloon, previously stolen from Woodford, which they presumably thought would be ideal to manoeuvre in traffic. Unfortunately for them, the engine failed to start. The owner was later to tell me that it had a faulty petrol pump, which played up from time to time and she was in the habit of hitting in with a stick to get it working. This was to prove the downfall of the two robbers; for having failed to start their 'get away' vehicle, they were obliged to abandon it and decamp on foot down Chesterfield Gardens where the vehicle had been parked. Whilst so doing, one of them threw the sawn off shotgun into a front garden where it immediately discharged, drawing further attention to the pair of them. On reaching the junction with Warwick Gardens they ran across the road and into a block of council, lock-up garages, which happened to be in the process of being re-decorated. An elderly decorator was bent over busily painting one of the doors, but had left a ladder propped against the boundary wall, which abutted the grounds of St. Ann's Road Hospital. West, seeing the ladder ran to it climbed up and disappeared over the wall much to the surprise of the painter. He was immediately followed by Cornwall who called out to the painter "Don't worry mate, I'll catch the bastard," whereupon he also ran up the ladder and jumped down into the grounds of the hospital. Various police units attended the scene and searched the surrounding streets for the two suspects and any witnesses.

West having made his way to the far side of the hospital grounds, some half mile away, was next seen as he scrambled down a railway embankment alongside a bridge, onto the footway of Hermitage Road and ran into a nearby block of flats. His actions were observed by a woman, whose suspicions were aroused, by having just previously seen and heard a lot of police vehicle activity in the area. Fortunately, the spot where West appeared, was in fact only some two hundred yards from the rear of St Ann's Road Police Station where the Police, District Transport Garage for 3 area (D.T.3) was also located. This witness hurried down Hermitage Road and into the Garage Office where she informed an officer of what she had seen. It was in fact the Sergeant in charge of this Traffic Patrol Garage that she spoke to, P.S. Archibald, and an officer who would not normally be operationally involved in crime matters. Archie, as he was known to all, jumped into a police car and took the witness to locate the block of flats where West had last been seen. There on a first floor landing, he found West, who he arrested, although at that moment in time, Archie would not necessarily have been aware of what exactly West may have been wanted for.

Cornwall however made good his escape, although a search of the hospital grounds and the railway embankment alongside revealed a brown pullover and a balaclava, which he had abando-ned. The shotgun was recovered from the front garden where thrown and must have been in the cocked position, to have discharged on impact with the pathway. Mick Strapp and I interviewed West, who answered the description of one of the robbers. I subsequently charged West with the robbery. He had previously served a five-year term of imprisonment for armed robbery and had a number of known criminal associates. During the ensuing days I concentrated on trying to identify his accomplice. I believe that it was as a result of a stolen driving license found on West, that my enquiries ultimately focused on Cornwall, who I then endeavoured to trace. He had not long been released from a ten-year sentence of imprisonment for armed robbery. Cornwall was fortunately arrested at Kings Cross a few weeks later, in connection with offences relating to a Stolen Vehicle Excise License. He was interviewed by me and subsequently placed on an Identification Parade at St. Ann's Road. Two witnesses identified him, one being the council decorator, who recognised him, as the second man who ran into the yard and up the ladder. He was then charged with the robbery and the pair of them were subsequently committed to stand trial at the Central Criminal Court.

When West and Cornwall appeared at the Old Bailey, on the morning that their trial was due to start, I was informed by Prosecution Counsel that the defence were seeking an audience in Chambers, with the trial judge in order to 'Plea Bargain'. This process involved both Defence Counsel, in the presence of Prosecuting Counsel sounding out what Sentence the learned Judge might be minded to impose on their clients, if a 'Guilty' plea was entered by them, thus saving the need and expense of a trial. Afterwards, Prosecution Counsel informed me that the learned Judge indicated that in view of the serious nature of the offence and their past records, he would be thinking of seven years and upwards. This clearly did not meet with the approval of either West, or Cornwall, as they decided to take their chance with the jury and both pleaded 'Not Guilty' to the various charges. On conclusion of their trial however, the jury found both men guilty. West was sentenced to seven years imprisonment and Cornwall to twelve years imprisonment. Shortly after the conclusion of the case my Area Commander awarded me a Commendation, for 'Initiative and ability leading to the arrest of and conviction of two criminals for armed robbery'. It was however only to be some five years or so, before Cornwall came to my attention again, but this time in a most tragic and unexpected way.

Whilst some individuals like West and Cornwall progress to become 'Career Criminals', It is a fact that the majority of crime is committed by young males, under the age of twenty-one, most likely in the thirteen to seventeen age group, many of whom turn away from crime as they mature. Sometimes, once they have gained regular paid employment, or formed some sort of relationship with a girl, so they are no longer hanging around the streets with no particular purpose. This fact was brought home to me one evening, whilst I was having a drink in the Woodberry public house in Seven Sisters Road. The Woodberry was very much a family pub, well run by a jovial Irishman, Mick Mc Carthy and his wife Julie, who I had known since my days as an Aide to CID. A young chap, who had been drinking with friends in the public bar, came round to the Saloon and said to me, "You don't recognise me do you?" I told him I had seen him in the bar before but was unaware of his identity. He then said "Bob Hardy. You nicked me for housebreaking, when I was a schoolboy." I immediately knew him, but his appearance had changed considerably in the six or seven years since I had last seen him. He was in fact the lad whose address Bob Chambers and I had been watching, on the morning of the armed robbery at Maynards sweet factory, albeit at that time he was suspected of handbag snatches. He then went on to tell me that he had left all that behind him, he was now earning good money in the building trade and had a steady relationship with a young lady, who would certainly not tolerate him getting into any trouble. He insisted on buying me a drink, by way of apology for his conduct as a youngster, although I would happily have bought him one, for his help in restoring my faith in human nature.

The Woodberry was but one, of a dozen public houses situated on our Section and certainly one of the friendliest and well-kept establishments. As an investigating officer, it was useful to get to know as many of the various licensees as possible and call in occasionally when passing, if time permitted, introducing oneself to any new managers or tenants, as they could be a valuable source of information. A visit also provided an opportunity to assess the clientele, lest any particular pub became the resort or meeting place of known criminals, or a clearinghouse for stolen property. Some establishments were more welcoming than others, both by the decor and the attitude of the licensees and their staff. We were fortunate in that the four public houses nearest St Ann's Road Station, The Dagmar in Cornwall Road, The Victoria in St. Ann's Road, the Oakdale in Hermitage Road, and the aforementioned Woodberry, all had good licensee's. They were pleasant places in which to have a quick game of darts and a sandwich, work permitting, at lunchtime, or a sociable drink at the end of a tour of duty.

Working the long and unpredictable hours that were required of an investigating officer, it was necessary to be able to get away from it all some days, by not dining in the Station Canteen and being able to just chat about anything unrelated to the job. Being a Sectional Station with only a few staff, we had a much closer working relationship, than was possible elsewhere.

Consequently we enjoyed meeting up off duty, from time to time with our respective wives, either for a meal, or when attending various Dinner Dances, or other Police social functions. Pat Lynch and his wife Betty were the licensees of the Oakdale, just a few hundred yards from our station and this friendly Irish couple, together with Mick and Julie, from the neighbouring Woodberry, would often attend such functions, at our invitation, becoming firm friends with us and our wives.

Noeleen and I had managed to save enough for a deposit to buy our own house during the first fifteen months of our marriage. We were therefore, able to vacate our furnished flat in Hornsey, in the autumn of 1966 and move to a semi-detached house in a quiet cul-de-sac in Waltham Abbey. When she became pregnant the following year and when the birth became imminent, it was a great comfort for both of us, to know that if she telephoned me at the office, whoever happened to answer the phone, be it Margaret the typist, or one of my colleagues, it would be someone she had met and knew personally. It was also pleasing for me to know that we had some good neighbours who she could call upon for help or support, if at any time some protracted enquiry were to keep me away from home, for overly long hours.

It was in fact Margaret, who took Noeleen's call in December 1967, which resulted in me booking off duty, early one afternoon, before driving to Waltham Abbey and then down to the Mothers' Hospital in Hackney, where it had been arranged that our first child should be born. By the time we arrived however, Noeleen's labour pains had slowed down and so we sat outside the hospital for some time, before she decided she needed to be admitted. Later that night another chap and myself were the only two expectant fathers in the waiting room, when he told me he was going outside for a cigarette. No sooner had he left, then a little Chinese nurse entered the room and beckoned me to follow her. She then ushered me into a small room where a proud mother was holding a new-born child in her arms. The poor girl must have been as surprised as I was, for it was not Noeleen's room I was in, I quickly explained to the nurse that the baby's father had gone outside for a cigarette. Later that night our first daughter Helen, was born and it was the early hours when I finally bade the two of them farewell and left the hospital, to discover a layer of snow covering the ground. Driving past Chingford Rugby Club a short while later, I came across two men pushing a car and feeling elated and on a high I stopped to see if I could be of assistance. The car had run out of petrol, but as I was in the habit of carrying a spare can of petrol, in my boot, they were in luck, as I knew there were no nearby garages still open. Once refuelled, their car started and having declined their offer of any money I watched them drive off up the road, the car swerving from side to side. Only then did I realise the driver had obviously been drinking, but it was too late now, I just hoped they arrived home without mishap.

Chapter Eight

The Murder of Maud Dibbs

The one crime that can make the biggest demands on man hours, is of course murder, particularly during the first week or so, when so much needs to be done whilst people's memories are fresh. I did find myself seconded to a Murder Squad at Winchmore Hill Station, for a few months, to assist investigations into the murder of a young French girl, Odette Du Maurier, who was working in the Oakwood area as an au pair. This young lady was attacked and sexually assaulted on her way home, after a night out, and her body was later found, in the front garden of a house in Prince George Avenue. A witness was traced who had seen what he thought was a couple, embracing in the garden, but he had unfortunately passed on by and no further useful description was obtained from him. Despite intensive investigations by Detective Superintendent Harry Tappin assisted by Detective Inspector White, this dreadful crime was to remain unsolved.

Fortunately it was some three years after my posting to St. Ann's Road, before we were to have a murder committed on our Section and this came about on 27th March 1969. The victim a Mrs Maud Dibbs, was a 75-year-old widow, who lived alone at 7, Culross Road N.15., just a short distance from its junction with the busy West Green Road. The premises, which she rented, consisted of an end of terrace dwelling house on two floors, with the lower front room used as a shop, from which she sold confectionery, cigarettes and groceries.

Her body was discovered on the morning of 28th March by her next door neighbour, at No 5, a Mrs McKenzie. Earlier that morning Mr Mc Kenzie had noticed that their side gate, which separates the two premises, was ajar some 18 inches, despite him having bolted it shut, at around 10.45pm the previous night. This gate was somewhat unstable and could be lifted, thereby releasing the bolt from the ground where it was held in place. He had also noticed a pair of leather gloves lying on the ground near his fence and he informed his wife of these facts before leaving for work. Mrs Mc Kenzie's suspicions were further aroused by her elderly mother a Mrs Eason, who at 9am noticed that the newspaper was still projecting from the letter box of the front door of the shop, which did not appear to be open for business. The two rear gardens were only divided by a two strand wire fence, so Mrs Eason, fearing Mrs Dibbs was unwell, crossed to the rear kitchen door of No. 7 and found it was unlocked. On entering she noticed that everything seemed to be in a state of disorder.

Mrs Eason then called her daughter for assistance and the latter, after getting no reply to her calls, went upstairs where she found Mrs Dibbs lying on the landing. She was obviously dead. Police were called and a uniform officer attended the scene and after seeing the body of Mrs Dibbs, summoned the assistance of the Criminal Investigation Department. Being the senior CID Officer present at St. Ann's Road when this call was received, I attended the scene.

I was to find the victim fully clothed but covered with an eiderdown, lying on the first floor landing, with the top half of her body projecting into a room used as a store. All rooms in the house were in a state of disorder, and bore all the hallmarks of a burglary having taken place. In a room behind the shop, the television was still switched on and washing up liquid had been squirted over the television screen, as well as two mirrors and a wall. The rear kitchen had a door leading into the garden, which could be secured by three bolts. It was this door that had been found open and used by the neighbour to gain entry, before finding the body.

Having summoned the assistance of the various support services and informed my Detective Inspector, Ken White, at Tottenham Police Station, I spend my time making notes and trying to memorise the scene of disarray, in an endeavour to envisage what had taken place and what might have been stolen.

Once the scene had been photographed and fingerprint examination had been made of the front hallway, stairway and landing area, the body was removed to Hornsey Mortuary, for further examination by Dr David Bowen, a Home Office Pathologist. He had also attended the scene at the request of Superintendent Jim Crane. As the first CID Officer at the scene, it was deemed prudent that I become the Exhibits Officer, in this case and I therefore attended the post mortem to deal with further samples and exhibits, as directed by a Laboratory Liaison Officer. Cause of death was established as Asphyxia due to pressure on the neck.

An Incident Room was set up at St. Ann's Road Police Station with additional staff loaned from neighbouring Sub Divisions. House to house enquiries were instigated, in the immediate environs of Culross Road, in an endeavour to establish, who had last seen Mrs Dibbs alive and if anyone had seen any suspicious activity around her shop. It was also essential to identify any friends or relatives of Mrs Dibbs, who may have had some knowledge of her daily routine and her personal possessions, with a view to establishing exactly what may have been stolen from her person, or dwelling quarters. Likewise, suppliers of her shop merchandise needed to be traced, to establish what may have been stolen from the shop. As Exhibits officer I raised many of these enquiries from names and telephone numbers on various papers, bills and correspondence found at the premises.

We traced a sister of the deceased, a Mrs Mc George who lived with her husband in Agar Grove, N.W.1. She had last visited Mrs Dibbs at the shop on the weekend prior to her demise. She was aware that one of the few items of any value that her sister possessed, was a fur coat. This item was missing from the premises. She was also aware that her sister had recently purchased a new radio. Although no such radio was found at the premises, I had found a fairly new box for a Red Dansette Gem radio, which was being used by Mrs Dibbs, to store some of her invoices and correspondence. Knowledge of these two missing items was later to prove particularly poignant in this investigation.

Our enquiries revealed that Mrs Dibbs was last seen alive at about 7.25pm on Thursday 27th March, by a Mr Dennis Humphreys who passed by on his way home and noticed Mrs Dibbs standing in the shop, as two small boys left the premises. It was at 6.30am the next morning, when Mr Mc Kenzie found his side gate unlocked and noticed the leather gloves lying by his front fence. At 7.50am Stephen Shrimpton a schoolboy employed by a local newsagent had delivered the morning paper to Mrs Dibbs locked shop, but noticed nothing untoward.

Further enquiries established the house and shop to be owned by a Mrs Kate Murrell who called each month to collect her rent. Mrs Murrell was aware that Mrs Dibbs kept cash in the room at the rear of the shop and that the business was not making a particularly good profit.

A close friend of Mrs Dibbs was identified as a Mrs Winifred Bowyer who lived nearby, she was able to inform us that the deceased kept money in a drawer of a wall dresser in the room adjoining the kitchen. She was also able to describe in detail the fur coat and a watch owned by the deceased, which was also found to be missing. She was also aware that Mrs Dibbs kept a police type whistle on a table beside her bed.

A number of salesmen and deliverymen who supplied provisions to the shop were also traced and interviewed. They added little of value to the enquiry in the initial stages other than to describe the type and quantities of merchandise supplied, which merely confirmed the small nature of the business conducted from the shop.

So within a few days of this murder having been committed, we were aware that a Dansette Gem Radio, a ladies fur coat a ladies gold watch on an expanding bracelet and probably a quantity of cigarettes, tobacco, cash and possibly grocery provisions, had been stolen. There had however, been no positive sightings of any possible suspects and no forensic evidence to point us in the direction of the culprits.

Routine house to house enquiries were still continuing. Details of the stolen property had been circulated and extensive press coverage had been given to the incident. The records of all local criminals were being checked for suspects, who may have convictions for shop breaking offences and various possible leads, from members of the public, were being followed up.

One routine line of enquiry on any murder, was a check of local Missing Persons Registers and at St. Ann's Road Station, there was a report of a fourteen year old schoolboy, named James Colbert, who had been reported missing about a week prior to the murder. Colbert who was known to me and other CID officers was due to appear at Tottenham Magistrates Court on 2nd April for dishonestly handling two stolen pedal cycle wheels. He failed to appear on that date and a warrant was issued for his arrest. He was not considered a serious suspect for the murder, but an Action had been raised for him to be traced and interviewed and eliminated from the enquiry.

A more interesting line of enquiry, had arisen, when our house to house enquiries were extended and reached the Blackboy public House, in Blackboy Lane, some half mile from the murder scene. A young barmaid informed us, that an eighteen-year-old youth. Simon Garratt, who she knew from her school days, had offered to sell her some cigarettes at a low price, presumably thinking she would re- sell them over the bar to customers. Initial enquiries about Garratt revealed he had two findings of guilt recorded against him, but his current address was unknown.

As with most murders, in view of the importance and urgent nature of initial enquiries, all officers on the enquiry team, worked through the first weekend of the enquiry, without taking their rostered rest days. As the following weekend was the Easter Holiday, it was decided that each officer would take one day leave, that weekend. With Mick Strapp and I being the two Detective Sergeants on the enquiry, it was arranged that only one of us would be off duty at the same time. By a stroke of good fortune, Mick took Sunday 6th April as his rest day, whilst I was due to take the Bank Holiday Monday.

Mick lived with his wife Peggy and young daughter Julie, in Enfield. On the Sunday afternoon, Mick drove the family to the nearby Broomfield Park in Palmers Green and there, he was playing ball with Julie, when he saw two lads sitting on a park bench, one of whom he recognised as James Colbert. Mick kicked the child's ball nearer to the bench to enable him to get a closer look at the two of them. Any frustration Mick felt at spotting Colbert – who was by no means a strong suspect – on his day off, was immediately dispelled when he realised his associate an older youth, was holding a red transistor radio.

Mick then requested his wife to telephone for police assistance, whilst he remained in the vicinity of the two suspects, keeping them under observation, whilst kicking the ball around with his daughter Julie, who remained oblivious to what was occurring. Once assistance was to hand, Mick approached the two youths and on speaking to them, Colbert initially denied his identity and when questioned about the radio, the older youth claimed he had found it in a dustbin. He gave his name however, as Simon Garratt, the name of the suspect who had offered cheap cigarettes, for sale in the Blackboy public house. The pair aged 14 and 17 respectively, were arrested and taken to Southgate Police Station, where Mick put in a hurried phone call to me, in the Incident room, before arranging transport home for his wife Peggy and daughter Julie, whose day out with Mick had been so eventfully interrupted.

Mick Strapp had confirmed that the transistor radio in Garratt's possession was a red Dansette Gem, such as had been stolen from Mrs Dibbs premises. As I drove over to Southgate with other officers, I could not believe what a fortunate breakthrough this appeared to be, particularly as there had been no indication that Colbert and Garratt were acquainted, prior to this chance sighting.

On arrival at Southgate Police Station after liaising with Mick, I saw that amongst Garratt's property was a letter, stamped ready for posting, which Garratt said he was due to post for a girlfriend. I decided to open the letter and found that it had been written by a person named Jenny, with an address of Wilberforce Road, Finsbury Park, N.4. More importantly, in the letter, Jenny mentioned having just come into possession of a fur coat, which she intended to pass on to the recipient of the letter, a female relative, when they next met.

Wilberforce Road was just round the corner from Highbury Vale Police Station, where I had previously served. It was well known to me, as a road comprising of large terraced Victorian houses, mainly let off as bed-sit flats. It was adjacent to the infamous, Queens Drive, the haunt of Prostitutes and other undesirables, and known as the 'Red Light' area of Finsbury Park.

The two youths were transferred to St. Ann's Road Police Station, where they were detained. Together with the Detective Superintendent, Jim Crane, Mick Strapp and other officers I went to Wilberforce Road, where the author of the letter was found to be a 21-year-old female, Jenny Paterson, who described herself as a singer and who lived there with her boyfriend, Raymond Jenkins. Although I did not know them personally, both had previously come to police attention.

I questioned Jenny, concerning the fur coat mentioned in her letter and she produced the coat and readily admitted that Garratt had given her it, together with a ladies gold watch. At the same time, Garratt had also given her cigarettes, containers of Target washing up liquid, packets of Fairy Snow soap powder and about 2lb of Brooke Bond Tea. These latter items all were products identical to items sold, from Mrs Dibbs shop.

Whilst I was interviewing Jenny Paterson, I became aware that Jim Crane had entered the room behind me, having been engaged elsewhere. I continued with my questioning but not being used to working in the company of such a senior officer and conscious that he was the S.I.O., I was unsure of the protocol, I therefore paused and turning towards Jim Crane, said,

"Did you want to interview this lady Sir?" to which he replied,

"No, carry on Ron, you're doing fine".

In answer to further questions, Paterson said, the aforementioned items had been brought to her house, when Garratt and Colbert came back just after midnight, on 'the Thursday, a week before Good Friday'. I.e. the night of Mrs Dibbs murder. Jenny Paterson had at the same time, seen Garrratt in possession of a radio, a Post Office Savings Book, an alarm Clock and some cash. Both youths had been sleeping at the flat, and had gone out earlier that evening. From conversation she had with the youths upon their return, she was fully aware that the property they had brought back with them had been obtained by way of theft. Garratt had in fact burned the Post Office Savings Book in her presence.

Jenny Paterson's boyfriend, Raymond Jenkins who was interviewed by other officers, recalled that in the early hours of Friday 28th March He had left the room where he had been sleeping to go to the bathroom. As he passed the kitchen he saw Garratt and Colbert in there, together with Jenny and two men, with whom she sang as part of a pop group. He noticed two suitcases in there and Garratt told him they had 'done a shop'. He had returned to bed, but later that morning Jenny had shown him a fur coat, which she said Garratt had given her. Garratt had later told him he had got the coat from the back room in the shop. Jenkins had also seen a red Dansette gem radio, which one of the youths told him, had also been stolen. Later he became aware that one of the suitcases, which Garratt kept, locked in a bedroom, contained cigarettes.

Following these initial interviews Jenny Paterson and Raymond Jenkins were taken, with various items of property, to St Ann's Road Police Station. In view of the vital evidence they could supply, despite their admitted involvement in knowingly handling stolen property, they were treated as witnesses and after further interviews, detailed witness statements were taken.

During examination of the murder scene, I had found a rubber-covered torch, on an easy chair in the room adjoining the kitchen, at 7 Culross Road. Whilst it was thought this may have been used and left behind by the intruders, the possibility that it belonged to Mrs Dibbs had not been eliminated. When Jenny Paterson was shown this item at the Station she stated that it was identical to a torch brought to her address by Colbert, who told her he had stolen it from a car in Wilberforce Road. In fact her small son had been permitted to play with it. Furthermore on 28th March she noticed that it was no longer in the house and Garratt when asked where it was, replied that he had left it in the house where they had been the previous night.

The two members of the group, with which Paterson sang, referred to by Jenkins, were also brought in for questioning.

One of them, Robert Dawson recalled that on 28th March, Paterson in the company of Garratt and Colbert had called at the address where he was staying. Paterson was wearing a fur coat and invited him and his roommate Colin Fullalove the other group member, to return to her flat where a party was to be held. All five had then returned to her address. Whilst at the party Dawson was sold a packet of cigarettes by Garratt and a few days later Garratt showed him a lady's gold watch and Jenny Paterson gave him an alarm clock.

Fullalove in recalling the party stated he had seen two suitcases in the kitchen and had in fact sat on them and had noticed a Dansette radio on the mantelpiece. He had also seen Paterson handing the alarm clock to his flatmate Dawson.

Detective Superintendent Crane, in company with Detective Inspector White interviewed Jeffrey Colbert, in the presence of his parents. He admitted going to the premises trying the front door and seeing a light on in a room at the back of the shop. He claimed, however, that after assisting Garratt to climb over the wooden side gate, he'd remained outside the premises until about an hour later, when Garratt unlocked the gate and let him through. He stated that he had then entered the premises and found two suitcases and two shopping bags ready packed. He admitted looking in the ground floor rooms and noticing the T.V. set being still on, but denied ever having gone upstairs or being involved in any assault upon Mrs Dibbs. He recalled Garratt abandoning a pair of gloves, as they were leaving the premises, before taking the suitcases to a mini cab, which Garratt had apparently requested, using Mrs Dibbs telephone. On conclusion of his interview Colbert made a written statement under caution.

Garratt initially denied all knowledge of the event but later admitted that he had in fact been into the premises. He claimed however, that Colbert had been with him throughout and that they had effected entry by climbing the sloping roof to the bathroom window, which they had then opened. He denied killing Mrs Dibbs, claiming that as he went up behind her to prevent her raising any alarm, he slipped and both fell to the floor. He claimed he saw blood and realised she had cut herself. Garratt stated that he then took an eiderdown off the bed and put it over Mrs Dibbs. He was however uncertain if she was still alive and so had taken a mirror from the bathroom in an effort to determine if she was still breathing. The mirror was still where Garratt said he had left it, when I arrived at the scene.

Garratt admitted having used a rubber torch and leaving it at the scene, also the pair of gloves abandoned outside the premises. Although he admitted taking cash from the premises he claimed Colbert had taken the watch and a Post Office Savings Book. He was adamant that the two of them had been together, throughout the venture. He also made a written statement under caution on conclusion of his interview.

Enquiries were also made at the mini cab premises, in Blackstock Road Highbury, which Garratt had used to secure transport from the scene of the crime. Mr Gemal the proprietor was able to confirm that his records showed, a telephone call being received from a male person, requesting a car to attend West Green Road and wait outside the Fox public house. This public house was almost opposite the end of Culross Road.

The driver, a Mr Irvin Braithwaite, had attended the venue at about 11.10pm. He informed us that after a five-minute wait, Garratt, approached the car from the rear in company with another youth. Garratt had a suitcase with him and said that he, "had some stuff to put in the boot". Braithwaite remained in the driving seat and was therefore unable to describe what was put in the boot. He did recall that Garratt was holding an alarm clock in the car.

After a short call to Friern Barnett, where Garratt left the car for a short time, Braithwaite was requested to drive the two youths to Wilberforce Road, N.4., where he remained in the car, whilst the youths removed their luggage from the boot.

After reading Braithwaite's statement, I recall making a mental to note, to ensure that in any future murder enquiries, local car hire companies should be included in follow up enquiries. Although in this instance the company Garratt had used, was not local to the venue, but local to his address.

Both youths were ultimately charged with the murder of Mrs Maud Dibbs. Their clothing was submitted to the Metropolitan

Police Forensic Science Laboratory, for examination. This did not however, reveal any evidence to connect them with the murder scene or the victim.

When any person is arrested for crime, background information as to their antecedents is sought, both for police record purposes and to inform and assist the judiciary, when their case finally comes to trial. Whilst nothing in any person's background can justify their taking another's life, it was not uncommon to learn that arrested persons had been the products of failed marriages or a disturbed childhood. I was to learn that such was the case with Garratt and Colbert.

Simon Garratt's parents had divorced when he was seven years of age and his mother had re-married. His father remained his legal guardian but about a year before his arrest he had moved out of his father's home and went to live with an uncle and aunt in West Green Road. An affair had developed between Garratt and his 27-year-old aunt, but he had become violent towards her, assaulting her on two occasions in a violent manner. He was finally told to leave about two months before his arrest. Since leaving school aged 15, he had had a number of employments of short duration and had two findings of guilt recorded against him at Juvenile Courts.

James Colbert had lived with his parents in Tottenham, until the age of 11, when on the advice of a Child Guidance Clinic, had been sent to a school for maladjusted children, in Sussex. His parents had removed him from this school some two year later, following an indecent assault being made upon him by one of the masters. Thereafter he attended a local comprehensive school, but had failed to attend for a period of two months prior to his arrest. He had also left home for no apparent reason, a few days prior to the murder and been sleeping rough and associating with Garratt during this time. He also had two previous findings of guilt recorded against him.

When this case ultimately came to trial the prosecution accepted a plea of 'guilty' to an alternative charge of manslaughter. Garratt was sentenced to three years imprisonment whilst Colbert was sentenced to Borstal Training.

Without a doubt, a major factor in solving this case, had been the good fortune of Detective Sergeant Mick Strapp deciding to chose to visit Pymmes Park on his day off. Thereafter, his initiative, ability and devotion to duty, had ensured the arrest of Garratt and Colbert. For, although, our enquiry had already produced the names of the two culprits, we had no evidence that they were associated, or had committed this particular crime. Had they been traced at a later date, when no longer in possession of the radio, or after the incriminating letter divulging information about the fur coat, had been posted, the result could have been entirely different. On conclusion of the proceedings, Detective Sergeant Strapp deservedly received a Commissioner's Commendation for his actions, in effecting the arrest of the two youths. The District Commander awarded me a minor commendation for 'Valuable assistance' in this case.

This murder enquiry occurred at the time when Noeleen was pregnant with our second child, so I was grateful that it did not become a long drawn out enquiry. Soon after Helen was born, I had successfully sat the Promotion Examination, for First Class Sergeant; a supervisory rank between Sergeant and Inspector, known as Station Sergeant, in the uniform department and denoted by a crown, worn above a sergeant's chevrons. (This rank was to be discontinued in later years, but not until I had served well over three years in the rank). Having passed this examination, I need to acquire more service in the rank of Detective Sergeant, before being considered for recommendation to attend a Promotion Selection Board. It would have been around the summer of 1969 that I was successful on such a board, for our second daughter Jane was born in the August and within a few weeks I learnt I was to be transferred to 'N' Division, on promotion to Detective Sergeant (First Class).

Chapter Nine

First Class at Islington

Notification of all matters affecting police personnel, including courses; new legislation; promotions and transfers were published twice weekly in 'Police Orders' a small loose leaf document, dispatched to all stations and departments and compulsory reading by all. Whilst on most occasions one might learn of an impending transfer, by way of a telephone call from a senior officer, Police Orders were the first indication to other officers that changes were afoot. It was force policy that a promotion was always coupled with a transfer to a new Division or Department, to facilitate severance of any close bonds with colleagues of similar rank, and allow the opportunity for one to exercise your new authority in a fresh environment. Naturally, once you knew that a promotion and transfer was imminent, the next thing you were anxious to ascertain was, which station you were being posted to on your new Division and whether you were already acquainted with any of the staff there. Likewise whenever someone, particularly a supervising officer, was due to leave a station the personnel there were always interested to know, who the replacement was going to be.

The first indication I had that my new posting was to be at Islington Police Station with effect from15th September 1969, came in a phone call from my last aiding partner, Sam Pollock, who was currently serving there as a Detective Constable. Sam related the names of the other staff at Islington, a few that were known to me, but the majority I had yet to meet. It was good to know that there would be a few familiar faces at my new posting. The excitement of my promotion however, was tempered with the knowledge that with it, came the responsibility of supervising about fifteen officers, comprising Aides; Detective Constables and

Detective Sergeants some of whom were far more experienced than I.

Unfortunately I knew that the amount of experience an officer had did not always make him a more efficient officer. I was not happy therefore to learn that one of the Detective Sergeants was Jeff Riley who had served at the neighbouring Tottenham Sub Division, whilst I was at St. Ann's Road. Our paths had crossed over a particular case whilst I was on 'Q' Car duties and without going into detail, I knew he would require close supervision. In this observation I was to be proved right, as some months later, as a result of an incident whilst he was deployed as the Divisional Night Duty CID Officer, he was suspended and later charged and sentenced to two years imprisonment for corruption. Fortunately this incident did not occur whilst he was directly under my supervision and had not involved any other of my staff.

One of the other Detective Sergeants – Stan Morten, had worked at Highbury at the same time as I and was both experienced and possessed of a keen sense of humour, he was to prove a useful ally. Another Detective Sergeants who I had not met before, was a keen young officer named Brian Reynolds, whose career was to culminate in his becoming the Chief Constable of Kent Constabulary. The staff included two typists Rose and Joyce and an elderly CID clerk, Les Sharp, a retired uniform officer, who I was to learn, required more supervising than some of the serving officers.

On arrival I was to see little of my immediate superior a Detective Inspector who was due to transfer himself within two weeks. He was replaced by DI Pat O'Brien whose brother Mick had been the First Class Sergeant at St. Ann's Road for short while, during my time as an Aide. Pat O'Brien having transferred in after a posting to the Regional Crime Squad, was perhaps even more like a fish out of water than I was, as there had been considerable changes both with regard to legislation and procedures regarding Crime Registers during his absence from Divisional CID work. Whilst he was based at Islington, he also had responsibility for Caledonian Road CID a Sectional Station of Islington Sub-Division.

When I was first appointed as a Detective, CID Officers investigated all crimes, albeit there was a separate register for offences relating to thefts of, or from, motor vehicles, known as the 'Motor Vehicle Crime Book'. With the continuing increase in crime, petty thefts, minor assaults and acts of criminal damage etc. were categorised as 'Minor Crimes' for which a separate 'Minor Crime Book' was created and these offences were allocated to uniform officers to investigate. This practice was brought about around the time that the 'Home Beat Officers' scheme was introduced in the Metropolitan Police, where specially selected officers were permanently allocated a Beat, to get to know intimately and build up personal relationships within the community on their 'Home Beat'. These officers were then tasked with investigating all 'Minor Crimes' and 'Motor Vehicle Crimes', which occurred on their beats.

Whilst an experienced uniformed officer, was appointed to allocate and supervise these Beat Crime investigations, the ultimate responsibility for ensuring that all relevant enquiries were responsibly carried and crimes correctly classified, with arrests effected where possible, fell to the lot of the First Class CID Sergeant. So, in addition to arranging duties and supervising crimes under investigation by my own CID staff, much of my time was to be spent training Home Beat Officers in the art of investigating crimes particularly where there were suspects to be traced or interviewed. Whilst this was time consuming on my part, I was fortunate in that most of the officers were not only quite experienced but also keen to undertake this new investigative role.

Part of my duties also involved reading and checking the various typed reports and accompanying statements, emanating from crimes under investigation. Mostly these reports were being sent to the Metropolitan Police Solicitors Department at Scotland Yard, seeking directions or representation in forthcoming court prosecutions. There was of course a need for correspondence with other police forces or public bodies, where assistance was sought with enquiries in various parts of the country, either tracing witnesses or suspects.

Despite the amount of time these supervisory duties took, I was still keen to get involved with investigations of my own, usually for crimes of a more serious nature such as robbery or sexual offences. At weekends however when there was limited staff on duty, I might find that there were only one or two other officers on duty with me. If one was required at Court, or there had been a heavy overnight report of burglaries or assaults, I would willingly undertake or assist in any investigation, as an excuse to get out of the office and meet people and provide a break from purely supervisory duties.

One such opportunity arose however on a weekday afternoon when the uniform Station Sergeant, informed me that an emergency call had been received from the local Nat West Bank in Upper Street, indicating that an armed robbery was in progress. The usual police response vehicles had been dispatched by way of radio messages from Scotland Yard's Information Room. As the bank was only four or five hundred yards away from the Station, I decided that it would be quicker to run to the bank on foot rather than try and use my own or any available police transport. So together with a colleague I ran along Upper Street to the bank arriving about the same time as the Area Car.

Typically there was a certain amount of shock and confusion at the premises with customers and staff in small groups conversing about what had occurred. I was directed to the manager's office where two other men were present. The manager introduced me to one of them as a customer who had tackled a man who had threatened his staff with a gun. What he did not do immediately, was inform me that the other man present who was sitting on a chair looking rather sheepish, was in fact the would-be robber who had been disarmed and detained by that customer.

It transpired that the customer, a heavily built man in his forties, had an appointment with the manager to discuss an overdraft facility for his carpet-laying business. The manager's office was situated at the far end of the banking counter and accessed by a door, which could only be opened from within. During the course of their meeting the suspect had entered the bank and passed a female cashier a carrier bag and a note bearing the words 'Put the money in the bag I have a gun'. Looking up she found herself staring at the barrel of a gun. She duly pressed an internal alarm button, which in addition to sending a call to Scotland Yard had alerted the manager, who ushered out his customer into the banking hall, before investigating the reason for the alert.

Once in the hall the customer found there was only a nine inch vertical brick pillar, shielding him from the view of the would be robber, a slightly built man of about 21 years who was pointing a gun at the female cashier. Unable to re-enter the manager's office he sized up the situation and made an instant decision to tackle the offender, which he did by lunging at him in a bear hug, thus throwing him to the floor. The man offered little resistance once tackled and the gun was then found to be a plastic toy.

Once all was explained, I searched the offender and found in one of his pockets a screwed up piece of paper bearing the words 'Put the money in the bag I have a revov'. The last word had been deleted, indicating our would-be robber was obviously unsure of his spelling of the word 'revolver'. He had therefore torn off the top half of the notepaper and revised his demand, using the word gun on the rest of the page, which he had proffered to the cashier. An indication of the mentality of this individual was to be seen on a further piece of folded paper I found on him, which showed plans for building a raft and was accompanied by a shopping list of items to take on his journey, the last item being a parrot.

For the cashier who had been faced with this situation however, this was a traumatic experience, staring at the end of a gun barrel she had no way of knowing whether it was real or whether her life was in danger. I was to later learn that the offender had committed a similar offence previously, at a branch of Barclays Bank Highbury Corner. On that occasion having been given some cash, he had fled down the nearby underground station, but had been pursued and apprehended, being easy to recognise as he was still wearing a scarf masking the lower half of his face. For that offence he had been sentenced to eighteen months' imprisonment. He was to receive a sentence of two years for his latest offence. A report I submitted bringing the customers action to the notice of the relevant authority resulted in his bravery being recognised by a monetary award from the High Sheriff of London. During conversation at the time of the presentation, I learnt that he had had no problem in negotiating his overdraft once his appointment had been re-scheduled.

Within a few months of my arrival at Islington I began to feel more comfortable with my role as a supervising officer having reorganised things to suit my preferred way of working and set up systems to enable me to adequately supervise all areas of my responsibilities. One area that I knew from past experience could cause problems was what was loosely termed 'Prisoners Property'. This included all property taken from persons on arrest either from their person their vehicle or a search of their premises, including the proceeds of any particular crime they were in the act of committing. It also included items such as jemmies screwdrivers or knives discarded during the commission of crimes, where no immediate arrest had been effected.

Once everything was listed and recorded in the relevant registers it then had to be stored in a suitably secure storeroom until such time as it was required by way of an exhibit at court during a prosecution. It was not uncommon however for some items to remain in the store long after a prosecution had finished. This was either because an officer had not got round to restoring property to its rightful owner, or in the case of implements used in the commission of crime, or property for which no owner had been traced, the officer needed to complete a report. He could thereby transfer the items to a central 'Prisoners Property Store', located at Chalk Farm, where it would ultimately be disposed of at auction.

With available space in any police station being at a premium, it was not uncommon for a cell to be taken over as a store for bulky items such as electrical goods, or car parts. In such instances it was often a question of, 'out of sight, out of mind', and unless an officer had occasion to visit the store he might overlook the fact that he still had items in their awaiting disposal. Failure to keep on top of the property situation could easily result in items becoming lost or mislaid.

The panic that ensued soon after my arrival at Islington, on the morning a trial was due to commence at court, and the officer in the case was unable to locate a small envelope, containing a thin stiletto blade used in a stabbing incident, highlighted the need for improvement. In that event the officer, an experienced Aide, had to attend court without his exhibit. It was later found to have slipped down from a shelf and become concealed behind bulkier items on the floor. Fortunately it was found in time to have no serious effect on the outcome of the case, but it proved a useful lesson to all, and justified my purge on officers, regarding the need to reduce the amount of items being stored at the earliest opportunity.

It was often the case that some of the keenest young officers particularly Aides were only too keen to get out on the street and effect crime arrests but needed a certain amount of advice and guidance when dealing with the paper work emanating from their efforts. I knew from experience the problems that could ensue if correspondence was not dealt with promptly and systematically. As a supervising officer I was conscious of the need to set good standards in all aspects of detective duties, particularly with regard to younger inexperienced officers. To this end I was grateful, that I myself had been set high standards, particularly with regard to report writing, by supervising officers during my own service.

One area where I felt I had to put my foot down quite firmly involved Les Sharpe the elderly CID Clerk, a former Aide who had a retired as a uniform constable. This came about when I discovered that he and a few of the Aides had been in the habit of playing cards in the CID Office during the lunch break. The practice had been curtailed on my arrival but once Les got to know me, he broached the subject one day to see if I would have any objection. When I asked why they could not play in the canteen, as was common practice in many police stations, I discovered it was in fact a poker school he was talking about, which involved gambling. During my early days living in Section Houses when we were paid weekly in cash, I had on occasions seen officers lose a week's wages in a few hours and knew the problems that could arise from such practices. I had no qualms therefore, in rejecting Les' proposal in the interest of maintaining good order and discipline with my staff as well as a responsibility towards the wives and families of the officers.

I was disappointed therefore, a few weeks later, to discover that Les and his cronies had made use of a little used office in the basement to continue the poker school and I made my feelings very plain to all concerned. On my arrival at Islington I had let it be known, that if any of the staff needed their duties re arranged or covered to enable them to indulge in representative sporting pursuits, I was more than willing to assist them – work permitting. I knew from my own experience that such attitudes helped build esprit de corps and trust. With C.I.D. work in particular one never knew when the assistance of a number of Aides might be needed for an urgent observation or to assist with a search or arrest operation. It was important therefore to know of staff availability at any given time and know that what was recorded in the Duty Book was a true record of the activities officers were involved in, particularly their expected time of return to the station.

In some ways I felt a bit sorry for Les Sharpe, as he had separated from his wife many years before and lived a bachelor life, in a flat in Holloway. He was always came to work smartly dressed in a suit and was efficient at his job which involved maintaining registers of the various criminal record files and all correspondence and reports that passed in and out of the office. He was a likeable individual and always courteous and respectful. A good friend who had at one time been his Aiding partner – Don Saunders, had pursued a successful career in the CID, rising to the rank of Commander. Don had called into the office a couple of times when in the area, to look up his old colleague, but it was clear to me that Les' work was the main source of his enjoyment. One day he told me that out of the blue he had received a letter from a firm of solicitors, informing him that his wife was seeking to tidy her affairs and for that reason was seeking a divorce. Les was not contesting the divorce and was not therefore required to attend the hearing. As the day approached however Les asked me if he could have the afternoon off to attend the Law Courts. It was apparent that he just wanted to see his wife who he knew would be there. That evening at home I read a two line entry in the Evening Standard newspaper, mentioning an unnamed man had collapsed and died on the steps of the Law Courts that afternoon. My heart missed a beat when I read this and my suspicions were confirmed the next day when I was informed that Les had suffered a massive heart attack and died. I never found out if he had seen his wife, the occasion had obviously been too much for him.

Les' next of kin was his elderly sister and having made contact with her I was able to offer her help and assistance regarding the funeral, which was well attended both the many uniform and CID officers who had come to know Les.

Civilian staff were always the responsibility of the Receivers Office of the Metropolitan Police and had their own civil service grades, so it was to this department I looked in order to find a suitable replacement CID Clerk. I was a bit surprised to learn that although they would advertise the vacancy, the responsibility for vetting and interviewing applicants would fall to me.

The position was an ideal one for a former police officer, who would not only be aware of police procedures, but familiar with the various files and paper work emanating therefrom. The Receivers office however, had become somewhat protective towards job opportunities for civilian employees and I was informed I could not seek to recruit a retired or ex police officer, as the vacancy had to be advertised to the public at large, by them, through their own Circulations.

From the various application that were received, I interviewed three or four and selected Laurie, a short dapper middle aged man who had worked 30 years for his previous employer and was seeking a change of environment. As the task of training Les' replacement would doubtless fall to me, I was anxious not to select a younger person who might have decided on a career move within a few months, whereby I would have to undergo the whole process again. Although Laurie had no experience of police work I felt sure he had all the attributes to become an efficient clerical officer and long after I had left Islington, he was still in service there.

On 17th June 1970 the bodies of, Sarah Blatchford aged 11 and George Hanlon aged 12, who had been reported missing from their homes in Ponders End, some 10 weeks previous, were found in a small wood just off the Sewardstone Road, on the borders of Waltham Abbey and Chingford. They were discovered in a hide made of branches and twigs, by a farmer out shooting with his dog. This location was but a few hundred yards from a road along which I drove daily, on my way to and from work. Living locally I had followed closely the publicity surrounding the disappearance of the children so the thought that I had passed so close to where their bodies lay undiscovered during this time, sent a chill down my spine as I passed by on subsequent days.

Owing to decomposition and the time the bodies had been exposed to the elements, the pathologist, Professor James Cameron, was unable to give a cause of death and the Coroner subsequently recorded an open verdict. Detective Chief Superintendent 'Nipper' Read, the officer in charge of the case, who had carried out extensive searches and enquiries, remained convinced however that the children had been murdered, as Susan's jeans had been ripped completely down each seam and some of her underclothes were missing. He was to be proved right eventually, but not until some 30 years later, when Paedophile Ronald Jebson, 61, who was currently serving a life sentence for killing eight year old Rosemary Papper in 1974, admitted the killing at the Old Bailey in May 2000 and was jailed for life.

Driving past the scene of this horrendous crime just after the bodies were discovered I had no way of knowing that within a few months I too would soon become engrossed in a sordid murder enquiry, fortunately not one involving such innocents.

Chapter Ten

The Murder of James William Cameron

The area policed by Islington Sub-Division encompassed most of Cannonbury, so in addition to the usual council estates there were many large houses, some set in squares, which were inhabited by the professional and managerial classes. Towards the Angel where Upper Street merged with Essex Road was Islington Green, a small triangle of parkland adjacent to which was Camden Passage, where twice weekly a busy antiques market was held. There were a number of quality restaurants in the Camden Passage area and it was to one such establishment that arrangements had been made for the Islington CID staff and their partners, to socialise and enjoy an evening meal during the early evening of Wednesday 14th October 1970.

That afternoon the CID Office was deserted with the exception of myself and a young Detective Constable, Bill Wooding, who had recently transferred to our office and for some reason was not going to participate in the social function that evening. I had arranged with my opposite number at Kings Cross for his staff to cover our office with Bill that evening. With the exception of a pair of Aides who were out patrolling, I had let the rest of the staff off early to return home wash and change in order to return with their wives or partners for the meal.

With our daughter Helen not yet three years and Jane only 13 months, our social life had been somewhat restricted, so we were both looking forward to an evening out, unencumbered. Noeleen had arranged for Marian, one of her former-nursing friends, to baby-sit that evening when she had finished her shift. Knowing we would not be able to leave for the restaurant until the last minute, there was little point in my leaving the office too early. I was therefore busy dealing with correspondence, when Sergeant Bill

Hughes the Station Officer entered the CID Office and said, "I think you might have to cancel your meal tonight."

"Why is that Bill" I replied.

"Well two of my officers have just had to break into a house in Burgh Street, and have found the owner dead on his bed, with his hands tied behind his back. They think he's been shot through the head."

I then learnt that the victim was believed to be James William Cameron, the Marketing Services Director for the Beecham Group Ltd., on the Great West Road Brentford, who had failed to turn up for work on Monday 12th, or keep appointments made for that day. Telephone calls to his house by his Secretary had not been answered and the following day when he again failed to arrive for work, after ringing several contacts, she had finally spoken to Julia Hunter, a friend of Mr Cameron, who lived nearby in Noel Road. Mrs Hunter and her husband had called at Cameron's house and receiving no reply left a note, which was still there on the doormat on Wednesday lunchtime, when she had made a further visit.

As a result of receiving this information, the Personnel Director for Beechams had telephoned Islington Police Station and spoken with the Station Officer, who had dispatched PCs Alan Evans and Geoffrey Wightman to the house at 3.15pm. These officers, after calling at 4 Burgh Street and getting no reply, had liaised with Mrs Hunter before entering the house via a rear first floor window, which was closed but unlocked.

In a ground floor front room they had found an electric fire was turned on. They had then searched the house and in a first floor front bedroom found the deceased, dressed in pyjamas, lying on his right side on a bed. His hands were tied behind his back with a necktie, and there was material over his face which was covered in blood. The officers had then telephoned the duty officer, Sergeant Hughes at Islington, with their findings.

I telephoned Noeleen to inform her of the situation and the fact that it looked like our evening out would have to be postponed. I knew that the next few hours would be taken up with getting the various Scenes of Crime Support Services, to the scene and carrying out a detailed examination of the house. I saw little point therefore in spoiling the evening for the rest of my staff and their partners, particularly as I knew they would all be busy in the coming weeks. Bill Hughes confirmed there were sufficient uniform officers available, to carry out some initial 'House to House' enquiries, but I knew I would need a good 'Exhibits Officer' straight away. I spoke therefore with my opposite number at Kings Cross; to advise him that I was about to visit the scene of a murder and would need to call on his resources a little earlier than planned. I knew that Det Sgt Stan Blunden was one of the officers who was due to cover for us. 'Tim', as Stan was affectionately known – probably on account of his huge bulk – was a mature experienced detective and not only was he readily available, but was an ideal officer for the task.

Burgh Street was one of the more sought after addresses on our section, with its neat Georgian style terraced houses situated only a few minutes' walk from the Antique Market of Camden Passage and the various transport facilities available at the Angel. Adjacent to Burgh Street was Noel Road, where the playwright Joe Orton had resided, until being murdered just three years previous, by his lifelong companion and lover, Kenneth Halliwell who had then committed suicide.

I drove to the venue with Bill Wooding, my only available staff member and as we entered Burgh Street from Great Peter Street, Bill remarked, "If number four is on the left hand side at the other end of this road, I have been there recently."

He then explained that he had carried out an enquiry for another Police Force, which had requested that enquiries be made to try and arrest a man who was believed to be staying at the address, and was wanted for a serious assault. Having called at the house, Bill had been surprised that such a person might be associated with the tenant who seemed a respectable man, living in a desirable neighbourhood. The owner had advised him that the person he was enquiring after was no longer staying there. There was however, another man in the house and although he did not fit the description of the wanted man, Bill had spoken to him to satisfy himself that he was not the subject of the enquiry. At this point the male resident had become somewhat abusive, objecting to police coming to his house and interviewing his guest. Bill suspected that the relationship between the two men might have been homosexual. As we neared the venue Bill confirmed it was the same address, but little did I know, just how significant Bill's remark was to prove, during subsequent enquiries.

Number 4 was a two-storey house with a railed basement area. Three stone steps bridging the basement area provided access to the front door, which was now guarded by the two uniformed officers, who only a short while previous had made the gruesome discovery.

The Officers directed us to the first floor front bedroom. Turning to my right as I passed through the doorway I found myself confronted with a view of the arms of the deceased, a heavily built middle aged man, with his hands bound behind his back with a necktie and a leather belt. The back of his head was hidden from view, by a folded pillow. Dressed in pale blue pyjamas, he was lying on his right side in a single bed his lower body covered by the bedding. Simultaneously I got a view of the front of his body, for the length of the far wall was furnished with a built in wardrobe, its full length mirrored doors reflecting the macabre view from a different perspective. A folded towel, heavily bloodstained, was wrapped round his face so only the top of his head and his lower jaw was to view. A further necktie was protruding from beneath the towel, as was a bloodstained handkerchief that appeared to have been placed in his mouth. There was stuffing escaping from a jagged hole in the folded pillow behind his head, indicative of a firearm discharge. The body bore signs of decomposition, confirming our suspicions that death had probably taken place a few days beforehand.

Having summoned the assistance of a Scene of Crime Photographer, Fingerprint Officer, Forensic Science Liaison Officer and the Coroners Officer, I informed my Detective Chief Superintendent, at Kings Cross who at that time was Bill Wright who had recently joined the Division. Having explained the staffing situation, I was pleased that he concurred with my decision not to cancel the meal. He said he would be at the scene within half an hour, so pending his arrival and that of the support services, I made a cursory examination of the remainder of the house, mindful not to disturb anything prior to the scene being photographed. I was looking for any clue as to what had preceded this dreadful act and also to learn something about the way of life of the deceased.

There was no sign of any forced entry to the premises. It was apparent that Mr Cameron lived alone in the house which was generally untidy and although furnished with quality antique furniture, both the bathroom and kitchen were in need of redecoration, with signs of some unfinished building alterations. In one corner of the bedroom a quantity of correspondence was scattered on the floor together with shoe cleaning brushes and an open tin of shoe polish. On top of a chest of drawers adjacent to some books, packets of Ryvita and sugar, a jar of pickle and an empty cereal bowl, indicated that food had been consumed in the bedroom.

Once Detective Chief Superintendent Wright had visited the scene, he decided he would like the pathologist to see the body in place before removal to the mortuary and accordingly, the Forensic Pathologist Hugh Johnson MA, MB, B.Chir. M.R.C.Path., D.M.J., was contacted and attended. He examined the deceased and after photographs had been taken, was able to make a more detailed examination, removing the folded towel to the custody of Tim Blunden the Exhibits Officer. He then found a circular firearm entry wound to the back of the head and an exit wound to the right side of the forehead. He also found what appeared to be powder burns, round a hole on the inside of the folded pillow with a further hole in the sheet and mattress below the forehead.

Dr Johnson was of the opinion from the severe decomposition of the body that it had been dead in position found for some days. A Post Mortem Examination of the body was arranged for 7.15pm that evening, once the body could safely be removed, on completion of fingerprint and forensic examination of the staircase. During that post mortem examination it was found that a handkerchief had been used as a gag held in place over the mouth by the necktie which was protruding beneath the folded towel. With the exception of the firearm entry and exit wound, no other injuries were found and there were no other contributory causes of death other than the firearm wound to the head. There was evidence that the deceased had participated in homosexual practices, but no evidence of recent interference.

Meanwhile initial 'House to House' enquiries by uniform officers had revealed that several neighbours had seen a man calling at Cameron's house a few days previous. Mrs Jessie Blackwell, a next door neighbour, had seen the suspect on Friday 9th October in the afternoon. She described a man aged about 25 of slim build, with long dark shoulder length hair, wearing dark glasses, a dark coat and carrying a rolled umbrella. She has first seen him knock twice at number 4 and then walk off after getting no reply. She had also seen him when he returned at about 5pm and on this occasion when he got no reply he had sat on the doorstep and waited. Later that evening between 6pm and 7pm she had again heard someone knocking at the front door of No. 4 and then heard the person being let in, but had not looked out to see who it was.

On the Saturday morning just before 12 noon, she had seen Mr Cameron alighting from a taxi with some shopping; he was alone. That was the last time she had seen him but recalled that on the Monday 12th at about 3.30pm whilst returning to her house, she had heard music coming from what she thought was the first floor front of Mr Cameron's house. She was able to furnish the information that Mr Cameron had quite a lot of men coming and going from the house, usually in the evening.

Another neighbour, Angela Baillie an elderly pensioner, had been standing outside her house at No. 1, between 2pm and 3pm on the Friday and had also seen a man knocking at No. 4. After getting no reply the man had walked towards her and as he passed remarked, 'Nobody answers me, do you know where he works?"

She had then seen the man walk on and stand at the corner of the road as she went indoors. Mrs Baillie had described the man as about five feet one inches tall with short dark hair and long sideboards. He was wearing a black overcoat and carrying a black umbrella. She however, had seen this same man the following day when she went shopping at about 2pm. He was dressed in the same clothes and was standing on the corner of Burgh Street and Danbury Street. He was still there on her return ten minutes later.

Penelope Phillips had only moved into her house opposite No. 4 a week prior to the murder. She also had seen what appeared to be that same man on two occasions. Firstly on the Friday she had seen him sitting on the steps of No. 4, for a period of about an hour before leaving at about 9pm. Then on the Saturday afternoon around 1.30pm she had seen him in the same position, although at no time was he seen to enter the premises. She described the man as about 25 years of age five feet ten inches tall, very thin pale face with straight hair parted and combed to one side and wearing dark glasses. On the first occasion she had seen him he was dressed in a dark jacket and trousers, light coloured shirt and dark tie. He carried a black umbrella. On the next occasion he was dressed the same with the exception of wearing a black high-necked sweater.

Once the various Scenes of Crimes personnel had arrived at the scene and been briefed and arrangements made for the body to be removed to the mortuary, I returned to Islington CID Office to begin setting up the necessary equipment and system, to operate a major enquiry. There were no dedicated Major Incident Suites available at that time so it was a question of reorganising the CID Office which fortunately consisted of two connecting rooms and was reasonably spacious. Bill Wright had promised to enlist the help of officers from other Stations on the Division with effect from the following day, but I knew how important it was to have a dedicated system in place at the outset, so no relevant information was lost.

Having been informed of the death of their friend and colleague, Barbara Heitzman, Cameron's Personal Secretary and Vaughan Shaw the Divisional Personnel Director of Beecham Products Division, both attended Islington Police Station that evening to assist in whatever way they could. His Secretary who had last seen him on Thursday 12th described a black leather document case that Cameron used for his correspondence and which she knew was not at the office. This item was also missing from the house, which indicated that the papers strewn over the bedroom floor might have been tipped out of it by his murderer and taken from the scene. Mr Shaw who had known Cameron for some three years as a work colleague, but had never socialised with him. He described him as extremely able and competent as a Market Researcher, but without any close friends in the company, tending to be an individualist who rarely used the firm's communal dining room. Asked whether he had any reason to suspect that Cameron was homosexual, he replied in the negative, although he had formed the impression that he did a fair amount of entertaining which may have been in connection with business.

Julia Hunter, the friend of Cameron who had been contacted by his Secretary, had told us that she had known him for some twelve years, first meeting when they both worked at the same advertising agency. They had become good friends and kept in touch and Cameron had bought a house nearby to her address some two years previous. Unaware that Cameron had failed to turn up for work on the Monday, she had telephoned his home that evening to invite him round for a meal with her and her husband, but received no reply.

It was late that night when I finally left Islington to return home, but I felt we had made good progress. Whilst the pathologist had not been able to be too specific in establishing the exact time of death – due to the electric fire having been left on, thus advancing the process of decomposition – we had established that Cameron was last seen getting out of a taxi on the Saturday lunchtime. It was reasonable to presume therefore that he had met his end sometime later that day or possibly the Sunday. There was increasing evidence that he was a practising homosexual who encouraged male visitors to his house. We had traced several witnesses who gave similar descriptions of the man with the umbrella who had made repeated calls at the venue and waited in the vicinity just prior to the murder. This man who clearly had been very determined to meet up with Cameron, needed to be traced and eliminated from enquiries if possible. Whilst the exact motive for the murder was unclear, we knew Cameron's briefcase had been taken, presumably to convey other items from the premises, so robbery was a strong possibility.

The following day I had to select some of my own staff to work on the Murder Squad whilst leaving sufficient experienced personnel to continue with the day to day crime investigations. This was never an easy task as most officers enjoyed the challenge of a murder enquiry, as well as the opportunity to work additional overtime and the financial reward that entailed. Fortunately the increased police activity that a murder enquiry generally brought to a particular neighbourhood, often resulted in a reduction in local crime, which in turn reduced the pressure on those officers left to carry on routine crime enquiries.

I was aware that our Area CID Commander Mr Marchant had accompanied Bill Wright to the Post Mortem and his interest doubtless resulted in a number of CID officers from other Divisions on 3 Area, being seconded to the Murder Enquiry. This was in addition to the 'N' Division personnel, which Bill Wright was able to arrange. I knew the role of Office Manager would fall to me, and once aware of my full complement of staff I was able to assess their skills and pick suitable individuals to assist me in the incident room. The remainder would be engaged on outside enquiries known as 'Actions' on any major incident.

Once the squad had been briefed with the nature of the crime and progress to date, there were several obvious objectives. Firstly we needed to continue with 'House to House' enquiries in an endeavour to trace further witnesses to any comings and goings from 4 Burgh Street, particularly over the last weekend. Secondly we needed to interview as many of Cameron's work colleagues and business associates as we could trace, in order to glean as much information about him as possible. In particular about his habits, his friends and anyone who might have visited his address in recent times, or telephoned his house over that fateful weekend. Finally once the forensic examination of the house had been completed, we needed to examine any diaries notebooks telephone records and correspondence therein, which could prove useful, not only to trace contacts, but assist us in establishing what items may have been stolen.

One priority was for Tim Blunden the Exhibits Officer to search for and retrieve the bullet, which had become lodged somewhere in the mattress. This was in fact recovered later that day and found to be a 9mm bullet, which at least gave us some indication as to the type of weapon involved.

Another priority was to formally identify the body as that of Mr. Cameron. In the absence of any know relatives this task may well have fallen to his secretary or Mr or Mrs Hunter, but they were to be spared this unpleasant task. With news of the murder being passed to the media at the outset, together with appeals for assistance from anyone who knew Mr Cameron, we were fortunate to establish that he was known to a serving police officer on the Division. Detective Constable Dick Roberts possessed skills as a driving instructor and he informed us that four years previous he had taught Cameron to drive, giving twice weekly lessons over a period of three months. Although he had not seen Cameron since he had passed the driving test, having attended St. Pancras Mortuary, he was able to formally identify the body to Bill Wright and myself.

Arrangements were also made for a photo-fit picture of the suspect with the umbrella, to be compiled, with the assistance of the various witnesses who could describe him.

Mr Hodges, the manager of the Midland Bank, Beecham House Branch, Great West Road Brentford, read about the murder as soon as the story broke on Thursday 15th October and realised Mr Cameron was one of his bank's customers. The following day, when five cheques, recently drawn on Mr Cameron's account, were received for payment, he contacted the Incident Room. This was a significant lead, particularly due to where the cheques had been tendered, so I allocated this enquiry to Detective Sergeant Harry Wilkins, one of the officers seconded to the enquiry from 'H' Division.

When interviewed by Sgt Wilkins, Mr Hodges handed over the cheques, which the officer preserved for future fingerprint examination. The cheques were in a series, with the earliest one dated 10th October, for the sum of £7.15 payable to 'David Stanley'. The second one dated 11th October, was payable to British European Airways for £20. This cheque had been endorsed with the flight number 'BE 5392'on the rear and some other reference numbers. The third cheque dated 11th October, was made payable to 'Self' for £5 cash and bore the stamp of 'Barclays Bank at West London Air Terminal'. The fourth cheque also dated 11th October was made payable to 'Cash' in the sum of £20 and bore, the stamp of the Midland Bank Ltd., Terminal 1 Branch at Heathrow. The fifth and final cheque originally dated 11th, but altered to 12th October, payable to 'Cash' for £20, bore the stamp of the Clydesdale Bank Ltd, Sauchihall Street, Glasgow. Mr Hodges was certain that all the cheques had been written and signed by Mr Cameron with the possible exception of a signature adjacent to the date alteration on the last cheque.

Further enquiries regarding these individual transactions were now a priority. Barbara Heitzman, Cameron's secretary had no knowledge of any reason why he should need to visit Glasgow and had he done so on Monday 12th, she would have expected a telephone call from him in view of his prior appointments. Doubt about the signature on the date alteration, on the cheque tendered in Sauchihall Street, cast further suspicion on the possibility that whoever murdered Cameron may have made this trip. With all available evidence indicating that someone known to him had murdered Cameron, we now had to consider that the offender might have been able to induce Cameron to write these cheques. Possibly under duress, if threatened with a firearm, particularly as the pathologist was of the opinion that death had ensued 'some days' before discovery of his body on Wednesday 14th.

Enquiries regarding the first of these five cheques established that it had been tendered in payment for a pair of men's shoes, at David Stanley Shoes, 358, The Strand W.C.2. A new shoebox had been found at 4 Burgh Street but not the shoes it had contained. The part time salesman, who had taken the cheque, was unable to remember the particular transaction, or describe his customer(s). The manager after investigating his till rolls was able to estimate that the sale had probably occurred around 12 noon on Saturday 10th.

Further evidence that Mr Cameron had been shopping in the West End of London, that Saturday morning, was provided by the manager of the hosiery department at the Savoy Taylors Guild, 94 the Strand, W.C.2. a Mr Clover who had been employed there for some 48 years, the last four of which he had known Mr Cameron as an 'Account Customer'. Mr Clover had contacted the Incident Room on reading about the murder and I had personally interviewed him on 16th, the same day that the cheques first came to light. He recalled seeing Mr Cameron in his shop between 11am and 12noon, when he purchased two shirts and four pairs of socks on his account, which was in credit. There has been no conversation regarding Cameron's proposed activities that weekend and he was on his own, as usual.

Enquiries made of BEA at West London Air Terminal, regarding the second cheque, revealed that it had been used there at about 9.30am on Sunday 11th October, to purchase a ticket in the name J.W.Cameron, on the London to Edinburgh Flight BE 5392. The flight was due to leave the West London Terminal at 2.10pm and depart from Heathrow at 3.10pm. Staff were unable to recall the customer who tendered the cheque other than having recorded the name. The passenger had also booked a Return Flight from Edinburgh to London Flight No BE 5413 'Y' for the next day, Monday 12th October. This flight was due to leave Edinburgh at 8.50pm

Further enquiries were also made of British European Airways Accounting Unit in South Ruislip to trace and recover the outward and return flight coupons forming part of the ticket. It was then learnt that the return coupon had been re-validated to be used on the same day as the outward journey i.e. 11th October.

Enquiries regarding the third cheque drawn on Cameron's Account, made payable to 'self' for £5, traced a Mr Leslie Johnson employed by Barclays Bank at the West London Air Terminal Branch. He recalled the cheque being tendered soon after 9am on 11th October and whilst he was unable to recall any details, he was of the opinion the customer must have produced some evidence of identity such as a driving licence, as it was out of normal banking hours. More importantly he recollected the customer as aged 30-35, sallow complexion with hollow cheeks, darkish hair parted on one side. He believed he was carrying a heavy raincoat and had an executive type briefcase. This was a description very similar to the suspect seen loitering outside 4 Burgh Street prior to the murder. Shown a photograph of Mr Cameron, he was unable to recognise him as the customer.

Enquiry at the Midland Bank Branch at Heathrow, regarding the fourth cheque, traced a Mr Brian Charman who recalled being asked by a man, on Sunday 11th October, to cash a cheque for £20 drawn on the Beecham House branch of their bank. On learning that the man did not have an arrangement to cash the cheque and was not in possession of a bankcard, he had sought identification and the customer had produced a driving licence and an airline ticket in the name J.W. Cameron. He was asked to sign the back of the already endorsed cheque and fill in a form giving his name and address, thereafter Mr Charman wrote details of the driving licence and flight number on the form. Needless to say it was James Cameron's details that the suspect had written on the form. Although he was unable to describe the man, Mr Charman did recall him asking which bank in Scotland was affiliated to the Midland Bank. He had informed him it was the Clydesdale Bank.

Norah Mc Ardle was identified as the young Bank Clerk at the Sauchiehall Street Branch of the Clydesdale Bank, in Glasgow, to whom the last of Cameron's cheques had been tendered. Although the date on this cheque had been altered from 11th to 12th October, it was in fact on Tuesday 13th October that this cheque had been presented, sometime between 10am and 11 am. The cheque made payable to 'Cash' in the sum of £20 was presented by a young man, who complied with her request for some form of identification, although she was unsure exactly what documentation he produced. She did however tell the customer she would have to telephone his bank to check there were ample funds, as the maximum allowance was £10. The man mentioned that in London he could draw £20 without the necessity for a phone call. Enquiries were however made and she handed over £20 cash and then asked the man for 3s 6d for the cost of the phone call. The man remarked that this was very cheap for the time of day.

The description of the man given by Miss Mc Ardle was very similar to that of the witnesses in Burgh Street, with the exception that she was better able to put an age to the suspect – about 22/23 years. She described him as clear spoken and polite, but without a noticeable accent. What struck this witness most was that he bore a remarkable similarity to a male acquaintance of hers. With the assistance of officers from Glasgow, who had interviewed Miss Mc Ardle on our behalf, this acquaintance agreed to pose for a photograph and when viewed by us it bore a remarkable likeness to the photo fit picture of our witnesses.

With the assistance of police in Edinburgh, BEA staff at Turnhouse Airport, Edinburgh, who had dealt with the return flight, were traced and interviewed. When shown the return portion of the ticket used by the suspect, Mr Andrew Erskine a Traffic Assistant recalled having accepted this ticket from a passenger and subsequently noticed it was for the following day. With some 108 passengers on the flight in order to save time he had not followed normal procedure for re-validating the ticket, but had made the manual alteration of the date from 12th to 11th. When spoken to the passenger had informed him that he had completed his business quicker than anticipated and wished to return to London as soon as possible. Shown photographs of both Cameron and the photo-fit of the suspect he was unable to recognise either or provide any sort of description of the passenger.

At this stage of the murder enquiry it was evident that the suspect seen loitering and calling at Cameron's house on Friday and Saturday 9th and 10th October, appeared identical with the person who had used Cameron's cheques. The cheques used to fly to Edinburgh on the morning of Sunday 11th and then return to London later that night, only to be sighted back in Scotland on Tuesday 13th, at the Clydesdale bank in Glasgow.

The shopping trip to the Strand, complemented by his neighbour's sighting of him alighting from a taxi with some shopping around noon, was to prove the last sighting of Cameron. Continuing 'House to House' enquiries had traced an elderly Italian lady, resident at No 1 Burgh Street who claimed to have been woken from her sleep in her rear attic bedroom at about 3am on Sunday 11th, by the sound of men shouting and fighting and a call for help. She had then heard a noise like a revolver shot after which everything went quiet. She had been too frightened to look out of her window or call anyone but knew the sounds had come from nearby. A further witness had been traced who had seen a man answering the description of our suspect, at 9.30am on Monday 12th, as she was pushing a pram along Danbury Street. The man had walked out of Burgh Street in a hurry, almost colliding with her pram. If this were in fact the suspect, it would indicate he might have returned to the scene for some reason.

In an endeavour to trace potential witnesses, who may have seen or spoken to our suspect on either of the two flights he had used, further enquires were directed towards BEA to establish the identities of other passengers. It soon became apparent however, that only in the case of persons who had made prior bookings, would there be a paper trail to trace these passengers. Where tickets had been paid for in cash on the day of travel only passenger names would be traceable. BEA provided a seating plan of the Vanguard 951, which had been used on the two flights. Where witnesses were traced, not only were they shown photographs of Cameron and the photo-fit of the suspect, but they were also invited to indicate the seating positions, their personal description and that of any accompanying passengers, in their statements.

Soon after the Fingerprint examination of the Cameron's house and contents had been completed, I had been informed by a Senior Officer of fingerprint Branch, that a good number of the finger impressions they had lifted, appeared to be from the same person. These marks had not been eliminated as having been made by Cameron or anyone else with known legitimate access to the premises. They were confident therefore that if they belonged to anyone with a criminal conviction recorded, they would soon be able to identify them and a dedicated team were working on this task. This was good news to all on the investigating team and certainly raised expectations that our enquiries may yet prove fruitful.

A few days later I received another phone call from the same Senior Officer at Fingerprint Branch, this time he informed me that his team had identified a suspect. This suspect, who I will refer to as Peter Bailey although this is not his real name, resided in Essex at a coastal resort not far from Southend. A small team from within our squad were then tasked to draw Bailey's Criminal Record File, in order to obtain as much background information regarding him and his habits as possible and then effect his arrest. This objective was achieved first thing the following morning and Bailey was brought to Islington Police Station for interview. Questioned about Cameron, Bailey admitted having met him and claimed to have stayed at his house for a few weeks whilst indulging in a homosexual relationship with him. He claimed Cameron had met him at a location frequented by homosexuals and invited him back to his address after which he had stayed on, but Cameron had terminated this arrangement a few weeks prior to the murder.

Nothing had been found at Bailey's premises which could be identified as Cameron's property, various items of clothing were seized and submitted to the Forensic Science Laboratory for examination, although none bore any visible signs of blood staining or firearm residue. Although witnesses had given differing heights for the suspect seen waiting for Cameron, most had agreed the photo-fit was a good likeness, but it could not be said to resemble Peter Bailey. Further enquiries were therefore made to check on Bailey's movements, as related by him for the weekend of the murder. During subsequent questioning Bailey recalled that whilst staying at 4 Burgh Street, a Police Officer had called at the premises making enquiries of Mr Cameron about another man who was wanted by police. Having been told the man was no longer staying there, the officer had spoken to him, to confirm his identity, which had made Cameron angry.

Whilst I was not involved in the interviews with Bailey, on hearing of this I recalled the remark Bill Wooding had made to me, as we drove into Burgh Street on the first visit to the murder scene. Bill – who had not been deployed on the Murder team but engaged on routine crime investigations – was consulted and was then able to confirm that Peter Bailey was the man he had seen at the house. This was almost as good as providing Bailey with an alibi, for it established that his fingerprints – found only on mundane items around the house – could have been in place prior to the murder. Although we still had to check Bailey's movements for the relevant times and await completion of the forensic examination of his clothing, this proved a great help in eliminating him from the enquiry.

Although our hopes of success had been raised and then dashed within a few days, the fingerprint identification of Bailey was not wasted, for it had enabled us to trace someone who could tell us more about the seamier side of Cameron's life. It was apparent from our enquiries to date that Cameron certainly enjoyed good food and was well known in restaurants around the Warren Street and Tottenham Court Road area of the West End of London, where enquiries were currently being made. What we had been lacking was knowledge of where he frequented to meet other homosexuals. Bailey was able, not only to fill us in on these details, but agreed to help our enquiry by taking officers to point out some of the establishments and locations Cameron may have frequented, where photographs of Cameron and our suspect were shown. To this end Bailey was happy to remain in custody at Islington for a few days more, whilst these enquiries were made and pending completion of forensic examination of his clothing, doubtless relieved at the prospect of being cleared as a murder suspect.

Enquires meanwhile to trace passengers on either of the two flights, had met with some success, resulting in a Miss Gillian MacMeekan an assistant editor with a London Publishing House, being interviewed by Detective Constable Chris Abbey. Shown the suspect's photo-fit picture, Miss MacMeekan who was on the return flight from Edinburgh following a visit to her parents, recognised the picture as that of a man who had sat next to her on the plane and engaged her in conversation during the flight. She was also able to identify her seating position, which faced towards the rear of the aircraft and the majority of the other passengers.

The man sitting in the middle seat next to her, had told her he worked for a chemical company which she felt sure was Beechams, either in sales or marketing. Asked where he worked he'd informed her it was Nottingham. He also spoke of having recently worked for Imperial Leather soap at one time He told her he had flown from London that morning and travelled by train to meet some friends at Kilmarnock but had to return to London for business. He had a Scottish accent similar to a Kilmarnock one, according to Miss MacMeeekan. During the flight this man had also spoken about flying solo, from which she understood that he was just learning, although he had not mentioned a particular flying school. She described the man as aged about 25 years, 5' 8" to 5' 9"; slim build; pale complexion; thin features; dark straight hair parted on one side but not as thick as the photo fit and with slightly longer sideboards. He was dressed in a dark suit shirt and tie and as he left the aircraft he carried a small briefcase and a mac but had no luggage.

We were fortunate to trace two other passengers who recognised the photo-fit picture as that of a fellow passenger. Mr Martin Findley a Director of Whitbreads Brewery, returning to his London home that evening, had sat in the aisle seat of row seven, on the left, or port side of the aircraft. He recalled a man coming onto the plane very late and sitting in the block of seats on the starboard side in row six. The man sat in the middle seat facing the rear of the plane next to a young lady (Miss MacMeekan) in the aisle seat.

Mr Findley saw the man place a brief case and coat on the luggage rack, before asking the lady if he could get a newspaper on the plane. When he left his seat to get a paper, Mr Findley had asked the man if he would mind getting him one, which he had done. Later he was aware that the man carried on a long conversation with the lady next to him, during which time he ordered a beer for himself and the young lady. Mr Findley gave a similar description as that given by Miss Mac Meekan, although he put the man's age as 28 to 32 years.

The other passenger a Mr Malcolm Mc Dougall, a journalist was travelling from his home in Scotland to London, which necessitated him taking the flight. He sat in the row of seats directly opposite and facing the suspect and the young lady in the aisle seat. His attention was drawn to the man because he bore a remarkable likeness to a former colleague and fellow journalist. He saw that this man had engaged the young lady beside him in conversation and bought her a drink. Mr Mc Dougall who had been interviewed, with the assistance of officers from Glasgow was shown the photo fit picture of our suspect which he did not consider to be the best likeness to the man he had seen, he therefore agreed to compile a photo-fit picture of the man himself.

This latest photo-fit picture was in fact very similar in facial shape and features to the one witness in Islington had compiled, with the exception that the suspect's hair parting was on the opposite side. Whilst the original photo-fit had been released to the press and received limited publicity, the suspect still remained unidentified. Confident that our photo-fit had proved good enough to trace witnesses on the flight, there was a need for more widespread publicity. With the assistance of our Press Bureau, it was arranged for the Cameron murder to be featured on a Police Five Special, television broadcast, hosted by Shaw Taylor.

The programme was broadcast on 22nd November some five weeks after the event. Shaw outlined the location of Burgh Street and the circumstances surrounding the last sightings of Cameron; the discovery of his body; sightings of the suspect in that vicinity and the flight made to Edinburgh, including details of the conversation with Miss MacMeekan on the return flight. Finally the photo-fit picture of the suspect was shown to viewers, whilst Shaw Taylor read out his description and appealed for anyone who thought they might recognise him, to contact our Incident Room.

A total of eighty-four calls were received in the next few days following the appeal, from people in various parts of the country. The remarks to Miss Mac Meekan on the flight, about his having flown solo, resulted in calls from members of flying clubs. There were calls from people who thought the suspect resembled a work colleague or someone at their sports club. There was however one which immediately aroused my interest, as I read through them endeavouring to prioritise the follow up enquiries. This message had come from a young salesman, Martin Burgon, employed by Vauxhall Stores Ltd., which had premises in Vauxhall Bridge Road and Wilton Street, London, S.W.1. The gist of the message was that during mid-October, he had sold an umbrella to a man fitting the description of our suspect. The man had paid by cheque and when asked for proof of his identity he had produced a Firearms Certificate, details of which Mr Burgon had recorded on the rear of the cheque which had subsequently been returned from the bank, marked 'Refer to drawer'. This seemed almost too good to be true and I would happily have dropped everything and gone out and interviewed Mr Burgon and pursued this enquiry myself, but that was not my role. I had enough to do reading all the messages and statements emanating from the enquiry and raising further actions there from.

One of the officers seconded to the murder squad, was a young Detective Sergeant, Brian Belch who had been loaned from Thames Division. We had not met before and I had been interested to discuss his role on Thames Division and the different types of crime he found himself investigating on the river. It was apparent that he was not as busy as he had been previously, when working in the East End of London. Brian had impressed me by the diligent and enthusiastic manner in which he pursued his enquiries, doubtless pleased to have his feet back on the ground and to be on a murder squad. I was anxious that the enquiry regarding the purchase of the umbrella was pursued with all due diligence and so allocated this enquiry to him.

Brian interviewed Mr Burgon and took a detailed statement from him regarding the transaction. It transpired that around the middle of October whilst working at the Wilton Street Branch, the customer had selected a gentleman's umbrella and then asked if he could pay by cheque, which Mr Burgon had accepted, subject to needing proof of identity. The man had then asked whether a Firearms Certificate would suffice and Mr Burgon had agreed and at this point his interest in this particular customer was raised, as he himself had an interest in guns and was a member of a sporting club. When the customer tendered the Firearms Certificate with his cheque, Mr Burgon asked him whether he preferred a revolver or an automatic, to which the man had replied that he used a revolver. Mr Burgon had then asked the customer if he shot a good score with the revolver and he had replied that his score was in the 80's, which Mr Burgon knew to be a good score. He had then asked him what make of gun he used and the man said that he was going to get a .38 with a 2" barrel. Thinking this unusual Mr Burgon asked the man how he was going to hit a target with such a gun and the man had replied that, 'you didn't have to hit the target as long as you were shooting at it – that was the important thing'. Mr Burgon was somewhat puzzled by this reply as he knew that such a short barrelled gun would be inaccurate and was designed for use only at close range.

There was some further discussion between the two of them regarding the timing of applications for firearms Certificates, from which Mr Burgon learnt that the customer had applied for his firearms Certificate in Scotland. The name of the firearms club to which the man belonged was also mentioned, but Mr Burgon could not remember the name other than that it was in the North of England. The man had written his address on the back of the cheque and Mr Burgon added the firearms Certificate Number. He later learnt that the cheque had not been honoured and was returned by the bank, where after it had been forwarded to Cheque Indemnity Ltd., a debt collection agency. He was unable to recall the name of the customer.

When Mr Burgon had watched the 'Police Five Special' programme, he realised the customer answered the description given of the murder suspect. Not only was his facial appearance similar, but also his physical appearance and attire included the fact that he wore dark glasses. He was sure he would recognise the man if he saw him again.

Naturally there was great interest amongst members of the murder squad when Detective Sergeant Belch returned with Mr Burgon's statement. Not only were we on the trail of someone who physically resembled our suspect and was dressed the same and in possession of an umbrella, but also this was someone familiar with firearms with a Scottish connection.

Cheque Indemnity Ltd., were a London based company that specialised in recovering, or attempting to recover money or assets, by tracing persons who had tendered dishonoured cheques in payment for goods. Many small businesses subscribed to this organisation, paying an annual fee for which they were guaranteed to receive a small percentage of their loss, on any given cheque, whether or not Cheque Indemnity were able to recover funds. The majority of such cheques were 'Refer to drawer' cheques where a customer did not have sufficient funds in his account to meet payment. We were fortunate that the cheque tendered by the suspect had been forwarded to this company as they worked closely with police. It was with little difficulty that Det. Sgt Belch making follow up enquiries, was able to recover the relevant cheque, together with another four drawn on the same account; all recently tendered at other London locations.

The cheque in question was found to relate to an account at the Meadows Branch of Barclays Bank Limited, 1, Arkwright Street, Nottingham, in the name M. Bennett. The cheque made payable to Vauxhall Stores Limited was dated 2nd October and Signed 'M. Bennett', with the address 'Western Boulevard, Whitemoor, Nottingham', in the same handwriting on the back. Also written on the back was the words 'Firearm Cert No 98', which Mr Burgon subsequently confirmed as his writing, the cheque being the one, tendered in payment for the umbrella.

Recovery of this cheque was to generate a number of enquiries not only to trace John Ernest Bennett, as the bank confirmed was his full name, but also to establish his movements both immediately before and after the murder. The four other cheques recovered from Cheque Indemnity Ltd., were all for small purchases in central London stores between 15th September and 5th October 1970. Enquiry of Barclays bank however, revealed that there had been insufficient funds to meet cheque payments since August and some twenty nine cheques had been drawn on the account since then, all of which had been returned marked 'Refer to drawer'.

Five of the unpaid cheques had been used for the purchase of rail tickets from British Rail and it was learnt that a Detective Sergeant Burkett of the British Rail Police had been making enquiries to trace the person responsible. Brian Belch therefore contacted this officer and learnt that he had established that Bennett was employed at the British Sugar Corporation, at Colwick, Nottingham and with the assistance of officers from the Nottinghamshire Combined Constabulary, arrangements were in hand to effect his arrest. On learning of this development I instructed Brian to liaise with the officers concerned and hold back from arresting Bennett for the cheque offences, until I had chance to update Bill Wright on this development.

Although Bill Wright was the Senior Investigating Officer, he still had divisional responsibilities. Once the investigation had been set up and was running to his satisfaction, he was able to return to his office at Kings Cross and keep in touch with the enquiry by phone making periodic visits to read statements and discuss progress. I was happy to manage the day to day running of the enquiry but knew we had reached a stage where his further involvement was necessary, so I telephoned him and arranged an urgent meeting at Islington. Once he had been fully apprised of the situation it was agreed that the officers in Nottingham should be requested to effect Bennett's initial arrest, but that once in custody he should not be questioned regarding the cheque offences but be detained pending interview by us regarding the murder.

What did please me was that Bill Wright requested that Brian Belch and I both accompany him to Nottingham once the arrest had been effected. Having been primarily office bound for the past six weeks as Office Manager, there had been little opportunity for me to become involved in outside enquiries. I was however fully conversant with all aspects of the enquiries to date and I immediately set about filling my briefcase with a set of statements, photographs and any item I thought would be of assistance in interviewing our suspect away from the Incident Room location.

At 2.30pm on Thursday 3rd December 1970, Detective Officer Brian Marshall, stationed at Hyson Green Police Station, Nottingham, accompanied by Detective Sergeant Dennis Burkett of the British Rail Police visited the premises of the British Sugar Corporation, at Colwick, Nottingham and there saw John Ernest Bennett. Marshall cautioned Bennett and told him he was making enquiries about a number of cheques passed by Bennett, which had not been honoured, by the bank. Bennett replied that he was expecting an insurance policy to come up but there had been some trouble with it. He was then arrested and conveyed to Police Headquarters, where he was told he would be detained pending the arrival of officers from the Metropolitan Police. Amongst property in his possession when searched was a pair of sunglasses; a Firearms Certificate No FC 98; a cheque book drawn on Barclays Bank and a piece of paper bearing details of amounts paid on his cheques.

Detective Officer Marshall established that the firearm subject of the Certificate had in fact been sold to a local gunsmith in Mansfield Road, he therefore visited these premises and recovered a Star 9mm Automatic Pistol, from the proprietor.

Once informed that Bennett's arrest had been effected we drove up to Nottingham where later that evening we liaised with Brian Marshall and his senior officers. A girlfriend of Bennett was in attendance at the station and after a brief interview with her she handed me a black umbrella which belonged to Bennett. Due to the lateness of the hour it was decided that we would not commence an interview with Bennett that night. The following morning Brian Marshall handed me the various items of property he had taken from Bennett, including the pistol recovered from the gunsmith. At 10.15am in company with Brian Belch and me, Bill Wright commenced interviewing Bennett, whilst I recorded notes of the conversation.

Meeting our suspect for the first time, it was interesting to study his face and compare his features to those of the photo-fit impression. There were marked similarities, although his hair was parted slightly higher and more off the forehead. He was 24 years old a native of Cupar in Fife, well-spoken and neatly attired, unlike the average person of his age that finds himself being interviewed by police. I'm sure both Bill Wright and Brian Belch must have shared my sense of excitement and anticipation as to how the interview would progress. Particularly as to what explanation might be given for the manner in which Cameron had met his end, for there seemed little doubt that we had finally come face to face with his killer.

After introducing us, Bill Wright informed Bennett that that he was making enquiries into the death of James William Cameron whose body had been found at his home address, – 4, Burgh Street, Islington, on Wednesday 14th October 1970. He then showed Bennett a photograph of Cameron; this was not a crime scene photograph but an enlargement of his passport photograph that we had been using to show potential witnesses throughout our enquiry. Bennett was then asked whether he knew the man, which he denied. He agreed that he knew Islington but denied knowing a man named Cameron. Asked when he was last in Scotland he replied that it was about the end of September the beginning of October. He confirmed that his parents lived in Scotland and that he was married. He was then questioned about a man whose business card was found in his possession and was asked whether the man was a homosexual, which he denied. Bill Wright then asked Bennett whether he himself was homosexual, and he said he was not. Referring to the sunglasses he had on him when arrested, he was asked whether he wore them often, he confirmed that he did, stating his eyes were sensitive to the sunlight.

He was then asked where he had been living recently and stated he had stayed a few nights in bed and breakfast and had also stayed at his shooting club. When asked if he had flown from Edinburgh to London on the evening of Sunday 11th October, and spoken to a woman passenger, Bennett replied, "Yes I bought her a lager."

Bill Wright said, "You must have met Cameron then?"

Bennett replied, "I met a gentleman called Cameron, yes."

He then went on to confirm that it was at the end of September, at which point Bill Wright cautioned him, before being asking him if he had been to Cameron's house. Having confirmed that he had, he was again shown the photograph of Cameron and then said, "Yes that's him."

Bennett was then shown the Star Pistol and asked if it was his and after examining it, he agreed that it was. In answer to further questions he said he had sold the gun because he was short of money and had last fired it about three months previous. He claimed to have used up all the ammunition he had, at the Trent range.

Bill Wright then showed him the umbrella handed over by his girlfriend, which he agreed was his and when asked where he obtained it, he admitted using one of his cheques to purchase it in London.

Bill Wright then said, "Did you sleep with Cameron?'

To which Bennett replied, "He suggested the first night I go to bed with him. I declined and slept on the sofa."

He was then asked what the background was to his knowing Cameron. Bennett then related that his wife had left him and their two young children in April, and gone off with her uncle. He had been unable to cope but with the assistance of his parents made arrangement for the children to be looked after while he came to London looking for his wife. He stated he had found out where she had been and telephoned her a few times, but she didn't get in touch. After staying with some friends in Nottingham he became depressed and fed up and returned to London. Eventually he became short of money and stated he met people in pubs who offered him places for the night and one night he had met Cameron.

Bill Wright then said, "Where did you meet?"

Bennett replied, "I came out of a pub in Tottenham Court Road and bumped into him. He was drunk, he asked me where I was going and I said 'Euston'. He said he was going the same way. I told him of my difficulties and he was sympathetic. He offered to let me stay with him. I realised he was queer but thought I could look after myself. We took a taxi back to his place, He came straight out with it and offered me the choice of sleeping on the couch or with him. I declined and slept on the couch. In the morning I went off. He said 'Come back at any time'. I then went to Scotland."

Bill Wright said, "did you see Cameron again?'

Bennett replied, "Yes, it was late at night. He sympathised with my difficulty and offered to help, and that was that. I read in the paper he was dead. I didn't want to be involved."

The interview then continued as follows:

Q. When was it that you saw him again?'
A. "On the Friday before I read about it. I stayed there that night and on the Saturday night also. On the Saturday he said he was expecting someone on the Sunday, a Portuguese. He also said that he was expecting an old friend from the country."
Q. "Did you take anything from him?"
A. "Yes some cheques."
Q. "Where is the driving licence?"
A. "I threw it away."
Q. "Did you tie him up?"
A. "I didn't tie him up that man is big."
Q. "You were involved weren't you?"
A. "I was involved, yes."
Q. "How were you involved?"
A. "I knew him, I had some of his cheques which I used."
Q. "Where is the cheque book now?'
A. "I threw it out of the train."
Q. "What train?"
A. "Between Edinburgh and London."
Q. "How many cheques were left in the book?"
A. "About three or four."
Q. "Where did you use the other cheques?"
A. "I cashed one at the air terminal, one for a ticket and one in Glasgow."
Q "Where is the briefcase?"
A. "I threw it in the Trent."
Q. "Whereabouts?"

Fortunately there was a large area map on one wall of the interview room and Bennett was asked to pin point the location. He indicated a point on the river Trent by a railway bridge.

By this time I felt confident that we had our man. Whilst Bennett had not yet been asked directly about the murder, he was by his answers gradually incriminating himself by his admissions, which were clearly the actions of a guilty man who had stolen from the deceased. I had not previously been involved in any investigation with Detective Chief Superintendent Wright, but I was pleased that he had approached the interview with Bennett in a similar vein to how I would have done. I was a great believer in skirting around the minor issues in the first instance and letting a suspect commit himself to giving answers to what may seem innocuous or irrelevant questions. This not only served to get a suspect talking but also tended to make him feel more relaxed and so likely to be unguarded about his answers. Unless the burden of guilt is such that a suspect could not wait to confess to his crime, I would have expected most people in Bennett's position to deny being responsible for the murder, certainly in the first instance. Mentally however, I would have expected them to prepare an explanation for having come under suspicion, or being known to have been at the scene of the crime. In such cases they would hope to convince an interviewing officer of their innocence by answering questions truthfully, lying about only those they felt might directly implicate them. What they could not do is anticipate every little question and its significance in establishing the truth.

As the interview continued Bennett admitted that he had put stones in the briefcase to ensure it sank and that it had also contained about six neckties. He also admitted throwing away his own shoes and which he claimed had worn out and selling a pair of desert boots to a local second-hand shop. When asked about Cameron's shoes he admitted to throwing them in the canal together with a shirt, which he claimed Cameron had given him with the ties, but which was too small for him.

Bennett also denied taking any money from Cameron, but claimed to have been given a couple of pounds the first time he met him. Asked when he last left the house, Bennett stated it was six o'clock on the Sunday morning after which he had walked to the West London Air Terminal. He claimed that having flown to

Turnhouse Airport he had taken a taxi to Edinburgh. When asked where he had gone in Edinburgh, Bennett replied, "I just waited around. I tried to phone Mr. Cameron several times but got no answer." Asked if he had the gun with him he said, "No, I hid it before I left Nottingham."

The interview then continued as follows:

Q. Are you a member of a flying club?"
A. "Yes, I am a member of the gliding Association.
Q. 'What went wrong whilst you were in London?"
A. "Well things went wrong after I got married. We went to a friend's wedding and then to a local dance hall. My wife was acting funny and wanted to stay up there in Scotland. I didn't want to as I already had a good job in Nottingham. We had been talked out of getting married, but after the baby was born we did. Later we had a son who died, so I wouldn't want to kill anyone."
Q. "Weren't you short of money?'
A. "I was bumming along all right."
Q. "Did he upset you?"
A. "No, he was pleasant."
Q. "Why did you return Sunday?"
A. "I rang him several times, I couldn't get any answer. I knew something was wrong. I went back to the house on Sunday night but couldn't get in."
Q. "Are you sure you didn't go in?"
A. "I didn't go in I knocked and there was no reply."
Q. "Were you in Burgh Street on Monday morning?"
A. "No."
Q. "Where were you?"
A. "I was looking around various dry cleaning shops for my wife. I saw her on one occasion come out of a shop in the West End, but she said she wasn't my wife and spoke with a foreign accent. I am sure now it was her. On the Monday night I went to Glasgow by train."

Bennett then started crying.

Asked by Mr Wright why he was so upset Bennett said, "I am prepared to admit that I am mentally upset by my wife leaving me, but I didn't kill him, I didn't rob him, I didn't tie him up." Mr Wright then said, "Why did you say you didn't rob him?"

To which Bennett replied, "I thought that was what you inferred when you asked me about his belongings."

Mr Wright then asked, "Did he want to be tied up?"

Bennett replied, "No, he wanted me to go to bed with him, but I declined."

He was then asked a number of questions regarding how he came to acquire the ties and shirts from Cameron, which he claimed he had been given. He denied taking any new shirts from the premises. When asked whether he had had a bath whilst at the house, Bennett said, "He offered me a bath but I didn't want to have one in case he came and tried to mess me about. I was worried about it."

The interview then continued as follows:

Q.   "Did you turn any drawers out?"

A.   "I was in the living room, I spent the night there"

Q.   "Where was he when you left him last?"

A.   "He came down and let me out and locked the door behind me."

Q.   "What about the previous nights?"

A.   "He always adopted the same procedure. He would see me to the door and ask me to call at any time."

Q.   "How did you get him to write the cheques out?"

A.   "He offered to help me. He wanted me to go to bed with him. He said he would give me anything. I told him I wanted to visit my parents in Scotland."

Q.   "Where did you get the briefcase from?"

A.   "He gave it to me."

Q.   "Did you empty all the contents over the bedroom floor?"

A.   "No I don't remember where the briefcase was. He was alive all the time I was in the house. When I called there on Saturday he was entertaining someone and he asked me to call back. I called back at 5 o'clock and he said he was going out, so I called about half past ten to quarter to eleven. There was a party going on across the road."

Q. "What time did you call there on Sunday night?"

A. "About 11.30."

Q. " Where did you sleep that night?"

A. "I went to the Adelphi Hotel, I had some cash. I used the name Duncan, it's a family name."

Q. "Where did you get the money from?"

A. "From cashing his cheques."

Q. "Did he give you some shoes?"

A. "Yes."

Q. 'What did you do with your old shoes?"

A. "I put them in the briefcase and threw them away in York."

Q. "Why take them all the way to York to throw them away?"

A. "I don't know."

Q. "Did you have intercourse with him?"

A. "No, I didn't."

Q. "Are you willing to be medically examined if necessary?"

A. "Yes, all he ever said was that he liked young boys and he said he liked fucking men. He told me to sort out my problems and come back on the Monday and live with him, he was to get me a job with his firm. He said it was Beechams. He also said he had a wife in Australia."

Q. "Why did you stop looking for your wife?"

A. "Because she got in touch with the welfare people and I came back to Nottingham and tried to pick up the threads. I knew you would eventually find me but I hoped you would catch somebody else for it. I know it's only circumstantial the evidence leading up to me."

This last reply was to confirm my suspicion that Bennett, knowing there were no witnesses to the murder and being intelligent enough to realise that Cameron's life style would throw up any number of potential suspects, thought he could get away with it. To this end, he was prepared to explain away his involvement with Cameron and the use of his cheques. We had yet to pursue fully the matter of the recently recovered pistol that Bennett had owned at the time of the murder, which hopefully, could be identified as the weapon that had fired the fatal round. Whilst he might have known there had been insufficient time to have it test fired and comparisons made with the murder bullet, I felt he must surely realise this would occur. I was curious as to how he expected to resolve this issue; little did I know that there was a reason for his apparent confidence about this. Similar thoughts may well have been going through Chief Superintendent Wright's mind at that point, for his questions then turned to that subject.

Q. 'When you fire your gun, does it make a loud bang?"
A. "Yes, I know, I fired it once in my house and know it makes a bang, it nearly deafened me."
Q. "Did you shoot Cameron?"
A. "I don't remember doing it."
Q. "Why did you go with him to this house of you thought he was homosexual?"
A. "I let him pick me up, I thought I could handle myself, I can use karate."
Q. "Did you have the gun with you when you were at Cameron's house?"
A. "No, I had it in three parts and hidden at the shooting club."
Q. "Did you go to bed with Cameron?"
A. "He invited me up to his bedroom. I told you I declined."
Q. "Did you dine with him."
A. "All I had there was a coffee."
Q. "Did you get drunk?"
A. "No, when I was there on the Saturday afternoon there were about two glasses of scotch in the bottle. He had one and I had one. I remember that when I called there on the Sunday night and got no answer, I was walking away and across the road was a big Rover car with two men in it, one got out and this car drove up past me, one of the men had walked over towards Cameron's house. The man in the car followed me up to Pentonville Road. I think it was a blue Rover. The driver was a young man my age with blond hair and tough

looking. I got a taxi to the Station and this car passed me again in the taxi. I left the taxi and walked up a side street and lost the chap that was following me and then I got a taxi again."

Q. "Why did you use the name Duncan at the Adelphi Hotel?"

A. "I thought people would be looking for me because I had gone off and left my children and I had been using bad cheques and I wanted time to get myself together."

Bennett was then asked if he would take us to the River Trent and the canal and point out exactly where he had thrown articles away, which he agreed to do.

A short while later Bennett was accompanied by Detective Chief Superintendent Wright and Detective Sergeant Belch to a police vehicle, on entering the vehicle Bennett said,

"Can I make a full statement? I would like to tell you all about it?"

Mr Wright said, "Are you now admitting Shooting Cameron?"

Bennett replied, "Yes, but I would like to explain how it happened."

Mr. Wright then cautioned him and told him he could make a written statement on their return. Bennett replied "I must also tell you that I altered the rifling of the gun before I sold it."

Asked by Mr Wright, how he had done this he said, "With a file. If you examine the gun you will see for yourself."

Having entered a second police vehicle accompanied by local officers, I was unaware of this conversation as we drove to a railway bridge over the River Trent, where Bennett was to indicate where he had thrown the briefcase into the river. As we alighted from the vehicles I could see a very satisfied grin on the face of Brian Belch as he beckoned me over, before imparting details of Bennett's admission, so I could share in the satisfaction of knowing for certain we finally had our man.

Once Bennett had pointed out the exact spot from where he had thrown the briefcase I remained there with officers of Nottingham Constabulary's Underwater Search Unit, who had been briefed to conduct a search for the briefcase. This search was however to be without success. Bennett meanwhile directed the others to a railway siding near Castle Boulevard, which had a canal running alongside it. He pointed out a high wall over which he claimed to have thrown some shoes and a little further along the shirt. He was unsure whether these items had gone into the canal on the far side of the wall, as he had not heard a splash. Gaining access to the towpath of the canal the shirt was found hanging on a bush and identified by Bennett, as he admitted having torn off the label. A little further along, a pair of gent's brown shoes were recovered from some thick grass, where they had fallen. Inside one shoe was a pen, which Bennett admitted had belonged to Cameron.

Bennett was then returned to Nottingham Police Headquarters where he elected to make a written statement under caution, which was taken down by Brian Belch. In his statement Bennett related how he had first literally bumped into Cameron on the late evening of Thursday 29th September, after leaving a public house in Tottenham Court Road, much the same as he had outlined in his previous interview. Having stayed that night on the settee at Cameron's house, he had left at 6am the following morning, as requested by his host, who had told him "I like to be discreet, will you leave when I get the alarm call."

Bennett claimed he'd been invited to return at any time and had done so on the evening of Friday 9th October, only to find Cameron was not at home on the two occasions he had visited. He had then returned the following afternoon and spoken with Cameron who advised him from his bedroom window that he was occupied, but suggested Bennett return at 5pm. On this later occasion he was received by Cameron in his dressing gown and they having consumed a glass of scotch, Bennett was requested to return at about 10.30pm – 11pm. Bennett duly complied with this request and was let into the house at 11pm by Cameron who was in his dressing gown and pyjamas.

Bennett claimed that Cameron had propositioned him saying, "There is the settee but I prefer it if you come to my bed." Bennett said that he having declined this offer – telling Cameron, "I'm not like that, I'll sleep on the settee." Cameron had told him he was very disappointed with him and felt that owing to his circumstances, he should have been willing to share his bed. Then having brought a pillow and some blankets Cameron had attempted to embrace him. Bennett stated that after he had pushed Cameron off, he had gone off to bed whilst he himself settled down to sleep on the settee having removed just his coat, boots, jacket and tie.

It was alleged by Bennett that he subsequently awoke, to find the light was on and Cameron was sitting beside him, fondling Bennett's private parts, whilst leaning over and kissing his forehead and cheeks. Pushing him off, Bennett had threatened to leave if Cameron refused to desist, whereupon Cameron had continued trying to embrace him saying he needed to have a boy that night.

Bennett stated that he had left his gun inside a blue bank bag, within the fold of his coat, which was on a chair beside the settee. Feeling sick and upset, he felt unable to handle Cameron who made yet another move upon him, so he took out his gun, cocked back the hammer and pointed it at Cameron, telling him to stand back. Cameron had allegedly laughed saying "You won't shoot me, I bet the gun isn't even loaded." Bennett stated that he had four bullets in the magazine, so he loaded a bullet into the chamber by pulling back the slide, thus cocking the gun, after which he claimed to have put the safety catch on. This had the effect of quietening down Cameron who went and sat down by a bureau, whilst Bennett proceeded to put his boots on, intimating he was leaving. According to Bennett, Cameron begged him not to leave, offering to give him anything he wanted if he would go to bed with him.

At this point Bennett told Cameron he needed to go to Scotland and asked how much money he had. Cameron not having very much on him had allegedly offered to write a cheque for an air ticket if Bennett went to bed with him and then wrote out a cheque to B.E.A. in the sum of £20, which he had signed. Bennett stated he had informed Cameron the cheque would be no good, whereupon Cameron had insisted it would be and handed over his driving licence, telling him to use it. Bennett admitted to being tempted by this offer, but claimed he declined and told

Cameron he would not go to bed with him and was leaving, which resulted in Cameron saying he would not let him go, as he liked him too much. Bennett stated he had then told Cameron he detested him and would shoot him if necessary, to get out and when Cameron told him this would make too much noise, Bennett claimed he lifted up a pillow, folded it over the gun and said, "It won't make a noise now." Thereafter he made Cameron go upstairs to the bedroom, at gunpoint and when Cameron had intimated he was going to call the police, he told Cameron he was going to tie his hands up.

Bennett alleged that by now Cameron had not only offered him as much money as he wanted and a job at Beechams and was writing furiously in his chequebook asking Bennett how much he wanted. Bennett knowing he could cash a £5 cheque at the Air Terminal claimed he told Cameron to make a cheque out for five pounds. Having done this, Cameron had allegedly told Bennett he would need more than this and would write another cheque for twenty pounds. Bennett claimed that although Cameron was a bit frightened about the gun he continued trying to get Bennett into bed. Having put his chequebook down on a bedside table, he had removed his dressing gown and tucked himself into bed saying he was going to sleep and Bennett could do what he liked.

According to Bennett he has then placed the gun, still inside the pillow, on a chest of drawers and walked over and picked up the chequebook, to see if Cameron had actually written out the cheques. At this point Cameron had lunged at him trying to embrace him, so stepping back, Bennett had retrieved the gun and told Cameron to, lie on his face with his hands behind his back. He had then tied a necktie round his wrists after which he began rummaging through Cameron's belongings. Having told Cameron that there was some nice stuff there, which unfortunately would not fit him, Bennett alleged that Cameron told him about a blue shirt in a drawer that might fit Bennett, as it was too small for him. Having found the shirt Bennett stated he had put this on as well as a pair of socks and then found a newish pair of shoes, which fitted him. He maintained that Cameron kept up a dialogue throughout, in an endeavour to persuade him to join him in the bed but eventually said to Bennett, "Before you go, leave the key in the lock, I'm expecting a friend."

Leaving Cameron on the bed, Bennett said he had gone down to the kitchen and returned with a tin of grapefruit which he had eaten in Cameron's bedroom, the latter declining to eat some himself. After returning to the kitchen Bennett had heard Cameron moving about on the bed and ongoing back up, thought he had been trying to free his hands, so used another tie and a belt to secure them before disconnecting the telephone. He had also gagged Cameron with a handkerchief held in place by a necktie, as he was persisting in talking. Bennett stated that he had then continued with a search of the premises emptying the contents of Cameron's briefcase on the bedroom floor, before placing the shirt, some ties, aftershave and spare socks into it, together with his shoes the cheques and Cameron's driving licence.

Thinking that Cameron might suffocate, Bennett had taken the gag off him and then wiped everywhere he had touched to remove fingerprints, but as Cameron continued talking he decided to re-gag him and claimed to have placed a towel over his head and eyes to shield them from the light. Bennett stated that having taken the briefcase and contents down stairs, he had gone back up to retrieve his gun which was still in the pillow. He then realised he could not hear Cameron breathing, so still holding the gun in the pillow he had leaned over the bed with the pillow touching Cameron's head and the next thing was, the gun went off with a thud.

Bennett sought to explain that as he was wearing gloves, he must have released the safety catch and pulled the trigger at the same time. He denied meaning to kill Cameron, but saw blood on the towel after which he put out the lights, then taking Cameron's keys, he let himself out of the house, taking the keys and the briefcase and contents with him. Knowing the gun was recorded on his certificate he decided he couldn't throw it away but walked to Kings Cross, where he threw the five house keys away in separate locations.

Travelling by underground, Bennett had reached the Air Terminal, then situated at Gloucester Road, where, using Cameron's cheques, he had purchased a return ticket to Edinburgh and obtained five pound in cash. On reaching Heathrow he had cashed the further cheque for twenty pounds before flying to Turnhouse Airport and taking a taxi to Edinburgh. Bennett claimed that, having got a rail ticket to Dundee, in order to confuse matters he had got off at Kirkaldie intending to stay with friends. He had not however left the station, but not wanting to believe that Cameron was dead, he claimed he had telephoned Cameron's house but received no reply. He had then returned to Edinburgh and caught a flight back to London.

Once back in London Bennett claimed that he had gone back to Burgh Street that Sunday night and knocked on Cameron's door. He claims to have seen a man in a car outside and thinking it may be a police officer, he became frightened and scarpered. The next night he had caught a train to Glasgow where he subsequently cashed another of Cameron's cheques for twenty pounds.

Believing police were after him, Bennett said he had been trying to confuse them and had therefore caught a train to Berwick where he had stayed at a bed and breakfast place for one night. Thereafter he had gone to York and finally Nottingham, where he had sold his firearm a fortnight later.

Bennett concluded his written statement by apologising for the pain and trouble caused to Cameron's family before reiterating that he never intended to kill him. Having signed his statement Bennett remarked, "I'm pleased it is over. When I first saw that picture in the daily papers I thought you had published my photograph. I walked round the Market Place that day to see if anyone would identify me, in fact I nearly gave myself up, then I thought I was safe, you didn't know it was me, so I started work yesterday." At this point Detective Chief Superintendent Wright told Bennett he was arresting him for the murder of James Cameron and he would be taken to London to be charged with the offence. After being further Cautioned Bennett intimated that the key to Cameron's briefcase was to be found in his locker at the shooting club. Although I later took possession of this key, the briefcase was never recovered.

How much of Bennett's explanation of what occurred in Cameron's house was true, only he knew. What my colleagues and I did not believe, was his account of how the gun came to be discharged in the pillow behind Cameron's head. It would seem likely that Cameron would have made homosexual overtures to Bennett and doubtless the hospitality of his company and his house was extended with this in mind. Armed with a firearm however, and the element of surprise, Bennett had the upper hand and could have left at any time, or could easily have just robbed Cameron if so minded.

During the subsequent journey back to Islington, Bennett mentioned that he had only taken the gun to London to persuade his wife to return home with him. Not having found her, he said he tried to get a ticket home but the cashier refused to accept his cheque. Why he should volunteer this statement remains unknown. It is hardly likely that he could have used the firearm to persuade his wife to return to him. With regard to the second part of his remark, this would also seem untrue as he had on five occasions purchased rail tickets using his own dishonoured cheques. Two such cheques were used during the period between his first meeting with Cameron and the weekend of the murder. Had he in fact planned to rob Cameron and returned to Nottingham to collect his gun with this venture in mind? All these questions were now a matter for a jury to consider in due course. It was however very satisfying to have reached this stage of our investigation.

Bennett was later charged at Islington Police station and then remanded in custody from Old Street Magistrates Court, pending his Committal for trial at the Old Bailey. In this intervening period, the examination of various exhibits by the Metropolitan Police Forensic Science staff at Holborn was completed. No forensic links to the murder scene were found on any clothing traced to Bennett's possession. The mouth and anal swabs of the deceased taken at post mortem were found to be without trace of any semen, indicating that no sexual activity had taken place around the time of death.

The bullet recovered from Cameron's mattress together with the pillow and Bennett's Star automatic pistol was examined by John Mc Cafferty employed as a Senior Experimental Officer at the Laboratory. He found gunshot damage and associated powder marks on the pillow indicative of the pistol having been fired through the pillow whilst folded around the weapon. The bullet was from a fired round of 9mm pistol ammunition. The pistol was a Spanish 9mm self-loading pistol in good working order. Mr Mc Cafferty found that the rifling in the bore of the barrel showed fresh damage marks consistent with having been caused by a file as described by Bennett. This damage did preclude indisputable identification, by way of comparison of the rifling marks on the murder bullet, with any test rounds Mr Mc Cafferty fired. Significantly it was found that the trigger required a minimum pressure of 4.5 pounds in order to fire the weapon once cocked and the safety thumb catch was effective and in good working order.

The Star pistol had been handed to our Exhibits Officer, Tim Blunden on return from Nottingham and he had dealt with submission of the various items to the Laboratory. It was therefore a pleasant surprise when I later received the Statement of Mr John Mc Cafferty and realised this was the former Detective Inspector who I had first met some fifteen years previous, whilst a Cadet attached to the laboratory at the Old Scotland Yard. It was to be some months later at Bennett's trial before we were to meet again.

Following Bennett's arrest and charge, his wife Karen was traced to an address in Chelsea. She was interviewed by Detective Inspector Pat O'Brien who took a detailed statement from her dealing with her knowledge of her husband and their association, from the time of their first meeting in Cupar in Fife in 1965, until she had finally left him in April 1970. There had been three children of this union the second of which had unfortunately died when aged only three and a half months. Bennett's wife outlined how the marriage had not been a success from the beginning, it being precipitated by the birth of their first child out of wedlock. She had subsequently fallen in love with an older man and left her husband and the children whilst they were living in Nottingham. She later learnt from contact with her husband and her aunt that the children had been taken into care. She was aware that John had been interested in guns since she had first known him, buying and selling a variety of weapons and ammunition and attending a Shooting Club. Despite describing him having a mania for guns she considered him to be of sound mind.

Prior to his arrest for the murder, Bennett had only come to police attention on one previous occasion, on 14th August 1965 a few weeks before his nineteenth birthday; he had been fined £10 in Edinburgh for Loitering with Intent.

His trial for the murder of James William Cameron, commenced at the Central Criminal Court on 29th March 1971 before Mr Justice Eveleigh. Bennett, who was represented by Mr C Salmon and Mr. Ryman of Counsel, pleaded 'Not guilty' to the charge. The prosecution was conducted by J. Mathew of Counsel assisted by Mr R. Hamar of Counsel. The majority of the prosecution evidence was not contested, the defence being primarily that the firearm had been discharged accidentally. John Mc Cafferty was one of the few witnesses called to give evidence in person, so that he might be cross-examined by the Defence. Subsequently whilst Bennett was in the witness box he was asked by his counsel, to demonstrate how he had been holding the pistol before it had 'accidentally' discharged. Bennett was duly handed the firearm exhibit by the court usher and proceeded to demonstrate. At this point the Honourable Mr Justice Eveleigh with a look of alarm on his face, turned to me and said, "could the officer assure members of the Jury and the Court that this gun is not loaded and is perfectly safe?' I was happy to oblige.

On 1st April 1971 the Jury returned a verdict of 'Guilty' on the charge of murder, clearly not having believed Bennett's explanation for what had taken place at Burgh Street. The learned Judge then sentenced Bennett to Life Imprisonment, remarking that at no time throughout the trial had he shown the slightest remorse and he was therefore making a recommendation that he serve a minimum of seventeen years.

Bennett's arrest and subsequent conviction brought a successful conclusion to a protracted enquiry into a horrendous crime. This success however, may not have been achieved without the publicity of the photo-fit picture of the suspect, afforded by the 'Police Five Special' programme. Also the good fortune that it was viewed by Mr Burgon, who was public spirited enough to come forward in response to Shaw Taylor's appeal. For Brian Belch and myself there was some further satisfaction arising from this enquiry, when on the recommendation of Chief Superintendent Wright we were both subsequently awarded a Commendation by the Commissioner for 'Valuable assistance in a case of murder.'

It was not uncommon when a Murder Squad had been running for some time and eventually an arrest had been effected, for there to be a celebratory drink arranged. This was to thank all persons who had served on the Squad and those support services that had played their part in assisting the investigation. Accordingly such a function was arranged to take place in the Fox public house at Islington Green and Shaw Taylor was one of the people invited. It was an enjoyable evening marred only by a power cut, plunging the bar into darkness. We were obliged to continue our drinking by candlelight, an event that Shaw still recalls when we have met for a social drink in recent times and reminisced about past cases.

Some fourteen years after the Cameron murder however, whilst serving on the Flying Squad as a Detective Superintendent, I was reminiscing one evening with two night duty telephonists – both former police officers – just before leaving the yard to make my way home. I mentioned I had previously served at Islington Police Station. One of them then remarked that whilst a Detective Sergeant with the British Transport Police he had been involved with a case involving cheque frauds and his suspect had been pinched off him, as he was wanted at Islington for a murder. To add insult to injury, he had not been invited to the murder squad's celebratory drink after the suspect was charged. He was clearly referring to the Cameron murder. I was flummoxed to say the least, but quickly let him know of my involvement as Office Manager on the case, before he said anything else that might embarrassment either of us. Whilst I could fully justify the murder taking precedent over the cheque offences, there clearly had been an oversight if no one had thought to invite him to the final celebration. Not having had personal contact with him at the time, I had erroneously presumed he was a Nottingham based officer, I could only therefore, offer my belated apologies.

Chapter Eleven

Skeleton in my Cupboard

On 5th April 1971 as part of my career development, I commenced a six week 'Advanced CID Course', at the Metropolitan Police Training Centre, at Peel House in Regency Street, Pimlico, where I found I was one of thirty students of similar rank. Nineteen were from various Constabularies around England and Wales and eleven were from my own force. Four of latter, were Special Branch officers, only one of whom I had met prior to his joining the Branch. Being unacquainted with any of the officers from the various Constabularies, I was pleased to see a few familiar faces, from the remaining officers. They included my old friend Dave Norris who had arrested George Ince for me, back in our aiding days; Dave Hall, who had been a D.C. at Carter Street when I served there and Gordon Maxfield, who I knew from 'Y' Division.

The purpose of the Course was to update us on the various Legislative Acts that had come into operation in recent times as well as to familiarise us with any recent 'Stated Cases' that had affected past legislation. In addition we were to be apprised of the various developments with regard to 'Scenes of Crime' examination and forensic developments and analysis. There was also a 'Media Awareness' element included, as most of us were on the threshold of promotion to Inspector rank, which would inevitably entail involvement in more serious crimes and their subsequent publicity. For the Constabulary Officers this was a residential course, whilst the remainder of us were able to commute to Peel House on a daily basis. As Gordon lived just half a mile from my home we readily agreed to travel together, alternating the driving duties as far as the nearest Underground Station.

As the last course I had attended had been the 'Junior Course' at the Detective Training School, some seven years previous, it was a pleasant break from routine detective work to attend Peel House. In addition to providing an opportunity to learn and discuss some of the anomalies that had arisen from recent legislation, such as the Theft Act of 1968, it gave us the opportunity to get acquainted with, colleagues from around the country. It also provided an opportunity to discuss their particular problems and methods of policing and investigation. By the end of six weeks studying and socialising together, many new friendships and useful contacts had been made by all.

There has always existed a common bond between officers from different parts of the country, who from time to time the need to enlist each other's help. I was shocked therefore some three months later, on 23rd August 1971, by the news that Detective Superintendent Gerald Richardson of Lancashire Constabulary, had been shot dead, after a robbery by an armed gang at a Jeweller's Shop in Blackpool. The lead story in most news media outlined how, following the robbery, a prolonged chase had occurred involving several unarmed police vehicles and Superintendent Richardson had been shot in the stomach whilst attempting to persuade one of the robbers to surrender his weapon. He had died later that day. During the chase, Police Constable Carl Walker, driving a police car had used it to block the path of the robber's car, which was then reversed into the side of his vehicle. Constable Walker had then pursued the robbers on foot until being shot in the groin. The courage and bravery of these two officers was ultimately to result in awards of the George Cross. The media also reported that at least one member of the gang had been arrested.

I was to be even more shocked a couple of days later when on my arrival at Islington Police Station, I read the latest edition of the Police Gazette which gave photographs and descriptions of persons wanted throughout the country for various crimes. The lead item referring to the Blackpool robbery and murder published a photograph of a Francis Sewell who was allegedly responsible for the actual shooting. It also gave details and descriptions of others involved in the offence and finally the name of one of the men that was already in custody for the offence. To my horror I recognised his name as that of my Uncle Dennis, my mother's younger brother.

I had first discovered that my Uncle Dennis was involved in crime when I was a young schoolboy. I became aware something untoward was afoot, by conversations between my parents being abruptly halted when my elder sister Marian or I, entered the living room. On one occasion I noticed my mother fold the local newspaper and place it behind the radio, which occupied a small shelf in a recess beside the fireplace. I knew it must contain something I was not intended to see – not that I was in the habit of reading the local paper at that time. As soon as my mother's back was turned, I retrieved the paper and perused the pages. I did not have to look far before reading about an armed robbery involving the use of pick axe helves and seeing the name of my uncle Dennis as one of those arrested and remanded in custody for the offence. This was a great shock to me and although I confided in Marian, we did not feel able to speak to my parents who clearly wished to conceal events from us.

Although I had seen very little of Dennis during my childhood, I was always pleased to see him, which was usually whilst visiting my grandmother's house in Fernlea Road, Balham. This was probably because one of my earliest recollections in life was at the age of three, being carried to safety by him, down the stairs of the cellar of that house, during the frequent night time Air Raids of the Second World War. My mother was at that time living in the upstairs flat with Marian and I, whilst my father was serving abroad in the army. I also recall Dennis who would have been a teenager at that time, showing me his collection of shrapnel and other war memorabilia. He was to serve a lengthy term of imprisonment in respect of that earlier arrest for robbery, which I was to learn later, was not the first time he had been in trouble.

It would have been about the time I applied to join the Police Cadets, that I first recall discussing, Dennis's criminal past with my parents, as I was concerned that this might in some way impede my application. Fortunately that was not the case and with me serving mainly on the far side of London our paths never crossed. On the few occasions when Dennis was under discussion, my mother whilst not condoning his criminal past, was naturally protective about him, explaining that he was the youngest of five children with four sisters, she being the eldest. Their father had been hospitalised on the other side of London, with Parkinson's disease for some ten years before his death, when Dennis was still a young teenager. It was soon after this that he had become involved with another boy, in breaking into a local shop, despite having attained a place at a local Grammar School. As a child my recollections of Dennis were that of a smartly dressed and well-spoken individual. As a teenager I was saddened to think that his criminal activities had robbed him of so much of his liberty and myself of the only uncle on my mother's side of the family.

Now as a Detective Sergeant with twelve years police service, reading of his arrest for the Blackpool Robbery, I could only be thankful for his sake as well as that of my mother and her sisters, that he was not the one responsible for discharging a firearm. I realised however, he would inevitably be facing a lengthy prison sentence. The Police Gazette item gave contact details of a senior officer on the Flying Squad who was assisting Lancashire Constabulary, to trace and arrest Sewell and the other gang members, who were London based.

Although I had had not seen Dennis since joining the police service, I felt a compulsion to make contact with someone, to offer any assistance I could. It was as if I felt guilty by association that someone who clearly was the black sheep of my family could become involved in such an enterprise. I therefore decided to contact the Flying Squad office. This resulted in a visit from a Detective Superintendent who I had not previously met. Detective Constable Peter Holman who had only recently transferred from my staff to the Flying Squad accompanied him.

Peter had come to Islington on his appointment as a CID Officer and had been on my Leave Party, working weekend duties together. I had found him to be an excellent officer and we had worked closely on a number of investigations, so I was pleased to see him in these unusual circumstances. I explained my relationship to Dennis and the fact that we had had no contact during my time in the force. I pointed out I merely wished to put on record the fact that we were related and if there was any way I could be of assistance to the enquiry, I would be only to willing. A few names of associates were discussed but there was very little I could help with as most of the news I received about Dennis had been passed on through the family from one or other of my mother's sisters who kept in touch with him.

On 7th October 1971 Sewell was arrested in a Dawn raid on a house in Birnham Road Holloway and subsequently charged at Blackpool Police Headquarters. On 17th March 1972 at Manchester Crown court, Frederick Joseph Francis Sewell was found guilty of the murder of Superintendent Gerald Richardson and sentenced to life imprisonment with a recommendation that he serve not less than 30 years. He was given concurrent sentences of 15 years for robbery, 20 years for the attempted murder of Sergeant Carl Walker and fifteen years for conspiracy to use firearms. John Patrick Spry aged 37 was sentenced to 20 years for manslaughter; 25 years for attempted murder; 15 years for robbery and 15 years for conspiracy to use firearms to prevent arrest. Dennis, in the name Geoff Bond then aged 43 together with Timothy Flannigan aged 43 and Colin Haynes aged 43 had been cleared of the murder of Mr Richardson. They were however sentenced to 15 years 13 years and 10years respectively for the robbery.

It was to be another sixteen years before I next saw Dennis, which was at my parents' Golden Wedding Anniversary Celebrations, in South London. By that time I was myself a Detective Superintendent, having just served four years on the Flying Squad in that rank, before transferring to 2 Area Major Investigation Pool, to deal almost exclusively with Murder Investigations. Dennis and I exchanged a few pleasantries and I introduced him to Noeleen and my daughters. I was introduced to his wife Pat who had stuck by him for so many years. No mention was made of his past or my service in the Police Force, although I'm sure Dennis must have heard from one of my Aunts at some time of my career progress. What did surprise me was his height; he was no more than about 5' 7". I'd never realised he was quite small, but then I had not seen him since I was a teenager.

Apart from seeing him briefly at the funeral of my one of my mother's sisters, it was another eighteen years before we next met. He attended the 90th Birthday Celebrations of my mother, at the house of one of my sisters, in Essex. Now quite elderly and frail he had been driven there from South London by his daughter. Although I was aware Dennis had a son, whom I first met at my aunt's funeral, neither I nor my brother and sisters, had been aware that Dennis had a daughter. This new found cousin was a charming young lady, who was equally pleased to be introduced to my mother and all our side of the family. Nothing was said however of the reasons why our paths had not crossed before. Dennis and I did engage in a lengthy conversation for the first time, it was however purely about health related matters and problems he had experienced after an operation at his local hospital. It was neither the time nor the place to discuss his criminal past, much as I would have been interested to hear his version of some of the events that had kept us apart for most of his life.

Chapter Twelve

The Paedophile Painter

I had served over three years in the rank of 'First Class CID Sergeant' at Islington, when the Metropolitan Police decided to abolish this rank and its uniform equivalent rank of 'Station Sergeant'. This meant that in future, officers of the rank of Sergeant, would be promoted directly to Inspector, or Detective Inspector rank, in the case of CID Officers. As a result of this decision, existing First Class CID Sergeants were either upgraded to 'Acting Detective Inspectors', or where suitable vacancies existed, promoted to the full rank of Detective Inspector. Don Mann my opposite number at Caledonian Road – our Sectional Station, had served even longer than I in the rank and was promoted to DI and transferred off Division. I was therefore transferred to 'The Cally' as it was euphemistically known, to replace him as an acting DI, with effect from 22nd January 1973. Noeleen was some eight months pregnant with our third child by this date but any hope that my workload might be a little lighter at my new posting, were to be quickly dispelled.

There was a much smaller staff at Caledonian Road, but a good mix of youth and experience, including Detective Sergeant Peter Wilton, who I had first met at the Hendon Police Training College, where like myself, he had volunteered to take part in the Boxing Training. During my second week at the Cally, Peter was rostered to be the Divisional Night Duty C.I.D Officer. I arrived at my office one morning, to find a large number of brown paper Exhibit Bags stacked by my desk, a sure sign that a crime of some significance has occurred overnight. I opened the 'Night Duty Occurrence Book', on my desk, to read Peter's report.

It transpired that the previous evening a man had called at Tottenham Police Station and alleged that a painter named 'Brian', employed by Haringey Borough Council, had committed buggery with his twelve year old son, who I shall refer to as Brian Long. It was also learnt that another boy, aged thirteen, who I will refer to as Paul Yates was out in the company of Brian, that same evening and was expected to be driven back to his home in White Hart Lane, N.17. At about 10pm.

Police constables Meadwell and Redman were deputed to keep observation in the vicinity of Yates' address and at 10.10pm a Morris van drove up and Paul Yates alighted from the vehicle and entered his house. The officers stopped the van a short distance away and the driver; a 54-year-old man named Herbert Dearden, was arrested and taken to Tottenham Police Station.

Paul Yates was also taken to Tottenham Police Station soon afterwards, with a parent and interviewed concerning his relationship with Dearden. He alleged that Dearden who he knew as 'Brian' had committed various acts of indecency and buggery with him over a period of about a year. The last offence of buggery, having taken place that very evening at Dearden's flat which was identified as being in Hartham Road, Islington, and N.7.

As a result of information supplied by both boys, in written statements concerning their relationships with and offences committed by 'Brian', the names were learnt of four other boys with whom he had been associating. Arrangements were therefore made for these boys to attend Tottenham Police Station the following morning, in order that they could be interviewed and medically examined.

At this stage of the enquiry, which was being conducted by Detective Constable Murphy, all the offences disclosed had taken place at Dearden's flat, which was situated, on the Caledonian Road Section of Islington Sub Division. Pending the possible disclosure by the other boys of any offences having occurred in the Tottenham area, it was decided that Dearden would remain in custody overnight at Tottenham Police Station. Relevant clothing of Yates and Long were taken by Detective Murphy, for future forensic examination, he also consulted with Detective Sergeant Peter Wilton at Caledonian Road and requested that Dearden's flat be searched and various items of clothing and any other relevant items be preserved for forensic examination. Dearden had declined a request to consent to a medical examination by the Divisional Surgeon, however Peter took possession of the trousers and underpants worn by him at the time of his arrest and these together with other potential exhibits, now occupied my office.

Confronted with this situation on my arrival the following morning, I initially liaised with colleagues at Tottenham CID. I then arranged for one of my staff – Detective Sergeant John Reynolds, to attend there and assist in determining the nature and location, of any other offences that had been committed, against the four boys due to attend that morning. The boys concerned were eleven year old twins James and Keith; their nine year old brother Martin and Nigel aged ten, all of whom resided on the White Hart Lane Council Estate. Once again pseudonyms have been used to protect their true identities.

Each boy alleged that 'Brian' had committed various acts of indecency with him at one or other of two flats he had occupied in Islington, during the period of their association. Detective Sergeant Reynolds also saw Dearden and requested him to consent to a medical examination which he again declined, despite being informed that it could be in his own interest if he had not committed any offence. The six boys were however medically examined by the Police Divisional Surgeon, who found evidence that at least three of them had been the victims of acts of buggery.

It was apparent from the written statements supplied by the boys that with one exception, all the various assaults and acts of indecency had either occurred at Dearden's flat at Hartley Road, N.7. Or his former address, a room in Isleworth Road, N.7. After consultation I arranged that Detective Sergeant Reynolds should transfer Dearden to Caledonian Road, where we would continue with the investigation.

In order to prepare myself to interview Dearden, after a briefing by John Reynolds, I studied the various statements of the victims. It was apparent from the outset that I was dealing with a most obnoxious and cunning individual. Criminal Records had confirmed that Dearden had been before various courts on no less than seven occasions charged with offences of indecency with boys and had received sentences of imprisonment totalling 21 years and 6 months. He had been employed as a painter, for just over a year, by Haringey Borough Council and deployed painting their housing stock on the White Hart Lane Estate. This had brought him into contact with the various boys all of who lived on this estate.

In his spare time Dearden was in the habit of frequenting jumble sales and street markets buying and selling curious. Every room in his flat contained many such items, including numerous knives, daggers and swords, which he allowed the boys to play with, thus encouraging them to visit, despite his nefarious attentions.

Paul Yates claimed to have known Dearden for about a year and had accompanied him to various jumble sales. The first act of indecency towards him had occurred some six or seven months previous when he had visited Dearden's basement room in Isleworth Road, after returning from a jumble sale. Deaden had undone the boys flies and played with his private parts. Similar acts had occurred on later occasions both in that room and at the flat in Hartley Road when Dearden moved premises. There were no witnesses to any of these offences nor did Yates make any complaint. A few weeks before Dearden's arrest he had committed an act of buggery on the boy, in his bedroom, using a Vaseline as a lubricant. Peter Wilton had recovered a jar of which in his subsequent search of the flat.

On the night of Dearden's arrest, Yates had met Dearden at about 6pm and gone with him in his van to Hartham Road, to help with painting Dearden's kitchen. On completion of this task the two of them had gone up to Dearden's bedroom, where the latter committed indecent acts culminating in his coercing the boy to commit an act of buggery on him. This doubtless was one of the reasons Dearden declined to be medically examined after his arrest, as he would have known that swabs would have been taken and traces of the boy's semen may well have been detected.

Yates had also been present at the Hartley Road address some two months previous, in the company of Brian Long, the pair of them having been driven there by Dearden in his van. On that occasion Yates had sat watching television whilst Dearden had taken Long up to his bedroom, where after the promise of payment, the boy had consented to removing his trousers. Thereafter he was indecently assaulted and buggered by Dearden. Yates claimed that he was unaware of what had taken place upstairs.

Similar accounts were given by the other boys some of whom had been invited to attend jumble sales with him and on one occasion four of the boys had been taken back to his flat so Dearden could wash their feet before taking them swimming. On the latter occasion Dearden had invited nine year old Martin to sit on his lap to have his feet washed and he had taken this opportunity to touch the boy inappropriately, causing him to run from the house. His older brother James was one of the others present and although he had not witnessed the offence, once told by Martin what had occurred he claims to have remonstrated with Dearden about his conduct.

What was apparent was that although Dearden had on many occasions invited more than one boy to his flat, he was crafty enough to ensure that his indecent acts were not witnessed. None of the boys had made any complaints to their parents and their association with Dearden had prevailed over several weeks or months. The statement of Keith mentioned a seventh boy, twelve year old Mike Radford, who had also been subjected to Dearden's indecent attentions.

Having commenced to interview Dearden in company with Detective Sergeant Reynolds, I soon realised what an arrogant obnoxious individual he was. Mindful no doubt, that I knew about his sordid past, he was quite boastful of his experiences in dealing with previous allegations and other investigating officers. He readily agreed to having befriended the various boys, whilst engaged in decorating their homes over a period of months. He also admitted taking some of them to Jumble Sales, to help him acquire various artefacts and to letting them visit his premises to play with the swords and knives in his collection. He flatly refused however, to discuss any of the various allegations of indecency which I attempted to put to him. He endeavoured to justify his association with the boys by denigrating their respective parents, saying he had taken more interest in them. He used the occasion when he had taken four boys home to wash their feet before going swimming, as an opportunity to criticise their home conditions and lack of personal care and parental interest. He was too shrewd however, to answer any questions I put, regarding allegations of indecency. He also declined a further request to be medically examined.

On conclusion of the interview I charged him with an offence of buggery committed upon Paul Yates, the boy who he dropped off home in his van, just prior to his arrest. The following day he appeared at Old Street Magistrates Court where, in view of further enquiries I needed to make regarding other offences and legal advice I needed to obtain, I sought a remand in custody. With allegations from seven boys and his previous convictions, there was no way he was going to get bail and he was remanded in custody.

Both at the Station and the Court, Dearden had declined the opportunity to be legally represented. Before I left the Court, he took great pleasure in displaying his personal knowledge of Court procedures, by informing me that he would not be consenting to the statements of the boys being tendered to the Court at committal proceedings. He further intimated that he would not seek to be legally represented prior to committal proceedings as it was his intention to cross examine the boys personally with a view to seeking the dismissal of as many charges as possible.

Whilst a number of alleged offences had been disclosed by the various boys, it was apparent from their statements that they were unsure of any specific dates when offences had occurred and many discrepancies existed in the accounts they gave, particularly on occasions where other boys were at the flat. It was therefore going to be necessary to re interview some of them to try and clear up these ambiguities.

Indecent assault on a male person was an offence contrary to Section 15(1) of the Sexual Offences Act 1956. One of the protective provisions of this act was that a male person under the age of 16, could not consent to being indecently assaulted. I knew from my training and past experiences that it would be necessary to strictly prove the age of the boys concerned, in order to negate any defence of consent. I would therefore need all their respective parents to produce the boy's birth certificates.

I sent the various items seized from Dearden's flat off to the Forensic Science Laboratory for examination. In view of Dearden's refusal to be medically examined, which would have involved providing intimate swabs, I held out little hope that much corroboration would be forthcoming from that direction, particularly as most of the offences had taken place over such a lengthy period. In order to establish accurately the dates when Dearden had lived at either of the two addresses concerned, I arranged for statements to be taken from the respective landladies.

At this stage of the enquiry I had not personally met any of the victims or their parents, as John Reynolds and officers from Tottenham had taken the initial statements. In the absence of any of the parents being of sufficient means to afford a telephone, it was necessary for me to visit their addresses in order to update them as to the progress of the enquiry and arrange to take further statements where necessary. I also needed a parent of each boy to make a statement formally producing their child's birth certificate. Fortunately all the victims lived within a close proximity to each other, on the White Hart Lane Estate. With the exception of ten year old Nigel I was to find that all the boys came from large families and their home conditions were very poor. When I saw the state of their squalid living conditions, it was not surprised that most parents were unable to locate their boy's birth certificates and I was subsequently obliged to make applications to the local Registrar of Births, to obtain duplicates on their behalf.

Finally I submitted a report with statements of all the evidence to the Metropolitan Police Solicitors Department, for their consideration as to what further charges should be preferred. I was aware that apart from the evidence of the Police Divisional Surgeon, there was little to corroborate any particular allegation as Dearden had been careful not to let his actions be witnessed. Had he denied the boys had ever been to his premises, we could have proved otherwise by their knowledge of the contents, but he was clever enough to know that he could not deny association, but stood a good chance of eluding conviction by denying the offences. I knew that ultimately, much would rely on whether the trial judge was happy for the boys to give sworn evidence and then the manner in which their evidence was given.

It was decided that Dearden would face a total of nine charges, three of buggery and six of indecent assault against six of the seven victims. As Dearden stuck to his decision to represent himself prior to Committal Proceedings, I was obliged to serve copies of all the statements on him personally, which I did at one of the remand hearing at Old Street Magistrates Court. A short while later whilst I was passing his cell door dealing with another matter, he called out through the wicket door of his cell saying, "I see you are producing birth certificates, I was hoping you might forget to do that. I got off a charge once when they didn't prove age."

Fortunately having experience of this type of case previously, I was not going to make that mistake. Unbeknown to Dearden however I could easily have been distracted around that time for on the day before one of the remand hearings, on 28th February Noeleen gave birth to our third daughter Ann.

Dearden's remark only served to remind me that I knew little about the background to this cunning individual and his past misdeeds. Although his Criminal Record listed his previous convictions and sentences, there was sparse detail of the circumstances of each case. Had any of Dearden's convictions occurred within the Metropolitan Police Area, I would have accessed the past case papers, to assist my handling of his prosecution. Unfortunately his previous arrests had all been outside the Metropolis, so this facility did not exist. If Dearden's remarks were true, an officer inexperienced in such matters may well have dealt him with in the past. Unfortunately for him, I had already gained considerable experience in dealing with cases involving indecency with children and young persons.

Shortly before leaving Islington, I had dealt with an equally nasty individual, who was living the life of a gypsy, on the northern outskirts of London, earning a living collecting scrap metal. His misdeeds had only come to my attention as a result of a teacher at Islington Green School reporting seeing an alleged kidnapping. Outside the school one afternoon she had witnessed an assault on one of her fourteen-year-old male pupils, by two older youths, who then bundled the boy into a car. The victim's twin brother, who was nearby, was then told by the driver to get in, which he had done and the car was driven off. Enquiries of the boy's family revealed that he had recently been staying with the gypsy who owned a similar vehicle. This individual encouraged his nephews and their friends to frequent his campsite, to help look after his horses and help with his scrap collection, sleeping over at weekends and during school holidays. The respective parents were either related or acquainted with the gypsy and consented to this. When the boys returned home later that evening, the alleged kidnap was found to have been no more than a dispute concerning the alleged mistreatment of a horse by one of the twins. Having commenced enquiries into this matter however, both boys were interviewed and I had them medically examined. This resulted in the discovery that during previous visits the gypsy had committed various acts of indecency and buggery with them as well as with his nephew and another boy.

The boys targeted by Dearden however, were much younger and certainly more innocent than those involved with the gypsy. It was with a sense of some satisfaction on my part, when Dearden was finally committed to the Central Criminal Court to stand trial on the nine charges, despite his best attempts to avoid this.

Dearden's trial commenced on 5th July 1973, before His Honour Judge Marnam at the Old Bailey and whilst the prosecution were represented by Mr J Connors of Counsel, Dearden still confident of his own abilities and experience with such matters, chose to defend himself. Such a decision was unprecedented in my personal experience. His Honour Judge Marnam did his best to advise Dearden of the dangers of not having qualified legal representation and offered him a last chance to change his mind, but to no avail.

With the passage of time since the offences occurred and the trauma of giving evidence in such august surroundings, I anticipated that the evidence forthcoming from some of the boys would not be of a sufficient standard to convince a jury beyond reasonable doubt that particular offences had taken place. There was virtually no forensic corroboration, but we did have the Divisional Surgeon's evidence that three of the boys had been the victims of the offence of buggery, although he could not say who had committed these acts. As the trial progressed and the boys gave their evidence, as anticipated, a couple of them were either vague embarrassed or simply chose not to recount fully, the intimate details of what had taken place with the defendant. I could see that the jury would be obliged to return 'Not Guilty' verdicts on some Counts. Dearden himself did a good job when cross-examining witnesses, to highlight matters in his favour. Naturally he was anxious to stress that all the boys had visited his premises of their own free will and he had looked after them, taken them to places where he was purchasing curios and given them food when they were hungry.

On conclusion of all the evidence when the Judge was summing up, he directed the Jury to return verdicts of 'Not Guilty' to offences of buggery and indecent assault against Keith. This was purely on the grounds that there was a lack of corroboration to the evidence of this eleven-year-old boy. He also directed them to return a verdict of 'Not Guilty' to offences of indecent assault upon Morris Redmond and buggery with Paul Yates, as no evidence of these offences had been forthcoming from these alleged victims. This left some five Counts for the jury to consider when they retired to consider their verdicts. As with all such cases, the jury were warned by the judge that each count had to be considered on its own merits and the fact that several boys had made allegations of separate incidents, was not in itself corroboration that any particular offence had been committed.

After due consideration the jury returned verdicts of 'Guilty' to a Count of Buggery against Brian Long, the twelve year old boy who had initiated the original complaint. They were therefore discharged from giving a verdict to an alternative Count of Indecent Assault, in respect of this matter. They also returned a verdict of 'Guilty' to a Count of Indecent Assault, against 13 year old Paul Yates, the boy who had been in Dearden's van on the night of his arrest. His evidence regarding the more serious offence of buggery had had not been forthcoming during his testimony. With regard to the remaining Counts of Indecent Assault against eleven-year-old James and his nine-year-old brother Martin the jury returned verdicts of 'Not Guilty'.

From the prosecution point of view we were more than happy with this result. With the lack of corroboration and the difficulties of children giving evidence, it was anticipated that Dearden would evade conviction on some Counts. But with two guilty verdicts and one for the serious offence of buggery, we knew the learned Judge would be able to impose a suitable sentence. At this stage of my career I had long given up anticipating the length of sentence any particular Magistrate or Judge might impose against any offender I had brought to justice. The satisfaction of arresting a culprit and his ultimate conviction were rewarding enough for me. I was however totally unprepared, when, after I had acquainted the Court with details of Dearden's antecedents and criminal convictions, the learned Judge sentenced Dearden to 'life imprisonment', for the offence of buggery and 'five years imprisonment' on the Indecent Assault Count.

It is not often that Judges passed maximum sentences for offences, but in this case, in view of Dearden's past and in order to protect other potential victims, he certainly deserved it.

Chapter Thirteen

The Murder of Laurence
William Everett

When Derek Pitt walked down Hollingsworth Street, Islington, at 9.45 a.m., on the morning of Sunday 11th March 1973, he was just killing time. He was totally unprepared for what he was to see as he passed the entrance of a derelict house with its front door open, a short way into his journey. The front door in question being accessed by four stone steps from pavement level, meant that the floor of the passageway was a little below eye level. As he glanced into the front entrance passage of number 23, he realised he was looking at the sole of a man's shoe and one trousered leg, on the floor, protruding out from the doorway of a room on the right. Mr Pitt stepped from the pavement onto the first step of the house, to confirm what he had seen, then decided to seek assistance before venturing further.

Mr Pitt in fact lived in Highbury and the reason this 27 year old litho printer had found himself in Hollingsworth Street that morning was that he was one of a number of drivers, who were awaiting a delivery, at a yard and warehouse at 18a Hollingworth Street. Premises owned by D.C. Thomson & Co. Ltd., Newspaper and Periodical Publishers. This was not a regular occurrence but alternative arrangements made, as a result of a rail strike which was in operation and which had affected the delivery of 'The Sunday Post', a Scottish newspaper which would normally have been transported from Scotland by rail and collected from Euston Station. As a result of the rail strike, arrangement had been made for the newspapers to be flown down to Luton airport and then transported by lorry to the depot in Hollingsworth Street, where Mr Pitt and other drivers were waiting to effect their distribution to various news vendors in London.

After a period of waiting and there still being no sign of the lorry's arrival, Mr Pitt had decided to take a stroll. Now, concerned with what he had seen, he hurried back to the depot reporting his find to the other drivers and requesting someone to come with him to have another look at what he had seen. There was however no response from the other drivers, who were indulging in a card game and thought what Mr Pitt had seen was a drunk asleep in a derelict house. Not convinced, he decided to return alone to the street and was fortunate to see a police car cruising along Hollingsworth Street, being driven by Police Sergeant Croker.

Mr Pitt stopped the officer and, who told him what he had seen. The officer entered No. 23 and saw the body of man on his back in the doorway of the ground floor front room, with his right leg protruding into the passageway towards the front door.

There was blood on the head and face of the man and a pool of congealed blood on the floor of the passageway beside the body. There were also shoe impressions in blood leading from this pool and onto the stone steps down to the footway.

P.S. Croker then summoned the assistance of other officers and requested the attendance of the Divisional Surgeon, Dr. Sanjoy Chatterji, who attended shortly afterwards and confirmed death. Detective Sergeant Peter Wilton was on duty at Caledonian Road that Sunday morning so he attended and took charge of the scene making arrangements for the attendance of Technical Support Officers, as well as myself and Detective Chief Superintendent Tony Peel.

Noeleen had given birth to our third daughter Ann just twelve days previous and I was off duty at home looking forward to a family day, when the call came requesting my attendance at the scene. Fortunately Mrs Kelly, my mother-in-law had come over from Ireland for a few weeks, following the birth, to help out with Helen and Jane, who were by now five and three respectively. Knowing what demands a murder enquiry could make on my time, I was particularly grateful that Mrs Kelly was there to help Noeleen with the children. I was very fortunate to enjoy a good relationship with Mrs Kelly, who made herself busy in an unobtrusive way as well as making an excellent apple pie.

Hollingsworth Road was a short road running north to south between Sherringham Road and the busy Mackenzie Road, which provided access between Caledonian Road and Holloway Road. It was in an area of streets designated for redevelopment by the Greater London Council and during the previous few years, residents of Hollingsworth and surrounding streets had gradually been re-housed and demolition work was being undertaken in the immediate vicinity. This work has long since been completed. Hollingsworth Road no longer exists today, in its stead is a small green, appropriately named Paradise Park.

On 10th March 1973, only two houses in Hollingsworth Street were still occupied, the remainder were derelict and awaiting demolition. Number 23 was an end terrace house on the west side, bordered by a disused builders yard to the south, adjacent to which was a lock up garage situated in the rear garden of a corner house – No. 16 Sherringham Road.

To the north of No. 23, houses numbered 22, 21, and 20 were derelict and separated from the premises of D.C. Thomson & Co. Ltd., at 18a, by a levelled site formerly No.19. On the other side of the road was a levelled-bombed site, with a four-foot brick wall abutting the pavement. No buildings therefore overlooked the front of No. 23. It was to this scene that Detective Chief Superintendent Peel and I arrived at 11.30am that Sunday morning, to meet up with the various Scenes of Crime personnel who had responded to the incident. The house in question, was a two-storey house with a basement. Four stone steps bridging the basement area accessed the entrance door to the ground floor where our victim was found and a further flight of stone steps from pavement level, led down to the basement door.

Carefully avoiding the bloodstained footprints on the stone steps, we entered the front passageway. Passing a tobacco tin lying on the floor just inside the door, we were to see the body of a thin, middle aged man lying on his back in the doorway of a front room on our right. An area of blood staining on the linoleum covered floor, extended from beneath the body across the narrow passageway to the far wall. This was not a pool of blood but smeared blood indicative of the victim having moved after being injured or more likely an attempt having been made to move his body from the passage into the front room. There was blood on the head and face of the deceased who was on his back with his legs astride the hinged edge of the doorframe, so that his right leg protruding into the hallway towards the front door. His left leg, which was bent at the knee, was resting against the door inside the front room, thereby holding it fully open against the wall.

The deceased was fully clothed, wearing an overcoat, jacket trousers jersey, shirt, tie shoes and socks. Once the Scenes of Crime Photographer had taken the requisite photographs in the immediate vicinity of the body, it was possible to search the pockets of the deceased's clothing in the hope of finding some indication of his possible identity. This was undertaken by the District Laboratory Liaison Officer, Detective Sergeant Green assisted by Detective Constable Stuart Douglas – who'd been appointed as Exhibits Officer. Both trouser pockets were empty and no money was found about the body. There was a key on a ring, secured on a chain affixed to the left side of the trouser waistband. This was lying beneath the body rather than in the left pocket where one might expect it to have been kept. The right hand overcoat pocket contained a table knife; an adjustable spanner; a piece of metal and a button, whilst the left was home to five cigarette ends. An inside pocket housed tweezers; scissors; needles and cotton, which together with shaving accoutrements found in the inside jacket pocket, confirmed the deceased's nomadic way of life. Nothing was found however, to confirm his identity.

Whilst the body was being moved for conveyance to the Mortuary, an empty match box and some spent matches were found in the blood beneath the body. These together with the empty tobacco tin in the hallway were the only other items found at the scene that could be linked with the deceased.

There was no obvious murder weapon to be seen in or around the premises and a thorough search of all the rooms and garden, undertaken after completion of photography and fingerprint examination, also failed to trace a weapon. The room where the body was found contained a small settee, whilst a double bed with mattress and blankets was found in the rear ground floor room together with two chairs. A further double bed, table and chair were to be found in the first floor front room. The previous tenant subsequently identified these items and a few other sundry furnishings, as items discarded when he and his family had been re-housed some two months previous.

A cloth cap was found on the roof of the aforementioned garage in the rear garden of the corner house at 16, Sherringham Road. The tenant Mr Sliney brought the cap to police notice, soon after the body was discovered. Mr Sliney was certain however, that he had first seen the cap on his garage roof at about 9am some two days previous, on the Friday.

Whilst forensic and fingerprint examination of the premises continued, Detective Chief Superintendent Tony Peel and I returned to Caledonian Road Police Station, where a number of CID Officers had been summoned. Some of these officers had been on duty on other parts of the Division, whilst others like me had been called back to duty on their rest day.

At this stage of proceedings our priority was to commence house to house enquiries of the few remaining tenants in Hollingsworth Street and then houses and businesses in the surrounding area. Firstly we needed to trace any potential witnesses who had been in the vicinity of number 23 in the past few days and may have seen possible suspects in the area. We also needed to identify the victim, with a view to establishing any possible motive. Press Bureau at Scotland Yard was also contacted so that notification of the crime and appeals for witnesses could be instituted through the news media.

A post mortem examination by Dr Hugh Johnson, M.A., M.B, B.Chir., M.R.C., Path,. D.M.J., had been arranged for 4pm that afternoon at St. Pancras Mortuary. This was attended by Tony Peel and myself together with our exhibits officer Stuart Douglas and Det. Sgt Green the Laboratory Liaison Officer. It was thereby established that our victim had suffered a 1.5" laceration over his right brow; a 2" laceration on the top right of his head; a

1.5" laceration to the left side at the back of his head and bruising around both eyes and both sides of his head. There were also fresh abrasions on both shins but no obvious defence wounds on his hands or arms. Dr Johnson also discovered that these lacerations had resulted in several fractures to the skull, which was unusually thin, being no more than one sixteenth of an inch in the temporal region.

Dr Johnson gave the cause of death as 'cerebral contusions and fractured skull'. He was also of the opinion that the injuries to the head were in keeping with at least three blows from a blunt instrument.

When the fingerprint examination of the house had been completed, it transpired that there were very few finger marks found of sufficient quality for comparison with any suspects. This was perhaps not surprising considering the derelict condition of the house. The only marks found in close proximity to the body were on a wooden rail of the settee in the front ground floor room. This was to later be eliminated as that of the former tenant of the house. Other marks found were on the inside of a cupboard door in the top floor front room. There were also marks found on the rear of a picture on the stairway between the first and second floor. Neither of these offered much hope of being connected to the murder.

The initial 'house to house' enquiries had resulted in the identity of our victim being established that first day. A Mr James Starkey who lived in nearby Crossley Street was in the habit of walking his dog during the evenings and he recalled seeing a 'totter' that he knew as 'Spike', going into No. 23 Hollingsworth Street on five or six occasions in recent weeks. Further enquiries in the neighbourhood resulted in it being established that Spike's real name was Laurence Everett, a scrap metal dealer of no fixed abode. Like most persons engaged in this type of profession, Everett had come to police attention on several occasions for acts of petty theft of scrap metal and with his identity revealed we were able to inform his next of kin late that first evening.

Everett was a native of Islington with an elderly mother and a sister residing in Barnsbury. I visited them personally to impart the sad news that we suspected the victim to be Laurence. I learnt that he had not lived with them for the past twenty years, having chosen to 'live his own life with his barrow' as they described it. He had last visited his sister the previous Saturday. The following day one of his brother's formally identified the body to me at St. Pancras Mortuary.

With the assistance of members of his family, police records and enquiries made of local residents and publicans, a picture gradually emerged of the simple way of life the victim had lived for the past twenty-five years.

Laurence William Everett was a bachelor, 50 years of age at the time of his death. He was born on 16th April 1922 in Islington, the fourth child of a family of four boys and two girls. After leaving school at the age of 14 he had gained employment as a casual labourer until 1945 when he served in the Royal Pioneer Corps and was employed on guard duty at a Prisoner of War camp. Discharged in September 1946, he later obtained work with Islington Borough Council as a rodent operative and night watchman.

In 1948 he became self-employed as a dealer in scrap rags and metal, conducting this business as a 'totter' in the Holloway and Islington area. He had rented rooms in low class boarding houses or a Rowton House, but was generally of no fixed abode. He was a man of simple habits walking the streets, initially with a pram then a handcart and occasionally a hired horse drawn cart. In this way he would seek out any scrap iron or re-saleable items he could find, often entering buildings vacated for demolition purposes and scavenging property discarded by the departing tenants. Such scrap as Everett collected he would sell to local metal dealers dependent upon where his days meandering had taken him. He was also known to sell any items of slight antique value, to dealers in Camden Passage the local Antique Market.

It was apparent that Everett had lived virtually 'hand to mouth'. As soon as he made a sale he would seek out a nearby public house and purchase himself a pint of beer or enter a betting shop and wager a small amount on the horses. We also learnt that it was common practice for him to remove one of the wheels of his barrow and take it with him into a public house, to prevent his barrow being moved or stolen. During his working day Everett would not dwell in a public house longer than it took him to consume his drink. In the evenings however, he remained longer and on some occasions, had been known to indulge in a song and dance routine to any background music, apparently more for his own enjoyment than the amusement of other patrons.

He always worked alone and usually drank alone; save for indulging in casual conversation with such other persons present at the bar that might feel disposed, to pass the time of day with him. Practically everyone who knew him that we spoke to during our enquiries described him as a 'loner'.

It was also learnt that Everett was in the habit of pawning items of his personal possessions, such as a watch, lighter or cigarette case. He would sometimes redeem these pledges when he was in a better financial situation, but it was learnt that often he would sell his pawn tickets, in order to raise money for food, drink or a bet. A number of persons were traced who had been approached by Everett and asked to purchase his pawn tickets, either in public houses or betting shops.

Everett was a tall thin man some six feet in height. He usually wore a long dark overcoat or raincoat and a flat cap. He had become a familiar figure walking the streets of Islington, bent over his barrow. Despite being a local character however, not many people knew his true identity. A few knew him as 'Laurie', most knew him as 'Spike' whilst other merely referred to him as 'The Singing Totter'.

Our enquiries in the vicinity of Hollingsworth Street, were to establish that two suitcases containing items of Everett's clothing had been lodged for safe keeping with the licensee of the 'Waterloo' public house in Sherringham Road. The licensee, Mr Michael Finnegan stated that Everett would come into the pub and take clothes, as he needed them. This together with evidence gained from metal dealers that Everett was in the habit of washing and changing clothes on their premises, supported the conclusion that he had been sleeping rough in other places for many months, prior to No. 23 Hollingsworth Street becoming available.

In any murder investigation, tracing the last known movements of a deceased can be vital in establishing either a motive or the identity of possible suspects or witnesses. Our enquiries established that Everett was last seen alive on Saturday, 10th March 1973. He was seen on five separate occasions prior to about 1 p.m. He was seen on one occasion during the mid-afternoon and finally one occasion at about 10.20 p.m.

On the first four occasions he was seen by various people pushing his barrow around the streets of Islington. Between 12.30pm and 1pm he consumed a pint of beer in the Kings Head public house in Upper Street according to a barman. The afternoon sighting was in a Betting Office in Holloway Road. The final sighting of Everett was by sixteen-year-old Betty Scott. Miss Scott knew Everett by his nickname 'Spike' and had first spoken to him some two months before his death when she had told him her name.

On Saturday 10th March, Miss Scott left her house in Sherringham Road, to purchase some cigarettes from the Waterloo public house situated opposite her address, at the junction with Lough Road. Lough Road was to the West of Hollingsworth Street and ran parallel to it. At about 10.20pm as she was about to enter the public house she saw Everett in Lough Road on the West footway, walking from the direction of Sherringham Road towards Mackenzie Road. Miss Scott called over to him "Hello Spike" and he had called back "Hello Betty". This was the last occasion upon which we were able to establish that Everett was alive.

A barrow located outside the premises of R.B. Metals in Lough Road, on the morning of 11th March, was identified as belonging to Everett. It contained an old iron bath and was minus one wheel. Mr. Ronald Brett the proprietor of R.B. Metals had known Everett for about twenty years. He had last seen him on 7th March when he had left the barrow outside the premises and deposited one wheel with Mr Brett to prevent misuse of the barrow. This was confirmed by an employee Mr Ronald Birmingham, who also verified that Everett was in the habit of sleeping in derelict houses nearby. He could not specify which particular house.

Both men informed police that Everett used to have a khaki bag of tools, which he carried around when looking for scrap metal. This bag was never located. It was however considered that Everett may have sold the bag of tools, as this would not have been out of character with him.

It was on 13th March that our enquiries revealed that Everett had taken a lunch time drink at the King's Head public house in Upper Street on Saturday 10th as previously mentioned. It was then learnt from the licensee that whilst he personally had not seen Everett, who had been served by one of his staff, he had noticed a barrow used by Everett parked outside. This empty barrow was still outside secured with a padlock and chain. It was taken into police possession. The key found on the keychain attached to the waistband of Everett's trousers was later tried in the padlock, which it unlocked.

The barrow however, bore markings indicating it was the property of E. Howard & Sons (Barrow Builders) of 23 Wheeler Street, E.1. There was a record of it being reported stolen some six months previous from Spitalfields Market, whilst on hire.

During the course of our investigation, enquiries were being made of all public houses, cafes, betting shops, antique dealers, second-hand dealers, old metal dealers and pawnbrokers in the area. This was in an endeavour to trace persons who knew, or had been in contact with Everett just prior to his death and in order that evidence of possible motive might emerge.

One such business, just 100 yards from the King's Head public house, was an antique dealer in Theberton Street. Mr Newland the proprietor was found to have known Everett for two years, having purchased items from him. He felt certain that the last occasion he had seen Everett was Saturday 10th March when he called at his shop to ask Mr Newland if he wanted to buy a barrow, stating he had bought a new one. It was not established when or how this second barrow came to be in Everett's possession.

The first barrow, recovered from Lough Road, was also identified by its markings and number to belong to E.Howard & Sons.

This barrow had 'gone missing' from Spitalfields Market some 5 years previous whilst on loan. It was learnt that it was common practise for 'totters' in need of a barrow to visit Spitalfields Market and just walk off with one and this is probably the way Everett came by the two barrows traced to his possession.

Although there was no evidence that Everett had managed to exchange blows with his assailant, checks were made at local hospitals and all persons who had attended for treatment of injuries on 10th and 11th March, were interviewed and eliminated from the enquiry.

Dry cleaners were contacted and requested to report blood-stained clothing deposited for cleaning. Two such reports of such items were received, but one was found to be relating to a road traffic accident, whilst the other related to an assault for which a person had been arrested.

There was an element of local gossip soon after publicity of the murder, that Everett had recently won a large sum of money in a Betting shop in Bride Street, N.1. It subsequently transpired that his win had been on 6th March and amounted to a total of 85p. Specimens of Everett's betting slips were however obtained so searches could be made during enquiries at other such premises, for trace of a winning bet written by Everett on 10th March, but no such bets were found.

Detailed searches were conducted of the derelict buildings and grounds in the vicinity of the murder scene including drain searches, but without trace of anything that could be identified as the murder weapon.

In an endeavour to trace possible witnesses to events surrounding Everett's death, on Saturday 17th March, exactly a week after Everett had last been seen alive, I arranged for a roadblock to be operated in the general vicinity of the scene at Hollingsworth Street. This was a line of enquiry I adopted in any major investigation, as past experience had shown that many persons were creatures of habit and had a regular routine for a particular day of the week, either for social or business reasons. This could be particularly useful in tracing potential witnesses who resided outside the locality and may not therefore be aware of a crime having been committed in a location frequented by them.

All pedestrian and vehicular traffic was stopped between the hours of 7pm and midnight and proformae were completed in respect of the person's movements that evening, the previous Saturday and any knowledge they had of the deceased. Some 264 persons were stopped, of which 95 were found to have known Everett by sight, if not personally. It was during the course of this operation that Miss Scott was first contacted, she being the girl who had spoken to Everett at 10.20pm the previous Saturday and the last to see him alive.

Eighty-four of the persons stopped were teenagers who were attending a disco-dance at a local youth club known as the 'Factory Club', which was situated in Sherringham Road near the junction with Liverpool Road. It was learnt that the majority of them had been attending a similar function the previous Saturday, which had terminated at about 10.30pm. In an endeavour to trace all the persons who had attended the disco-dance on the night of the murder, statements were subsequently taken from all the club members stopped and names of other persons who had been present on the previous Saturday were obtained. These persons were, in turn, seen and statements obtained respecting their movements and those of their friends at the club.

None of the club members interviewed recalled seeing Everett on the evening of Saturday 10th March and no evidence came to light to indicate any connection between the death of Everett and the activities of the club members.

Despite national publicity regarding the murder in various newspaper editions and widespread publicity in two local news-papers over several weeks, only one witness had come forward. This had been one of the persons who had seen Everett with his barrow on the morning of 10th March.

From enquiries at second-hand and antique dealers, we learnt that Everett was known, at 32 out of 52 premises visited. With the exception of Mr Newland, to whom he offered the barrow for sale, none of them recalled seeing Everett on Saturday 10th March.

Everett was well known at 20 of the 23 old metal dealers where police enquiries were made. There were however no reports of Everett having visited any of them on 10th March. Further visits were made to second-hand dealers and old metal dealers in the general vicinity of the places where Everett was seen on Saturday 10th March, with particular emphasis on tracing where he disposed of variously described items seen on his barrow that day. These enquiries were abortive and unless he had disposed of the items to some private individual as he often did, it may well be that such dealers as he did visit were loath to divulge the information to police because they had failed to record the transaction in their books.

Enquiries we made at pawnbrokers were not only to assist in tracing Everett's recent movements but also to determine what items of property he might have had in his possession, which could have been stolen from his person, had the motive been one of robbery. It was learnt that Everett was a regular customer at 4 of the 7 pawnbrokers within the area of the enquiry.

Mr Quigley, the manager of Barrett's Jewellers and Pawnbrokers at 271, Caledonian Road, N.1., had known Everett for the eight years he had been at the shop. He recalled having sold Everett a cheap watch, some three weeks previous, together with a Ronson Veraflame lighter.

Mr Berry the manager of the Upper Street branch of Barrett's Jewellers and Pawnbrokers had also known Everett as a customer for many years. He had taken a watch in pawn from Everett on 21st February, which had been redeemed by him on 24th February.

Mr Shepherd was the manager of Charles Coley Jewellers and Pawnbrokers of 236 Holloway Road. Both he and his wife, who also worked at the shop, knew Everett as a customer. Mr Shepherd had a record of Everett pawning a watch on 6th February, which he had redeemed on 20th February. A further record showed that Everett had again pawned a watch on 26th February and that pledge had been redeemed on Saturday 10th March, the day before Everett was found murdered.

The redemption of this pledge had been dealt with by Mrs Shepherd and when, on 16th March she was asked to recall the incident she was certain that it had not been Everett who had collected the watch. She described two men who she thought had collected the watch. The descriptions given were recognised by her husband as that of a Mr Wright and one of his two brothers, who were also regular customers. The shop records also showed that Mr Wright had renewed a pledge on a pawned ring on 10th March. Mrs Shepherd was then uncertain whether she had been right in her recollection, but was sure that no one had redeemed two pledges on the day in question.

On 17th March the three Wright brothers were interviewed at Caledonian Road Police Station. They were all able to give satisfactory explanations of their movements on Saturday 10th March. Mrs Shepherd, when confronted with one of them, recognised him as the man who had renewed the pledge on his ring. She was certain that he was not the person who had redeemed Everett's watch.

In an endeavour to elicit further help from the public regarding the murder, we managed to secure the services of the London Weekend Television Programme, 'Police 5', with a view to being included on their broadcast on Friday 23rd March. It was essential to show a photograph of Everett. The only photograph of Everett considered a good likeness was a Criminal Record Photograph which we had been using to show potential witnesses during our enquiries, but which had not been made available to the press.

In the absence of any family photographs, his mother had initially refused permission for this photograph (suitably re-framed) to be used to assist appeals through the medium of press and television. She subsequently changed her mind however and agreed to the photograph being used for the 'Police 5' programme.

Film of the scene at Hollingsworth Street and the vicinity of Charles Coleys, Pawnbrokers, Holloway road were shown, together with the picture of Everett. An appeal was made for whoever had redeemed Everett's pawned watch, to contact police. It was particularly disappointing that only four telephone calls were received, none of which contributed towards the enquiry.

From routine enquiries during the course of the investigation, it had been learnt that a conversation had been overheard in a public house, indicating that a man had spoken of owning a watch formerly belonging to Everett. That man was traced and found to be a local decorator who I shall refer to as Mr Maddox. When interviewed on 6th April he admitted having redeemed Everett's watch from Charles Coley, Pawnbrokers, on Saturday 10th March. The watch was still in his possession. Maddox claimed that he had first met Everett two months previous in a public house and then five or six weeks later had seen him again in the Edinburgh Castle public house in Caledonian Road. On the latter occasion he had been induced by Everett to buy the pawn ticket for £1, having first declined Everett's request for £2.

Thereafter Maddox had left the pawn ticket in his room until Saturday 10th March, when, being unable to work as a result of a injuries sustained in a fight with his landlord, he decided to redeem the pledge and had thereby obtained the watch Maddox's landlord was interviewed and he confirmed having had a fight with Maddox on 8th March. He was also able to confirm that two or three weeks before the fight Maddox had mentioned having bought a pawn ticket from a totter.

Another tenant residing at the same premises stated that Maddox had shown him a pawn ticket some four or five weeks previous and later after Everett's picture had appeared in a newspaper, Maddox had indicated that this was the man from whom he had bought the ticket.

Maddox's address was searched and various articles of his clothing and footwear were submitted to the laboratory where they were examined, but without trace of blood or any connection with the scene. From the known history of Everett in relation to his pawn tickets and the corroboration of Maddox's account, it was thought that he was speaking the truth and was in no way involved in Everett's death.

On 29th March a 53 year old, unemployed man, who I shall refer to as Alan Hunt, was arrested on a warrant and charged at Caledonian Road Police Station for an offence of being drunk and failing to appear at Old Street Magistrates Court some three months previous. Hunt was in the habit of sleeping rough in a derelict shop in Mackenzie Road and was well known in local public houses. He was interviewed by murder squad officers and found to have known Everett by sight but there was no evidence to connect him with his death.

When details of Hunt's previous criminal record were seen, a conviction for assault occasioning actual bodily harm for which he had been discharged conditionally for 12 months some two years previous, gave cause for concern. The circumstance of the offence were that, whilst sleeping in a derelict house with another man he had, during the course of an argument struck the man with his fists and kicked him, causing injuries.

Hunt was re-arrested on 10th April and brought to Caledonian Road Police Station. He was further interviewed and his shoes and clothing were submitted to the laboratory for examination and comparison with the footprints but no evidence was found to connect him to the murder scene.

On 8th April, during a routine search of derelict houses in Ponder Street, N.1., bloodstained clothing, food and bedding was found, indicating some persons were in the habit of sleeping at one of the houses. Observation was kept and at 10.50pm a 26 year old man was seen to enter the house; he was detained overnight at Caledonian Road Police Station.

The following morning, when interviewed by members of the murder squad, he stated that he had been sleeping rough at the house for the past 5 or 6 weeks, with two other men who he named and who he had met in the Kings Cross area. He claimed that the bloodstained clothing belonged to one of the men who had been assaulted a few weeks previously, in a betting shop in Kings Cross.

The victim of this alleged assault was traced and interviewed a few days later. He claimed to have been assaulted by a woman whereby he had received a head injury, for which he had been treated at the Royal Free Hospital. His explanation was verified by the hospital and the alleged assault had been recorded at Kings Cross Police Station. Police Officers concerned were able to verify that the bloodstained clothing was that worn by the victim at the time.

Mr Patrick Barber was the Superintendent of a children's Home at 11, Sherringham Road, N.7. When interviewed in the course of the enquiry he made mention of a man named Mick whom he had known for about two years and who was in the habit of visiting him at the home. Mr Barber recalled Mick had visited the home at about 11.10pm on Saturday 10th March, in a drunken state, and asked if he could stay the night. Mr Barber had refused and after a few minutes conversation Mick had left. In view of the incident and the close proximity of the home to Hollingsworth Street, enquiries were made to trace the man Mick.

On 28th March Mick again visited the Children's Home and police were informed and attended. Mick was found to be a 39-year-old general builder who I shall refer to as Michael Stevens. He gave an address in New Cross Gate, S.W.4. A statement was obtained from him concerning his movements on 10th March. He stated that he had known Everett and drunk with him on occasions when they met in public houses. With regard to his movements on the late evening of 10th March Stevens could only recall being drunk and getting a mini-cab home. He was unable to state where he obtained the services of the mini-cab.

Enquiries were made of local mini-cab offices but no record could be found of the journey referred to by Stevens. Enquiries were made at the address given by Stevens and it was found to be false. Officers were deputed to trace Stevens and re-interview him regarding this discrepancy.

On 24th April Stevens was traced and brought to Caledonian Road Police Station where he was further interviewed. It transpired that the address referred to by Stevens did exist, but although he had given the correct house number, as the house was on a corner he had inadvertently given the name of the adjacent road. The house was unoccupied and in the process of re-decoration. Stevens had been employed re decorating the premises.

Stevens who had been detained whilst enquiries were being made regarding his movements subsequently admitted that he had in fact only stayed at the New Cross address for a few nights. In answer to further questions he admitted that since the beginning of March he had been living rough, sleeping in a derelict house at 20, Lough Road and it was to this address that he had gone on leaving the children's Home on the night of 10th March. The reason given by Stevens for not divulging his true place of abode when first interviewed was that he was too ashamed.

The derelict house at 30 Lough Road was searched and various items of Steven's clothing were seized and, together with the clothing and shoes he was wearing were submitted to the forensic science laboratory for examination. Stevens meanwhile, was further interviewed and a detailed statement under caution was obtained from him. On completion of various enquiries and the laboratory examination, no connection could be proved between Stevens and the scene of the offence. He was therefore released after spending three days in Police custody.

In his statement Stevens had referred to three Irishmen who were also sleeping at 20, Lough Road. Two of these men a 37-year-old labourer and a 33-year-old cleaner were still doing so. They were interviewed and confirmed that Stevens had been staying at the house since the beginning of March. In view of their mode of living they also were interviewed respecting Everett's death but could not be connected with the enquiry.

As enquiries into Everett's death continued, it was becoming clear that two aspects were proving to be obstacles to furthering our enquiry. Firstly the lone lifestyle of Everett meant that he did not have close friends or associates. There was therefore, no one to whom he might have confided any fears or threats he may have experienced, or details of his intended movements on the night of Saturday 10th March. Secondly the remoteness of the premises where his body was found inhibited any chance that there were any witnesses to what had occurred.

The only vehicle found parked in the general vicinity of the scene was a coach, parked in Sherringham Road opposite the junction with Hollingsworth Street. The coach driver was traced and interviewed. He had parked this vehicle at about 5pm and could not assist the enquiry.

The men employed in the various demolition gangs, working in the vicinity of Hollingsworth Street, were interviewed, as were former tenants of the houses there. Three former tenants gave information and descriptions of a prostitute who had been in the habit of frequenting derelict house in that street with her clients. The prostitute was identified and traced but no evidence was forthcoming to connect her or a client with the murder.

It also became apparent that nobody had been able to supply information as to the whereabouts of Everett during the late afternoon or early evening of Saturday 10th March. His brother Charles had informed us that he used to be fond of the cinema. Enquiries were therefore made at local cinemas but none of the persons seen could recognise Everett's photograph as that of a patron on 10th March.

The result of scientific examination of Everett's Stomach contents and urine sample had been without trace of any drugs or alcohol, or any recent intake of food. The possibility that he may have spent this time in a public house was thus eliminated. The results of a detailed study of the foot impressions in blood on the passage lino, by Mrs Butcher a Principal Scientific Officer, were however of some value. She was of the opinion, that a shoe, almost certainly with a plain sole, of at least size ten, made them. She also concluded that the most likely explanation for the position of the prints is that the wearer was staggering.

This development furthered a growing suspicion that whoever committed the murder may well have been someone who was intoxicated and chose the same house as Everett to sleep that night, thereby leading to an altercation, with the theft of any possessions merely an afterthought.

During our enquiries information was received that various alcoholics were in the habit of frequenting the gardens of Mary Magdalene Park in Liverpool Road, opposite the junction with Sherringham Road. One such person in particular was described as a ginger haired Irishman, who had a particular reputation for being violent when in drink.

This man was eventually identified and I shall refer to him as Patrick Whelan. At the time of his identity being established this 36-year-old man was in fact serving a term of two months' imprisonment imposed on 4th April for an offence of criminal damage. Whelan's clothing was examined at Pentonville Prison on 11th May and bloodstaining was found on his jacket sleeve lining.

His clothing and shoes were submitted to the laboratory for further examination and on 14th May, when Whelan was released from prison, he was detained and brought to Caledonian Road Police Station where he was interviewed by me and a statement obtained.

Whelan admitted to being an alcoholic but could not recall his movements on 10th March. He stated that he had been staying in a derelict building in Elthorne Road, Holloway, prior to his arrest. The buildings referred to were thoroughly searched but nothing incriminating was found. In answer to questions regarding the bloodstaining on his clothes, Whelan stated he had cut his head in a fall, two days prior to his arrest and a priest had called an ambulance for him.

Father Joseph Power a priest of lady Margaret Road, N.W.5., confirmed knowing Whelan and verified that on 25th March, Whelan had called upon him with blood on his face and clothes. When the result of tests at the laboratory were made known, it was learnt that the blood on Whelan's jacket was consistent with being his own and not that of Everett. Comparison of Whelan's shoes with the footprints left on the lino at the scene showed that they did not make the marks.

Whelan an amiable enough fellow whilst sober, was content to enjoy the hospitality of Caledonian Road Police Station for the three days it took to make our enquiries and complete the forensic comparisons. On his release having been provided with a clean suit and new shirt and shoes courtesy of H.M. Prison Pentonville, he was smart enough to attend a job interview had he been so minded.

Sadly a few weeks later, arriving for duty at Caledonian Road Police Station early one Sunday Morning, I was to see a very dishevelled Whelan taken out of the back of a police vehicle by two uniformed officers. He was still dressed in the same attire we had provided, except the shirt and suit were now crumpled and dirty and the once shiny black shoes were badly scuffed. On enquiry I learnt that he had been detained for begging, after a complaint that he was stopping pedestrians and asking for money. He was clearly still intoxicated from the previous night's drinking.

He was however sober enough to recognise me and greet me like a long lost brother.

I explained to the officers how Whelan had recently spent three days in custody whilst we made enquiries to eliminate him from the Murder. They had no wish to waste much more of their time processing him on a begging charge, as the twenty four hours he would be detained before attending court, would doubtless be his sentence. It was mutually agreed that Whelan would be given a cup of tea and some toast and be allowed to continue on his way shortly with a warning as to his future conduct.

On 24th March a 30 year-old man giving the name of Kenneth Smith, with an address in Peckham, attended Caledonian Road Police Station and volunteered information respecting the murder which he had seen publicised. The man gave details of three youths that he alleged he had seen acting suspiciously in Hollingsworth Street on a date, which he thought was 15th March. Later investigation was to prove the statement to be false, as was Smith's identity. He was in fact identified as a local resident with a criminal record. He was arrested and in a written statement under caution admitted that his first statement was false and had been made in the hope some reward might be forthcoming. During the course of enquiries, evidence came to light that he had stolen property from his employers on 24th March and he was charged with the offence of theft. On learning of the circumstances of his arrest, the Learned Magistrate at Old Street Magistrates Court remanded him for medical reports, before imposing a fine of £20.

Throughout the enquiry house-to-house enquiries continued in the neighbourhood. In all some 977 persons were interviewed and although 285 of these persons knew Everett by sight, no persons were traced who could supply information of the events surrounding his death.

A total of 195 public houses were visited and of these, Everett was known in 84. Where there was any evidence that Everett had been seen recently, drinking in the company of any person, such persons were traced and interviewed. No useful information was obtained respecting events that led to his death.

Everett was known in 69 of some 143 local cafes and 15 of some 59 betting shops visited, but once again no useful information as to motive was forthcoming from these enquiries.

Despite the various avenues of possibility explored and investigated, no positive motive was ever established. There is little doubt from the nature of the injuries and the confined area of blood splashing around where the body was found, that the injuries were inflicted inside the house.

The absence of money on the average person would tend to indicate a robbery motive, but not so with someone of Everett's station. Alternatively were his death merely the result of an outburst of violence not intended to kill, it would not be unnatural for the assailant to search the body, seeking some means to further his escape.

Everett was a convicted thief and his whole mode of existence was centred on what he could scrounge or steal. Doubtless such a hazardous way of life always carried with it the possibility of some form of retribution from an aggrieved loser of property, be it a fellow totter or an irate householder.

The very nature of the area where Everett chose to sleep made him an ideal target for anyone looking for a victim to rob. With such a motive his attacker(s) could lie in wait in the house for his return were it a planned venture, or follow him into the house without fear of being seen or overheard if an opportunist.

Much evidence was unearthed during the enquiry indicating that the derelict properties in the area were a constant haunt of numerous persons without a permanent address. Such places being occupied by families squatting, others by poor class labouring types who either could not or did not wish to pay high rents for accommodation, often little better than that provided by the derelicts.

Methylated spirit drinkers and alcoholics are another breed of person found to have sought refuge in that area. To the likes of such people a good 'skipper' as such places are known, is a thing to be cherished especially when comfortable bedding was to be had. Was Everett to have returned to his habitat and found another there, or been there when another entered seeking shelter, there would doubtless have been a dispute between them and this could have resulted in Everett being struck the blows, which caused his demise.

The fact that the murder weapon was never found, despite the most intensive search of the area leads to the conclusion that the assailant took it with him. This gives rise to the possibility that there was some value attached to it, such a piece of lead pipe were his assailant a fellow totter or a bottle containing alcohol were he attacked by an alcoholic. The latter possibility would be consistent with the conclusions of Mrs Butcher the Scientific Officer that the footprints were made by someone who was staggering.

The degenerate condition of some of the alcoholic types found to be frequenting the local parks and gardens was such that were his assailant to be one of them he may well have been unaware of his actions.

The manner in which Everett's cap came to be on the garage roof, adjacent to 23, Hollingsworth Street the Friday before his death was never satisfactorily explained. One possibility was that young children playing in and around the derelict house could have found it and thrown it up there.

Dr D.R.Chambers (H.M. Coroner) sitting with a Jury at St. Pancras Coroner's Court on 21st June 1973 conducted an inquest into the death of Everett. After evidence from relevant witnesses had been given, the Jury returned a verdict of 'Murder by person or persons unknown'.

Enquiries into Everett's murder continued thereafter with officers chasing up loose ends and enquiring into any fresh information that was forthcoming. There was however a growing realisation that the value of the scientific evidence was dwindling daily as it was unlikely that the offender would be found wearing the same attire and footwear as on the night of the murder. The two outstanding fingerprints being remote from the ground floor where the offence had occurred were not considered likely to be connected with the offence. The only hope therefore was the remote possibility of some unforeseen information coming to light, which might lead to the identity of the person responsible. No such information however, was forthcoming.

With Everett being such a loner, this investigation presented a real challenge to the officers involved in the case and it is to their credit that within a very short space of time, so many people were traced who knew Everett or whose premises or facilities he frequented. This enabled us to gradually piece together details of how he lived his life. Sadly it did not enable us to determine who was responsible for bringing about his demise.

Chapter Fourteen

Detective Inspector at Holloway

On 2nd July 1973 just as the enquiry in the Everett's murder was drawing to a close, I was promoted to Detective Inspector and a little flattered to be retained on 'N' Division by being posted to Holloway Police Station, situated in Hornsey Road N.4. This was a relatively new building, which had been built to replace its war damaged predecessor, situated a few hundred yards away, with which I had been more familiar, during my days as an Aide on the Division. Little did I realise that in the course of this posting I would find myself dealing with the most complex and demanding role of my career to date, involving numerous acts of bravery by various officers' intent upon arresting dangerous armed criminals.

My role was much the same as it had been at Islington in the now defunct rank of First Class Sergeant. I was responsible for the allocation and supervision of all criminal investigations. To this end I had a staff of about twenty officers including Aides to CID. I was fortunate in that I knew the four Detective Sergeants, who were experienced officers with similar service as myself. Two of them, 'Buzz' Goodingham and Tom Moore, had been in the same class as me at the Initial Detective Training Course. Another, Peter Kent-Woolsey had been a PC on my relief in uniform as well as having assisted on the murder squad investigating the death of James Cameron. Whilst most of the Detective Constables and Aides were new to me, they represented a good mix of youth and experience.

One familiar face I was pleased to see was the late Ralph Fewell, who having retired as a Detective Sergeant was then working as a civilian CID Clerk. It was ironic that it had been Ralph who had prompted me to make an early application for

Aide to CID duties, following my probationer C.I.D. attachment at St. Ann's Road.

I was pleased to learn that most of the uniformed constables investigating 'Minor Crimes' and 'Motor Vehicle Crimes' on their respective Beats were experienced in this role. A young uniform Sergeant, Gavin Robertson, ably assisted by Constable Ian Graham, supervised Beat Crimes. I had known Ian since my days in Stoke Newington Section house where we had mutual friends, although he was not a resident there. We soon established a good working relationship and whilst Gavin was somewhat new to his role he was very keen to learn and take on more responsibility seeking my advice as necessary. This made my supervisory role much easier. It was not surprising that Gavin later transferred into the CID where he pursued a very successful career.

My immediate supervising Officer was Detective Chief Inspector Trevor Lloyd-Hughes, who occupied an adjacent office. We had barely got to know each other however, before he was transferred elsewhere. I received the news that his replacement was to be Alec Eist, with very mixed feelings. Although we had known each other as Detective Sergeants on 'Y' Division where I had assisted him with arresting the team that were engaged in 'smash and grab' raids at electrical stores, we operated on different wave lengths. I was in fact a little surprised to learn of his promotion to Chief Inspector. He was renowned as an active thief taker with a great knowledge of the local criminal fraternity, particularly those engaged in the theft of lorry loads of valuable stolen goods. He had many useful contacts and informants and his skills were ideally suited to working on a team such as the Flying Squad. From my personal experience I knew paperwork was certainly not his forte, so quite how he would operate as a Divisional Chief Inspector I was unsure.

Needless to say he greeted me like a long lost brother on his arrival, whether from genuine affection or the knowledge that I would be a reliable deputy, I'm not sure. Having transferred from St. John's Wood Division he initially made numerous trips back there for what he would describe as a 'meet'. Alec always played his cards close to his chest, so one never knew what he was involved in. I knew a 'meet' could be a meeting with one of his informants or merely a social drink with one of his cronies. Whilst I was not in a position to object to such absences, his tendency to use our one CID car with some young Detective Constables as his driver did prove inconvenient on occasions.

Obviously when an officer like Alec Eist had the ear of useful informants, such information as they were minded to pass on would not necessarily relate to activities on his current Division. This would necessitate passing on the details to whoever was dealing with any crime that had been committed, or to suitable Operational Squad officers where information related to crimes that were merely at the planning stage.

On a personal level I liked to get involved in the investigation of some of the more serious crimes that happened wherever I was working and so when an allegation of Incest was made, not having experienced such a case before, I decided to deal with the investigation myself.

The complainant was a West Indian lady working as a nurse at a North London Hospital who discovered her thirteen year-old daughter was pregnant. I was horrified to learn that this was the second such occasion this had occurred. On the first occasion Islington Social Services had dealt with the matter by arranging for a medical consultation, resulting in a termination of the pregnancy. For some unknown reason they had not thought fit to inform police that it was the girl's father who had made her pregnant. The mother, who I shall refer to as Mrs. Brown, imposed the only form of punishment by refusing to sleep with her husband, banishing him to a spare room. After a few months however, she had relented and normal relations were resumed between husband and wife.

Not content with this however Mr. Brown had continued to have intercourse with his daughter taking advantage of his wife's absence from their home through shift work and now she was pregnant again.

Having obtaining relevant statements from both mother and daughter and learnt that Mr. Brown was a painter employed by British Rail, I contacted the British Railway Police at Kings

Cross Station and they were able to detain him for me on completion of his days' work. When interviewed by me, Mr. Brown had little choice but to admit to the offence and in due course he received a sentence of 3 years imprisonment for the offence of Incest. The daughter's pregnancy was however at such an advanced stage that termination was not viable on this second occasion and adoption of her child was arranged with the assistance of Social Services.

Doubtless had Social Services informed police from the outset when the child first became pregnant this second pregnancy could have been avoided. I never received any satisfactory explanation as to why police had not been informed in the first instance. Fortunately due to a number of high profile cases of child abuse, it was soon to become mandatory for multi-agency Case Conferences to be held when anyone suspected a child may have been a victim of neglect or abuse.

The next serious crime that I was to deal with was an allegation of rape by a young teenage girl. The allegation arose during the early hours of one morning when the girl escaped from a house in Fonthill Road, Finsbury Park where she had been taken and made her way to a telephone kiosk from where she telephoned her boyfriend's mother. Police were informed and she was brought to Holloway Police Station, where she recounted her story of having met a young man the previous day and subsequently accompanied him in his car to a house of some of his friends in Islington. She claimed that after being induced to swallow some amphetamine sulphate tablets, she had been taken to a bedroom by the man where he had indecently assaulted her. She had subsequently been driven to his house in Fonthill road where the alleged rape had occurred, despite the presence of another young female in the flat.

The initial investigation into this allegation had been undertaken by the night duty CID team, who in addition to obtaining a detailed statement had arranged for the girls examination by the Divisional Surgeon. Finally they had taken the girl back to Fonthill Road where she had been able to identity the house where the alleged offence had occurred.

Confronted with details of this allegation on my arrival at Holloway it was merely a matter of getting a small team of officers together and raiding the house where we arrested the suspect who I shall refer to as Graham Cook. Also present and arrested, was his seventeen-year old girlfriend who I shall refer to as Mandy. During the arrest Cook was seen to throw a small package out of a rear window which when retrieved from the garden was found to contain cannabis. Details of the pair were searched at Criminal Record Office and Cook was found to have numerous convictions recorded for a variety of crimes including acts of violence. Mandy had several convictions for soliciting prostitution.

When interviewed by me, Cook did not deny having chatted up the alleged victim and taken her to a friend's house, before returning with her to his flat. Whilst not denying the various sexual acts that the victim had alleged, he claimed that everything was done with the girls consent. He denied inducing her to take any drugs.

At the time of these allegations the victim had been residing with her boyfriend and his parents in a flat on the Woodberry Down Estate, Manor House, having become estranged from her own parents. It was for this reason that she had telephoned her boyfriend's mother once she escaped. Whilst not a witness to any of the alleged offences I knew that the boyfriend's mother's evidence that the victim telephoned her in a distressed condition as soon as she was free to do so, was admissible in any proceedings, as evidence of 'recent complaint'. A statement was taken from her accordingly.

During interview the victim had expressed some concern at the thought of her boyfriend's mother becoming involved. It transpired that this was due to the fact that her boyfriend's father was one half of a well-known singing duo. I subsequently received a telephone call from him in Blackpool where he was currently appearing. Whilst expressing concern for the wellbeing of the victim, he was also concerned that his name should not be divulged in any proceedings.

Enquiries were made at the premises in Islington and such persons as were present when Cook brought the girl there, were interviewed. Needless to say all denied any knowledge of drugs being taken or offered to the girl in their presence. Although there was some confirmation of Cook and the girl having spent some time in one of the bedrooms no evidence of any complaint by the girl were forthcoming.

The medical examination of the victim had revealed some evidence of bruising to the girl's thighs, which could tend to corroborate her allegation. In view of Cook having admitted to consensual intercourse I knew any subsequent evidence from laboratory examination of the various swabs that had been taken, would not further the case.

Mandy, the girlfriend of Cook was interviewed regarding her association with him and in view of her convictions for prostitution was questioned as to whether Cook was exercising any control over her or living on her immoral earnings. She denied that this was the case, stating that Cook was merely her boyfriend and had his own flat in Bow but did stop over at her flat on occasions. The fact that she was able to corroborate that Cook had brought another female i.e. the victim, to her flat and made use of her bedroom with this girl was evidence of the control Cook had over her. She was however unable to corroborate the girl's allegation as to what had occurred in the bedroom.

Cook was charged with the offences of rape and possession of Cannabis and in due course committed for trial at the Central Criminal Court. After considering all the available evidence it was the opinion of counsel appointed to prosecute the offences, that in view of Mandy's convictions for prostitution they did not propose to call her to give evidence at the trial.

On the day of the trial the victim, a well-endowed young lady, unfortunately turned up dressed in a short skirt and a bright orange tee shirt which clearly evidenced the fact that she was not wearing a bra underneath it. The defence team must have been delighted as to her appearance as it made her look a cheap floozy rather than the naïve young girl I knew her to be. Her appearance clearly did little to convince the jury that she had not consented to the various acts she recounted in her evidence for they subsequently acquitted Cook on the Rape and

Indecency Charges. He was however convicted for possession of the Cannabis. After details of his previous convictions had been made known to the court he was sentenced to nine months imprisonment.

During my time at Holloway a prostitute was found murdered near some lock up garages on Highbury Vale Section and Alec Eist having responsibility for that Section headed up a murder squad at Highbury Vale, investigating her death. During the course of his enquiries Alec enlisted the services of the Police Five Programme resulting in a visit by Shaw Taylor the presenter. Whether the two were previously acquainted or not I am unsure, but shortly afterwards I learnt that Alec had invited Shaw to his Silver Wedding Anniversary Celebrations which Noeleen and I were due to attend.

The function was held at Quaglino's Restaurant in the St James's area of London's West End. I had been a little surprised when Alec invited Noeleen and I as no one else on his staff was invited and we had only briefly met Alec's wife Ruby when sharing a coach to attend Divisional CID Dinner Dances. Never the less it was an opportunity to enjoy a good night out with good food and wine, whilst the highlight for Noeleen was having danced with Shaw Taylor whose company we were pleased to enjoy that evening.

Whether Alec had a personal contact at Quaglino's I know not, but it was certainly an establishment that would have been out of my price range for a meal out, let alone inviting the number of guests that attended. The restaurant was to feature in Alec's plans on another occasion during my time at Holloway, but this time in a completely different context.

Alec and a group of friends and local businessmen became involved in a venture to raise funds for the Lion Boys Club situated in Hoxton. With the assistance of contacts at Waltham Forest Boxing club, they had decided to promote a Charity Boxing Dinner, to be held at Quaglino's Restaurant. I soon found myself co-opted onto the committee and there followed a number of meetings to discuss progress and the logistics of holding such an event at premises which had not previously been used for this purpose. I was given the responsibility for the provision and supervision of stewards on the night. I had no trouble in obtaining the services of a number of volunteers, some from our current staff as well as other local officers who I knew to have an interest in boxing.

In due course the event, which was a black tie affair, was held and well supported, including the attendance of a number of well-known faces from the criminal fraternity, doubtless cajoled by Alec into parting with some of their ill-gotten gains to support the local youth. There was the usual raffle and an auction of sporting memorabilia, some provided by local football teams, thus enabling a significant financial contribution to me made to the funds of the Lion Boys Club on conclusion of the event.

On another occasion Alec Eist informed me that through one of his contacts, he had been asked to provide stewards for a forthcoming concert by Frank Sinatra, at the Royal Albert Hall. This was an unofficial 'duty' and he recruited a number of our staff including myself who were prepared to attend in their off duty time. This rare opportunity to see the great man in person was reward enough to enable Alec to enlist the help of about a dozen officers. When I mentioned it to Noeleen she was quite envious knowing that whilst I preferred the voice of Nat King Cole, Frank Sinatra had always been her favourite. When I told Alec he had no hesitation in telling me to bring her along. Noeleen was delighted and on the evening of the concert we met up outside the venue where Alec issued everyone with including her with a 'Steward' lapel-badge. Our duties were perfunctory with each of us allocated a particular entrance in which to loiter, once the doors were opened for public admission. We were however not allocated any seating to view the performance but once the concert commenced I was able to join Noeleen who was waiting for me in one of the bars and I managed to find her one of the pull-down usherette seats on one of the upper tiers from where we were able to view the event.

Alec Eist was certainly a larger than life character with numerous contacts in the criminal underworld and the upper echelons of society and show business, but I breathed a little easier when he was ultimately replaced by the late Don Mann who had served as the First Class Sergeant at Caledonian Road when I had first been promoted to that rank at Islington.

In the opening paragraph of this chapter I spoke of my involvement with a case involving numerous acts of bravery by officers facing a group of armed and desperate criminals. In order to do justice to that case and the officers concerned, my next chapter is entirely devoted to it.

Chapter Fifteen

Siege at Crouch Hill

On Friday 19ᵗʰ October 1973 at about 5.30pm, 66 year-old Granville Howells was about to lock up the front door of his Sub-Post Office and stationers business in Marlborough Road, at the junction with Sussex Way in Holloway. The only other person present was his Post Office Clerk Mrs. Isabella Hughes who was in a room at the back of the office placing stock into a safe. As Mr. Howells reached the front door it was pushed open and three men burst in.

The men were William Stuart aged 29, Brendan Carey aged 30 and Frank Shevlin aged 33. Outside waiting at the wheel of a stolen Ford Corsair was a fourth man Alexander Sudding aged 26. Mr. Howells was forced to lie down behind the counter by Shevlin who was holding a sawn-off shotgun. He was then covered with a car rug and struck on the head and shoulder when he dared to move, his legs were then tied together.

Mrs. Hughes was made to lie down in the back room, a chair was placed over her head and she was tied hands and feet with chiffon scarves. The contents of the safe consisting of cash, Postal Orders, Premium Bonds, Postage and Insurance Stamps, Savings Certificates and other Post Office sundries, to a value of £13,890 were stolen.

Whilst this robbery had been taking place, Malcolm Payne a Bank Manager was passing by and his suspicions were aroused by the presence of the Ford Corsair with its engine running, driver at the wheel and both nearside doors partly open. As he walked over to have a look at the driver he saw the other three men leave the post office with a large mailbag. As the vehicle was driven off at speed north along Sussex Way, he entered the Post Office where his suspicions were confirmed and he then assisted Mr. Howells to telephone Police.

Police Constable Bryan Pollard was on duty that afternoon driving 'November 4' R/T Car with P.C. Charles Hipkin as his radio operator. Both officers were attached to Holloway Police Station, and were patrolling that Station area. At 5.30pm, fortuitously, they were driving west along Marlborough Road when they saw a Ford Corsair being driven at a fast speed out of Hatchard Road and into Marlborough Road in front of their vehicle. At this time details of the robbery had not yet been made known to police, the vehicle having only been driven some 200 yards from the Post Office.

Aroused only by the manner in which the Corsair was being driven, the officers pursued it. On reaching the junction with the busy Holloway Road the vehicle was driven right, across the path of oncoming traffic without stopping. P.C. Pollard followed with P.C. Hipkin communicating details of their route to all police vehicles in the area, in order that any available officers could come to their assistance. Almost immediately the Corsair turned right again into a side road and P.C. Pollard continued in his pursuit of the vehicle through various back streets of Holloway and the Crouch End area of neighbouring 'Y' Division. During the pursuit it struck four other vehicles and was driven on the wrong side for much of the time, the officers established however that there were four occupants of the vehicle.

Some two miles into its pursuit, whilst being driven along Coleridge Road Hornsey, Stuart who was seated in the front passenger seat, leaned out of the car window and pointed a gun at the pursuing police car. P.C. Pollard was obliged to drive over to the offside of the road to place his vehicle out of the line of possible fire.

Shortly afterwards having turned left into Crouch End Hill a shot was fired by Stuart at the pursing Police Car. Both P.C.'s Pollard and Hipkin instinctively ducked, but nothing struck their car. Doubtless through keeping a healthier distance from the Corsair thereafter the officers lost sight of the Corsair but almost immediately, they were informed by the Crew of Yankee 1. R/T Car that they were now pursing the vehicle.

P.C.s Ryan David and Charles Graham attached to Hornsey Police Station were driving 'Yankee I' R/T Car in Landrock Road, Hornsey when they saw the Corsair driving towards them. P.C. David had tried unsuccessfully to block the road and as it was driven past them, they saw Stuart holding a shotgun in the front passenger seat and Carey holding another shotgun in the rear. P.C. David reversed the police car and immediately drove in pursuit whilst P.C. Graham took over the commentary for the benefit of other police vehicles in the area.

Whilst driving behind the Corsair in Crouch Hill at a distance of about twenty yards the two officers saw Stuart lean out of the front passenger door window and point his shotgun towards them. Stuart then fired at the police officers and pellets struck the front windscreen of the police car in front of P.C. David. Undeterred the officers continued in their pursuit.

When I subsequently made an examination of this vehicle, in addition to finding pellets embedded in the rubber windscreen surround on the driver's side, I found that pellet marks from the shot spread, measured some twenty two inches in height and twenty eight inches in width in the region of the front bonnet and windscreen. These marks extending from the extreme offside of the vehicle towards the centre, i.e. the driving position.

P.C.s Anthony Fitzsimons and Steven Coburn attached to Highbury Police Station were the crew of 'November 3' R/T Car that afternoon and having received details of the pursuit, P.C. Fitzsimmons had driven over to Crouch Hill to render their assistance. On hearing that the Corsair was being driven south in Crouch Hill towards them, P.C. Fitzsimons decided to block the Corsair's escape and he did this by parking his Rover police car broadside across Crouch Hill, adjacent to an already parked car. This was at a bend in the road, just south of the junction with Sparsholt Road, the latter turning being a cul-de-sac.

Both officers then alighted from their police car and stood to the rear of their car, thus completing blockage of the full width of Crouch Hill. They saw the Corsair approaching them at a fast speed, before braking and turning right into the junction with Sparsholt Road. As it passed them, Stuart fired his shotgun towards them through the passenger door window, at a range of 25 to30 feet. The Corsair came to a halt having mounted the south footway of Sparsholt Road and as it did so, P.C.s Fitzsimons and Coburn saw a further shot fired from the same car door window. Fortunately neither officer was struck by any pellets from either discharge.

P.C. David in pursuit of the Corsair had brought his police Rover to a halt alongside the Corsair's offside in Sparsholt Road, with the front of his vehicle touching the front of the Corsair preventing any further forward movement. P.C. Graham being seated in the front passenger seat of the police Rover found himself alongside the driver's door of the Corsair and seeing the driver about to leave he forced the front passenger door of the police car against Sudding's door thus enabling himself to alight from the police car whilst preventing Sudding's escaping.

Once the Corsair was stationary P.C.s Fitzsimons and Coburn ran towards it as Shevlin started to get out of the rear nearside door. Seeing these brave officers approach, Shevlin decided to get back in the car but P.C. Fitzsimons pulled the door back open and the two officers managed to arrest him, despite his attempt to re-enter and shut the door on the officers.

Shevlin when searched was found to have 105 £5 notes and 180 £1 notes in his right coat pocket, he was however unarmed and was detained at the scene in 'November 4' R/T Car by the arresting officers who could therefore take no further part in what was to follow.

P.C. David ran from his police Rover round to the passenger side of the Corsair and through the open window grabbed hold of the shotgun, which Stuart was holding and had pointed at him. Carey in the back of the vehicle then struck P.C. David's left forearm and when this failed to dissuade the officer to release his hold on the firearm, Carey said, "Shoot the Bastard." Seeing Carey place a fresh cartridge in his own shotgun, P.C. David wisely relinquished his hold of Stuart's gun and ran to the other side of the car. He then arrested Sudding the driver of the Corsair, with the assistance of P.C. Graham and P.C.'s Geoffrey Parker and Stephen Hughes from Hornsey Police Station who had just arrived in their Panda Car. Incidentally, P.C. Hughes was on his fourth day of 'Learning Beats' since leaving the Police Training School.

Station Sergeant Michael Peffer and Sergeant David Dixon, had both arrived at the scene from Hornsey Police Station, at this time and were appraised of what had already occurred and saw that two men (Carey and Stuart) each armed with sawn-off shotguns were still in the Ford Corsair. Carey in the rear was waving his gun around in all directions and appeared agitated. Sgt Peffer was also aware that a request had been made for officers to attend the scene with Police Issue Firearms from Hornsey Police Station. Various officers present at the scene were either seeking refuge behind parked vehicles or at a distance out of range of the firearms.

With Crouch Hill being a busy major road and these events taking place at a time when pedestrian traffic was at its peak, members of the public had begun congregating in the general vicinity, eager if somewhat foolishly wishing to see what was taking place, despite efforts by some officers to clear them from the area. S.P.S. Peffer having assessed the situation feared that when armed police officers arrived a gun battle could most likely ensue, during which serious of fatal injuries might befall either of the two armed men, police officers or member of the public. He therefore decided to attempt to talk Stuart and Carey into surrender.

Revealing himself to the two armed men in the Corsair he walked slowly towards them from the offside of the car. Stuart seeing the officer approaching pointed his gun at him. The officer continued until he reached the bonnet of the Rover police car Yankee.1 which was alongside and touching the front of the Corsair. At that time S.P.S. Peffer was spotted by Carey, who also pointed his gun at the officer. Then standing exposed some six or seven feet from Stuart he told him that he wished to speak with him to which Stuart replied "Get away or I'll fucking well kill you." S.P.S. Peffer then held out his hands telling the two men that he was not armed.

Stuart further indicated that he did not wish to discuss matters or surrender even after being told that the assistance of armed officers had been sought. S.P.S. Peffer however persisted in his efforts undaunted by the two sawn-off shotguns now pointing at him and spoke for several minutes endeavouring to persuade the two men to surrender. It was apparent to the officer that his efforts had been in vain when Stuart wound up the window of the driver's door and began to reverse the Corsair back in an arc, still keeping his gun trained at the officer. He then drove it forwards again until a stationary police vehicle obstructed his path.

PC David Brady from Hornsey Police Station had arrived at the scene in a police panda car at the time when S.P.S. Peffer was talking to Stuart and Carey. Seeing both men armed with shotguns he at first took shelter behind a parked police vehicle. As Stuart reversed the Corsair and drove forward, P.C. Brady threw his truncheon at the driver's window, but it struck only the door and Stuart then reversed again until the rear of the Corsair collided with a metal bollard on the footway outside an off-licence, at the northwest corner of the junction. P.C. Brady, realised that despite the positions of the various parked police and private vehicles, one possible avenue of escape for the Corsair existed in the southern section of Crouch Hill, the direction in which Stuart had manoeuvred the Corsair to face.

P.C. Brady therefore ran to the abandoned Rover police car 'Yankee 1' formerly driven by the now injured P.C. David, started the engine and reversed the Rover at a fast speed towards the Corsair, holding the door open with his right hand through the door window on the outer handle.

PC Raymond Collett from Hornsey Police Station was sitting in the driving seat of a police van, which he had parked in the Centre of Crouch Hill just north of, and facing the junction with Sparsholt Road, when Stuart commenced driving the Corsair. As the Corsair was reversed towards him, PC Collett saw Carey in the rear aim his shotgun at him and fire through the Corsair's rear windscreen, which shattered but no further damage or injury was caused. Carey then seeing Brady reversing the police Rover towards him, fired another shot in his direction through the broken rear window.

Fortunately the bulk of the shot from this discharge penetrated the boot lid of the Rover police car as it collided with the rear offside door of the Corsair, although some pellets struck the rear windscreen and P.C. Brady received a slight wound on his right hand from where he had been holding the door open.

P.C. Collett in the police van then saw Stuart exchange his shotgun with Carey and in order to try and prevent their re-loading or firing further shots, he decided to ram the nearside of the Corsair with the Police van which he did twice.

P.C. Terence Southwell was the Collator at Hornsey Police Station and on the afternoon of that day was on duty in plain clothes in his office when he heard details of the pursuit broadcast over his personal radio. On hearing that the Corsair had been stopped and the occupants were firing on police, he being an authorized police firearms user, immediately volunteered his services to be issued with a firearm and go to the assistance of his colleagues.

He arrived at the scene at about the time that Stuart had taken over driving the Corsair in an attempt to drive away, and on arrival he heard a shot being fired and then witnessed the shotgun being discharged towards P.C. Brady in the police Rover. P.C. Southwell to his credit remained calm and fully conscious of both the danger to his colleagues and the public and he called out to the two men in the car that he was an armed police officer. Stuart unheedingly pointed his shotgun towards P.C. Brady and fearing that a further shot might be fired at the officer, P.C. Southwell fired at Stuart. The shot penetrated the front windscreen of the Corsair but did not hit Stuart or fortunately anyone else.

P.C. Brady meanwhile having rammed the rear offside of the Corsair and been fired upon, then leaped from the Police car and ran round towards the rear nearside door of the Corsair, stooping to pick up his truncheon on the way. He opened the door to come face to face with Carey who was lying on the back seat with a sawn-off shotgun in his hands and his feet up towards the officer.

P.C. Brady then struck Carey with his truncheon causing the latter to drop the gun.

P.C. Richard Coombes attached to Hornsey Police Station had attended the scene in the van driven by P.C. Collett and having witnessed the efforts of S.P.S. Peffer and the attempt by Stuart and Carey to escape the scene, he ran after P.C. Brady and assisted him in overpowering the still struggling Carey after removing him from the Corsair.

One of my Detective Constables – George Peel together with Temporary Detective Constable Paul Priest were the crew of 'November 11' 'Q' Car being driven by P.C. Robert Wyness. Having initially arrived at the scene whilst S.P.S. Peffer was talking with Stuart and Carey on the far side of the Corsair, both D.C. Peel and P.C. Wyness had attempted to get to the nearside of the Corsair whilst the occupants attention was distracted. Carey had spotted them however, and thwarted their efforts by pointing his shotgun in their direction.

Stuart's attempt to affect the escape of Carey and himself in the Corsair combined with P.C. Brady's brave actions, prompted all officer at the scene to act in unison by rushing the car from all directions. D.C. Peel and T/D.C. Priest having armed themselves with pieces of brick threw them at Corsair breaking the glass in the front windscreen then rushed the car from the nearside with P.C. Wyness in an attempt to arrest Stuart but found the front nearside passenger door to be jammed. S.P.S. Peffer ran to the offside of the car and by putting his head and shoulders through the shattered rear offside passenger door managed to place one arm around Stuart's neck and restrain him. P.C. Collett having twice rammed the Corsair, left the safety of his van and ran to break the window of the driver's door with his truncheon allowing P.C.Wyness to reach in and open the door. He then together with T/D.C. Priest was able to remove Stuart from the Vehicle.

Whilst Stuart and Carey were being taken to Hornsey Police Station, P.C. David after searching the Ford Corsair took possession of two sawn-off shotguns each containing a spent cartridge as well two live cartridges, which but for the brave actions of the various officers would doubtless have been used by Stuart and Carey in their bid for escape. Fortunately, the only injuries sustained by police officers were bruising to P.C. David's arm, from being struck by Carey's shotgun and a small incised wound to Brady's right hand sustained when ramming the Corsair.

At 5.30pm on the Friday afternoon when the post office robbery occurred, I was in the C.I.D. Office at Holloway Police Station contemplating whether to have a quick drink with a few of my staff before returning home after yet another busy week of investigative and administrative work, when I received a visit from the Station Officer. He informed me that the crew of 'November 4' R/T car were in pursuit of a Ford Cortina containing four men one of whom had fired shots at them. He also related that a report had just come in of an armed robbery at Marlborough Road Post Office and as 'November 4' had started their pursuit in that road, it was presumed the two incidents were connected.

After dispatching a couple of officers to the scene of the armed robbery, I went downstairs to the communications room to monitor how the pursuit was progressing, only to find that the Cortina had been stopped in Crouch Hill, since when little radio traffic had been heard other than a request for the attendance of firearms support, indicating that some form of siege was prevailing. I decided to visit Crouch Hill, which I did with one of my staff and some difficulty, as traffic in the surrounding streets was in gridlock. On arrival I was to find that the four men had been taken to Hornsey Police Station where the majority of the officers and transport involved were based.

Fortunately two Traffic Patrol Officers were in attendance at the scene endeavouring to sort out the traffic and one of them showed me the two shotguns and cartridges, which had been placed in the boot of their vehicle for safe custody by P.C. Ryan David. The Ford Cortina had every window shattered and everybody panel dented or scratched and was still wedged up against the metal bollard outside the off licence. The police Rover November 4. Was still broadside across the entrance to Sparsholt

271

Crescent with its rear end about a foot from the severely damaged door rear offside door of the Cortina where P.C. Brady had rammed it.

As most of the officers directly involved in the incident had departed for Hornsey Police Station with the prisoners before my arrival, I was not aware at that time of exactly what had taken place as only brief details were recounted to me by those officers still at the scene. The sight of the shotgun damage to the front windscreen of the police Rover and the shotgun hole in its rear boot lid together with the extensive damage to the Cortina, bore silent witness to the drama that must have preceded the arrest of these four desperate and dangerous armed men. The full extent of the bravery by some many officers had yet to unfold.

As the initial armed robbery had taken place on Holloway Sub Division it was clear to me that despite firearms having been discharged during the police chase on 'Y' Division, the investigation of all that had taken place leading up to the arrest of the offenders, would have to be dealt with by me at Holloway. Having arranged for the attendance of a Police Photographer and Scenes of Crime Officer at Sparsholt Road and instructed the Traffic Patrol Officers to deposit the shotguns at Holloway Police Station once their duties permitted, I departed for Hornsey.

On my arrival I found the Station to be in a state of euphoria with small groups of officers in various parts of the building relating to their colleagues details of their particular involvement, or what they had seen or heard during the pursuit or arrest. Having served briefly at Hornsey as a Detective Sergeant I knew many of the uniform officers and after speaking with some of them briefly I realized my biggest difficulty would be to establish the exact chronology of the various events that had taken place in particular at Sparsholt Road. I also became aware that many officers from three different Station areas had acted in the finest traditions of the Metropolitan Police by their concerted and often brave actions in effecting the arrest of four dangerous armed criminals.

My opposite number at Hornsey Police Station was Detective Inspector Jerry Fallon an officer I had known for a number of years, we having served at neighbouring police stations on several occasions. I found him in his office with a glass of scotch to hand. A smile crossed his face on seeing me as he remarked, "It looks like this job is down to you Ron."

"Don't worry Jerry I'm well aware of that." I replied.

He then informed me that the prisoner Stuart was in the process of making a written statement under caution to D.C. George Peel, and was admitting they had committed an attempted robbery the previous day at a Sub-Post Office in Grange Road, S.E.1 using the same vehicle, the index number of which had been noted by a witness. After assuring Jerry that I would arrange transfer of the prisoners to Holloway as soon as practicable I set about organizing a general de-brief of all officers concerned.

Having assembled all the relevant officers in the parade room, I got each to relate brief details of their actions and observations both throughout the pursuit and in particular once the vehicle had been stopped at Sparsholt Crescent. This proved to be a most useful exercise not only for me in determining the exact sequence of events, but also it enabled all officers to identify the parts their colleagues had played at various stages of the siege.

What was foremost in my mind was that once the prisoners had been prosecuted I would need to make recommendations for certain officers to receive Commendations and in some instances Bravery Awards. Whilst I had previously caused deserving officers to receive Commendations, I had not previously handled a case where Bravery Awards were appropriate and I needed to do justice to all concerned. I left Hornsey that evening knowing that a difficult task lay ahead with so many brave or commendable actions having been highlighted and corroborated by those officers. I knew that publicity surrounding the events would arouse interest amongst the hierarchy within the force within a short space of time so I needed to be fully aware of each individual's involvement. It was however the practice that any recommendation for Commendation or Bravery Awards where persons had been arrested, would only be submitted once all legal proceedings had been concluded.

My immediate task therefore was to continue with the investigation and evidence gathering regarding what now involved two armed attacks on post office personnel. To that end the Ford Cortina having been photographed at the scene of the ambush was conveyed to Holloway Police Station as were the four arrested men.

Twenty nine year old William Stuart was a native of Bolton with two findings of guilt as a juvenile and some twenty previous convictions recorded against him, the majority for petty theft. He had been released from prison some seven months prior to his arrest after serving an eighteen-month sentence of imprisonment for taking a vehicle without consent and stealing property from it. He has been divorced from his wife for two years and there were five children from this marriage. He had been employed mainly as a labourer but unemployed for the past four months, he was currently residing with his mother at an address in Bolton.

Twenty-six-year-old Alexander Sudding the driver of the Corsair, was a native of Huddersfield and somewhat surprisingly had only been before a court on one previous occasion when he was fined £10 for theft. He was currently living with his wife and two children at an address in Bolton. His employments had mainly been as a dairyman, but he was employed as a labourer at the time of his arrest.

Thirty year-old Brendan Carey was a native of Derry with some eleven convictions recorded against him. He had been released from prison some eleven months previous after serving a term of seven years imprisonment imposed at Leicester Assizes, for robbery with violence and possessing an imitation firearm with intent to rob. He had recently become divorced from his wife and there was one child of this marriage. He was currently living with the estranged wife of a former associate, in Islington. His employments had mainly been as a casual labourer on building sites.

Frank Shevlin a native of Belfast was the oldest of the group at 33 years of age. He had fourteen previous convictions recorded for a variety of offences and had only been released from a sentence of 21 months imprisonment some two months previous. He was a single man and was living in a house frequented by squatters in the Holloway area. His employments had mainly been as a casual labourer on building sites.

The Ford Corsair had been reported stolen from a car park in Coventry two days prior to the robbery. In company with Detective Sergeant Trevor (Buzz) Goodingham I searched this vehicle on its arrival at Holloway Police Station and from it recovered the post office sack containing the proceeds of the Marlborough Road Sub-Post office robbery and a further three empty shotgun cartridges. Stuart and Sudding when interviewed admitted taking the vehicle from the car park when Stuart found his own car keys fitted the ignition of the Corsair.

The fact that this vehicle had been used in an attempt to rob another Sub-Post Office at 165 Grange Road S.E.1 the previous day, would have been broadcast to all officers involved in the pursuit, once the crew of November 4 had relayed information regarding the vehicle to Scotland Yard. Enquiries of colleagues in South London into the circumstances of that offence revealed that it had also occurred in the late afternoon when 52 year-old Mr. Jack Rose the Sub-Postmaster was alone in his office. Three men had entered, one of who approached the counter and after saying something which Mr. Rose could not hear, pointed a sawn-off shotgun at him through the glass protective screen over the counter. Mr. Rose then ran to the back room, actuating an alarm as he did so. He then saw the shotgun discharged splintering the protective screen. Looking out of a window Mr. Rose saw the men get into a Brown Ford Corsair and noted the index number. He was only able to give a description of the man with the gun and that description fitted William Stuart.

When interviewed by Detective Constable George Peel and in his written statement under caution, Stuart admitted his part in the Grange Road Sub-Post Office, attempted armed robbery. Further that Carey, Shevlin, Sudding and a fifth man whose identity he did not know, also participated. He disclosed that he had been staying temporarily at St. Chads Hotel, Kings Cross, as a result of which George Peel and other officers later searched his room and took possession of a suitcase which in addition to items of clothing was found to contain a sawn off shotgun barrel, a live shotgun cartridge, a small hacksaw and a stolen driving licence. Stuart was later to admit to having purchased the licence from a woman in a café in Holloway Road, whilst the owner who resided in Hackney, had not realized his licence was missing until informed of its recovery by police.

As a result of the mention by Stuart, of a fifth man involved at Grange Road, Detective Sergeant Goodingham and I interviewed the other three prisoners late that evening and whilst all admitted their involvement in the attempted robbery at the Grange Road Sub-Post Office, Carey and Sudding denied knowing the identity of the fifth man, claiming he was a friend of Shevlin. The latter declined to supply his name and he was never identified.

The following day I returned to Hornsey Police Station to make a detailed examination of the police Rover 'Yankee 1.' Which P.C. Ryan David had been driving in company with P.C. Charles Graham, prior to P.C. David Brady using it to ram the stolen Corsair. I removed a number of shotgun pellets from both the rubber surrounds of both front and rear windscreens. The assistance of a mechanic had to be gained to remove the rear bumper before it was possible to open the boot, which had been holed by one of the shots fired by Carey. I was to find that shotgun pellets had not only penetrated the boot lid and it's inside cover, but also the petrol tank cover. I also found the retaining wadding from the shotgun cartridge inside the boot, indicating of just how close the barrel of the shotgun had been when discharged.

Returning to Holloway I conducted further interviews with Carey and Shevlin who both made written statements under caution. Carey admitted his part in both the Marlborough Road and Grange Road offences, but Shevlin whilst verbally admitting to the Grange Road offence requested that his written statement contain only reference to the events at Marlborough Road. It was thought this was due to his wish to protect the identity of the fifth man who the others claimed to be his friend.

George Peel meanwhile interviewed Sudding who admitted taking the Ford Corsair with Stuart and his involvement in both the Marlborough Road and Grange Road offences. He also confirmed what Stuart had previously admitted to George Peel, that the pair of them had acquired the guns from a man in Bolton.

During the course of our enquiries on 20th October, information was received from a Detective in Bolton that Stuart and another man had been concerned in a further offence of robbery at a Post Office in the Euston area of London some four weeks previous. Both Stuart and Carey during the course of interviews by myself in company with George Peel, admitted this further robbery. This offence had taken place about six weeks previous, between 5th and 6th September at a Sub-Post Office at 209 Royal College Street, N.W.1 they both made written statement under caution regarding this third robbery and enquiry of the officers involved in that investigation revealed the following.

Mr. Mahashbhal Patel was the Sub-Postmaster of that office, a ground floor terraced property the upper floors of which were unoccupied. At 5.30pm on 5th September Mr. Patel secured and left the premises. Fifty-six year old James Kelly who resided next door at number 211 was out that evening and returned home at about midnight and retired for the night in his 2nd floor flat. He was soon aroused by noises outside his flat and upon investigation found two men on the stairs, one of which stated they were Police Officers. He was then assaulted by being punched and kicked and he saw that one man had a knife, He was then tied up in his room with his own neck ties, apparently whilst the men searched the premises and shortly afterwards he was untied and questioned about the Post Office next door. In his statement Stuart had admitted that they entered the wrong building in error.

Mr. Kelly was allowed to dress and then taken by the men out onto a flat roof at the rear between 1st and 2nd floor level and across to an adjacent roof at No. 209 where the men entered the premises via a window. He was then obliged to spend the remainder of the night in an empty room over the Sub-Post Office guarded by the two men. At around 7.30am he was again tied up and the two men went downstairs.

At 8.45am that morning Mr. Patel arrived, unlocked his Sub-Post Office and began arranging things for his day's business.

Two men who were armed with a knife and an iron bar then accosted him. He was obliged to hand over his keys and one of the men struck him on the leg with the iron bar. Some £3,633 was stolen from the safe despite an alarm system, which actuated, then after Mr. Patel's hands had been tied with string the two men ran off.

Mr. Kelly although tied, had managed to make his way down the stairs and was released with the assistance of a passer-by, just prior to the arrival of police. A Mr. Derek Stone a skip-driver was working near the Post Office that morning and he described two men who he saw running from Royal College Street.

On conclusion of the various interviews with the four arrested men they were initially charged with the robbery of the Marlborough Road Sub Post Office and detained to appear at North London Magistrates Court on the Monday morning. They were then all remanded in custody in order to enable me time to complete outstanding enquiries and obtain statements from all relevant witnesses to the various offences, before finally preparing a detailed report for the information of the Director of Public Prosecutions.

In any complex investigation fraud or otherwise, I was well aware of the value of producing a Schedule setting out relevant details, particularly where matters that, although contained in statements of evidence, needed further clarification in order to be understood or better appreciated. There were three civilian and seventeen police witnesses in relation to the events following the Marlborough Road robbery. With this number of officers becoming involved at various stages of the incident, they had each witnessed or participated in different events. From the initial robbery until the final arrest of the last of the four men responsible there had been some nineteen separate events, such as the discharge of a firearm or ramming of a vehicle or attempt to affect an arrest. I therefore prepared a 'Schedule of Events', which ran to five-pages, which was forwarded with my report and copy statements and documents to the director of Public Prosecutions. This was to prove most useful throughout future proceedings.

When I next crossed paths with Frank McGuinness my Detective Superintendent, a few days after submitting my report via his office to Scotland Yard, He said, "Somebody at the Yard was very impressed with that report you submitted on the robberies. It was a very good report" He mentioned no names and knowing the report would go to C.2. (5) Department which handled case papers I could only presume he may have been referring to Commander Roy Habersham who was in charge at that time. Whilst it was pleasing to get such feedback after all the hard work that had gone into the investigation and preparation, it was to be some eighteen months later that my mind would reflect back to this remark.

Because of the complex nature of this investigation and the number of offences and persons involved, some two months was to elapse from the date of the arrest until submission of my report. During this time the prisoners were making weekly appearances at the magistrate's court when further remands in custody were sought and granted. (Fortunately in recent years this requirement has been changed, thus saving the waste of everyone's time that this used to cause). On one such occasion William Stuart requested the return of a navy blue jacket, which he said would be in the suitcase officers had recovered from the St. Chads Hotel, where he had been staying at the time of his arrest. The following week before leaving for court I retrieved the jacket from the suitcase, which had been kept in our prisoner's property store. I decided to check through the pockets and was glad I had, for in the top pocket I found a small folded piece of paper, which upon examination proved to be a Metropolitan Police Fixed Penalty Ticket. A traffic warden had issued the ticket at 8.48m on 6th September 1973 in Royal College Street, in respect of a motor vehicle registration number GKF 328D. Folded with the ticket was a form HO RT 1 issued by P.C. 1320 Martins of Leicester and Rutland Constabulary, at 7.30 p.m. on 4th September, to William Stuart in respect of a Morris Mini Index No, GKF 328D. This form indicated that the Driving Licence and Certificate of Insurance were to be produced at Kilburn Police Station.

Later that morning I saw Stuart at North London Court when I handed him his jacket. I then said to him, "By the way I found a parking ticket in the top pocket for Royal College Street, on 6th September 1973, the day of the robbery there. I don't suppose you've paid that have you?" He said, "No, that was on there when I went back to pick the motor up later on." I then discussed the form for production of his driving documents and told him I would contact Kilburn Police and let them know what had happened to him.

On 6th December 1973 the four men appeared at North London Magistrates Court when on the directions of the Director of Public Prosecutions I further charged them with some thirteen further offences. Stuart and Sudding for taking and driving away the Ford Corsair; all four defendants for the attempted robbery at Grange Road Sub Post Office; Stuart and Carey for two offences of burglary at 211 Royal College Street and robbery at 209 Royal College Street; Shevlin for possessing a firearm in Marlborough Road with intent to resist arrest; Sudding for dangerous driving at Crouch Hill; Stuart and Carey for making use of a firearm with intent to resist arrest, possessing a firearm with intent to endanger life and possessing a firearm with intent to commit an indictable offence, namely robbery. In addition Carey for wounding P.C. Brady with intent to resist arrest. They were then committed in custody to stand their trial at the Central Criminal Court, Old Bailey.

I was a little surprised a few weeks later on receiving instructions from the Director of Public Prosecutions, to make enquiries regarding notices of alibi, received from Defence Solicitors in respect of all four defendants in relation to the attempted robbery at Grange Road and in particular in respect of Stuart and Carey in relation to both offences at Royal College Street.

During my earlier years in the force it had not been uncommon for the Defence to spring surprise witnesses at Court Trials, providing an alibi for the defendant at the time and date of the alleged offence. This usually took the prosecution by surprise and provided little opportunity for any checks to be made to refute the alibi, before conclusion of the trial. Legislation had subsequently been passed whereby evidence of alibi could not be adduced in court unless prior notice had been served on the prosecution thus enabling police to interview alibi witnesses and make any necessary enquiries with Defence Solicitors being given the opportunity to be present at any proposed interviews.

Despite any admissions made by prisoners on arrest, once remanded in custody and having time to reflect on their likely future sentence, often assisted by fellow inmates, it is perhaps not surprising that their thoughts turn to the weight of evidence against them, particularly once in possession of all prosecution statements.

William Stuart's alibi in respect of the Royal College Street burglary and robbery, was that he had been in Bolton between 2nd and 6th September, 1973. Stuart clearly had overlooked the fact that I had found the parking ticket for his vehicle dated 6th September and had evidence of him being stopped by police whilst driving in Leicestershire on 4th September. This potential evidence having only having come to light after submission of my report to the D.P.P. had not been included in Committal Proceedings. Nevertheless, Stuart named two brothers in Bolton whose company he claimed to have been in. I therefore caused enquiries to be made by Bolton C.I.D. and appointments having been made by an officer to interview both men, they failed to keep the appointment. When a further attempt was made to re-arrange an appointment with one brother he adamantly refused to supply any statement of alibi or keep any appointment. The other brother admitted to having had a drink with Stuart in Bolton but not during the relevant dates as he had been working elsewhere at that time.

In view of this intimation that Stuart was seeking to deny his involvement in the Royal College Street offences I arranged for a statement to be made by the officer who had issued him with the form to produce his driving documents. It transpired that Constable Paul Martin of Motor Patrol Headquarters in Leicestershire had stopped Stuart at 7.30pm on 4th September whilst he was driving south on the M.1. towards London, in his Morris Mini saloon. In answer to questions regarding his journey Stuart had stated he was going to London where he was working for a construction company at Selfridges in Oxford Street. He supplied details of an address in Kilburn and stated that he was en route from his mother's address in Bolton. The officer's statement together with one from the traffic warden who had issued the parking ticket and a further statement from myself regarding my finding the items and discussing them with Stuart was subsequently forwarded to the D.P.P. as additional evidence.

As far as the attempted robbery at Grange Road was concerned it was claimed by Stuart and Sudding that they spent the whole day together driving around London and at one point had visited a building site at Selfridges at about 3:30pm where Stuart spoke to two former work colleagues. Only one of the men could be traced and whilst he stated he had met up with Stuart for a drink on about three occasions, it had always been at lunchtime. Stuart had however been in the company of another man on one of the occasions.

Brendan Carey's alibi notice regarding the attempted robbery at Royal College Street on 6th September was merely that he could not remember where he was or who he was with that day. In relation to 18th October, his only recollection was of drinking in the Nags Head in Holloway Road. This had been mentioned in his statement under caution and those of his co-accused wherein they had admitted to having left that public house and driven to Grange Road where they attempted the robbery there.

Frank Shevlin in his notice of alibi claimed to have been in the Nags Head until leaving at 3:15pm and then returned home some 20 minutes later. He named a girl who resided at the same address who he had seen that afternoon, but as the address had been a house frequented by squatters and was unoccupied and boarded up by the time of my enquiries, the girl could not be traced.

It was the recommendation of Prosecution Counsel that in view of the notices of alibi, the four defendants should be given the opportunity of identification parades in respect of the robbery at Royal College Street and the attempted robbery at Grange Road. Defence Solicitors subsequently agreed to this proposal and on 27th February 1974, Identification Parades were held at Brixton Prison involving Stuart and Carey in respect of the robbery at Royal College Street. On the first Parade in which Stuart participated Mr. Kelly the neighbour who had been tied up, identified another participant in the Parade. Mr. Stone the skip-driver failed to make any identification. On the second Parade however, Mr. Kelly identified Brendan Carey and again Mr. Stone failed to recognize anyone.

Mr. Patel the Sub-Postmaster at 209 Royal College Street was unable to attend the Parades as he had been hospitalized for some time. Arrangements had been made for the attendance at the Prison of Mr. Rose the sub-Postmaster from 165 Grange Road, but unfortunately on the previous evening he was again the victim of an offence of robbery at his Post Office and was not in a fit state to attend.

On 11th March 1974 at the Crown Court, Old Bailey the four prisons appeared before His Honour Judge Edward Sutcliffe, Q.C. Brendan Carey, William Stuart, Alexander Sudding and Frank Joseph Shevlin each pleaded 'Guilty' to the following Counts

(1)   Attempted robbery at the Grange Road Sub Post Office
(2)   Robbery at the Sub Post Office in Marlborough Road
(3)   Possessing two shortened shotguns with intent to commit robbery on 19th October 1973.
        Carey and Stuart also pleaded 'Guilty' to a further Count
(4)   Making use of a firearm with intent to resist or prevent the lawful arrest.

Carey and Stuart both pleaded "Not Guilty' to robbery at the Royal College Street Sub Post Office and assaulting Mr. James Kelly. All four also pleaded 'Not Guilty' to a further joint offence of making use of a firearm with intent to resist arrest on 19th October. No plea was taken in respect of a firearm offence at Grange Road on 18th October relating to all four or a Count of wounding P.C. Brady against Carey and Stuart.

In view of the gravity of the offences all four had pleaded 'Guilty' to and the length of sentences that could be imposed, Prosecution Counsel took the view that little purpose would be served other than wasting court time, in pursuing the offences to which 'Not Guilty' pleas had been made. Doubtless Defence Counsel had either anticipated this or reached agreement with the prosecution in what is generally known as 'Plea Bargaining'.

After full details of the circumstances relating to the admitted offences and antecedents of the defendants, had been outlined to the court by Prosecution Counsel, His Honour Judge Edward Sutcliffe, Q.C. sentenced Carey, Stuart and Shevlin each to 10 years imprisonment on Count (1); 12 years imprisonment on Count (2) and 8 years imprisonment of Count (3). Alexander Sudding was sentenced to 8 years imprisonment on each of charges (1) and (2) and 6 years imprisonment of Count (3). Carey and Stuart were also sentenced to 14 years imprisonment on Count (4) all sentences to run concurrently. The Judge also directed that the remaining Counts were not to be proceeded with without leave of the Court or the Court of Appeal (Criminal Division) as was usual procedure in such instances.

At the termination of the trial after the defendants has been sentenced His Honour Judge Edward Sutcliffe, Q.C. commended all those concerned in the arrest in the following manner:-

'One of the difficulties of mentioning people who seem to have behaved in the most praise-worthy way is that if you mention some you must also miss out others, but I do think I should mention Mr. Payne who showed his public spirit by taking notice of what was happening, and taking the right action about it. I would be glad if the thanks of the Court, and of the public – that is what I am speaking for – could be conveyed to him. Also Mr. Rose, the sub postmaster at Grange Road, who kept his head sufficient to get the alarm going.

I have probably missed someone out as far as civilians are concerned, but I cannot help it, and they will have to forgive me. One of the redeeming features of this case is that everybody seems to have acted early.

I turn to the police and Sergeant Peffer, although again, it may be wrong to pick him out signally because it seems to me, that all behaved with the utmost heroism: words fail me. All I can do is express my great admiration to those men who behaved in this way in the face of firearms like this. They really deserve the highest commendation, all those who took part, each in their way, in the arrest of those men, and I feel sure it will be passed on, and I know that it is right that it should be.'

Subsequently in a letter date 19th March 1974 the Director of Public Prosecutions also commended the officers involved.

The trial having been successfully concluded my attention then turned to compiling and submitting a report making recommendation for suitable recognition, for the bravery and commendable actions the various officers had displayed. Awards for gallantry by serving police officers were certainly very rare and when details of Commendation or High Commendation were published in Police Orders they usually only concerned a handful of officers at most. By my reckoning the arrest of these four desperate, dangerous armed men had only been affected by the combined efforts of some seventeen officers, each of who had at some time displayed courage initiative or determination.

I had been clear in my mind from the first day that some officer's actions were worthy of their receiving bravery awards rather than the usual Commendations for good police work.

P.C. Ryan David had singularly handed tackled and attempted to obtain possession of Stuart's shotgun after just previously been fired upon whilst driving in close pursuit.

P.C.'s Anthony Fitzsimons and Steven Coburn who knowing they were dealing with armed and dangerous men had placed their personal safety in jeopardy by blocking the path of the Corsair and then having been fired at on two occasions, without hesitation run to the Corsair containing the four men and effected the arrest of one of them, before the assistance of the various officers that were later to arrive.

S.P.S. Michael Peffer had placing his personal safety in jeopardy in his persistent attempt to prevent further injury to all parties present at the scene by endeavouring to talk the armed men into surrender.

P.C. David Brady had made a courageous and determined effort to prevent the escape of the armed men using an abandoned police car, before leading the final assault and tackling Carey whilst he was still armed with a sawn-off shotgun.

I therefore made a recommendation that the actions of these five officers be considered for bravery awards.

My next recommendation was that that the actions of three other officers had been worthy of being 'Highly Commended'. And these were P.C. Bryan Pollard Charles Hipkin the crew of November 4 R/T Car and P.C. Raymond Collett the driver of the police van.

P.C. Pollard for the determined and capable manner in which he drove in pursuit of the Corsair under hazardous conditions even after being fired upon.

P.C. Hipkin for an outstanding R/T commentary, given in the most difficult conditions, resulting in other police vehicles being able to position themselves to prevent the escape of the offenders.

P.C. Collett for his courage and initiative in ramming the Corsair after personally being fired upon, and so preventing any further escape attempt by Stuart and Carey.

In addition I recommended Commendations for the remaining nine officers, who had all acted within the best traditions of the Police Service by displaying determination and ability in effecting the arrest of these four dangerous criminals.

Finally I recommended that suitable letters of thanks be forwarded to Mr. Payne and Mr. Rose for the valuable assistance they afforded.

Subsequently all seventeen officers involved in the pursuit and arrest of the four armed men received either Commendations or High Commendations from the Commissioner of Police.

On 18th March 1975 Constables David Brady and Ryan David together with Sergeant Michael Peffer were each awarded the Queen's Gallantry Medal. Police Constables Steven Coburn; Raymond Collett; Antony Fitzsimons and Charles Graham were each awarded the Queen's Commendation for Brave Conduct.

Chapter Sixteen

Detective Inspector at Highbury Vale

During the early part of 1975 I moved across to take charge of Holloway's Sectional Station – Highbury Vale, situated in Blackstock Road a short walk from the Arsenal Football Club.

The staff at Highbury consisted of a couple of Detective Sergeants and four Detective Constables. One of the Sergeants, the late Graham 'Robby' Robinson was an old acquaintance of mine from 'Y' Division and a very shrewd investigator another was Pat Ford who had been an Aid to C.I.D. at Hornsey when I'd worked their briefly. Pat had lived nearby to Noeleen and I following his marriage and had the driest sense of humour I've ever encountered. Although I knew most of the other officers by sight I'd never worked with any of them but I soon got to know their various attributes and one young Detective Constable, Keith Manktelow, proved to be a particularly able investigator.

Crime at Highbury was pretty much the same as I had been used to and I soon found myself dealing with some unsavoury characters. I recall one such person who lived in Conewood Street who I arrested and interviewed in relation to an allegation of Buggery with a 17 year-old youth. This individual admitted to picking the youth up at Victoria Station bringing him home and checking him over to see if he was infected by any sexually transmitted diseases before allowing him to sleep in a spare bed in his bedroom. He denied committing any offences in relation to the youth, who he claimed was just one of some twenty individuals who over a period of time, he had tried to help get back on their feet usually after having run away from home. The complainant in this case was found upon medical examination to have been the victim of an offence such as that alleged, but he proved particularly unreliable and without any corroboration it was not possible to proceed further.

Another particularly nasty individual I found myself dealing with, borrowed a van, armed himself with a knife and broke into a Women's Refuge in Leconfield Road during the night. He then forced his ex-girlfriend to return to his flat under duress. The poor girl had sought and been granted shelter in the Refuge to escape previous acts of violence directed at her by the boyfriend who somehow had managed to locate the address where she was staying.

Part of my responsibilities at Highbury Vale was supervision of a Divisional Crime Squad, run by the late Detective Sergeant John Mullally a keen West Ham Football Club supporter. My service in the Tottenham and Highbury areas had enabled me to attend football matches at Spurs and Arsenal from time to time, however I still considered myself a Fulham Supporter from my childhood days of attending all their home games with my father.

As luck would have it, Fulham although currently in the Second Division, but captained by Alan Mullery, were due to play West Ham in the Cup Final on 3rd May1975. The former West Ham and England Captain Bobby Moore then in the twilight of his career had recently transferred to Fulham and with West Ham Captained by Billy Bonds, having the likes of Frank Lampard and Trevor Brooking in their team, it promised to be an interesting Final.

Through contacts John had at West Ham, he was able to purchase us a couple of tickets for the game and so I attended my first Cup final. Unfortunately West Ham won 2 nil but it was an enjoyable day with great sportsmanship displayed by both sides.

Situated only a short distance from Highbury Vale Police Station was Blackstock Road Fire Station, above which were a number of married quarters for firemen and their families. With both emergency services often working in conjunction with each other a good rapport normal exists between personnel. It was therefore particularly disturbing to finding myself having to investigate an allegation of Incest directed at a 41-year-old serving fireman resident in those flats in July 1975.

This allegation came to light after the estranged wife of the fireman discovered that her 16-year-old schoolgirl daughter, had become pregnant. When interviewed the girl reluctantly admitted that after her mother had left home she had subsequently shared her father's bed on occasions and ultimately he had committed various acts of indecency with her, eventually culminating in full sexual intercourse. The girl was also admitted that on an occasion when she had left home for a couple of weeks she had stayed at the neighbouring flat of another fire officer and claimed to have slept with his 19 year old son during this time.

In company with Pat Ford, I interviewed the girl's father, he was clearly embarrassed and very shame faced, but to deny the offences would have been to call his daughter a liar, he therefore took the only course open to him and made a written statement under caution admitting his daughter's allegations. He was later charged with three offences of Incest.

When his neighbour's son was interviewed although he admitted he had been out with the girl in the past he denied that she had stayed at his parents flat or that he had been intimate with her. When later confronted with the fact that his father confirmed the girl had been allowed to stay at the flat, he admitted this was true but continued to deny having had intercourse with her. He further stated he had seen her taking three boys into her own flat when her father was absent.

Full details of the girl's allegation regarding this lad's involvement and his subsequent denial were reported to the Director of Public Prosecutions together with the facts concerning her father but ultimately only her father was prosecuted.

One day I received a telephone call from Frank Mc Guinness my Detective Superintendent. He informed me that Commander Roy Habersham the Head of the Bomb Squad had enquired whether I would be interested in transferring to that Branch. I was a little taken aback as I had never met Roy Habersham and had no real knowledge of how the Bomb Squad operated. Frank told me to have a think about it and that was that.

The only person I knew to be working on the Bomb Squad, which was currently C.1. (4) Department at Scotland Yard, was

P.C. Fred Titchener, who I knew from my days at Hornsey. I was aware that Fred had transferred there as a Collator. I decided to ring Fred and ask him about the Bomb Squad and what the duties and responsibilities of a D.I. were there. Fred gave me a very brief resume of work on the Bomb Squad and explained that his particular role was the collation of bomb fragments, such as parts of timing devices, detonators or other materials recovered from the sifted debris after bombing incidents. I soon realized the work would be completely different from anything I had previously experienced and provide an exciting challenge.

A few weeks later I had another call from Frank Mc Guinness who mentioned that Roy Habersham had spoken to him again and wanted to know if I had made any decision about transferring to the Bomb Squad. We had a brief discussion concerning the merits of this possible transfer and Frank assured me that it would be a good career move and so slightly flattered by the thoughts of my services being sought after and tempted by the opportunity to become part of a specialist team at Scotland Yard, I agreed to accept the transfer.

Following the initial telephone call from Frank Mc Guinness I began thinking as to how my name should have come up in relation to this proposed move. I was aware that Frank and Roy Habersham were old buddies and my thoughts went back to the remark Frank Mc Guinness had made some months previous regarding the report I had submitted on the Post Office robbery at Holloway. I realised that Roy Habersham was at that time working in C.2. (5) Department, which handled Case Papers and I concluded he must have been the person who had been impressed with my report. Whatever the reason, notification of my transfer to C.1. (4) Department (Bomb Squad), with effect from 8th September 1975, was published in Police Orders soon afterwards.

Chapter Seventeen

Death of a Bank Robber

On 7ᵗʰ September 1975 a family out blackberry in Hertfordshire, discovered a shallow grave containing a body wrapped in a bedspread. I first learnt of this when reading a newspaper report of a man's body being found in Hatfield Forest. I thought little more of it until a few days later when I received a telephone call from a Detective Inspector from Hertfordshire who was enquiring about my knowledge of Michael Cornwall, who together with Michael West, I had prosecuted for the Barclays Bank Robbery at Haringey some seven years previous. This was the case where the get-away car failed to start and the two robbers decamped on foot. Cornwall being the one who having used the painter's unattended ladder to escape into the grounds of St. Ann's Road Hospital had initially managed to evade arrest, whilst his associate West was caught when spotted leaving the hospital grounds.

I was more than a little shocked to learn that fingerprints had revealed it was 37 year old, Michael Cornwall whose body, shot through the head, had been discovered in Hatfield Forest. My first remark was to question how this could be, as I presumed him to still be inside serving the twelve-year sentence he had got for the robbery. The D.I. then informed me that Cornwall had later appealed against the severity of his sentence and it had been reduced to one of nine years imprisonment and he had been released from Hull Prison on 18ᵗʰ October 1974. Whilst unaware of the circumstances that had led to his demise, I could not help thinking that had he not appealed he might well be still alive. We had a brief discussion about various associates of Cornwall but I could add little to help the Hertfordshire Murder Enquiry.

It subsequently transpired that a friend of Cornwall, William Moseley, a well know character from Holloway's criminal fraternity, had been released from prison a month before Cornwall, but whilst serving his sentence had received visits from a Mrs. Elaine Bright with whom he had been conducting an affair for several years. Her husband, Ronald Bright had himself been in prison for part of this period and Moseley's affair with Mrs. Bright was known to several of his friends.

Between 5th and 15th October 1974, five parts of Moseley's body were washed up at separate locations on the Thames foreshore in Essex. The head and hands were not found at that time, with the result that for a while identification remained uncertain, although the remains were suspected to be those of Moseley. The first post-mortem examination gave little insight into what had happened to Moseley immediately before and after his death, apart from the fact that he had probably died as a result of a head injury. A later post-mortem revealed that he had been tied up and tortured before being killed by severe violence to the head; and that his body had been dismembered when he was either dead or (possibly) unconscious.

Commander Bert Wickstead undertook enquiries into the murder and when Cornwall was himself interviewed and learnt of the disappearance and suspected murder of his friend Moseley he became upset. Soon afterwards he had let it be known that he intended to find out for himself who was responsible.

Unbeknown to me at that time police enquiries soon centred around two well-known Holloway Criminals, Reg Dudley and Robert 'Bobby' Maynard. Whilst I had had no personal dealings with either of them, I was aware of them as local criminals and knew Reg Dudley by sight, as he had lived in an adjacent road to where Noeleen and I had rented a flat when first married. I was also aware the he was a confident of my former Detective Chief Inspector, Alec Eist. As Alec always played his cards close to his chest I was never made aware of the nature of any meetings between Alec Eist and Reg Dudley. It was however apparent to me that Dudley was used by Alec as a conduit into the activities of the local criminal fraternity and I suspected that this arrangement might also operate in reverse.

In January 1976 at the conclusion of a long and painstaking investigation during which Commander Wickstead's enquiry into Moseley's murder became linked with the Hertfordshire enquiry into Cornwall's murder, seven people, including Dudley and Maynard were arrested. In April 1976 Reg Dudley; his daughter Kathleen Bailey; Robert Maynard; his brother Ernest Maynard; Charles Clarke; Ronald Fright and George Spencer, were committed from Epping Magistrates Court to stand trial at the Old Bailey in London, charged with various offences relating to these gangland killings.

The brief background relating to the arrest and trial of the aforementioned were that Bobby Maynard had been a close friend of Moseley and was the key holder of his flat whilst he was in prison. It was alleged that soon after his release the two had fallen out possibly as Moseley suspected Maynard of disclosing details of his affair with Mrs. Bght, to a third party. In addition Moseley had allegedly put it about that Maynard and his mate Dudley were both informers; and Dudley had another reason to resent Moseley, in that several years earlier he had come off second best in a public house brawl.

Moseley was last known to be alive on the afternoon of 26th September 1974, when he borrowed a friend's car to use that evening saying that "he had some business tonight". There was some evidence that Moseley was due to meet up with Ronald Bright that evening but the latter was to claim that he was late and Moseley did not appear. Dudley and his daughter arrived in England that afternoon, by hovercraft on the last leg of a journey from Spain. The car was not returned the following day as arranged and was reported missing. It was eventually found on 30th September outside a public house, undamaged but with one of the doors unlocked.

It transpired that Cornwall had a regular girlfriend called Gloria Hogg but whilst maintaining that relationship he had affairs with other women including Kathleen Hailey the daughter of Reg Dudley. From January 1975 however, he had based himself with the Saggs family in their Islington flat. Fifteen-year-old Sharon Saggs lived there with her mother and three brothers, her father being in prison at that time.

I recall meeting Colin Saggs at the Old Bailey on the day Cornwall's trial commenced for the Bank robbery charges. Having introduced himself as a friend of Cornwall he had posed the question, "Is there anything that can be done?" Such words were not unfamiliar coming from accused persons or their associates when seeking help to lessen the gravity of charges or in some way bring about a "Not guilty' verdict. Whilst innocent enough on their own, I considered them, a prelude to an attempt to pervert the course of justice, by opening up a dialogue in an endeavour to see if an officer was open to some form of inducement, to refrain from carrying out his duty in relation to the case. His words had been wasted on me.

Enquiries were to reveal that between January and July Dudley and Cornwall met on several occasions and that what was initially a reasonably friendly relationship deteriorated to the extent that Dudley was openly expressing his dislike of Cornwall. There was a suggestion that these centred around possible accusations by Cornwall that Dudley was a police informer and Cornwall's association with his daughter Kathleen Hailey.

Early one morning in July 1975 Cornwall had left the Sagg's flat in a hurry never to return. From evidence given later by Sharon Saggs, he seemed to be expecting that someone would be coming for him. Shortly after Cornwall's departure, two men had actually arrived at the flat looking for him. Sharon Saggs was to subsequently identify photographs of Dudley and Maynard, shown to her by police, as being the two men who arrived. Other evidence showed that Cornwall had in fact then gone to live with Gloria Hogg, staying with her until 5th August when he left saying he would be back in two days' time. He did not return.

She became worried and towards the end of August saw Maynard in a public house and asked him if he knew where Cornwall was, but he said he did not. It subsequently emerged that two witnesses had seen Cornwall on 22nd August in London, one of whom spoke to him briefly. This was the last day on which any witness saw Cornwall alive. It was never ascertained where he had been living in the interim period.

On 30th August someone walking in woodland in Hertfordshire, found a place where turf had been cut back and earth disturbed. He did not notice anyone around and made no further investigation. Subsequent events showed that he had come across Cornwall's grave, either before or after the body had been placed in it, as it was to be another week before a family out blackberry picking came upon the same spot. This time they looked further and found a body later identified as that of Cornwall, wrapped in a bedspread.

During a period prior to Committal Proceedings the defendants, Dudley, Robert Maynard and Clarke were remanded in Brixton Prison where they were in contact with Anthony Wild another prisoner on remand who had a serious criminal record. Wild by his own account was anxious to ingratiate himself with the police for his own purposes, which included a favourable outcome to current criminal proceedings against him. Wild did provide police with a good deal of information including the fact that whilst the three aforementioned were in his company, damaging admissions were made by them relating to both murders. Dudley allegedly boasted of taking a head in a bag to show to the licensee of a public house in Brighton, in which he had an interest, and leaving it there. Maynard and Dudley also described in graphic terms their involvement in the shooting of a man who was then buried in a forest. Wild gave the police information about these events over a period of time; but despite his general enthusiasm for providing information, did not begin to do so on this topic until October 1976, some six months after the alleged cell confession. He was later called to give evidence for the prosecution, against the aforementioned defendants.

It would appear that apart from the evidence provided by Wild, the case against the accused was largely circumstantial save for alleged admissions made to police officers at the time of their arrest and during subsequent interviews under caution. These admissions were strongly disputed by the accused at their trial.

Indeed the trial Judge Mr. Justice Swanwick on the first day of his summing up, in addressing the jury, said, "In no case here, none of the cases against any of the accused, is there any evidence directly connecting any of them with any of the crimes charged. There is no evidence of where or exactly when either Moseley or Cornwall died. There are no eyewitnesses of any crime; no murder weapon to connect any of the accused with either killing, and no written and signed confessions. The evidence against the accused consists largely, and in some cases almost wholly, of alleged oral confessions to police and others."

The Judge's summing-up took twelve days and the trial, which had lasted some seven months, was concluded on 17th June 1977, and proved to be the longest in British criminal history at that time.

Reg Dudley and Bobby Maynard were each convicted of murdering William Moseley and Michael Cornwall, and sentenced to life imprisonment. Kathleen Hailey, Dudley's daughter, was convicted of conspiracy to cause grievous bodily harm to Michael Cornwall and received a sentence of two years imprisonment suspended for two years, and Charles Edwin Clarke was convicted of conspiracy to cause grievous bodily harm to William Moseley and Michael Cornwall was to serve four years imprisonment.

Ronald Bright and George Spencer were acquitted of the murder of Moseley and other offences connected with his abduction. Ernest Maynard was acquitted of conspiracy to cause grievous bodily harm to and falsely imprisoning Moseley. Other counts involving Dudley and Maynard were ordered to lie on the file.

On 28th July 1977 police were called to a public toilet in Richmond Avenue, Islington where they were shown a human skull. The skull was examined by criminal pathologists soon afterwards and identified as that of a male person. A dark blue woollen balaclava accompanied the mummified head with holes cut in areas consistent with the eyes and mouth. It was wrapped in pages of the London Evening News dated 16th June 1977- the day that the trial had ended at the Old Bailey. The head and the balaclava were extremely cold and moist to the touch when found and appeared to be in a state of thawing.

Fractures were noted on both sides of the hyoid bone and X-ray evidence revealed a fracture of the nose and a double fracture of the lower jaw, with the loss of a molar tooth in the left upper jaw. All the facial injuries indicated that that the man had been subjected to severe blows just before death. The cuts in the neck structure were consistent with being made by an eighteen-teeth-per-inch, Eclipse high-speed hacksaw blade and were identical with those recorded from sections of the torso identified as that of William Moseley.

After he had been murdered and decapitated, Moseley's head had been stored in either a refrigerator of deep freeze cabinet. Sometime after the trial someone unknown had taken it out of frozen storage wrapped it in the newspaper and left it to be found in the public toilet.

Subsequent Appeals against conviction, by all four were dismissed on 2nd April 1979. Thereafter a number of representations, petitions and complaints were made by and on behalf of the unsuccessful appellants, principally Dudley and Maynard. These consisted of attacks on the police evidence regarding notes of interviews and upon the reliability of the witness Anthony Wild, who upon release from a relatively short prison sentence, publicly admitted that his evidence had been untrue. These representations were to drag on for a number of years until 31st March 1997, when the case was transferred to the Criminal Case Review Commission (CCRC).

Finally on 16th July 2002, at the Court of Appeal (Criminal Division), Lord Justice Mantell together with Mr. Justice Holman and Mr. Justice Gibbs, allowed the appeals of all four convicted persons on the grounds that their convictions were unsafe.

It was from the Report by Lord Justice Mantell, of the reasons for granting the Appeals, published by the Royal Courts of Justice, in the Strand, that details of the background and result of this case have been obtained.

But for the Criminal Appeal Act of 1995, which had enabled the establishment of the Criminal Cases Review Commission as an executive Non-Departmental Public Body, this result might never have been achieved. Prior to 31st March 1997 the Home Secretary dealt with applications by people claiming to be victims of miscarriages of justice and could refer cases back to the Court of Appeal. The appellants' solicitor, had made such an application in July 1992, but the then Home Secretary, had decided not to so refer this case.

Whatever the rights or wrongs of this case this final result came too late for three of the four appellants. Reg Dudley served 21 years before given parole in 1977. Robert Maynard was only granted bail pending appeal in November 2000. Charles Clarke who served a total of four years for the two offences, of which he was convicted, died in 1995 and his widow was subsequently granted approval to pursue the appeal on her husband's behalf. Reg Dudley's daughter Kathleen Hailey had received a suspended sentence.

In reviewing this case however, I can't but help cast my mind back to the initial thought that I had when I first heard that Michael Cornwall had been identified as a murder victim. Had he not been successful in his appeal against the severity of his 12 year sentence for armed robbery, he would probably be alive today.

Chapter Eighteen

Bomb Squad

It was with a mixture of excitement and trepidation that I reported for duty at New Scotland Yard on Monday 8th September 1975. Despite my sixteen years' service in the force mainly in the C.I.D. It had only been necessary for me to make the occasional visit to Scotland Yard, usually to liaise over some routine matter or to collect urgently required Criminal Record files or correspondence. Now however, I was about to join the Bomb Squad, C.1 (4), in the rank I had held on Divisional duties for the past two years, that of Detective Inspector. Whilst I had little knowledge of what my duties would entail, I was aware it was one of the most prestigious branches of Scotland Yard's Specialist Crime Department. Furthermore, from media publicity regarding the various atrocities of the current Provisional I.R.A. campaign, I was conscious that I was joining the squad at what was proving to be a most demanding time.

The Bomb Squad occupied a large suite of offices on the fifth floor at Scotland Yard where my first port of call was to their Reserve Room. Here a small team of officers was dealing with telephone calls and enquiries from the public, operating under Detective Inspector Dave Lamper a Special Branch officer seconded to C.1. (4).

Dave explained that as the nature of their investigations, included intelligence gathering and assessment as well as liaison with other Special Branches, both north and south of the border in Ireland, a small number of Special Branch Officers of all ranks up to Detective Superintendent, were attached to the bomb squad. A handful of C.I.D officers from other forces around the U.K. were also currently attached to the branch on a temporary basis, in order to gain experience in dealing with bombing incidents for the benefit of their respective forces.

After my initial meeting with my new Commander, Roy Habersham, he introduced me to Jim Nevill, the Detective Chief Superintendent. Jim was a tall distinguished looking man, with a head of tight grey curly hair; steely blue eyes; smartly dressed in a dark suit. Although we were not acquainted, I recognized him as a former officer of the Flying Squad that had been involved in the arrest of two men for robbery on St. Ann's Road manor, some years previous when I was serving there as an Aid to C.I.D. Having informed me that I was to take charge of 'C' team, he then mentioned that they were all currently engaged, investigating the latest bombing incident, at the Hilton Hotel, Park Lane. This incident had taken place the previous Friday 5th September, resulting in the deaths of two people with some 63 persons injured.

The Hilton Bomb had exploded at 12.18pm just as the majority of senior Bomb Squad officers were in Basingstoke, attending the funeral of 40 year old, Captain Roger Goad, BEM, a Metropolitan Police Explosives Officer, who had fallen victim to a Provisional I.R.A. bomb he had been attempting to defuse, on 29th August outside a shop in Kensington. Captain Goad was later to be posthumously awarded the George Cross for the heroism he had displayed on numerous occasions including that fateful day. The bomb he was attempting to defuse was later found to have an anti-handling device fitted.

Jim Nevill mentioned that he had debated as to whether to send me over to the Hilton to join my team, but as he had a very experienced officer Detective Sergeant Tony Polley, running the enquiry, he had decided to give me time to familiarize myself with my new department and its workings before committing me to any enquiry. To say I was grateful for this decision would be an understatement.

I was then taken to an adjacent office where I was introduced to Detective Superintendents Bill Hucklesby and Peter Imbert, the latter being a Special Branch Officer who from the moment I first met him, seemed to be permanently engaged in dual telephone conversations, with a telephone to each ear.

I learnt that my immediate Senior Officer was Detective Chief Inspector Dave Munday. Dave was one of the few officers with whom I was familiar, as he had previously served at Kings Cross on 'N' Division. He was however currently away on a training course at Bramshill Police College. His opposite number from Special Branch was detective Chief Inspector Graham Ison.

The Bomb Squad at that time comprised of three investigation teams of about ten Officers, Detective Sergeants and Detective Constables, each handpicked and under the command of a Detective Inspector such as myself. They were housed in one large office at the end of which was the D.C.I's and the D.I.'s office. I discovered that I knew one of the other D.I's, Malcolm Hackett who had been on the same initial Detective Training Course as I, some eleven years previous.

An additional team consisting primarily of Aides to C.I.D. supervised by a D.I. Dave Stephenson and occupying offices in a separate building near to Scotland Yard, were employed on surveillance duties, with a secondary role of acting as sweepers of debris whenever an explosion occurred. Plastic dustbins containing such debris would ultimately be taken to the Royal Armament Research and Development Establishment (RARDE), at Woolwich, to be sifted for evidence, under the direction of the Exhibits Officers. There were three dedicated Exhibits Officers on the squad, and they occupied their own office complete with an exhibits store.

With the assistance of Dave Lamper, arrangements were made for me to attend the Metropolitan Police Radio Station at Denmark Hill, in order to have my private motor vehicle fitted with a covert police radio. To this end I was allocated Call Sign 'Central 707'. Not quite James Bond, but near enough for me. In addition I received a permit authorizing the parking of my vehicle in the basement car park. Although there were a few pool cars, practically every Detective on the Bomb Squad was authorized to use his or her own vehicle, and each was fitted with a force radio. A list of the various Call Signs was also supplied and I learnt that C.13. had a dedicated radio channel, shared only with other operational 'C' Department Squads.

I was issued with a pair of Wellington boots, a protective Anorak and a hard helmet, and one of the reserve officers took me down to the basement to familiarize me with the Bomb Squad's Incident Van. This vehicle had been especially customised for the bomb squad so in addition to the usual blue flashing lights and police radio the rear interior was provided with two narrow writing surfaces on each side with swivel chairs to enable it to be used as a mobile office where witnesses could be interviewed and statements taken etc. There were numerous storage facilities for such items as rolls of tape for cordons, stationery, exhibit bags and labels, mains operated flood lighting, first aid box, step ladder, in short anything that past experience indicated could be of assistance at the scene of a bombing incident.

The practice was that each team operated a 24-hour reserve system and should any incident occur during their period on reserve, the team would attend the scene in the Incident Van and any other vehicles as required. It would then be their responsibility to secure the scene and commence their investigation, usually with an inner cordon to preserve all possible clues amongst the debris and an outer cordon to restrain the public. Thus enabling police and other emergency services to evacuate or deal with any injured persons and generally carry out their various duties unhindered. Local officers were generally used to implement the cordons and man them once suitable boundaries had been agreed by the investigating officers. Since many of the recent bombing incidents had been occurring during the late evening in central London it was practice for part of the reserve team to work a 5pm to 1 am shift in readiness to attend any fresh incident.

It was now important for me to try and learn more about the types of devices used and to assimilate what intelligence had been gathered regarding any suspects for the recent bombings.

Fred Titchenor the Collator and the person I had consulted when my move to the Bomb Squad had first been muted, was a veritable mine of information. He had an array of photographs and various mock-ups of devices that had been used in the past. He was also able to update me with data relating to all previous bombing campaigns and details where members of Active Service

Units (A.S.U.'s) throughout the country had been identified or arrested.

What was evident was that whilst the identities of the Provisional I.R.A. A.S.U. currently operating in London, were yet to be established, there was a high probability that identifiable finger impressions of at least some of them, were now recorded in the 'Scenes of Crime Section' of the fingerprint Department at Scotland Yard. In certain instances, Improvised Explosive Devices (I.E.D.'S) had been recovered intact, after being made safe by Explosive Officers. In such cases, after cursory examination for future reference, their component parts were made the subject of detailed examination by fingerprint branch. It was often the adhesive tape used to as a binding to secure the component parts together that yielded some of the best finger impressions. Furthermore in February that year, following the tragic shooting of P.C. Stephen Tibble in Kensington, Officers had raided a suspect's premises at 39, Fairholme Road which was found to be the address of an Active Service Unit. Although the suspects had fled hurriedly following the shooting before discovery of the address, they had left behind explosives, timers, detonators and other bomb making paraphernalia. Such items together with various books and documents had yielded vital forensic evidence and fingerprints.

Whilst as with many crime scenes one was seldom likely to recover the impressions of a complete hand, A finger and thumb impression, or two or three adjacent finger impressions, could often result from examination of any given surface, depending on how it had been held by a suspect. Over a period of many months a good number of such finger or hand marks had been recovered and each time a new mark was found it had been given an identifying letter of the alphabet. A confidential chart listing various bombing incidents or finds, correlated with the various alphabetical references where identifiable finger marks had been found, had been produced for intelligence purposes. I was afforded such a chart, which was to prove particularly useful in the months ahead.

It should be mentioned that the Metropolitan Police had employed Explosive Officers for a good number of years. I myself had called upon their services from time to time, particularly when dealing with incidents where explosives had been used for safe blowing and the like. Such personnel were usually retired army officers who had gained experience in dealing with ordnance and explosives during their service life. With the advent of the Provisional I.R.A. campaign their numbers had been increased to ensure a rapid response to any bomb related incidents and they together with their equipment and dedicated police drivers, occupied offices at Cannon Row Police Station, adjacent to the old Scotland Yard building in Whitehall.

As when any busy officer is transferred from one division or department to another it is never possible to make a direct transition. There are always case papers or correspondence to attend to, or court cases requiring your attendance. So it was with me for the next few weeks. During which I spent my time between Highbury Vale and Scotland Yard. In fulfilling my Reserve Duties on the Bomb Squad I was getting to know the various members of my team and other personnel. I was anxious to absorb as much intelligence and information as possible to enable me to fulfil my new role before the next bombing incident in London.

There was a great deal of information forthcoming daily from well-meaning members of the public. Some of the information was relevant to particular incidents as they occurred, whilst much of it was in response to general appeals that that had been made for any information regarding the possible identities of IRA activists. All this information had to be logged and assessed and actioned out for further enquiry where possible. Some matters reported by members of the public amounted to no more than complaints of loud Irish music being played in adjacent premises. Having personal knowledge of the Irish culture and I knew many such calls arose either from ignorance or intolerance of neighbour's habits.

Part of our duties involved carrying out search warrants and interviewing suspects whenever reliable information was received from members of the public or intelligence reports were received from Special Branch.

On 9th October at about 9pm a bomb exploded at a bus shelter outside Green Park Underground Station, close to the Ritz Hotel in Piccadilly. Although I was not the duty officer that night I was still on duty at Scotland Yard and went with other officers to the scene. This was an unusual location for a bombing and the fact that public toilets were adjacent to the bus stop led to conjecture that they may have been used for cover whilst the device was armed. It was also thought that the device could have been activated prematurely. A number of pedestrians were injured by the blast, which also shattered shop windows nearby. One male found unconscious at the scene and conveyed to hospital was initially thought to be a possible suspect for carrying the device, but this proved not to be the case. The man was subsequently found to have died of heart attack.

We were to learn a few months later that this device was intended for the Ritz Hotel but, the bomber having found the hotel lobby too busy for him to be able to conceal the device, had left and temporarily disarmed the device with a view to returning. He had later entered a cubicle at the Green Park toilets where he re-set the timer and again armed the device, but whilst he was putting it into a bag he became aware that the male occupant of the adjacent cubicle had apparently become curious, as he heard him stand on his toilet seat before peering over the side partition. Unsure as to how much the man may have seen, the would be bomber left and abandoned the bag in the bus shelter outside, before walking off.

A few days later another device was planted outside Lockets Restaurant in Marsham Street, Westminster. This high class dining establishment being just a half mile from the House of Parliament, was popular with MP's and the like and presented a an ideal target for the Provisional I.R.A. Fortunately a hotel porter on his way home spotted the bag and being suspicious reported it to the Manager at Lockets who in turn called police. On arrival outside the restaurant a police officer carefully unzipped the bag only to realise that it did indeed contain a bomb. Fortunately there was still sufficient time for Lockets to be evacuated, much to the annoyance of some diners and Major Don

Henderson was able to disarm the device before it could explode. Although I was not directly involved with this particular incident, I was rapidly becoming acquainted with the increasing intensity of the bombing campaign and its ever-changing targets.

Less than two weeks were to elapse before the attempted assassination of Sir Hugh Fraser in the explosion in Camden Hill Square, the incident with which I chose to commence these memoirs. In the ensuing days of that enquiry our efforts were mainly concentrated on eliminating the various suspects and suspect vehicles, which members of the public reported having seen in and around Camden Hill Square, late on the night of 23rd October and early hours of the following morning. The fact that Sir Hugh Fraser had not parked his vehicle outside his house until some three quarters of an hour after midnight, narrowed down the available time for the bomb to be placed under his car. Statements were taken from the various tenants whose premises had suffered blast damage as a result of the explosion, once details of repair estimates had been obtained.

As previously mentioned the blast had caused a premature fall of autumnal leaves from the numerous trees around the Square. This made the task of identifying any bomb components in the vicinity of the explosion all the more difficult, for these all had to be swept up and placed in dustbins for conveyance to the Royal Armament and Development Establishment (R.A.R.D.E.) at Woolwich. The wreck of Sir Hugh Fraser's Jaguar Car was also conveyed there and ultimately examined by Donald Lidstone, a principal Scientific Officer employed by the Home Office. I made my first visit to R.A.R.D.E. on 29th October with one of the Exhibits Officers, in order to familiarize myself with the staff and workings of this department.

Donald Lidstone's opinion was that the damage was consistent with the involvement of about 10lbs. of typical Nitro-glycerine based blasting explosive, set off by an electrical source, possibly a 1.5 volt battery. He concluded that the deceased Professor, Gordon Hamilton-Fairley was about four feet from the device when it exploded. He was also of the opinion that it was likely to have been an anti-disturbance device as opposed to a conventional time bomb.

Sir Hugh Fraser having ensured the safety of his staff and houseguest Caroline Kennedy, had been undeterred by his would be assassins and taken himself off to the House of Commons later on the morning of the explosion. Detective Superintendent Hucklesby interviewed him in company with Detective Constable Bob Allon, who wrote down his witness statement. As the enquiry continued I found it necessary to re-interview Sir Hugh at the House of Commons and take a further statement, to clear up certain ambiguities and ascertain whether his vehicle had ever had a House of Commons Sticker or other identifying feature affixed to its windscreen. Sir Hugh informed me that this had not been the case, which left open the possibility that he must have been under observation at some time either leaving the House of Commons or returning to his home.

An inquest touching upon the death of Professor Gordon Hamilton-Fairley had been opened by H.M. Coroner Gavin Thurston, on 27th October 1975 at Westminster Coroner's Court and adjourned until 4th February 1976 to enable further enquiries to continue.

Two days later, on the late evening of 29th October, another bomb exploded, this time it had been placed outside a window of the Trattoria Fiore Italian restaurant, situated at the junction of Mount Street and South Audley Street, in the prosperous, Mayfair district of Central London, about 100 yards from the American Embassy. Some seventeen persons were injured in this explosion six of them seriously.

Five days later on 3rd November another car bombing occurred this time in Connaught Square, a select neighbourhood close to the junction of Bayswater Road and Edgware Road. Just after 9am that morning Mr. Richard Charnley a Barrister left his nearby house and got into his Grey Mercedes Car, started the engine and was about to drive off whereupon a bomb planted underneath it, exploded. The vehicle was somersaulted onto its roof completely wrecking the vehicle, and leaving Mr. Charnley suspended by his seatbelt, which he had fortunately just fastened.

The front nearside wheel became detached during the explosion and crashed through the living room window of a house opposite. Police and other emergency services attended the scene and Mr. Charnley was safely removed from his vehicle and conveyed to hospital where he was found to have a fractured left leg. Enquiries were carried out into this particular crime by colleagues of mine on the bomb squad and it was suspected that Mr. Charnley was unlikely to have been the intended target as a number of other more prominent personalities resided in the Square.

The following Day, Ross Mc Whirter the joint publisher with his twin brother Norris, of the Guinness book of Records, offered a £50,000 Reward for information leading to the arrest and conviction of those responsible for the recent spate of bombings. This was to have a devastating consequence before the month was out.

The next intended Target of the P.I.R.A. was the former Prime Minister and Leader of the Conservative Party, Edward Heath who resided at 17 Wilton Street, Belgravia. On Saturday 8th November 1975, Mr. Heath was due to be the guest of Honour at a dinner at the Royal Yacht Club, in Lymington, Hampshire. Various events that day had conspired to make him late in leaving to drive to the event and having got into his Rover car outside his house, he slammed the door and quickly accelerated away at a fast speed, intent on making up for lost time. It would seem that his actions could well have inadvertently saved his life, in that they are believed to have caused a bomb attached to the underside of his vehicle to become detached and fall into the roadway outside his house.

A young couple looking for a convenient parking space later that evening duly parked their mini in the space vacated by Mr. Heath's Rover, but reversing into the space in the dark the device went unnoticed in the roadway. They did not return for several hours and when they did, perhaps mindful of police and government advice to check under your vehicle if it had been left unattended in the West End, they spotted the package. They immediately sought police assistance, the bomb squad was informed as were the Bomb Disposal Officers and Major Geoff Biddle attended the scene, conscious of the proximity of the suspect package to the address of Ted Heath. Local residents were evacuated and the area cordoned was off whilst major Biddle working by torchlight, lying in the gutter, managed to disarm the bomb and render the area safe.

When Ted Heath returned to Wilton Street at around 2am, he found the area around his address cordoned off and was then briefed by police officers as to what had occurred and was shown the disarmed device by Major Biddle.

Some four days later, on 12 November 1975, the Provisional I.R.A. was to strike again, this time reverting back to restaurant premises. Their target was the exclusive Scott's Restaurant and Oyster bar at 20, Mount Street in Mayfair patronized by the rich and famous and just across the road from the previously attacked Trattoria Fiore Restaurant. At 9.28pm a fused device, fitted with bolts and ball bearings, was thrown at one of front windows and having crashed through the glass, it exploded within the restaurant. Some diners hearing the crash of glass managed to throw themselves to the floor to avoid injury. One man received injuries from which he died, despite emergency surgery at St. George's Hospital, at Hyde Park corner. Fifteen other customers were injured in the blast. With the exception of one eyewitness who was able to tell police that he had seen three men drive off in a Ford Car at the time of the explosion, there was little evidence to further the investigation.

My enquiries were still continuing into the murder of Professor Gordon Hamilton Fairley but despite the extensive enquiries that were carried out into this crime no definite leads as to the identity of the culprits were disclosed in the initial stages and my enquiries were still continuing when a further bombing incident occurred on my watch.

Visitors to 121, Walton Street, S.W.3 today, would find it housing the Itsu Restaurant, a modern Sushi Bar. In 1975 it was the location of Waltons Restaurant a high-class establishment situated at the junction of Walton Street and Draycott Avenue, just south of the busy Brompton Road in Kensington.

On the evening of Tuesday 18th November 1975, Walton's restaurant was fully occupied to its capacity of some sixty-eight persons. It was to prove fortunate for some of the diners that the dining area consisted of three rooms. On entering the restaurant via the main entrance door in Walton Street, there was a small reception area. A doorway to the right gave access to the 'Grey Room', which had windows overlooking Walton Street and Draycott Avenue. Passing through the reception area there were two further rooms, the 'Terrace Room' on the right and the 'Mirror Room' on the left. Parked outside were at least two Rolls Royces as well as numerous other expensive cars, some with personalized number plates, indicating the financial status of the owners.

Just before 10pm a young couple a Mr. Graeme Hawley and a Miss Carol Ashby, were walking along Draycott Avenue towards Walton Street from the direction of Brompton Road, when Miss Ashby, saw two men standing in Walton Street by one of the windows of the restaurant. As one of the men began to walk away from her direction down Walton Street, she saw the other man crouch down and then saw sparks close to the man, as if from a firework. Although she had not seen anything in his hands, when he began to run down Walton Street, perhaps conscious of the current bombing campaign in London where some three restaurants had recently been targeted, she realized it might have been a bomb. So she shouted to her companion, "It's a bomb" and the pair of them flung themselves to the pavement, hearing a loud explosion as they did so.

Also in Walton Street that night was a Miss Sally James who had been visiting a friend in nearby First Street. When she was about 10 to 15 yards from the restaurant, her attention was drawn by the sound of running feet and she saw three stooped male figures, running away from Walton's Restaurant across Walton Street and get into a dark coloured car parked opposite. At that moment there was an explosion at the restaurant and in her confusion she did not notice the car drive off.

Meanwhile inside the restaurant one of the waiters, Mr. Donato Chezzi, was standing by the bar in the reception area looking out of one of the reception room windows, which were fitted with blinds covering their top section. Through the space below the blind, he saw a man in Walton Street and noticed the man bending down with his right arm back in a throwing position facing towards the Grey Room, the blind however obstructed his view of what the man had in his hand. Realising it might be a bomb; Mr. Chezzi began to run away from the window but tripped over a table and fell to the floor. He then heard the window break, followed by a loud explosion.

Seated at the first table inside the 'Grey Room' adjacent to the windows were two couples, Gerald Edgson and his wife Audrey together with their friends, Sidney Lewis and his wife Joan. The two men were seated side-by-side facing the window with their respective wives seated opposite them with their backs to the window. These windows were fitted with heavy drape curtains and pelmets obscuring much of the view into the street outside. Mr. Edgson was to recall that suddenly there was crash of glass in front of him and a bomb landed on their table. Mr. Edgson instinctively stood up and was intending to fetch an ice bucket from another table in order to dowse the fuse, but as he got to his feet the device exploded. Somewhat surprisingly he was able to give a good description of the device before it exploded, as follows: 'It was about the size of a half-gallon tin of paint and was cylindrical in shape. It appeared to be wrapped in cello tape and I think it was brown paper wrapping. The fuse was exactly like the stub of a cigar; it was about three quarters of an inch in diameter and was about an inch long. There appeared to be sparks coming from it and a smell of sulphur or sort of firework smell.'

The accounts later given by Mr. and Mrs. Lewis coincide with that of Mr. Edgson, with the addition that they recalled the bomb knocking over a table lamp and Mr. Lewis recalled that the device fell onto the floor before exploding.

Seated at a table adjacent to the one where the device landed were two other couples, Theodore Williams, and his common law wife Josephine and their friends Ivy and Sidney Brent. Both women were seated with their backs to the window with their partners opposite them. During the course of their meal

Mrs. Williams heard the sound of breaking glass and then saw a sparking object fly through the air to her left. Realising what it was, Mrs. Williams shouted, "It's a bomb", pushed the table away and ran towards an alcove.

What anyone who saw the device before it exploded would not have known, was that the explosives were laced with a mixture of nuts, bolts and ball bearings. These would have been taped around the outside of the explosives, to act as shrapnel and intended to inflict the maximum amount of carnage to the diners in the restaurant and carnage and mayhem was certainly the result.

The unfortunate occupants of these two tables were to suffer the worst injuries; for both 44-year-old Mrs. Audrey Edgson and 49-year-old Mr. Theodore Williams from the adjacent table, were to die from the result of their injuries soon after their arrival at the local St. Stephen's Hospital. In addition some sixteen other diners as well as Mr. Chezzi the waiter received injuries from the blast.

Trevor Davies was driving his Triumph 2000 car past the restaurant just as the explosion occurred, with the result that the vehicle's front windscreen and offside windows were shattered causing multiple grazes to the 31-year-old drivers face.

Richard Forster a State Registered Nurse was nearby at the time of the explosion and he entered the devastated restaurant and rendered first aid to two injured male casualties.

The first Police Officers on the scene were P.C. 469 'B' Donald Mac Donald, who was off duty and in the nearby 'Queens Arms" public house and P.C. 683 'B' Stephen Steere who was on foot patrol in Sloane Avenue when he heard the explosion. P.C. MacDonald assisted injured persons from the restaurant whilst P.C. Steere radioed to Chelsea Police Station and then assisted to clear the area. Another off duty police officer P.C. 614 'B' Michael James was in the vicinity at the time of the explosion and he went to the scene to render what assistance he could. He assisted ambulance crew treating the injured Mr. Williams and accompanied him to the hospital.

As soon as information concerning this latest outrage was received at Scotland Yard it was passed to the Bomb Squad's

Incident Room where I and other members of my team were present on Standby duties. Quickly donning my protective clothing I left with others for the scene in the Incident Van whilst additional members on my team followed on in their respective vehicles. Although I was not familiar with the venue of the restaurant, on route I realised that Walton Street was also the location of the police building used as the Detective Training School some eleven years previous where I had attended my Initial Detective Training course.

We arrived within a matter of a few minutes and as we drove in from the far end of Walton Street the sight that greeted me was like that of a film set from a war film.

A few local uniform officers were already in attendance as were a fire crew. Two ambulances were parked in Draycott Avenue across the junction with Walton Street and a number of walking wounded were being helped into the back of one of them. Flames from the heavy window drapes were licking at the surrounding paintwork and smoke was billowing from the various broken windows of the restaurant from which injured person were still being assisted by fire and ambulance personnel. A number of less or uninjured diners were standing around amongst the glass debris on the footway with a look of shock and horror on their faces, inadequately clothed to face the cold night air, whilst others surveyed the damage to their prestigious vehicles.

Our driver parked our incident van alongside a row of parked cars on the far side of Walton Street about fifty yards back from the bomb scene and as I alighted I was conscious of a cacophony of alarm bells which only added to the drama of the scene unfolding before us. The burglar alarms, fitted outside a row of small shops opposite the restaurant had obviously been activated by the blast from the explosion but were unfortunately serving no useful purpose.

Seeing the ambulance door close as I approached the scene, I was conscious that we needed to ascertain details of the casualties and their injuries as well as preserve any bomb fragments with which casualties could have become embedded. In addition being unfamiliar with the area I was unsure which hospital(s) the casualties might be conveyed to, so seeing a young uniform Police Constable nearby I gave him a quick briefing as to the need to ensure no evidence was lost at casualty and directed him to jump in the back of the ambulance and report back in due course.

Whilst some of my bomb Squad colleagues were liaising with a local inspector regarding the placement of suitable cordons I realized that whilst those vehicles within the cordon would not be allowed to leave the scene for some time, the owners of other vehicles currently parked in the street were also potential witnesses, be they diners or not. I therefore instructed another constable to quickly note down the registration numbers of all vehicles in the vicinity and deposit it with our incident van crew, in order that any departing owners could be interviewed in due course.

Our vehicle had been parked adjacent to a small lock up shoe repairers shop and fortunately the owner resided there and he obligingly let us plug our mains extension lead into his power supply. This gave us a good source of lighting within the vehicle for officers engaged in taking statements or details from various diners or potential witnesses present at the scene.

The Duty Explosives Officer Ken Howarth had arrived at the scene at about the same time as us and immediately commenced his examination of the restaurant. He was of the opinion that the device had contained not more than 2lb. of high explosives, the effect of which was accentuated by the inclusion of numerous nuts, bolts and ball bearings. It soon became clear that the majority of the damage and injury to persons had involved the diners in the 'Grey Room'.

As with any serious crime the duty police photographer had been summoned to the scene and liaised with me regarding what photographs were required, both of the damage within the restaurant and the exterior of the premises including various vehicles affected by the blast.

As soon as the restaurant had been cleared of casualties and declared safe by the fire brigade and Ken Howarth, collection of the debris and various items for further examination was able to be undertaken by Detective Sergeant Vince Napolitano our duty Exhibits Officer working in conjunction with D.I. Peter Goodall the Metropolitan Police laboratory liaison officer. Our dedicated sweeping team also undertook a controlled sweep of debris in the area outside the restaurant. This also involved the preservation and transport of four of the damaged vehicles for further examination at R.A.R.D.E. in Woolwich.

Once I had been able to assess the situation in Walpole Road and determine what witnesses were readily available and gauge the number of casualties to be interviewed I dispatched several officers to St. Stephens Hospital to interview victims and effect recovery of any exhibits there. As usual, the C.13 Reserve Officers had passed news of this latest bombing to other senior officers at home and in due course Detective Chief Superintendent Jim Nevill and Detective Superintendent Peter Imbert attended the scene, whilst Detective Superintendent Bill Hucklesby attended the hospital to co-ordinate events there.

The damage to the restaurant was later to be estimated at £40,000 but Waltons was not the only premises to affected by the blast, four other premises in Walton Street and two in Draycott Place suffered damage mainly affecting glass windows. In addition ten motor vehicles suffered damage to their windows or paintwork.

All residents in the immediate area had obviously heard the noise of the explosion and lights were on in many residential premises with some residents looking out of their windows or chatting with neighbours in the street. Despite the lateness of the hour, it was therefore practicable to commence some house-to-house enquiries seeking potential witnesses, particularly regarding the description of the suspect vehicle and its occupants. One of the residents in Walton Street was in his front sitting room when the explosion occurred and immediately went out of his house to look up the street where he was to see the smoke and debris at the restaurant some 200 yards away. As he walked into the roadway a car drove towards him from the direction of the restaurant at a fast speed. The witness described the car as a fairly old saloon in the singer Gazelle Range, possibly green or cream in colour.

He also supplied two letters from its registration plate and stated that the car contained four people the front passenger being a blonde female aged about 23/4.

Having regard to the distance from the restaurant to the witnesses address and the timing described by him it was considered that the occupants if not directly concerned in the bombing must have been almost outside the restaurant at the relevant time and considerable publicity was given to the description of the vehicle with a view to tracing the occupants following the incident.

Another resident in Walton Street looked out of his front window on hearing the explosion and some 30 seconds later saw what he described as a dark blue saloon coming from the direction of the restaurant. This may have been the same vehicle which two other witnesses later reported as stopping in front of them alongside parked cars, some 50 yards after they drove into Walton Street at 9:45pm that evening. These two witnesses thought the vehicle was a Ford Cortina or Consul containing three men and a woman.

Our enquiries into this incident that night went on into the early hours of the next day and I must have been at the scene for about an hour and a half when I became aware that just outside our cordon at the far end of Walton Street a mobile stall was dispensing hot drinks and sandwiches. Welcome as a hot drink was, I was totally surprised to find such a facility there for the various emergency services. On enquiry of one of the ladies dispensing drinks, I was to learn that they were Salvation Army Volunteers and that it was a regular occurrence for them to be notified of such incidents and turn out whatever the time of day or night they received the call. In later years whenever I have come across Salvation Army personnel collecting for their charity, my thoughts have returned to events that night and I have been more than happy to support them.

If things were chaotic in Walton Street that night they must have been equally chaotic at St. Stephen's Hospital in Fulham Road, Chelsea, (Since replaced by the Chelsea and Westminster Hospital), for seventeen or the twenty injured persons were conveyed to St. Stephen's Hospital whilst three others were treated at St. Georges. Mr. Theodore Williams was examined on his arrival by Mr. Simon Shorvon the Medical Registrar, who found no signs of life. Vigorous resuscitative procedures were adopted but proved unsuccessful and death was certified at 10.40pm. His common law wife Josephine who had acted so quickly on seeing the bomb as it landed in the restaurant, fortunately escaped injury, but suffered emotional stress on hearing of her husband's demise.

Mrs. Audrey Edgson when seen by Dr Zoltan Slekely was found to be in a state of collapse with an absence of pulse and blood pressure and had numerous external wounds. Attempts at resuscitation were unsuccessful and she died at 10.45pm that night. Her husband Gerald received serious lacerations and penetration wounds to his lower torso and upper parts of both legs. Consultant Surgeon Mr. D.A. MacFarlane M.Ch F.R.C.S. and Mr. J.G. Jones Surgical Registrar operated him on. Two ball bearings and two china fragments were removed from his body.

Mr. Sidney Lewis the dining companion of the Edgson's received minor blast injuries to his left thigh and a penetration wound to his right thigh from which a metal fragment was removed by a Dr Malpass. His wife Joan was seriously injured and was treated by Dr El-Borai for a double fracture of her left leg; a fracture of her right leg; a fractured rib; lacerations to her face and right eye and a perforated right ear drum. Three ball bearings were recovered from her wounds.

Mr. and Mrs. Brent the dining companions of Mr. & Mrs. Williams were also injured, Mr. Brent receiving abrasions to his face whilst his wife received a small puncture wound to her left elbow and grazes to her face and right thigh.

The injuries suffered by other diners consisted of penetration wounds from which other fragments were removed and lacerations to various parts of their bodies; many also suffering from perforated eardrums. Needless to say the shock and trauma of events that evening must have had a lasting effect on everyone in the restaurant whether or not they were physically injured.

In any murder enquiry it is always vital not only to prove accurately the identity of a deceased victim, but where death, or the certification of a person's death takes place other than at the scene of a crime, it is important that there is continuity of evidence linking the body with the scene of crime. One of the ambulance crew who conveyed Mrs. Edgson and P.C. James who had accompanied Mr. Williams, were therefore able to identify their respective bodies to Detective Superintendent Hucklesby at the hospital, as victims from the restaurant bomb. Later, still in the early hours of 19th November, the legal wife of Mr. Williams has the unfortunate task of formally identifying the body of Theodore Williams to Bill Hucklesby and Jim Nevill.

Once all relevant action had been taken at the scene, an Incident Room was set up at Chelsea Police Station staffed by members of my team complemented by C.I.D. and uniform officers from 'B' Division. A post mortem examination was duly arranged to take place at 11.30am on the morning after the incident at Westminster Mortuary, which I attended. Prior to its commencement, relatives of Mrs. Edgson formally identified her body to Detective Chief Superintendent Nevill and Detective Superintendent Hucklesby who in turn were able to identify both bodies to the Pathologist.

The Post Mortem was conducted by Donald Teare, M.A., M.D., F.R.C.P., F.R.C.Path., D.M.J., Consultant Pathologist and Professor of Forensic Medicine. Mrs. Edgson was found to have numerous wounds and lacerations mainly to the right side of her body and three pieces of metal were removed from her wounds. The Cause of her death was certified as 'Bilateral Pneumothoraces due to Traumatic Emphysema due to an explosion'.

Compared to Mrs. Edgson, Mr. William's body had received only a few small wounds and lacerations. Two steel ball bearings and a sheared bolt were however removed from his body. I was surprised to see how small the ball bearings were, they being about 5 millimetres in diameter.

The lethal effect of them was brought home however when one of them was recovered from Mr. William's heart and the Professor certified death as due to 'Haemorrhage from a missile (ball bearing) wound to the heart'. I recall thinking how unlucky it had been, for had that ball bearing penetrated any other organ or part of the body I felt sure death would not have ensued.

From the beginning of this particular enquiry it was apparent that the persons responsible were members of the Provisional Irish Republican Army Active Service Unit, known to have been operating against similar targets within the West End of London. Whilst we had witnesses who had seen either two or three suspects outside the restaurant at the time the device was thrown, there was no evidence as to how long they had been there carrying out any form of surveillance beforehand and we only had the briefest descriptions of them and the vehicle used. In addition to local residents I considered it important therefore to trace and interview everyone who had dined at Waltons that evening, as well as the persons who had parked their vehicles in that vicinity for whatever reason, for any of these persons may have had a sighting of possible suspects when parking their vehicle or accessing the restaurant earlier in the evening.

In the ensuing days, in addition to house-to-house enquiries of the local residents, the owner of the various vehicles noted at the scene were traced and interviewed. With regard to the diners it was clear that apart from those that had been injured and conveyed to hospital many had naturally been anxious to depart from the scene as soon as possible after the explosion and had left before police were able to speak with them. Where customers were known or prior bookings had been made, we were able to trace some but not all of them.

In addition to appeals via the national newspapers, in an endeavour to trace other potential witnesses, I requested that details of all credit card transactions be obtained from the management. This did enable us to contact some of those who had either left the restaurant earlier in the evening or soon after the explosion. Unfortunately this particular line of enquiry was to prove particularly embarrassing for one poor woman. One of my officers having telephoned to make an enquiry of a credit card payment for two meals, spoke to the husband of the woman whose card had been used. The husband completely refuted the fact that his wife had been a diner in the restaurant on the night of the bombing. Later the same day a very embarrassed and apologetic husband rang the officer back to apologise, informing him that having since spoken with his wife, she had confessed to having dined at Waltons with a male friend on the night of the bombing and paid for the meals with her credit card, unbeknown to her husband. This did cause a little bit of light relief when the officer put down the phone and related the details to us.

Whilst our enquiries continued, staff at R.A.R.D.E. were examining the eleven dustbins of debris collected from within the restaurant and eight dustbins of debris swept up from the various areas of pavement and roadway outside, under the direction of the explosives officer Ken Howarth. In addition to a quantity of ball bearings and nuts and bolts that Ken Howarth had previously collected during his search of the premises, another 40 ball bearings were found amongst the general debris from within the restaurant as well as 19 from the carpet and underlay from the floor area under the point of the explosion. Five fragmented parts of 3 bolts with nuts attached were also found in that area. A further seven ball bearings as well as a bolt fragment, were retrieved from the debris collected from outside the restaurant.

Throughout the current bombing campaign, Detective Sergeant David Waghorn and colleagues working within an intelligence cell at the Bomb Squad were collating details of all relevant facts regarding the various incidents. A pattern was emerging regarding the times and locations of recent events, which were usually late on weekday evenings within a reasonably confined area of London's West End where so called 'establishment targets' were situated. Evidence indicated that at least three members of an A.S.U. would need to participate in the bombing incidents, one driving, one bomb thrower and another as a look out. Furthermore it was likely that the suspects using stolen vehicles would have to perform some form of recognizance prior to each incident. Dave Waghorm therefore submitted a report proposing that a covert operation be launched to swamp the streets of the relevant area with police officers in plain clothes, during late evenings, in an endeavour to enhance the chances of catching the bombers.

His report was favourably received and plans were drawn up to launch such an operation on 21st November, but the Evening Standard received leaked news of the operation and gave it headlines in that day's edition, thus alerting the ASU much to the frustration of all concerned. The operation was therefore suspended.

At 6.45p.m on 27th November Ross Mc Whirter was at home in Village Road Enfield, when his wife Rosemary returned home in the family's Ford Granada. As she alighted from her car in the dark, she was accosted by two men each armed with a handgun, who demanded that she hand over her keys, which she did. She then ran to her front door and being unable to let herself in, rang the doorbell frantically until her husband Ross answered it. As his distraught wife ran past him towards the kitchen, Ross was confronted by one of the gunmen who shot him first in the abdomen and then the head. The two men then decamped in the Mc Whirter's car, whilst Mrs. Mc Whirter ran to a neighbour's house to raise the alarm. Police and ambulance teams arrived at the address and Mr. Mc Whirter was conveyed to Chase Farm Hospital where he was pronounced dead on arrival.

The stolen car was soon found abandoned in Devonshire Hill Lane Tottenham, and confirmation that his assassination was yet again the work of the Provisional I.R.A. came when fingerprints found on the car were linked with certain of those found at 39 Fairholme Road, the address linked to the murder of P.C. Stephen Tibble. I was still busily engaged on the Waltons Restaurant bomb when Ross Mc Whirter was killed, and unbeknown to either myself or my colleagues investigating his death, this was to be the penultimate terrorist act this A.S.U. would commit before their eventual arrest.

Chapter Nineteen

The Balcombe Street Siege

Throughout 1975 Roy Jenkins the then Home Secretary was experiencing increasing political pressure to explain what measures were being taken to thwart the Provisional IRA bombers that had been wrecking carnage in Central London, particularly following the assassination of Ross Mc Whirter. It was therefore decided by senior officers at Scotland Yard to reinstate the plans made following suggestions by Detective Sergeant Dave Waghorn and 'Operation Combo' was re-launched during the first week of December.

Several hundred uniform officers working in pairs and in plain clothes were each allocated selected locations in central London, to patrol and observe and whilst they were equipped with a hand held force radio, they were unarmed. There were however a number of armed uniform officers of the Special Patrol Group (SPG), located at strategic locations within the area of the operation, ready to respond to any calls regarding potential suspects or bombing incidents.

Inspector John Purnell from Paddington Green Police Station and Sergeant Phil McVeigh from Harrow Road police station were one such pair of officers engaged on this operation that week and were detailed to cover the location of the Churchill Hotel and the Portman Hotel in Portman Square just north of Oxford Street.

Saturday 6ᵗʰ November 1975 was a particularly cold night for all officers engaged on this operation, however at about 9pm that evening things were about to warm up. For about that time, four members of the A.S.U. in a Ford Cortina car stolen a few hours earlier in Hammersmith, drove eastwards down Mount Street in Mayfair towards their intended target of Scott's Restaurant.

Officers posted in that vicinity saw the Cortina as it slowed to a halt containing the four suspects. They also noticed the barrel of a rifle pointing out of the front driver's window and heard two shots as they were aimed at the restaurant window. In the darkness they would have been unaware that all four men were armed with handguns and one of the men in the rear of the car was attempting to fire a stun gun, which fortunately had jammed. The vehicle was then driven on turning right into Park Street.

This was the opportunity the operation had been devised for and the officers wasted no time in passing details of the incident including a description of the vehicle, its occupants and direction of travel, to all officers on the operation via their police radio. Hearing this broadcast, John Purnell and Phil McVeigh realized that the vehicle was less than a mile away and could well be heading towards them in the one-way traffic system in Park Street. Knowing that the vehicle could turn left at Oxford Street before reaching their location, the officers hurried down Portman Street towards that junction, only to suddenly see the suspect vehicle approaching them in Portman Street.

The quick thinking officers hailed a passing taxi-cab and directed the driver to follow the Cortina. As the officers followed the suspects heading north from Portman Street into Gloucester Place, Phil McVeigh gave commentary on his radio for the benefit of police mobile units that were endeavouring to assist.

One such unit was a Police Personnel Carrier of the Special Patrol Group (SPG) containing six officers, two of whom were armed. Another unit that heard details of the shooting and immediately drove towards the chase was a team of four Flying Squad officers in a Ford Granada. This vehicle was crewed by Detective Inspector Henry Dowswell, Detective Sergeant Phil Mansfield, and Detective Constable Bob Fenton with Constable Peter Wilson as their skilled driver.

On reaching the busy Marylebone Road the Cortina was driven straight across and then into Park Road, bordering the nearby Regents Park. John Purnell had instructed the taxi driver not to get too close and arouse the suspicion of the occupants. The two men in the rear of the Cortina could however be seen to continually turn round and look back in their direction obviously anxious to ensure they had not been followed. A short distance into Park Road the Cortina turned left into Alpha Close a short cul-de-sac and John Purnell directed the taxi driver to pull up a short distance further on along Park Road.

Despite hearing the sound of Police Car Sirens in the distance there was no immediate assistance to hand as Inspector Purnell and Sergeant McVeigh alighted unarmed from the taxi. Anxious not to lose sight of their quarry, the officers walked towards Alpha Close and saw the four occupants had left the Cortina and one of them was carrying a holdall. The four men looked in the direction of the plain clothed officers, then turned and walked back down Park Road and then began to run. Purnell and McVeigh instinctively began to run and then came under fire as their actions confirmed the suspect's suspicions, that it was police officers that were following them. On reaching the first junction, the suspects turned right into Rossmore Road a road, which sloped upwards to traverse the rail tracks from nearby Marylebone Station.

Assistance finally arrived in the shape of the armed SPG unit and with Purnell and McVeigh keeping close to a side wall to avoid further fired shots, the four suspects could be seen jogging up the road. The SPG Carrier drove up passed the suspects and stopped a short distance in front of them. It was at this point that the man, who had been carrying it, abandoned the holdall and shots were fired in the direction of the SPG Carrier as the two armed officers alighted. They returned fire lying prone in the road beside the Carrier which after an exchange of shots resulted in the four ASU members turning back heading in the direction of Purnell and McVeigh.

Fearful of being shot either by the suspects or friendly fire from their SPG colleagues, Purnell and McVeigh turned and ran back and as they passed the abandoned holdall, John Purnell reached inside grabbing the first item his hand came into contact with, which happened to be a rifle barrel. Further timely assistance arrived at that moment, as the Ford Granada containing the four flying squad officers squealed to a halt, only to immediately come under fire from the suspects, with one bullet piercing the radiator.

The suspects in pairs passed either side of the Ford Granada and when the officers alighted a further shot was fired back in their direction, which lodged into the rear seat of the Granada.

As John Purnell and Phil McVeigh sought shelter behind a bus that had been obliged to stop behind the Ford Granada, the four suspects ran down some steps that led into the adjacent Taunton Place. Three of the men then ran left into Balcombe Street whilst the other ran on towards Boston Place. McVeigh passed details of their route over his police radio whilst Purnell decided it would be safer to follow the lone suspect. As Purnell turned into Ivor Place from Boston Place he noticed a lone male standing outside the door of one of the houses, and suspecting he may be his quarry he tackled the man only to realize then that he was not the man he had been pursuing.

Henry Dowswell and McVeigh had joined the pursuit and the latter had seen the four suspects meet up again as they all ran into Ivor Place. Some bystanders indicated to the pursuing officers that the men had continued down Balcombe Street and as Purnell arrived outside the Portman Arms public house, a woman indicated that she had seen them running into an apartment block opposite. The officer entered the pub and requested that police be contacted and informed of the location of flats concerned. On leaving he was joined by Henry Dowswell and the two officers took cover behind parked vehicles in the street opposite the flats.

The four ASU members were to find that the flats provided no avenue of escape to the rear, only a stairway leading to the upstairs flats in particular to number 22b where lights indicated occupancy of those premises. Inside 22b fifty-four year old Mr. John Mathews and his fifty-three year old wife Sheila, were settled down for the evening watching television. Hearing shouting from the direction of the street outside, Mr. Mathews stepped out onto his front balcony overlooking the street. John Purnell who was crouched down behind a car opposite the flats immediately spotted him and told him there were armed men around and that he should go back indoors for his own safety.

Having returned to the safety of his flat, the doorbell rang and thinking it may be the police Mr. Mathews opened the door to be faced with the four now desperate armed members of the ASU, who immediately pushed past him and entered the living room. After searching around for something to tie the unfortunate couple with, the men settled on some panty hose with which they then bound their hands and later their feet.

Outside in the street various police units were arriving but Inspectors Purnell and Dowswell having no intimate knowledge of the interior layout of the flats, were unaware of the exact location of the suspects. An armed unit was directed to enter the buildings and they went from door to door speaking to residents in their search for the ASU. Having rung the bell at 22b and announced that they were police officers, Mrs. Mathews at the behest of her captors told the officers to go away, a request reinforced in stronger terms by one of the four men.

Meanwhile at about 10pm that evening a telephone call was received at Scotland Yard's communication centre from one of the men, later identified as Joseph O'Connell, who stated that they were holding a couple hostages in Balcombe Street. In a subsequent telephone conversation with Deputy Assistant Commissioner Ernest Bond, O'Connell having confirmed that they were members of the Provisional IRA, demanded the services of a car to take them to London Airport and a plane flight to Dublin, in return for the safe release of the hostages. Mr. Bond declined this request insisting that the hostages should be released forthwith. He was warned that any attempt to forcibly enter flat 22b, would result in the death of Mr. & Mrs. Mathews. With the IRA taking this attitude and the ever-increasing police presence surrounding the flat, the 'Siege of Balcombe Street' was beginning to evolve.

By now the various news services had got wind of the developing incident and were quickly on the scene interviewing any potential witnesses with the result that events featured on the late evening television and radio news broadcasts.

This must have been one of the few Saturday nights of the year when neither the radio or television were used in the Chapman household, for that evening Noeleen and I were attending a social event at our local Church Hall, some five minutes' walk from home. We arrived home tired and weary after an enjoyable social evening and retired straight to bed. Unbeknown to me at that time Peter Imbert was also missing the late television news, having fallen asleep on the couch of his brother's home in Oxfordshire, where he and his wife were enjoying a well-earned weekend break with his brother and sister-in-law.

Peter later mentioned that when news of the latest terrorist incident broke on the news, his wife and sister-in-law were debating whether to wake him. His wife was quite understandably being reluctant to disturb him from his much needed sleep whilst the sister-in-law felt sure he would want to be woken to view events. The decision was made for them however by Jim Nevill, who having been called to the scene and knowing where to contact Peter that weekend decided to telephone him, initially with the intention of requesting him to attend the incident. After some discussion between these two officers it was agreed that as Jim Nevill was already there he would endeavour to talk the ASU out of the flat that night and that Peter Imbert would attend Paddington Green Police Station early on the Sunday morning to commence interviewing the prisoners.

The first I knew of the incident was at 7am the next morning when my bedside phone awaked me from a heavy sleep. The caller was Detective Constable Phil Stebbings who I believe was one of our surveillance team at the time but he was calling from the C.13. Reserve Room and his first words to me were "Governor can you get down to Dorset Square by 10am?' Having enquired where Dorset Square was and what required my attention, I recall Phil seemed most surprised that I was unaware that the Provisional IRA had been holding two people hostage in a flat since the previous evening. Phil quickly explained what had taken place after the shooting at Scott's restaurant and added that fingerprints found on the some of the weapons in the abandoned holdall, had already been confirmed as identical with some of our wanted provisional IRA suspects. He explained that Detective Chief Inspector Dave Munday had been called out late the previous evening, to set up an Incident Room in the British Rail Headquarters opposite Marylebone Station and I was required to relieve him and take over and run it for a twelve-hour shift starting at 10am.

Having quickly showered dressed and grabbed some breakfast; I headed down to the location given. Needless to say there was a heavy uniform police presence at the scene, with the whole of Dorset Square and Balcombe Street cordoned off. Having parked my vehicle and entered the cordoned area I could see that officers from D.19 our firearms department were strategically placed, with their weapons trained up to the first floor balcony area of a block of flats in Balcombe Street. A number of high-powered spotlights of the type used to illuminate scenes of major accidents were also in place facing the front of the building. A veritable army of journalists and photographers were assembled adjacent to the cordon in the southern section of Balcombe Street near Dorset Square, their camera lenses also trained on the first floor flat of 22b or recording the various movements of armed officers in the street.

I found the Incident Room had been set up in what was the Boardroom of the British Rail Headquarters and whilst not ideal, in that there were no desks, the sumptuous large boardroom tables had been re-arranged to suit out purpose. I learnt from the briefing Dave Munday gave me that a number of residents in the immediate vicinity of flat 22b Balcombe Street, including those opposite, had been evacuated for their own safety, the majority being re-located by Social Services into local hotels. Armed units of D.19 had occupied flats immediately adjacent to as well as opposite the Mathew's flat; in addition, a flat on the opposite side of the road had been commandeered for negotiating purposes. Officers of the C.7. Technical Support Branch was also at the scene, hoping to install surveillance equipment to monitor conversations and movements within flat 22b.

Overnight negotiations had been conducted by Detective Chief Superintendent Jim Nevill, but had failed to secure the release of the hostages. He was due to be relieved in this duty by Detective Superintendent Peter Imbert assisted by Detective Inspector Malcolm Hackett.

A small team of officers had been called in to man the Incident Room and carry out necessary enquiries, thus enabling those officers that had been on duty overnight to get some well-earned rest. In view of the numerous murders, bombings and shootings that this particular Provisional IRA ASU had been responsible for, it was anticipated that the siege could well be a long drawn out affair and it had already been decided that everyone involved in the negotiations or enquiries would work 12 hour shifts either 10am to 10pm or 10pm to 10am. Hence those officers called out in the first instance were to remain on the night shift.

A number of witness statements had already been made by the officers involved in the pursuit the previous evening. In addition to carrying out a criminal investigation into the shooting at Scott's restaurant and the subsequent shooting at pursuing police officers, the primary functions of the Incident Room and its staff was to support the efforts of the negotiators by ascertaining as much information about the two hostages as possible, including their mental and physical condition, the contents and layout of their flat and obtaining recent photographs from relatives if possible.

Some doubt existed initially as to whether all four members of the ASU had actually entered the flat particularly as they had been seen to split up whilst running from police, although as mentioned two officers had seen them join up again, but it was only unknown members of the public who had actually seen the suspects run into the flats.

It was important therefore that we made enquiries of all residents in Balcombe Street as soon as possible in order to trace and identify such witnesses. I learnt that the Commissioner Sir Robert Mark had been at the scene during the early hours of the morning and given a press briefing, indicating that police would not be giving in to the ASU's demands for transport to Dublin. Confidentially I was informed that once fingerprints lifted from the abandoned weapons confirmed the suspects were definitely those responsible for the recent atrocities, there was no way they would be allowed to leave the flat other than by their surrender. In the prevailing circumstances, although every effort would be made to bring about a negotiated surrender, the lives of

Mr. and Mrs. Mathews were considered expendable if these efforts failed and a breakout was attempted using the Mathews as cover.

A psychiatric team headed by Dr Peter Scott from the Bethlehem Maudsley Hospital, who had given valuable advice and assistance at the recent Spaghetti House Siege had been put on standby to assist with negotiations and the Home Office had made contact with the Ministry of Defence to alert the Special Air Service (SAS) that their assistance might well be required, if negotiations failed and it was deemed necessary to forcibly enter flat 22b.

In view of the fact that flat 22b had a front balcony overlooking the street below, the ASU potentially had a good view of what was occurring in the street, but fortunately they had so far confined themselves within the flat. Any officers however who needed to enter or leave any of the premises commandeered by police within this inner cordon, were considered at risk as potential targets. Therefore whenever it was necessary for such movements, D.19 officers were notified and took up positions in the street with their firearms pointing up towards the balcony of flat 22b to provide covering fire should it be required.

Such tactics whilst entirely necessary for the safety of police personnel, provided the news media at the southern cordon of Balcombe Street with the occasional photo opportunity, thus relieving what must have been a monotonous situation for them. An additional incident which gave rise to much press speculation occurred when a resident living in nearby Huntsworth Mews, having witnessed the police tactics, decided that a World War One four-wheeled armoured vehicle which he owned as a private collector, would come in useful to provide protection for police should a shooting incident develop in the street. As the vehicle was outside his home minus its engine, he decided to push it round into Balcombe Street.

In the media press briefing by the Commissioner Sir Robert Mark, during the early hours of that Sunday morning he had made clear that he considered the men involved to be no more than ordinary criminals and in order to ensure the safety of the hostages, police were prepared to play a waiting game and were prepared to surround the premises "until these people see reason". This was as much for the benefit of the ASU as the media, as it was presumed the ASU would have access to radio and television broadcasts within the flat. He also emphasized in response to questions, that no food would be sent into the flat and that people could survive on water alone for some considerable time.

What was not known by anyone other than the occupants of the flat at that time was that the ASU had confined themselves and their hostages to the front living room adjacent to the balcony, having moved furniture to block the doorway into the hall passageway. They had taken this action soon after entering the premises when under the misguided impression police officers had managed to effect entry to other parts of the flat. By so doing they had effectively cut themselves off from access to any food or drink in the kitchen as well as toilet facilities.

Deputy Assistant Commissioner Ernest Bond the head of 'C' Department had telephoned the Mathews flat at 7.30am and spoken to one of the ASU who had repeated their demand for a car to Heathrow and a flight to Dublin. Mr. Bond had again demanded the safe release of the hostages in the first instance and received the reply 'we'll see about that." In a press briefing shortly afterwards he was obliged to warn the press not to try and telephone the Mathews' flat themselves, as Technical Support officers of C.7 who were monitoring all telephone traffic, had informed him of numerous attempts being made to get through to the Mathews' phone number.

Overall control of the uniform police operation of containment of the area within the cordons and deployment of D.19 officers had fallen to Deputy Assistant Commissioner Wilford Gibson "A" Department, who had responsibility for all public order situations. He had commandeered a ground floor room at 20 Dorset Square on the corner of Balcombe Street across the road from number 22 where he proposed Peter Imbert should work from in his negotiating role. Peter however expressed a wish to "look down on his prey" from a psychological point of view and so an additional room on the third floor was put at his disposal.

Two major thoughts were at the back of all our minds from the onset of this siege. Despite the holdall of weaponry abandoned during the foot chase we had no way of knowing what guns, ammunition or possibly even explosives, the ASU still had in their possession which they might use to attempt an escape. Nor did we know whether the P.I.R.A. hierarchy would endeavour to affect their escape or release, by some other outrage committed elsewhere. It was therefore considered vital to prevent the ASU having contact with any potential outside help.

Disconnection of the Mathews' phone line was considered a priority; fortunately mobile phones had yet to be available. At 11.30am Jim Nevill therefore advised the ASU of police intentions, emphasising the need for a reliable, secure, confidential and uninterrupted means of communication between them and explaining that a hard wire battery operated field telephone would be lowered down to the balcony by way of replacement, providing direct contact between the two parties.

Once installed Peter Imbert used the field phone to make the first contact and established that the spokesperson for the IRA unit wished to be called 'Tom' whilst Imbert agreed that Nevill and himself would use their first names, Peter and Jim. Ever seeking to gain further intelligence, Peter requested the name of the other team members and was told "Mick and Paddy." A further request by Peter Imbert to be allowed to speak with Mrs. Mathews was acceded to and she was handed the phone. Asked how she was, she said she was well but in some pain due to recent dental treatment and the sitting position she was being kept in. Imbert agreed he would send down some painkillers, which were later lowered down and taken into the flat.

Located as I was in the makeshift incident room of the British Rail Headquarters Building, we were not immediately privy to the progress of the negotiations but were updated at convenient intervals as circumstances dictated, often by Malcolm Hackett who was acting as go between, assisting Peter Imbert. We were however furnished with a television monitor showing the view of the front of the flats and could watch any events taking place in the street or on the balcony. Shortly after seeing a plastic box containing the painkillers being lowered to the balcony of flat 22b, the box was brought into our room to be dusted for fingerprints by one of the fingerprint officers. Within a matter of hours we received confirmation from New Scotland Yard, that marks lifted from the box belonged to one of our most prolific bombers, despite his true identity still remaining unknown.

One of our priorities was to gain as much information as possible concerning from family or friends regarding the layout of the furniture within the Mathews' flat, in order to assist C.7, our Technical Support officers, in deciding the best location to attempt to insert sensitive surveillance equipment, by drilling from neighbouring premises. One surprise development that was to assist in this matter came during a brief conversation between Tom and Peter Imbert that morning. Tom mentioned that Mrs. Mathews wanted a drink of water to which Peter had replied "well get her one then." Tom then said "Not bloody likely your guys are all over the place".

This off the cuff remark made Peter Imbert realize that the ASU must have confined themselves to just the living room in the mistaken belief that police had entered other parts of the flat. This changed the whole perspective of the situation for it meant that neither the ASU nor the Mathews had access to food, water or toilet facilities and could only use whatever items were available in the living room. Conditions within the flat from a sanitation point of view would deteriorate considerably making it even more traumatic for the hostages to deal with.

Arrangement were therefore made for a supply of bottled water and a chemical toilet to be brought to the scene, to be lowered to the flat at a time convenient to Peter Imbert's continuing negotiations. It was now important for police to occupy the remainder of the flat at the earliest opportunity, not least to assist our Technical Support Officers who could confine their activities to just the one room. A need for stealth was important and any attempt to force the front door could result in a tragic confrontation. It was decided that the best means of access would be via a ladder placed at the rear of the flat and a supply of plimsolls was requisitioned from the Police Training School, for the team that needed to undertake this covert operation.

Whilst I had made use of certain technical equipment used by my C.7. Colleagues in the past, I was interested to learn from one of them of a piece of equipment I was not familiar with, a special low speed silent drill, which would take several hours to penetrate a wall. All the debris evacuated by the drilling mechanism was retained in a glass test tube type attachment held vertically. The result would provide a sample of the type of material that was being penetrated, very much like the coloured sands sold at coastal resorts like Alum Bay on the Isle of Wight, i.e. plaster initially and then brick dust and when plaster again appeared the operator would know that complete penetration was almost effected. The idea would be to just pierce the interior wallpaper enabling a fibre optic type probe to be inserted to view the interior of the room and its occupants. In view of the time and stealth needed for such an operation, a high drilling position was considered least likely to be noticed from within the room and less likely to be obstructed by interior furniture.

In a further press briefing that evening Commander Bill Fleming explained to the assembled media that the police had the suspects and their hostages confined in the Mathews' living room, with the result that the siege could be over quicker than first thought. Sir Robert Mark mentioned that in view of the force's policy of not surrendering to hostage takers demands it was inevitable that both Mr. and Mrs. Mathews could suffer some hardship, particularly as no food would be sent into the flat. He did however confirm that police would be consulting medical advice from time to time regarding the likely state of health of the hostages. His final remarks were to advise the hostage takers that the best course of action was for them to give themselves up and come out, as police were prepared to await this outcome.

One of the benefits of these regular media broadcasts was that it was almost certain the hostage takers would be monitoring the news media to learn what was occurring outside and it was therefore a convenient way of reinforcing the message that Peter Imbert and Jim Nevill had been trying to get across in their negotiations. There was also the added advantage that the message would get across without the interruptions that the negotiators experienced, as Tom was prone to lace his conversations with four letter expletives or abruptly put down the phone mid conversation.

Later that evening Peter Imbert informed Tom via the field phone that a chemical toilet had been obtained and would be lowered down to the balcony together with some bottled water to improve the sanitary conditions within the flat. Tom agreed to this move but his request for cigarettes to accompany the delivery were declined by Imbert, when Tom failed to agree to releasing Mrs. Mathews as part of the deal.

Back in the Incident Room I had been busy going through the various witness statements. One member of the public spoke of seeing a man in a light coloured raincoat leaning on a parked car opposite the flats, holding what looked like a firearm, which he was pointing up towards the Balcony area. This had been just after the suspects were seen to enter the flats, but none of the armed officers who had been at the scene had mentioned taking up such a position. It was important to ascertain exactly who this person was. I therefore arranged for all officers to make further brief statements detailing the clothing they were wearing that night. It transpired that Inspector John Purnell had been wearing such a garment. When details from the witness statement were mentioned to him, he recalled that on his arrival opposite the flats where the suspects had entered, he had taken cover behind a parked vehicle and still holding the rifle barrel retrieved from the abandoned holdall, in the heat of the moment he had instinctively pointed it up at the flats. It would of course provided little protection if he had been fired upon.

When my tour of duty finished that day I drove home wondering whether there would be any significant developments overnight. I knew I would be able to rely on the media to monitor the situation and the early morning bulletins the following day were without significant incident.

On the Monday morning one of the priorities of my enquiry team was to obtain detailed plans of the building structure from the local council. I had been informed that the SAS who were on standby, wished to make a mock-up of the flat layout at Chelsea Barracks, so they could plan and practice their entry into the flat should that necessity arise.

Some concern had also developed within the senior command group as to the likelihood of a counter strike by other Provisional IRA members. The possibility of a car bomb being used was taken into consideration and security round the outer cordon was strengthened, with vehicles entering the outer cordoned area being checked for explosives devices and members of the public resident or working therein, being issued with passes. Sandbag emplacements were also erected in Boston Place to the rear of the Balcombe Street flats, lest any attempt to assist an escape were attempted from that direction. Armed officers then manned these emplacements.

A further indication that police were prepared for a drawn out hostage situation was the provision of a mobile police canteen vehicle and a mobile police station brought into Dorset Square.

In an early morning call to the flat via the field telephone Peter Imbert spoke again with Tom who merely repeated his previous demands for safe passage to Dublin in return for release of the hostages. This stalemate situation was however causing some concern, firstly the hard line tactics adopted by Sir Robert Mark severely restricted the negotiating position of Imbert and Nevill furthermore it was the opinion of Dr Scott the psychologist that such tactics might force the ASU to become desperate enough to inflict their revenge on either of the hostages or place their lives in danger by attempting an escape using them as shields. A softening of this hard line attitude was therefore being proposed.

An opportunity to defuse the situation arose later during the morning when for the first time since the field phone had been set up, Tom instigated a call to the negotiators. Peter Imbert answered the call to receive a request from Tom for hot food and cigarettes to be sent to the apartment. Imbert's response was to agree to do this if Mrs. Mathews was released, a decision, which appeared to take Tom by surprise as he intimated he needed to think about the proposal or talk it over with the others.

In an endeavour to put further pressure on the ASU a press conference was then held by Deputy Assistant Commissioners Peter Walton and Ernest Bond, in which details were publicised of the police offer of hot soup and cigarettes being made available in exchange for the release of Mrs. Mathews. Mr. Bond even qualified the offer by saying he was prepared to send in the food merely on the ASU's word that Mrs. Mathews would be released shortly after it had been delivered. Some consideration was given as to whether Mrs. Mathews would refuse to leave without her husband, but in the event Tom later made contact declining Imbert's offer but still requesting food and cigarettes. Tom was not best pleased when fresh demands to release Mrs. Mathews were made by Peter Imbert and he expressed his displeasure by disconnecting the field telephone.

It was to be several hours of attempting negotiations with a hand-held megaphone before the field phone was re-connected by the ASU. During these periods of frustrated waiting there was much discussion as to what the ASU were hoping to achieve. There was a school of thought that perhaps they were merely playing for time to enable associates to visit their living quarters, wherever that may be, in order to retrieve any weapons, or bomb making materials. Foremost in everyone's mind however was the knowledge that we were dealing with men who had already killed and injured many innocent people and had little respect for human life in the furtherance of their political objectives.

Later that evening Sir Robert Mark in a final press conference of the day appealed to the general public for help in identifying the men. In particular he appealed to anyone who rented rooms, or were neighbours of young Irishmen who had not been seen at their premises over the past couple of days. He further emphasized that the primary aim of police was to save the lives of everyone in flat 22b.

By the third day of the siege, Tuesday 9th December, certain of the media in their search for something fresh to report, had taken to consulting with members of the medical profession, speculating on the likely medical condition of the ASU. One opinion expressed was that if police deliberately kept them hungry they could become 'bloody minded.' When Peter Imbert attempted to make contact with the ASU that morning, he was to find the field telephone had been disconnected and he was obliged to use a hand-held megaphone to communicate with them.

Later that morning during a press conference, Commander Roy Habershon informed the media that the disconnection of the telephone line would in no way impinge of the Met's overall strategy of patience. In addition DAC Peter Walton stated that should it become necessary, based on medical advice regarding the wellbeing of the Mathews, police were prepared to send in food and cigarettes. Sir Robert Mark added the rider that no attempt would be made to put drugs in the food in order to incapacitate the men inside the flat.

When the telephone line was later re-connected, communication between Imbert and Tom resumed, with the latter again requesting a hot meal for everyone in the flat, only for his request to fail when Imbert insisted on Mrs. Mathews release as part of the deal. A further disappointment for the ASU came when the Irish government intimated that under no circumstances would they be prepared to grant landing rights to any aircraft carrying the IRA men, or any other terrorist seeking sanctuary in the Republic.

During a midday press conference it was mentioned that police were aware that a man known as Michael Wilson a prominent IRA operative who was responsible for a number of bombings and shooting in recent months was believed to one of the hostage takers. This name had been given by one of the ASU responsible for renting the flat at Fairholme Road, but decamping after the shooting of P.C. Stephen Tibble and subsequently linked by fingerprints to various incidents. We were of course still unaware of the true identity of Wilson, he merely being Suspect 'Z' in the fingerprint collection built up from various IRA incidents.

During conversation over the field telephone during that afternoon Peter Imbert offered to replace the chemical toilet in the flat, an offer that was to be declined by Tom, presumably in an endeavour to maintain some control over negotiations. Imbert continued however to offer food without the promise of a hostage being released.

The BBC Six O'clock News that evening was to feature Sheila Mathews' sister, Mrs. Joan Royce being interviewed and being allowed to make direct statements addressed to her sister. The interview was arranged after Mrs. Mathews' family had offered to help in any way they could and was filmed in a police section house by agreement with Commander Roy Habershon. Mrs. Royce appealed to her sister not to lose heart, informing her that what was going on outside was quite fantastic and assuring her that the two daughters of John and Sheila Mathews were holding up under the strain of their parents situation. She also appealed to the ASU to let John and Sheila go stating there was nothing more to be gained from continuing with the siege.

Following this broadcast Peter Imbert called Tom on the Field Phone and in an attempt to capitalize on any impact the broadcast may have had, asked him what Daithi O'Connell, the IRA chief of staff would think of their actions in taking a middle-aged couple hostage. Describing their actions as pathetic, Imbert continued to taunt Tom until the phone suddenly went dead indicating Tom had yet again slammed the phone down.

Shortly afterwards the balcony doors of 22b opened and the field telephone base unit was thrown out into the street below. Peter Imbert was later to confide that he thought he may have gone too far in provoking Tom and he dreaded that a gunshot sound might follow from within the flat as a hostage was executed.

In an attempt to calm the situation down Imbert was obliged to resort to the use of the hand-held loudhailer to communicate with the occupants of the flat. His efforts were however met with a barrage of verbal invective-laden abuse from Tom and his comrades who were in no mood to converse with the negotiating team. In a further effort to bring the situation back under control Imbert ordered a supply of hot vegetable soup, coffee and cigarettes to be lowered down to the balcony of flat 22b.

Once the food had been lowered, Imbert use the loudhailer to inform the ASU of it arrival, for which he had asked for nothing in return. Somewhat surprisingly the food container remained in place dangling in front of the balcony windows, as the ASU exercising severe restraint, clearly wished to demonstrate that they were the ones in control of the situation.

The earlier appeal for the public to notify us of any suspicions they may have as to the premises where the ASU members had been living, had certainly resulted in a good deal of information being supplied and with the continuing public and media interest in the siege, the steady supply of information continued to keep my enquiry team busy. We were however no nearer to discovering their addresses.

By Wednesday 10th December the ASU had now gone without food for over four days. As someone who enjoyed his food and would be uncomfortable with just missing one meal, I found it hard to imagine how the hostages must be feeling, particularly when the decision had been made to leave the food container and its contents dangling outside the balcony window.

Working twelve hours shift in addition to the traveling time meant the siege was taking up most of my days, yet it was an all-consuming operation and I know I was not alone in almost not wanting go off duty lest I should miss some significant event whilst not there. The first thing I did on waking each morning was to turn on the radio or television to check the situation and as the days wore on I felt more sure that I would hear that the siege had ended but this was not to be the case.

With the field telephone having been ejected into the Street below, the negotiating teams were now faced with having to resort to the use of a loud hailer whilst standing in the street below the balcony of 22b. This was proving unsatisfactory in that everything the negotiators said could be heard by anyone in the surrounding area including the press, whilst on the occasions when Tom felt inclined to reply, his spoken words could barely be heard by the team in the street below. It was only when Tom was roused to shout invectives that the press heard his replies, so reporting of the dialogue had become rather stilted. Arrangements were therefore made for a microphone to be suspended over the balcony of 22b, to a position just out of reach by anyone on the balcony but low enough to pick up their speech. This microphone was connected to two speakers facing out into the street.

Since the commencement of the siege consideration had been given to disconnecting the gas and electricity supplies to the flat. We had established that there a was a small gas fire in the living room which would provide the comfort of heat to the occupants, whilst the television enabled the ASU to monitor everything that was being reported in the media and could serve to bolster their resolve at a time when they were seeking to gain the upper hand.

A decision was therefore made that both services would shortly be disconnected. Termination of the electricity supply would have the additional advantage in that a record player in the flat could no longer be used; this use had been preventing surveillance devices picking up conversations from within.

With the increase in pressure that these measures would have it was considered crucial to try and get food accepted into the flat and such was the advice of Dr Peter Scott to DAC Gibson who briefed Peter Imbert accordingly. Imbert's attempt to communicate over the loud hailer system were being met with no response so he requested a clipboard and pencil be lowered to the balcony of 22b, in order that the ASU could write down any requests which they did not wish to have broadcast over the loudspeaker system. This latest initiative also failed to get a response.

Using the loudhailer, Imbert addressed the ASU informing them that he had been advised to provide some Valium tablets for Mrs. Mathews. Shortly afterwards a container was lowered down to the balcony, but Imbert decided to include sandwiches and coffee along with the drugs in the hope they would be accepted. The container was retrieved by the ASU and taken into the flat however the sounds of shouting shortly ensued from the flat and the container and the untouched food and drink was then hurled from the balcony spilling its contents on to the street below.

Early on the morning of Thursday 11th December the fifth day of the siege, Jim Nevill managed to strike up a dialogue with Tom using the loud hailer in the street. He was seeking to ascertain the condition of the hostages and the conditions generally within the flat. Whilst Tom declined to comment on the condition of Mr. and Mrs. Mathews, he agreed to accept Nevill's offer of a new chemical pack for the toilet and some fresh drinking water and these items were then lowered down and accepted.

Later that morning when Peter Imbert took over negotiating duties he used the loud hailer to pass on various messages of support and encouragement from family and friends of the Mathews. There was no response from the ASU who appeared very subdued no doubt dispirited by the loss of the gas and electricity services to the flat.

There had been some interesting developments however regarding the true identity of the suspect Michael Wilson whose fingerprints had been recovered at Fairholme Road after the murder of P.C. Stephen Tibble; on the Ford Granada stolen after the murder of Ross Mc Whirter and on weapons abandoned by the ASU as they were pursued by police into the flat at Balcombe Street. In cooperation with the Irish Garda these finger marks had been checked with their records which provided a link to a man wanted in connection with an £8 million art robbery from the home of Sir Alfred Beit in County Wicklow in 1974 and a subsequent shoot out with Garda Officers. What had been puzzling both the Garda and our own fingerprint department C.3, was why neither force had been able to identify who this active IRA operative was. Fortunately C.3 decided to research the fingerprint records of IRA operatives whose reported deaths over recent years had caused their fingerprints to be removed from the current collection. Here they struck lucky for the fingerprints matched those of a Harris Duggan junior of Feakle Co. Clare who had reportedly been killed on active service for the IRA in Northern Ireland, whilst wanted for various offences.

Meanwhile there had been little sign of any activity within the flat that day and concern was growing about the need for the hostages to receive some food. Late that evening Imbert arranged for a supply of hot soup, sandwiches, coffee and cigarettes to be made ready in the flat above 22b. As the container was lowered to the balcony area below, Imbert addressed Tom on the loud hailer, stating that the food was for the hostages and being a public announcement the press would know if he refused it, when there was no response Imbert tried again saying "I presume you are taking responsibility, Tom to deprive these people, the food is on doctors' orders for Mr. and Mrs. Mathews."

This last remark had the effect of inducing Tom to come to the open window whereupon Imbert informed Tom he was sending in food for five people, remarking "You told me Tom, there are five people in there." Tom then queried how Imbert knew for sure the number of people in the flat to which Imbert replied, "How many are there? These are all the sandwiches you are going to get!"

The container of food continued to dangle in front of the balcony window whilst Tom and his comrades deliberated on what they should do, until suddenly the silence was broken by a shrill piercing scream emanating from Mrs. Mathews, "Take it!" she was heard to utter in a high pitched yell, indicative of the mental state the poor woman must have been in.

Finally some progress seemed to have been made when Tom returned to the window and requested of Peter Imbert that he send in food for seven people. Imbert however compromised by offering to send in food for six, which Tom agreed to. He then took in the container of food and two further meals were subsequently lowered down and taken into the flat, by which time it was late in the evening.

It was early on the morning of 12th December, the sixth day of the siege that Jim Nevill re-commenced negotiations with the ASU, still using the loudhailer. When Tom was asked how the hostages were doing he replied "Okay" but declined Nevill's request to let him speak with either of them. Intent on keeping the dialogue going Jim Nevill asked whether it would be possible for one of Mrs Mathew's relatives to come and speak with her. After appearing to consider this request Tom declined the offer stating that the experience would be too upsetting for Mrs. Mathews. Although this response indicated a degree of consideration for Mrs. Mathews it could equally be that Tom considered what an adverse effect a distraught Mrs. Mathews would have on the other occupants of the flat.

Jim Nevill managed to keep up a dialogue with Tom attempting to get him to agree to release Mrs Mathews but this request was declined, as was an offer to send in a replacement field telephone. An offer to supply fresh drinking water was however accepted.

Within the flat that morning however the mood had changed and the ASU had decided they had no alternative but to attempt a breakout using the Mathews as hostages. With this objective in mind the ASU had divided up their available cash so each had about £10 each should they become separated. Similarly they divided up their available ammunition so each member possessed a supply suitable for the calibre of weapon held. Mr. and Mrs. Mathews were untied and made to walk around the room in order to get their circulation going and one of the ASU swapped jackets with Mr. Mathews.

The surveillance team monitoring the flat picked up snippets of conversation indicting that something was afoot. Receipt of this news however only served to increase the tension of the negotiators and the senior Management team, in particular in view of Commissioner, Sir Robert Mark's policy that in no circumstances were the ASU to be allowed to escape, even if the lives of Mr. and Mrs. Mathews were put at risk. In short they were considered dispensable if all else failed.

In a hastily convened press briefing DAC Peter Walton talked with David Lay of the BBC, their discussion centred around the Met's preparedness for a shootout with the IRA men if necessary and included information that a detachment of soldiers from the Special Air Service was on standby and ready to enter the apartment at a moment's notice. This interview was broadcast in the 1pm news and picked up by the ASU who still had the services of a battery-operated transistor radio, with which they were known to monitor all news bulletins.

The ASU would have been fully aware of the effectiveness of the SAS and been in little doubt that if deployed none of them would be likely to survive. It was perhaps not surprising therefore that at 1.45pm, Tom shouted out of the balcony window requesting the services of a field telephone, much to the delight of

Imbert and Nevill. After the equipment had been lowered from the flat above, Peter Imbert used the loudhailer to inform Tom that the field telephone was in place and could be pulled into the flat from the balcony.

Once the phone had been taken into the flat, Tom's opening call to Peter Imbert posed the question, "What are the terms for our surrender?" The word surrender had deliberately been avoided all week by both negotiators who had no wish to antagonise their quarry. Taken aback by this sudden change of dialogue, Imbert replied, "You're not mucking me about are you?" But as the dialogue continued it was evident that the ASU had decided to capitulate and wished to ensure their safe passage from the flat into police custody.

The nature of how this might be effected had obviously been a matter of discussion between the negotiators, the senior management team and the firearms Department D.19, in the preceding days, bearing in mind that the front door to the flat was barricaded with sandbags. Peter Imbert informed Tom that first Mrs Mathews should be released onto the balcony area so she could be safely helped onto the adjacent balcony of a flat occupied by police. Thereafter it was agreed that a hot meal would be supplied for the occupants of the flat including Mr. Mathews, where after he would be released. Finally each member of the ASU would be invited to come out onto the balcony one at a time in a manner showing that they were unarmed and climb over the railings to the adjacent balcony where they would be met by police officers.

The first I knew of this sudden change of attitude was when Jim Nevill came down to the incident room accompanied by one of our technical support officers who handed me a small recording device. Jim Nevill explained that Mrs. Mathews was about to be released and he wanted me to accompany her in the ambulance, which we had had on standby throughout the siege. Ever one to play his cars close to his chest, he did not inform me that negotiation had reached a stage where it was anticipated that the four ASU members would shortly be surrendering.

My instructions were to debrief Mrs. Mathews about the numbers of ASU members, their intentions, their weapons and whether they were in possession of any explosives. In addition to obtain descriptions of the men and details of their clothing and any changes that had been made within the flat such as furniture moved to barricade doors etc.

Shortly afterwards at about 2.15pm, I witnessed Mrs. Mathews being assisted onto the balcony of 22b, by agreement between Tom and Peter Imbert the frail Mrs. Mathews was supported by one of the IRA team, (later identified as Eddie Butler), to the end of the balcony where she remained motionless until Butler had made his way back into flat 22b, keeping his arms raised above his head and acting under instructions from the negotiating team. Once Butler had left the balcony two officers appeared on the adjacent balcony and whilst one provided armed cover the other assisted Mrs. Mathews to climb the railings between the two balconies.

A W.P.C. finally accompanied Mrs. Mathews out of the building entrance and across Balcombe Street to where I was waiting with the ambulance. With University College Hospital being situated little more than a mile distance away I had barely time to introduce myself and re assure Mrs. Mathews before we arrived at the hospital. On our arrival Mrs. Mathews was whisked away surrounded by medical staff anxious to check her over. Having informed the nursing staff that it was important that I was able to speak with her briefly as soon as possible, I was obliged to wait a short while before being allowed in to see her again. Other than being very frail and totally exhausted Mrs. Mathews was reported to be in reasonably good health and willing to help me in any way she could. I elicited the fact that all four members of the ASU were armed with handguns, no mention had been made of explosives, one of them had exchanged jackets with her husband and the door into the sitting room was blockaded from the inside by furniture having been moved.

I telephoned into the Incident Room to pass on such information as I had and I was immediately informed that the four ASU members were in the process of surrendering themselves into custody and Mr. Mathews had now also been released. It had been agreed between Tom and Peter Imbert that Mr. Mathews would remain in the flat until two of the ASU had safely surrendered and then he was allowed his walk to freedom followed by another ASU member with Tom remaining in telephone contact with Imbert until finally it was his turn to leave. All members of the ASU had made makeshift hoods to protect their identities once on the balcony in public view, their weapons and ammunition having been discarded and left on the floor of the living room. Their eventual surrender commenced at 4.15pm that Friday afternoon and some ten minutes later all were safely in custody and Mr Mathews was on his way to University college Hospital for a medical examination.

So after six traumatic days for everyone involved, the Siege of Balcombe Street had finally ended. The police strategy of containment and patient negotiations had finally paid off with no serious injury or loss of life. Both Mr. and Mrs. Mathews were in reasonably good health considering their personal ordeal and were soon re-united with their two daughters and Sheila's sister Joan. Doubtless some inconvenience had been caused to local residents, but the arrest of four dangerous armed men responsible for numerous bombings and shootings in Central London meant that London would be a safer place for all in the run up to Christmas and until another IRA unit could be installed to replace those arrested.

Once flat 22b had been vacated, officers were able to gain entry to the flat, and finally take possession of four handguns and a quantity of ammunition left lying on the floor amongst the general debris that together with the stench of two chemical toilets, evidenced the appalling conditions that the Mathews had endured over the past six days. Roy Jenkins, the Home Secretary attended the scene shortly afterwards on behalf of the government, to congratulate Police on bringing the Siege to such a successful conclusion, he also made a brief visit to see the conditions within the flat.

Meanwhile the four ASU members Eddie Butler, Hugh Dougherty, Harry Duggan and Joseph O'Connell alias 'Tom', were all conveyed to nearby Paddington Green Police Station, where Peter Imbert had previously intimated to Tom that he and Jim would shortly be along to interview them.

In anticipation of when the siege would end a room had been set aside at Paddington Green Police Station, from which ongoing enquiries would thereafter be conducted and we lost no time in transferring our temporary Incident Room from the British Rail Headquarter Building to Paddington Police Station. It was there at about 6.30pm that evening when I first learnt that some progress had been made during the preliminary interview with the prisoners. Chief Superintendent Jim Nevill requested that I get a team together to search an address in North London where Edward Butler admitted he had been residing. He directed that I obtain the services of an Explosives Officer lest the premises be booby trapped.

The address given was 61, Crouch Hill, Hornsey N.4, a road I knew well having lived in a turning off Crouch Hill when Noeleen and I were first married. I knew the houses there to be large multi occupancy Victorian dwellings let out into various flats or rooms. Our search was to relate to a top floor flat.

Having obtained the services of Detective Sergeants Peter Fickling, Keith Blackmore (Special Branch), Vince Napolitano, one of our Exhibits Officers, Detective Constable Howard and several other officers, I arranged with Ken Howarth the duty Explosives Officer, to meet at the premises at 7.30pm.

I found No 61 Crouch Hill was situated at the Junction with Shaftesbury Road just some 100 yards from Ashley Road where I had once lived. Entry to the top flat on the second floor was via a locked door fitted across the top of the staircase, making it self- contained. After preliminary checks by Ken Howarth we were happy that it did not appear booby trapped and I put my shoulder to it to effect entry. Behind the door was an entrance hall with a doorway to a kitchen on the left and another door in front, which gave access to a bedroom. Once in the first bedroom another door on the left provided access to a second bedroom. Both rooms were sparsely furnished and in one corner of the second bedroom was a built in cupboard, which was locked.

Ken Howarth checked this cupboard out before forcing the lock and contained on the four shelves within we were to find all the accoutrements of a P.I.R.A. Active Service Unit.

On the top shelf was an Armalite Rifle wrapped in a piece of sheet, together with two Armalite magazines, 20 non electric detonators a length of safety fuse an electric detonator and some wire.

On the second shelf was a very significant item as far as I was concerned, a box of ball bearings, identical in size to those I had seen removed from the victims of the Waltons Restaurant Bomb. There was also a briefcase containing a few rolls of plastic tape, two London A-Z Geographicals, a large bolt with a nut attached, a spanner and screwdriver.

On the third shelf down was a pile of reference books and a suitcase, which contained a large quantity of assorted ammunition, 48 electric detonators and a length of detonator cord.

On the floor of the cupboard, were a large holdall and two plastic bags, which were found to contain a quantity of explosives wrapped in newspaper and several hundred rounds of ammunition. A total of some 586 rounds of ammunition suitable for use with six different calibre of firearm were recovered from that cupboard.

As soon as it became obvious that we had a significant find at this address, the assistance of a Police photographer and fingerprint officers were obtained before items were disturbed or examined further. The services of an explosives Dog were also sought to determine whether further explosives might have been concealed elsewhere. I was pleased find that the Dog Handler was Brian Sworn, a former colleague of mine from my days at St. Ann's Road. This search however proved negative.

As various other rooms in the house were let to different tenants we had to ensure that none of them were in anyway associated with Edward Butler and his flat mate, so whilst some of my team were involved with searching the top flat others were tasked with interviewing the various residents, partly to glean any intelligence available regarding their former neighbours on the top floor and additionally to ensure they themselves were in no way involved in P.I.R.A. activities.

There were four young Irish male tenants of two first floor rooms two of whom were brothers. During enquiries it transpired that one of the brothers had working at the Palace of Westminster in June 1974 during the time of a bomb explosion there. This resulted in the necessity for these four tenants being detained at Holloway Police Station that evening, under the provisions of the Prevention of Terrorism (Temporary Provisions) Act 1974, until enquires about them could be completed satisfactorily.

In addition to the aforementioned bomb making equipment and weaponry, a number of significant documents were found and I knew that some of them would need to be submitted by our exhibits officer for chemical treatment to check for any latent fingerprints. In order to facilitate urgent enquiries prior to such items being returned by fingerprint department, I directed that a schedule be prepared listing a detailed description of all documents or writings, together with a note of exactly where the item was found, prior to any item being bagged up as an exhibit.

Included amongst such documents were 10 press cuttings of prominent public figures, a note pad bearing a list of names and addresses of other notable figures. These items can only be described as a list of potential targets for this unit. Fortunately none of them had yet been victims of any terrorist act.

One of the reference books found was a copy of Whittackers' Almanac perusal of which revealed a number of manuscript numbers had been written on the inside front cover. These numbers were obviously page numbers of interest to the ASU as they relevant pages related to a list of Government Ministers; the Home Office; UK Defence and Ministry Personnel; the largest ships in Service and a list of Chief Executives of County Councils and Chief Constables.

One significant document found was a page torn from the Evening Standard dated 9th May 1975, on which had been drawn a rough sketch of the general vicinity of Scotland Yard including the position of the underground car park as well as a local public house and café. This newspaper had been in the suitcase containing the detonators and ammunition.

Other items found in the cupboard were various documents relating to a Ford Cortina motorcar PBV 789E. Subsequent enquiries were to reveal that this vehicle had been stolen between 7.15pm and 9pm on 18th November 1975, from outside the owner's address in Agate Road, W.6 and later recovered at Connaught Square at 10.40pm after three men were seen to drive up, park and hurriedly leave the vehicle. The significance of this event being that the bomb at Waltons Restaurant occurred at 9.52pm that evening.

The vehicle had been retrieved by police and forensically examined but to no good effect.

A stolen driving licence and two bank deposit books in fictitious name were also found in the flat as were a number of loose keys and a key fob, which were to prove to have relevant links in due course.

The forensic examination of the flat and listing and exhibiting of its entire contents was to take several days. The explosive materials were removed from the flat at the earliest opportunity and transported by Ken Howarth to Woolwich Arsenal for further examination.

A day or so after the search of the flat at 61 Crouch Hill, I was in the Incident Room at Paddington Police Station when Pat O'Connor one of our exhibits Officers showed me a photograph of a car key attached to a plastic key fob, bearing the image of the 'Bisto Kids' sitting on a seesaw. "You didn't see anything like this at Crouch Hill did you?" he asked. Then qualified his remark by informing me that such an item had belonged to Mrs. Mc Whirter and was stolen when her car was taken by the men who shot her husband. I immediately recalled seeing an identical key fob in a chest of drawers in the flat, albeit no key was attached. Subsequent examination of the various keys recovered from Crouch Hill identified a Ford Ignition key as the one belonging to Mrs. Mc Whirter, which she identified together with the key fob. This was a very useful piece of evidence.

The owner of the premises at 61 Crouch Hill resided in Enfield and he employed a part-time agent to look after the lettings of this address as well as four similar properties in

North London. The owner subsequently produced two rental agreements dated 22nd August 1975 relating to the letting of the top floor flat to two men using the name Mr. Anderson and Mr. J. Farley. (I.e. Doherty and Butler). These tenants had originally occupied a ground floor room at the same premises since the spring of 1975.

It was to be a few more days until another address occupied by O'Connell and Duggan came to light and this was as a result of a tip off by a suspicious member of the public. On 16th December, I together with Detective Superintendent Hucklesby, Detective Inspector Dave Stephenson and a team of officers raided a flat at 99 Milton Grove Stoke Newington. My activities were directed towards interviewing other tenants at the premises. Although no further explosives were found, a quantity of ammunition and bomb making materials were found behind a bath panel. Various other incriminating material was found including copies of the Army List, the Civil Service Year Book and a list of potential targets including, Roy Jenkins, Ted Heath, Sir Robert Mark and Commander Roy Habershon. In addition a number of press clippings and restaurant reviews were found, including one on Waltons Restaurant. Two spent .357 cartridges cases, believed fired during the murder of Ross Mc Whirter, were also recovered

The four ASU members had originally been detained at Paddington Police Station under the provisions of the Prevention of Terrorism Act and in view of the large number of offences they were suspected of having committed it was proposed that a series of Identification Parades should be held within the secure confines of that building before relevant charges were preferred. Since some potential witnesses were service personnel who were now serving out of the U.K arrangements were made with the Ministry of Defence for them to be flown home as soon as possible in time for the Parades, which were scheduled for 17th December.

Detective Chief Inspector Dave Munday had been appointed to plan and organise the identity parades in view of the number of potential witnesses involved regarding offences over several years. With the assistance of local uniform officers, arrangements were made for a number of male volunteers from local businesses or organisations, to attend the Station at various times as it was not deemed practicable to expect volunteers to remain at the station for the length of time the parades would take. Other officers in police transport were out on the streets appealing for volunteers and the public were a little more cooperative than usual, doubtless conscious of what matters the parades might relate to.

As a result of the parades several witnesses identified Joseph O'Connell in connection with different offences and one witness identified Hugh Doherty as one of two men who were concerned in causing an explosion at the Stage Door public house, in Arlington Street S.W.1 on 26th December 1973.

The Identity Parades had gone on late into the evening and before travelling home Dave and I were having some well-earned refreshment in a local public house when Dave reminded me that, having been identified for particular offences the usual practice was that the investigating officer would re-interview the suspect pointing out details of the offences for which he had been identified, caution the offender and invite any reply. Up until this point all interviews had been conducted by Jim Nevill and Peter Imbert, but they were no longer on duty.

Somewhat reluctantly we decided that being the only two senior officers available, we had better conduct such interviews ourselves. Having prepared ourselves for the interviews, it was a minute after midnight when we finally saw Joseph O'Connell in his cell. This was my first meeting with O'Connell and I was a little taken aback to find him to be such a slightly built individual with thin facial features a prominent nose and a shock of dark unkempt wavy hair. Dave Munday introduced us and having Cautioned O'Connell, pointed out that the first two witnesses who had identified him were police officers who had identified him as one of two men who whilst armed with a firearm had kidnapped one of the officers in a car park at Semley Place S.W.1 on 18th October 1974. The same place as where a bus inspector had been kidnapped a week before and forced into the boot of a car.

DCI Munday informed O'Connell that he had also been identified by a Mr. Bayley, as one of the persons responsible for a bombing and shooting incident at the Naval and Military Club in Piccadilly on 11th December 1974. Then the last four witnesses were police officers that had picked him out having recognised him as a man seen in the Lord High Admiral public house, on 11th November in the company of a man known as 'Spotter Murphy'.

O'Connell replied, "That's the four that puzzled me."

DCI Munday said, "The Lord High Admiral is just along the road from here, in fact the officers made up a Photo Pfit picture after they had seen you with Spotter Murphy and it is obviously you."

O'Connell nodded his head in agreement.

DCI Munday then asked, "What were you doing in the car park when the police officers obviously disturbed you?"

O'Connell replied, "We were just trying keys."

DCI Munday asked, "Did you know they were police officers?"

O'Connell replied, "Not until one of them showed his I.D."

DCI Munday said, "What about the bus inspector, was that you as well?"

O'Connell paused and DCI Munday continued, "I'm not asking you to tell me who you were with, were you one of the men who kidnapped the bus inspector?"

O'Connell replied, "Yes I was."

DCI Munday then said, "Do you admit being at the Naval and Military Club bombing?"

O'Connell said, "Yes."

DCI Munday then questioned O'Connell further about his knowledge or association with Spotter Murphy. I was familiar with this name as I knew he had been a target of our surveillance squad. O'Connell, however, declined to answer any further questions regarding this man.

Finally DCI Munday informed O'Connell we knew about his address at Stoke Newington, to which O'Connell replied, "What at 99?"

DCI Munday continued, "That's right, 99 Milton Grove. From what we have found out about you and fingerprints we now know to be yours on several bombs in the past, you have obviously been actively engaged in IRA terrorist activities, do you want to tell us about this?"

O'Connell replied, "You tell me what ones you are talking about."

DCI Munday then said, "Do you want to make a written statement about this matter?"

O'Connell said, "Yes."

It should be mentioned at this stage neither Dave Munday nor I had received any briefing as to what any of the four ASU members had said in prior interviews with Chief Superintendent Jim Nevill or Detective Superintendent Peter Imbert. It was however satisfying that O'Connell was prepared to cooperate with our enquiries.

At 12.25am he commenced to make a written statement under caution, which Dave Munday wrote down. I was in possession of my chart listing all the various terrorist incidents showing where fingerprint evidence had been recovered, only now we knew which of those outstanding marks belonged to the various ASU members we had in custody.

O'Connell began with recounting the events in the car park where a firstly bus inspector and later a police officer were kidnapped after they had disturbed the ASU whilst attempting to steal a cars for use on bombing incidents. He then continued to give brief details of some thirty-two bombing or shooting incidents, which his ASU had been responsible for during 1974 and 1975. He was not prepared to name individuals who had participated in particular events. When an offence was put to him he often answered "That was us", or "Yes I made that bomb".

It was apparent that often only three persons would participate in a bombing. He admitted having made many of the devices himself and justified the targets chosen as being 'establishment targets' or prominent politicians as in the case of two bombing incidents he admitted directed at Ted Heath and the other at Sir Hugh Fraser. In referring to the latter incident in which Professor

Gordon Hamilton Fairley, the Cancer Research specialist had been killed, O'Connell remarked "That was an anti-handling micro switch bomb. We didn't mean to get the professor. We didn't mean to get him. The target was Fraser. He was a well-known politician, a hard line Tory you know."

On a personal level as the investigating officer for this particular offence it was satisfying to hear this admission, despite the lack of any remorse being shown.

As the interview progressed I quickly became aware that in dealing with this self-confessed IRA bomber we were in the presence of an intelligent educated young man, who was quite prepared to discuss and justify his past activities in a cool calm matter of fact manner. He appeared fully prepared to admit to such acts as his ASU had been involved in, without any elaboration or bravado. He was obviously a political idealist who felt fully justified in his actions and appeared to have no conscience concerning the death and destruction he had been responsible for. He was certainly far removed from the various criminal types I had been dealing with for the past sixteen years.

When asked what he could tell us about the bomb at K shoes in Kensington Church Street, on 29th August, 1975, that killed an explosives officer Roger Goad, O'Connell's reply was, "I made that. That was an anti-handler, anti-lift micro switch. The one in Oxford Street the night before was to give a false impression because they had defused some. The Oxford Street one went off but if they had got to it, it would have given them a false impression, a come on. Our aim was to get an explosives officer, plus the fact that if we gave a warning on any bombs, they would have to stand off and use the wheelbarrow. The real reason was that if we gave a warning they would have to stand off and not defuse them, and it would give time to clear the area and not injure people."

For the benefit of the reader the wheelbarrow was a slang expression for the remote controlled device used to examine or disrupt suspect devices from a safe distance.

When asked what he could tell us about the Green Park bomb on 9th October 1975 that had killed a man having been left at a bus stop, O'Connell remarked "The time ran out on that one, it was just one of those things. The target was an establishment target in the area. One of the lads was blown off his feet in that one."

Asked if he had made this device O'Connell replied "Yes I made up that one. It shouldn't have gone off that one. He pulled the det out of that one. I suppose still in the confined space of the bag it still set it off."

When Dave Munday asked O'Connell what he could tell us about the Hilton Hotel bomb on 5th September 1975. O'Connell said "That was one of ours."

Dave then remarked "I don't want you to admit any of the bombs I put to you, for the sake of it. There were two people killed at the Hilton."

O'Connell continued, "I know. No, that was ours. There was a warning on that one. It was supposed to be like the Europa in Belfast. That's been bombed thirty times. The Hilton bomb was not meant to kill. It was put in the foyer just near the seats you know, under a table I think that was the last warning we gave."

Asked why that was, he replied "I don't know. We're supposed to give warnings on targets like that."

An indication that O'Connell was only taking responsibility for those acts committed by his particular ASU, came a little later in the interview when he was asked about bombs in the Prince of Wales Club in Lillie Road, S.W.6; the Army and Navy Club in St. James Square and Brooks Club. He denied responsibility for any of these bombings, which had occurred in late 1974.

O'Connell admitted to having resided at 99, Milton Grove, Stoke Newington for six or seven months having moved there from 39, Fairholme Road, Hammersmith.

This interview finally concluded at 4.35am, some four hours and ten minutes since we had begun. There had however been two breaks for coffee, sandwiches and cigarettes. On completion O'Connell signed the ten-page statement, which D.C.I. Munday had written whilst seated beside him on the cell bed. For myself it had not been the most comfortable night as I had been seated on the cell floor. It had however been one of the most fascinating and rewarding interviews I had ever participated in. I certainly never expected O'Connell to be so co-operative; had I known, I would probably have got myself a chair.

A few hours later O'Connell was briefly re-interviewed under caution by DCI Munday, again in his cell in my presence. Initially Dave Munday endeavoured to find out more about the aforementioned 'Spotter Murphy' who O'Connell had met in the Lord High Admiral public house. O'Connell insisted the man was of no significance and declined to divulge anything relating to him. The murder of Ross Mc Whirter on 27th November 1975 was then raised and O'Connell was asked what he knew about the murder. He replied, "That was ours."

He claimed however not to have gone on it himself stating, "It wouldn't need all of us.

DCI Munday then referring to a visit to Paddington Police Station by police officers from Surrey during one of the preceding days, said "Do you remember being asked about the Caterham Arms Bomb on 27th August 1975 by police officers from Surrey?"

O'Connell replied, "Yes that was ours, it was a military target, but I didn't go on it."

Asked whether it was his team he replied, "It was one of ours but as I didn't go on it myself I don't want to talk about what others have done."

He was then asked about a bomb at the Hare and Hounds public house Maidstone on 25th September 1975, to which he replied, "That was ours as well."

DCI Munday said, "Did you go on it?"

O'Connell replied, "What does it matter, it was one of our, we all knew it was going to be done."

Asked whether he had made the bomb, O'Connell said, "I don't want to say any more about that one."

DCI Munday then said, "What can you tell us about the Kings Arms Woolwich, a throw in bomb on 7th November 1974, two men were killed and a number seriously injured?"

O'Connell replied, "That was not one of ours."

Asked, "Who's was it then?"

He replied, "I don't know."

Having agreed that he had stayed at the Fairholme address O'Connell was then asked, "Tell us who shot PC Tibble?"

To which O'Connell answered, "It wasn't me. I don't want to talk about it. What else do you want to ask me?"

DCI Munday listed three other incidents in 1974, which resulted in O'Connell stating, "Don't bother mentioning any more, I've said all I'm saying for now. I'm not answering any more questions."

At which point we terminated the interview, it was now 6.45am.

We then saw Hugh Docherty in his cell and DCI Munday cautioned him, introduced us and said, "You have been identified as identical with a man, one of two who were concerned in causing an explosion at the Stage Door public house Arlington Street, S.W.1 on 26ᵗʰ December 1973."

Docherty's reply was, "I have nothing to say."

A number of further questions were put to him, however he refused to give answers to any of them and we terminated the interview after about 15 minutes, realising we were wasting our time.

As I recall Dave Munday and I were pretty exhausted by now having been on duty since 9am the previous day, however in view of the Statement made by O'Connell, we decided we would remain on duty until Jim Nevill or Peter Imbert arrived back on duty, so we could brief them personally about events.

Later that day the four members of the ASU were formally charged with various offences relating to events on the night of 6ᵗʰ December 1975 and the six days of the siege. The offences included possession of firearms with intent to endanger life, using firearms to resist arrest and unlawful imprisonment of Mr. and Mrs. Mathews. After a brief appearance before local Magistrates they were remanded in custody to Brixton Prison, pending further enquiries and Committal for trial.

Once the prisoners were no longer incarcerated at Paddington Police Station we were able to move our incident room and enquiries back to New Scotland Yard. With persons in custody for this long lasting terrorist campaign it was important that all enquiries into the various offences were completed and reported on at the earliest opportunity, outlining in particular what evidence fingerprint or otherwise existed to support charges. Detective Superintendent Bill Hucklesby was deputed to collate the various reports before submission to the Director of Pubic Prosecutions for consideration of further charges.

I therefore had now to complete and submit reports on the attempted assassination of Sir Hugh Fraser resulting in the death of Professor Gordon Hamilton-Fairley at Camden Hill Square on 23rd October 1975, the Explosion at Waltons Restaurant on 18th November 1975, resulting in the death of two persons and injuries to numerous others, and the Search of and findings at 61 Crouch Hill, on 12th December 1975.

The majority of the enquiries into the first two incidents had been completed and it would only be necessary to consider what additional evidence had been forthcoming from the interviews with the accused and the discovery of items at their two addresses.

My immediate enquiries were therefore concentrated on the findings at 61 Crouch Hill. Fingerprint examination of the newspapers contained in the suitcase with the explosives, were found to be identical with Doherty, Duggan and O'Connell. Doherty's fingerprints were also found, on a brown paper bag containing the box of ball bearings. During interview with Detective Chief Superintendent Nevill and Detective Superintendent Imbert both Butler and Doherty admitted possession of the various arms ammunition and bomb making equipment found at their flat.

Fingerprints of O'Connell were also found on a jotter pad bearing the name of intended targets, which Butler during interview admitted were list of people to be killed. Further fingerprints found on the copy of Whittackers Almanac in the cupboard were those of a Paul Gerrard Norney, who was part of another ASU and had been charged at Manchester on 3rd July 1975 with attempted murder.

Various fixed items in the flat at Crouch Hill bore the fingerprints of Doherty and Butler indicating their residence there. Other fingerprints found on a Geographers A-Z of Bristol and

Bath, were found to relate to a William Joseph Quinn who was known to be in the south of Ireland but wanted in connection with his fingerprints being found on three postal devices, as well as at a bomb factory in Westridge Road Southampton. He was also known to have been residing at 39, Fairholme Road W.14 until the day of the shooting of P.C. Tibble and wanted for interview regarding that murder. It was to take another eleven years before Quinn was brought back to this country and sentenced to life imprisonment for this murder.

Enquiries regarding the stolen driving licence revealed it to be owned by a man, resident in Glasgow who claimed to have given it to a friend to produce at a Belfast Car Hire company, where the two men were to hire a car to be driven by them both. When the owner asked for the return of the licence, his friend claimed to have lost it with his jacket one night whilst drunk. Coincidentally both men admitted to knowing Doherty but were unable to assist as to how he came into possession of it. Doherty admitted receiving the licence when interviewed.

A key found in a wardrobe at Crouch Hill, was found to fit the lock of an internal ground floor door at 39, Fairholme Road, the address which was being used as a safe house by this ASU at the time of the shooting of P.C. Tibble.

When the four men emptied their pockets onto the floor of 22b Balcombe Street before their final surrender they left a number of keys. These were found to fit locks at both Crouch Hill and Milton Grove and there were sufficient for each pair to have had a key to either premise.

One matter of some concern for Chief Superintendent Nevill arose from one of his initial questions to Eddie Butler after his arrest when he asked him to describe the first bombing he had embarked on. Butler replied that police had already put people away for his first job at Woolwich. He was referring to a throw in bomb at the Kings Arms public house on Woolwich on 7th November 1974, where an off duty soldier and a civilian were killed and a number of people were injured. Nevill and Imbert would have been aware that Paul Michael Hill and Patrick Armstrong had been convicted just two months previous for this

361

bombing. These two men together with Gerard Conlan and Carole Richardson, had also been convicted of two pub bombings in Guilford following their arrest by Surrey C.I.D. This heavily publicised and disputed case had resulted in their being dubbed 'The Guildford Four'.

Initially Nevill thought Butler was intimating that he had been involved with Hill and Armstrong, until he informed Nevill that he had never heard of any of the 'Guilford Four' until their trial and they had not been involved in the bomb-throwing incident.

The full facts were reported to the Director of Public Prosecutions, who must have been faced with the dilemma as to whether the 'Guilford Four' had been wrongfully convicted, or were their fellow Irishmen 'The Balcombe Street Four' against whom there was an abundance of evidence, merely trying to take the blame on their behalf.

A number of lawyers involved with the case of the 'Guilford four' and a related trial concerning the 'Maguire Seven', began to take an interest in this case and whilst remanded in Wandsworth prison, Butler, O'Connell and Duggan requested a meeting with Frank McGuire, the Member of Parliament for Fermanagh and South Tyrone, Northern Ireland. At the meeting on 27th May 1976, Butler, O'Connell and Duggan agreed to make statements admitting their involvement in the Woolwich and Guilford pub bombings, providing that a former member of their ASU, Brendan Dowd who had jointly been involved could also make a statement. Dowd was in custody elsewhere in England, charged with 3 counts of attempted murder.

Frank Maguire subsequently met with Dowd who agreed to make a statement regarding the Guilford and Woolwich pub bombs as he claimed to have participated in both incidents together with O'Connell. Subsequently all made detailed statements regarding their involvement in the two incidents, to Alistair Logan a solicitor acting for two of the 'Guilford Four'.

On 24th January 1977 the trial of the four members of the Active Service Unit arrested at Balcombe Street commenced at the Central Criminal Court, Old Bailey before Mr. Justice Cantley. Each faced a total of twenty-five counts of murder and bombings from December 1974 until December 1975. It had however been the decision of the Director of Public Prosecutions not to include the offences relating to the Guilford and Woolwich pub bombings.

When the Counts were put to the defendants all four declined to enter either guilty or not guilty pleas and O'Connell made a statement to the court as follows. "I refuse to plead as the indictment does not include the two charges concerning the Guilford and Woolwich pub bombings. I took part in both, for which innocent people have been convicted." Similar statements were made by Duggan and Butler.

As is usual in such cases the Judge had no alternative but to proceed as though not guilty pleas had been tendered. The prosecution evidence was commenced and was completed on February 7th. Mr Richard Harvey, Defence Counsel then informed the court that no witnesses were to be called by the defence, but Mr. O'Connell proposed to read a statement made on behalf of the four defendants.

The statement made by O'Connell basically attacked the British government for its involvement in Northern Ireland. Referring again to the Guildford Four case, he accused the director of public prosecutions of doing nothing, despite their admissions of responsibility for those offences. Claiming to be patriots and volunteers in the Irish Republican Army who fought to free their nation from bondage to British imperialism they refuted the rights of its representatives to pass judgement on them.

After considering all the evidence, the jury found all four guilty of the majority of offences, but not guilty of five offences of bombing various premises, including the Caterham Arms and the Portman Hotel. They also found them not guilty of murder in relation the Hilton Hotel bomb reducing the charge to one of manslaughter, because of perceived delays in the police passing on the warning given.

With Butler, O'Connell and Duggan convicted of some 20 counts, Mr Justice Cantley sentenced each of them to 12 life sentences, 21 years for manslaughter, six 20-year sentences and one sentence of 18 years. Doherty convicted on 18 counts received

11 life sentences, 21 years for manslaughter, five sentences of 20 years and one of 18 years.

In his summing up Mr. Justice Cantley had praised the bravery of Inspector Purnell and Sergeant McVeigh, Inspector Dowswell, Major Biddle and many others, before concluding with the statement, "I realise that there were other policemen who showed great courage and devotion to duty who were not identified in the trial. I hope they received the recognition they duly deserved. The public is very fortunate to have the protection of men such as these."

At an appeal by the Guildford four was heard in October 1977 before Lord Justice Roskill, Lord Justice Lawton and Mr. Justice Bernham, O'Connell, Dowd, Butler and Duggan appeared in person to give their accounts of how they had in fact committed the Guilford and Woolwich attacks. When this evidence was weighted against the alleged confessions and statements made by the Guildford four, the judges reached a conclusion that the two groups must have colluded in the attacks and rejected the appeal.

In 1977 John Purnell, Phil Mc Veigh and Henry Dowswell were awarded the George Medal, for their conspicuous bravery in chasing down the four, armed members of the ASU resulting in the six-day siege at Balcombe Street. Detective Sergeant Phil Mansfield, Detective Constable Bob Fenton and three Special Patrol Group Officers, were awarded the Queens Gallantry Medal for their bravery in the Rossmore Road shooting incident. Detective Sergeant Dave Waghorn received a Commissioner's Commendation for his ingenuity in conceiving the idea of Operation Combo.

Concern about a possible miscarriage of justice regarding the guilt of the Guildford four, was to result in a continuing campaign to overthrow their convictions, which was assisted by various investigative television programmes and the personal involvement of Cardinal Basil Hume and Chris Mullin, author journalist and MP.

A fresh investigation was finally ordered and conducted by officers of Avon and Somerset Constabulary, who found serious irregularities in the manner in which notes of interviews had been recorded by Surrey detectives. It was to be October 1989 before this second appeal was heard and at the hearing Roy Amlott Q.C. on behalf of the Crown, commenting on the results of the Avon and Somerset Police investigation stated "New evidence of great significance has come to light after a police enquiry" He then conceded "It has thrown such doubt on the honesty and integrity of Surrey Police Officers investigating this case the Crown is now unable to say that the convictions of any of the four were safe or satisfactory."

The Court of Appeal had no option but to agree with this claim and on 19th October 1989, quashed the convictions of the Guildford Four and set them free after serving 15 years in prison.

Home Secretary Douglas Hurd ordered an immediate judicial enquiry into the case as well as an official criminal investigation into the conduct of the officers. Three detectives were later charged with perverting the course of justice and stood trial but were not convicted on any offences.

In 1997 multiparty peace talks were held in Stormont in an endeavour to reach a power-sharing arrangement in Northern Ireland, they culminated in what became known as the Good Friday Agreement, which was signed in Belfast on 10th April 1998 by the British and Irish Governments. As part of this agreement some 131 Republican and 118 Loyalist prisoners were set free some three days later, including the four members of the ASU responsible for the IRA campaign in London in 1974/5.

Final thoughts

We sincerely hope you have enjoyed what you have read, there will be some of you to whom the events themselves bring back memories.

We did discuss trying to complete these memoirs between ourselves, as Ron left detailed notes and outlines of chapters to come, as well as persons to contact and follow-ups needed. However we all agreed that it would not be the same, as what makes these memoirs so unique is voice of the storyteller himself.

Other planned chapters included his time as Det Supt on the Flying Squad and Central Robbery Squad and The Murder of Miss Bhugaloo in Ponders End in June 1984. There was also the infamous 'umbrella murder' of Bulgarian dissident Georgie Markov in 1978. This case led to such notoriety that it is now featured amongst other infamous London crimes in the Metropolitan Police 'Black Museum' and it remained a constant source of interest to Ron, who had his own theories on this still unsolved case.

There was also going to be a chapter on the Billy Allen case and the final chapter, from what we can see, was covering his time at No 2 Area from January 1986 until November 1989. We hope you have enjoyed these memoirs and the memories you have of Ron.

We would like to thank the Metropolitan Police, past colleagues of Ron, in particular Andy Petter, Barry Howe, Peter Wilton and members of the Recidivists for their continued support to our family.

Ron's Service Commendations

<u>COMMENDATIONS, AWARDS, DECORATIONS</u> and details of accepted suggestions to improve force efficiency

DATE	AWARD
17.11.59	Commander2: Commendation for vigilance, initiative and ability in effecting the arrest of two men for office breaking and possessing H.B.I. by night. Also commended at Tottenham Magistrates Court.
30.6.61	Commissioners: For persistence and ability resulting in the arrest of a number of troublesome juveniles for larceny.
17.7.61	Commander 2: For devotion to duty whilst off duty and ability in effecting the arrest of a troublesome and violent thief.
9.2.62	Commissioners: For vigilance and determination in a case of housebreaking.
1.3.62	Commander 2: Commendation for devotion to duty whilst off duty, vigilance, initiative and ability in effecting the arrest of two men for stealing a motor car.
30.1.62	Commissioners: For ability and persistence in a difficult case of demanding money with menaces (with other Officers).
5.12.62	Commander 2: For vigilance and initiative in effecting the arrest of a man for housebreaking (4 cases) and receiving.
9.6.66	Commander 2: For determination and courage resulting in the arrest of a man for indecent assaults on women, whereby he sustained personal injury. Also commended at Highgate Magistrates Court.
7.12.66	Commander 2: For good team work and determination resulting in the arrest of three persistent breakers.
27.4.67	Commander 2: For perseverance and ability in a difficult case of malicious damage.

3.4.69	Commander 'C' (A&D): A minor commendation is awarded for initiative and ability leading to the arrest and conviction of two criminals for armed robbery.
4.8.69	Minor Commendation: For valuable assistance in a case of murder.
23.4.71	Commissioners: For valuable assistance in a case of murder.
31.12.76	Commissioners: For persistence and detective ability leading to the arrest of 4 men for conspiracy to cause an explosion.
21.2.78	Commissions: For persistence and detective ability in a case involving offences of murder, attempted murder and serious offences under the Explosives Substances Act 1883. Also at CCC and DPP.
CR 201/77/102	Commissioners: For his leadership and detective ability in a case of murder.
P.O. 28.7.81	Police Long Service and Good Conduct Medal.

N Division Boxing

Ron, seeing the funny side, with colleagues

Ron and Colleagues

Dad with Manfred (visting policeman from
Germany & life long friend)

Ron with Barry Howe & Colleagues

Ron's retirement do with family
and good friend Shaw Taylor

On the course with life long friends Peter Wilton & Andy Petter

Ron with wife Noeleen, Daughters Helen, Jane and Ann
and grandchildren Molly, Jack, Teddy, Martha and Ben

www.ingramcontent.com/pod-product-compliance
Lightning Source LLC
Chambersburg PA
CBHW030531100426
42813CB00001B/222